THE
POLITICS IN
UNITED STATES

FROM CARTER
TO BUSH

New Edition

Other titles in this series

Politics in Britain: From Callaghan to Thatcher (new edition)
Politics in China: From Mao to Deng
Politics in France: From Giscard to Mitterrand (new edition)
Politics in the Soviet Union: From Brezhnev to Gorbachev
Politics in West Germany: From Schmidt to Kohl

About the Series

Chambers Political Spotlights aim to provide a bridge between
conventional textbooks and contemporary reporting. Each title
examines the key political, economic and social changes of the
country, providing, in addition, a brief contextual background
to each development discussed.

Politics in the United States

Dr Ian Derbyshire was formerly a British Academy Post
Doctoral Research Fellow at Cambridge University. He
specializes in contemporary international politics and is
currently attached to the South Asian Centre in Cambridge.

POLITICS IN
THE UNITED STATES

FROM CARTER
TO BUSH

New Edition

Ian Derbyshire

Chambers

EDINBURGH   NEW YORK   TORONTO

First published by Sandpiper Publishing as a *Sandpiper Compact*, 1986
First edition published by W & R Chambers Ltd, 1988

This edition published 1990 by W & R Chambers Ltd,
43–45 Annandale Street, Edinburgh EH7 4AZ
95 Madison Avenue, New York N.Y. 10016

Library of Congress Cataloging-in-Publication Data applied for

ISBN 0-550-20750-3

Cover design by James Hutcheson

Typeset by Alphaset Graphics, Edinburgh
Printed in England by Clays Ltd, St Ives plc

Preface

In January 1977 an unknown southerner, Jimmy Carter, entered the White House promising a new era of frankness and honesty following the disgrace of the Watergate years. Four years later he was to depart in ignominy, having failed to exert his influence over Congress and having been held to ransom by Iranian students. His successor, Ronald Reagan, a 69-year-old former film star, was elected to office on a wave of patriotism and conservatism. He pledged to restore America's strength and to effect a radical economic and social reformation. The following two years saw the country plunged into a deep recession and a renewed east-west 'cold war'. The US economy, however, rapidly rebounded and, with the country's military might restored, President Reagan was re-elected for a second term with a landslide majority. Subsequently, during its closing two years, much of the sheen was wiped away from the Reagan presidency as it became embroiled in the 'Irangate' scandal. Nevertheless, in November 1988, Reagan's deputy George Bush successfully secured election as the country's new President in what was the Republican Party's fifth success out of the last six contests.

This *Spotlight* examines the changing political scene in the United States during the Carter, Reagan and Bush eras and the different policy programmes pursued. It examines the resurgence of Congressional power and the growth of political individualism; the operation of presidential government; the contests for national leadership; the revival in Republicanism and conservatism; the changing character of the Supreme Court; the rise of ethnic politics; the diminishing influence of trade unions; the implication of growth in the 'sunbelt' West and South; and it assesses changes in America's foreign policy and the success of the 'Reaganite counter-revolution'. In addition, it includes analyses of the 1986–7 'Irangate' scandal, the 1988 presidential contest, and assesses the opening year of the Bush presidency.

Contents

List of Tables

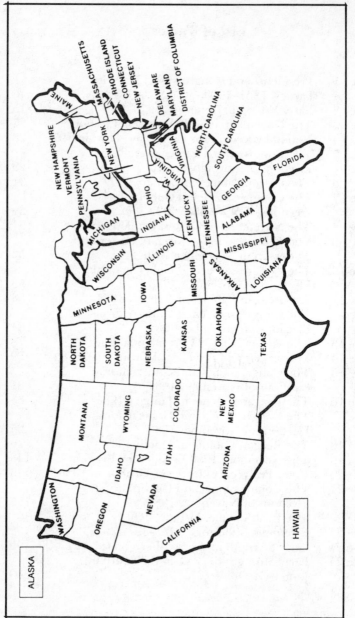

Figure 1 The States of America

Part One

POLITICAL FOUNDATIONS

Chapter 1

THE AMERICAN POLITICAL SYSTEM

Race, Region and Religion: The Politics of Diversity and Space

Three factors have played a determining role in American political development – geography; ethnic, religious and regional diversity; and the cultural and historical background to the country's creation and early growth.

The United States consists today of fifty States spread across a land mass of 3.6 million square miles – an area more than four times that occupied by the 12 nations of the European Community. Its population is not dense – totalling 246 million in 1988 compared to the EC 12's 330 million – but it is composed of an extraordinary mixture of ethnic, racial and religious groups. Around 30% can trace their descent from British and Irish stock, 8% from German, 5% from Italian, 3% each from Scandinavian and Polish; 23% are Catholics, 11% Baptists, 6% Methodists, 3% Lutherans, 2% Eastern Orthodox, 2% Mormons and 2% Jewish; 12% are black, 8% Hispanic and 2% Asian. The United States is thus above all a land of immigrants, with a constantly shifting frontier and centre of gravity, and it is a nation riven with strong vertical regional, racial and religious cleavages. However, it has been a land of final destination, not of transient immigration. Immigrants have been – the southern blacks excepted – variously thrust towards this 'New World' as a result of religious or political persecution at home, or, more recently, have been attracted by a desire for economic betterment. They have brought with them the spirit of self-reliance, independence and ambition which has come to characterise American culture. Conscious efforts have been made to inculcate these values and to develop a feeling of national allegiance through the educational system.

The political evolution of the United States has reflected this interplay of historical, geographical and social forces. The American constitution, framed at the Philadelphia Convention in 1787, soon after the successful outcome of the War of Independence (1776–83), drew heavily upon the settlers' experience of contemporary European political institutions, while at the same time seeking to overcome a number of their anti-democratic features. The new US constitution, which was consciously created and enshrined in statute, aimed to safeguard individual liberty and protect the powers of the Union's Constituent States and to prevent the concentration of power at any one centre. This was achieved through a system of checks and balances and through a thoroughgoing separation of judicial, legislative and executive powers, with designated circles of competence and a strict segregation of personnel.

The President At the apex of the system stands the President of the United States – to be elected every four years by the entire nation and restricted, since 1951, to a maximum of two terms in office. Each State is allocated a number of 'electoral college' votes (equivalent to the sum of its Congressional Representatives and Senators) for this election. Votes cast are counted on the first-past-the-post basis at the State level – simple majorities capturing all the State's college votes – and the candidate with an absolute majority of 'electoral college' votes gains the presidency.

Once elected to office, the President is placed at the head of the executive branch of government, head of the armed forces and Federal civil service, in charge of negotiating in foreign affairs, and he becomes the chief initiator of Federal legislation. He cannot be removed by Congress except through the singular act of impeachment. The President is served by an advisory cabinet of 14 non-elected departmental Secretaries which is appointed by and fully dependent upon the President. It includes experts drawn from universities and the business community and representatives from various ethnic, geographical and socio-economic interest groups but may not include members of Congress. Additional guidance is provided by the support teams of the

National Security Council (NSC), the Domestic Council, the Office of Management and Budget (OMB) and the Council of Economic Advisers (CEA), and by the ever-growing White House Office of personal aides and trouble-shooting assistants. (See Appendix E for the present extent of this executive machine.) Although the powers of the presidency have increased enormously during the course of this century as government interference and centralisation has progressed, the US constitution has, through the separation of powers, left the President dependent upon Congress for gaining approval for these programmes. In this respect the American President remains in a significantly weaker position than a British Prime Minister who sits in and commands a disciplined majority within the legislative assembly.

Congress forms the legislative arm of government and is bicameral – being composed, unusually, of two equally powerful houses. The *Senate* is the second or upper chamber and is composed of 100 Senators, two Senators representing each State regardless of size or population. A third of the Senate is elected biennially, each Senator serving a six-year term. The *House of Representatives* forms the lower chamber and comprises 435 members who are elected every two years from constituencies of roughly equal demographic size in which they reside. Control of the Senate is skewed towards traditionalist and sparsely peopled agrarian states, while the interests of members of the House of Representatives are unusually parochial. Thus the outlook of Congress and the President – elected by the whole people – invariably diverges.

However, Congress, despite this political perspective, wields significant authority in the American system of government and differs from European legislatures in its independence from direct executive control. It has sole powers of legislation and controls the purse-strings of government. The President thus needs to work with its support if his Federal programme is to be approved and funded. The leaders within Congress determine the priorities of legislation to be introduced and its members can add amendments altering the character of legislation which is passed. Items are scrutinised in detail by a system of powerful, expert and televised *standing, select and special investigative committees*, which call forth an array of important witnesses and which are composed of members drawn from both parties in broad accordance with overall party strength within the chamber and are chaired by senior members of the controlling party.

(See Appendix Tables D5 and D6 for the present number and composition of such committees and Appendix C for further details on the workings of the Congressional committee system.) Legislation requires the approval of both chambers of Congress before reaching the statute book, with special 'conference committees' composed of senior figures drawn from each chamber being established to bridge differences if they arise. The Senate has a number of additional powers – the consent of this chamber is required before key Federal (including presidential cabinet, diplomatic and judicial) appointments can be made and a two-thirds Senate majority is needed before foreign treaties can come into force, rendering the Senate's Foreign Relations Committee a most influential body. Small groups of intransigent Senators can attempt to block the passage of bills through the 'filibuster', engaging in unlimited debate until the leadership of the chamber is eventually forced to drop the measure unless it can muster 60% support in a 'cloture' action.

However, the powers of Congress are essentially individualistic and are often negative. Only the President can provide coherent national leadership to deal with contemporary problems – unemployment in the 1930s, racial and urban tension in the 1950s and 1960s, the energy crisis during the 1970s. He announces annual policy guidelines in the January State of the Union message, 'recommends' measures for consideration, and then sets about trying to persuade congressmen to propose and support these bills. This task is, however, never easy. Personal, party-based and ideological factions and coalitions emerge to attempt to thwart controversial measures. The President is thus engaged in a perpetual bargaining battle with Congress. He can grant subtle inducements (personal or regional patronage) to individual members; make a direct national appeal to the American public to build up pressure from below; or threaten to employ a veto which can only be overridden by a two-thirds majority in both chambers. These mutual checks and balances and such interdependence have forced the President and Congress to work together and engage in tit-for-tat compromise deals allowing each side to see a number of their most cherished schemes all the way to fruition. The success of a President and his cabinet team revolves very much around his ability to manage the complex and fragmented Congress system.

The *Supreme Court* stands at the apex of the third branch of the American political system – the judiciary. It plays a vital adjudicatory role, interpreting and safeguarding the nation's written constitution – ensuring that the correct balance is maintained between the Federal government and the constituent States and between Congress and the presidency; and that the individual liberties (the freedoms of speech, press, peaceful assembly and religious belief; the right to carry arms; the right of fair trial) enshrined in the Bill of Rights are upheld. The Supreme Court is composed of nine judges, who are appointed by the President with the Senate's approval. Once appointed they can only be removed by impeachment. The Court has played a crucial role in reinterpreting the often vague US constitution and in enlarging Federal powers so as to adapt an eighteenth-century constitution to the needs of the later twentieth century. It has built up a corpus of thousands of interpretive rulings which have become precedents and pointers for future decisions.

The appointment system for the Supreme Court has meant that its political outlook changes only slowly. This can cause considerable difficulties for incumbent Presidents. During the early 1930s a conservative-dominated Supreme Court clashed with and blocked many of the radical 'New Deal' initiatives introduced by President Roosevelt. Later, during the 1950s and 1960s, a strong liberal majority emerged in the Supreme Court of Chief Justice Earl Warren (1953–69) and took 'activist' steps in favour of civil rights reform. Gradually, however, these members retired or departed and were replaced by appointees of the Republican Presidents Nixon, Ford and Reagan (see Appendix Table B5). This turned the Supreme Court of Chief Justice Warren Burger (1969–86) and his successor William Rehnquist (1986–) into an increasingly cautious and conservative body. Such changes demonstrate that it is possible for a President, backed by a supportive Senate, to alter the balance of opinion in the Supreme Court, but it is a slow and uncertain process. There is invariably a gestation lag, which has left succeeding administrations needing to work with a Court tilted towards the political persuasion of the preceding presidency.

The numerous deliberate and fortuitous checks and balances built into the American political system thus place great barriers in the way of firm central control or the pursuance of major reform programmes unless a strong consensus for change has developed within the country. The American President when he attempts to foster new legislative initiatives is liable to encounter opposition from Congress and from outside interest groups. When acting as chief executive he can add his own interpretations and priorities to the functioning of the departments and bureaucracy at his disposal, but he may find himself challenged by a Supreme Court ruling or by intransigence on the part of the quasi-independent regulatory commissions. This has placed a premium upon the powers of persuasion and skills of bargaining and has made it unusually difficult to succeed with radical reform. For constitutional reforms, the obstacles to change are even greater. A two-thirds majority is first required from both houses of Congress and then support is needed from three-quarters of the nation's 50 State legislatures. The opposition of just 13 States – or, at its extreme, only 4% of the total population – is sufficient to quash a proposed measure. Thus, despite the introduction of more than 8000 proposed Amendments into Congress and the formal submission of 40 to the States, there have only been 26 Amendments (see Appendix F) to the constitution since it came into effect in 1789. Of these, only 11 have successfully been introduced this century.[1]

The final limitation upon strong central control in the American system of government derives from the very structure of its organisation – the Federal system. The constitution was established by the original 13 Union States after the War of Independence to give the Federal administration the minimum of powers required in defence and foreign affairs to enable it to resist attack from any potential foreign aggressor and thus prevent fragmentation and to give Washington the authority to co-ordinate 'inter-state' concerns. In most other matters the States retained autonomy and established their own duplicates of the Federal system, with their Governors, separate legislative chambers (see Appendix Table A2), State supreme courts and constitutions. Over the years the central government has impinged into more and more areas once reserved for the State administrations. Nevertheless the States still retain an unusual degree of power and influence – quite naturally when their sheer size is remembered – compared to the provinces and counties of Western Europe, acting in certain policy spheres as vital 'laboratories of innovation'. In 1988 expenditure by State and by the equally active local governments amounted to almost 80% of the sum expended by the centre. Moreover, more than 14 million workers were on the latter's payroll, compared with only three million on the Federal. The States frame much of their own civil and criminal law; they are involved in welfare, educational and health affairs; and they have retained substantial powers of taxation – raising funds from property and sales taxes and often from local income taxes. The operations of State and local governments are, however, circumscribed by the laws and guidelines set by the constitution and by the Federal administration and they remain dependent upon Federal grants for almost 20% of their income. This forces the centre and the States to work together and to agree to trade-offs and compromises in areas where State and national interests overlap.

Unifying and Fragmenting Bodies – Parties and Pressure Groups

The constitutional structure of American government has led to fragmentation and decentralisation in decision-taking and has placed great obstacles in the path of radical change and government intervention. In other countries such a system may have had an adverse, stultifying effect on both the economy and upon social relations. This system has, however, worked in the United States, with its continuing physical expansion and its burgeoning free-market economy, and it has reflected the wishes of a nation of tremendous geographical and ethnic diversity. There has nevertheless been the need for the creation of a number of umbrella organisations to bring together the disparate wishes of the nation's constituent States and social groups in the periodic elections for Congress and the presidency. Encouraged by the 'first-past-the-post' electoral system, two powerful parties, the Republicans and Democrats, have emerged and have come to represent important and unifying forces in American political life.

These political parties are grand 'catch-all' coalitions which differ substantially from the well-disciplined and often class-based parties of Western Europe. Ideological differences exist between the broad ranks of Democrats and Republicans, but they are minor in comparison to the differences evident in Europe and they are by no means uniform – within each party there exist wings and factions which regularly align with the majority opinion in the opposing party. Historical, social and regional factors play as much a role in political allegiance in the United States as ideology.

The Democrats The roots of the Democratic Party (established 1800) lie in the cotton-growing Confederacy States of the South which were defeated by the urban-based, industrial States of the north-eastern seaboard during the 1861–5 American Civil War. Slave-owning was replaced by sharecropping in the South, but a strong conservative plantocracy continued to dominate and this group made strenuous efforts to exclude the large black population of the region from the political process. The southern States became a stronghold for the Democratic Party, but elected Senators and Representatives of a conservative and illiberal hue. In the north-eastern seaboard States, major economic and social changes were experienced between 1865 and 1920, with almost 30 million immigrants flooding into the country as industrial and urban growth accelerated. The Democratic Party sought out and won over these new immigrant minority communities – the Irish, Poles, Italians, Catholics and Jews – thus establishing a firm new power base in the North. This was effectively cemented by President Franklin D Roosevelt during the 1930s 'Great Depression', when the Democratic Party pressed forward with his 'New Deal' programme of reform and interventionism to stimulate economic recovery and to alleviate the hardship experienced by depressed and marginal groups. These policies attracted such wide and diverse support that the Democrats became the dominant political party in Congress and secured the presidency for its candidate during 28 of the 36 years between 1933 and 1968. (See Table 1.) Liberalism came to dominate American political thinking during this period and the Democrats became skilled and renowned 'machine politicians', putting together coalitions of labour and ethnic groups and drawing upon union and community leaders to deliver their vote; they granted in return advice and aid in the field of welfare, employment and contracts.[2] As a party, the Democrats became identified with the working man and with an extended role for the Federal government.

The Democratic Party has never been an homogeneous unit. Major geographical and ideological faction divisions have always been evident. The most basic has been that between its southern conservatives and its north-eastern liberals. The divisions between these branches widened significantly during the 1960s as northern Democrats, who controlled the party's Federal leadership, pushed for civil rights reform – desegregation, equal opportunity and voting rights for the

black community. This created conflicts with the reaction-
ary and racist 'historical Democrats' of the South during
the Kennedy and Johnson presidencies. White support in
the South for the Democrats' presidential candidates crum-
bled and many southern Democrat Congressmen regularly
voted against the President on social issues. This led to
the southern branch of the Democratic Party being termed
the 'Congressional wing' and the northern the 'Presidential
wing'. During the later 1960s growing disillusionment with
the Vietnam War among northern liberals broadened such
divisions as the party's foreign policy consensus was shattered. This set in train a drive to democratise the party's
organisational structure and broaden its membership base.

The Democratic Party today is composed of at least five significant factions, excluding a multitude of smaller splinter and 'issue
groups'. A reduced southern conservative rump is to be found in
the Conservative Democratic Forum (CDF), comprising around
14 Senators and 40–59 Representatives. The swathe of northern liberals, moderate on defence, 'New Deal' interventionists
on economic and social issues, and highly rated by Americans
for Democratic Action (ADA), group together in the Democratic
Study Group (DSG) and still control the party. Closely allied to
this grouping are the radical liberals of the Midwest agricultural-
industrial States, heirs to the progressivist and prairie populist
tradition, who survive in the Minnesota Democratic Farmer-
Labor (DFL) Party. A smaller, but vociferous, faction are the
Trumanite 'Defense Democrats' who, while liberal on economic
and social issues, favour the pursuit of a firm, anti-communist
foreign policy – they have recently included Senator Patrick
Moynihan of New York and the late Henry Jackson of Washington. The final major faction operates radically at the fringes of
the party outside Congress and has sought, under the leadership of the black activist the Rev Jesse Jackson, to build a new
minority 'rainbow' coalition embracing blacks, Hispanics, feminists, students, peace campaigners and suburban liberals.

The Republicans The Republicans (established 1854) formed
originally the party of the wealthy and victorious industrialising
North. They added to this support from rural and small town
areas of the Midwest, which included the long-settled Protestant majority community, and the frontier States of the Pacific
coast, and put together a dominant electoral coalition up to the
1930s (see Table 1). The 'Roosevelt revolution' left the party in

**TABLE 1 PRESIDENTS AND CONGRESSIONAL
MAJORITY PARTIES, 1861–1990**

**1861–1932
THE ERA OF REPUBLICAN DOMINANCE**

PRESIDENTS*

A Lincoln†	R	1861–1865
A Johnson‡	U	1865–1868
US Grant	R	1869–1876
RB Hayes	R	1877–1880
JA Garfield†	R	1881–1881
CA Arthur	R	1881–1884
G Cleveland	D	1885–1888
B Harrison	R	1889–1892
G Cleveland	D	1893–1896
W McKinley	R	1897–1900
T Roosevelt	R	1901–1908
WH Taft	R	1909–1912
W Wilson	D	1913–1920
WG Harding§	R	1921–1923
C Coolidge	R	1923–1928
H Hoover	R	1929–1932

CONGRESS

REPRESENTATIVES		SENATE	
Republicans	1861–1874	Republicans	1861–1878
Democrats	1875–1880	Democrats	1879–1880
Republicans	1881–1882	Republicans	1881–1892
Democrats	1883–1888	Democrats	1893–1894
Republicans	1889–1890	Republicans	1895–1912
Democrats	1891–1894	Democrats	1913–1918
Republicans	1895–1910	Republicans	1919–1932
Democrats	1911–1916		
Republicans	1917–1932		

1861–1932: Total 72 years

Control of House	R–50 Years	D–22 Years
Control of Senate	R–62 Years	D–10 Years
Years as President	R–52 Years	D–16 Years

* Presidential terms are taken to run from the January after election to the December of the final fourth year, although, to be strictly accurate, terms in fact continue until 20 January of the following year.
† Assassinated in office. ‡ Union Party. § Died in office.

1933–1990
THE ERA OF DEMOCRAT DOMINANCE

PRESIDENTS*

FD Roosevelt†	D	1933–1945
HS Truman	D	1945–1952
DD Eisenhower	R	1953–1960
JF Kennedy‡	D	1961–1963
LB Johnson	D	1963–1968
RM Nixon§	R	1969–1974
GR Ford	R	1974–1976
JE Carter	D	1977–1980
RW Reagan	R	1981–1988
GHW Bush	R	1989–

CONGRESS

REPRESENTATIVES		SENATE	
Democrats	1933–1946	Democrats	1933–1946
Republicans	1947–1948	Republicans	1947–1948
Democrats	1949–1952	Democrats	1949–1952
Republicans	1953–1954	Republicans	1953–1954
Democrats	1955–	Democrats	1955–1980
		Republicans	1981–1986
		Democrats	1987–

1933–1990: Total 58 Years

Control of House	D–54 Years	R–4 Years
Control of Senate	D–48 Years	R–10 Years
Years as President	D–32 Years	R–26 Years

* Presidential terms are taken to run from the January after election to the December of the final fourth year, although, to be strictly accurate, terms in fact continue until 20 January of the following year.
† Died in Office. ‡Assassinated in office. § Resigned in midterm.

a minority at the Federal level for much of the 1930s and 1940s, but under Eisenhower the party came to accept these popular social and economic reforms and captured the presidency for two terms. There have remained, however, as in the Democratic Party, numerous diverse strands of Republicanism which have gained varying degrees of prominence during the past two decades.

The major cleavage within the party has been that between the sophisticated, well-schooled, monied and industrial urbanites drawn from the North-east and the expanding cities of the interior and the Pacific coast – the so-called 'Wall Street' Republicans – and the rural and small town communities of the Midwest and central States – the 'Main Street' conservatives. The 'Wall Street' Republicans were personified by Dwight Eisenhower and the late Nelson Rockefeller, being essentially moderate and consensual: accepting and supporting the welfare state, remaining tolerant in social matters and internationalist in foreign affairs, and supporting cautious Keynesian economic policies at home. They succeeded in gaining the presidential nomination for a man of their inclination in each of the contests between 1940 and 1956 and could then be termed the party's 'Presidential wing'. The 'Main Street' Republicans have been more traditionalist in their philosophy. They have retained a belief in the ideals of laissez-faire, seeing only a limited role for the State in economic matters; a respect for the family unit and Protestant mores in domestic social policies; and they espouse a virulent anti-communism in foreign affairs. Barry Goldwater (1909–)fought on an extreme version of this platform and failed miserably in the presidential election of 1964. However, 'Main Street' Republicanism, supported now in intellectual circles by the revival of monetarist economics and by a political breakthrough in the white South, gained ground during the 1970s, bearing fruit with the election in 1980 of President Reagan. This transformed it into the new 'Presidential wing' of the party, with the more conservative and extreme 'New Right' fundamentalists, led by the Rev Pat Robertson, flanking it to the right. Aided by economic and social changes – the growth in suburbia and the white-collar sector, increasing material affluence; and the upward mobility of the older Irish and Italian communities – the Republican Party has re-established itself as an effective national party and conservatism has become a challenging new ideology. The party has thus managed to capture the presidency for 18 of the 22 years between 1969–90.

It is clear from the above brief sketch of the development of
the Democratic and Republican parties that each party has and
continues to attract a number of specific regional, ethnic and
class groups. Surveys and elections have shown the Democrats
usually drawing in the bulk of the votes cast by lower-income
groups, blacks, Catholics, Hispanics, Jews, the unionised, the
South and the large city conurbations, and they have shown
the Republicans monopolising much of the vote cast by high-
income managerial and professional groups, rural and small town
Protestants, the Midwest and the Pacific coast. Such sectionalism
and regionalism has meant that almost half of America's States
are dominated by one party – although this might be internally
divided by competing faction groups. Each State party forms an
individual party of its own, impossible for the centre to control
and concerned with the local issues around which State, county
and city elections revolve. These are the true political parties in
America. Party leaders attempt, unsuccessfully, to enforce unity
in the House of Representatives and the Senate, and National
Party Committees exist, composed of representatives nominated
by the State parties. However, the latter body, with its National
Chairman, comes into serious operation only twice every four
years as the party first agrees upon its electoral rules before
later falling in behind its chosen candidate for the presidency.
In the absence then of an efficient and unified nationwide
party structure or ideology, it is not surprising that each party's national support is much less predictable than its State level
support. Presidential contests remain open and competitive, with
particularly large fluctuations being registered in the vote of
groups poorly enmeshed in the party machines.

The different regional and sectional groups voting for each
party have pressed upon them a multitude of diverse and often
conflicting policy interests. In such circumstances America's two
political parties lack clear, sharp ideological definitions and have
become true 'catch-all' coalitions. This broad church approach
to political affairs has been institutionalised through the meth-
od of selecting Congressional and presidential candidates – the
primary system. This system allows any member of the electorate
expressing an interest in supporting the party at the next election
to vote to select delegates to be sent to the National Convention,
which selects its presidential candidate. Participants do not have
to be fee-paying or card-carrying members of the party and in
extreme cases – in 'open primaries' – they do not even have

to express a wish to vote in the future for that party. The primary system was evolved by the Populist Movement to break the unsavoury monopoly held by the local party bosses who had kept a firm command over the choice of candidates through their control of the oligarchic caucuses and conventions of the late nineteenth century. Primaries acquired increased importance from the 1970s, following the democratisation reforms launched by radical Democrats who were disenchanted by the way in which Hubert Humphrey had been granted the 1968 nomination despite his lack of support among the rank and file.[3] The spread of the primary system has made contests more unpredictable, fragmented party organisations and lengthened campaigning seasons. In compensation, however, this selection system has enabled parties to reflect the diverse complexion and demands of each locality – facilitating the inclusion of ethnic candidates on the party 'ticket' – and has provided, in 'one-party States', a crucial electoral tier in which intra-party factional battles can be resolved.

The weakness of national party organisations and the divergent outlook of party members drawn from different regions has meant that party discipline inside Congress is extraordinarily low by European standards. Cross-party coalitions are frequently formed for particular issues, with the division between liberals and conservatives often appearing more important than between parties. The situation is exacerbated by the institutional absence of a single visible 'leader of the opposition' in the American system of government. Thus almost half the votes taken in Congress are bipartisan, with majorities from both parties voting in a similar manner. (See Table 2.) This lack of party unity has compounded the problems of the presidency. Presidents are unable to rely upon or compel regular support from their party colleagues and must seek to put together varying coalitions for the successful enactment of key policy initiatives.

The fragmentation of American society and its political and party system has provided, in addition, an opportunity for numerous diverse pressure and interest groups (for example, the oil, farming, medical and ethnic lobbies) to play a significant role in influencing the policy process. These groups are able to voice their demands and challenge unfavourable decisions at many stages and levels of the political process – at the State level, in primary contests, in Congressional committees, by lobbying the President, by building up extra-Congressional and public pressure through

TABLE 2 PARTY VOTING IN CONGRESS, 1970–89

Session	Total Recorded Votes			Bipartisan Votes* As % of Total			Party Unity Votes† As % of Total		
	Senate	House	Total	Senate	House	Total	Senate	House	Total
1970	418	266	684	65	73	68	35	27	32
1971	423	320	743	58	62	60	42	38	40
1972	532	329	861	64	73	67	36	27	33
1973	594	541	1135	60	58	59	40	42	41
1974	544	537	1081	56	71	63	44	29	37
1975	602	612	1214	52	52	52	48	48	48
1976	688	661	1349	63	64	63	37	36	37
1977	635	706	1341	58	58	58	42	42	42
1978	516	834	1350	55	67	62	45	33	38
1979	497	672	1169	53	53	53	47	47	47
1980	531	604	1135	54	62	59	46	38	41
1981	483	353	836	52	63	57	48	37	43
1982	465	459	924	57	64	60	43	36	40
1983	371	498	869	56	44	49	44	56	51
1984	275	408	683	60	53	56	40	47	44
1985	381	439	820	50	39	44	50	61	56
1986	354	451	805	48	43	45	52	57	55
1987	420	488	908	59	36	47	41	64	53
1988	379	451	830	58	53	55	42	47	45
1989	312	368	680	65	45	54	35	55	46

* Bipartisan votes refer to votes where a majority from both parties vote together on an issue.

† 'Party Unity' votes refer to votes that split the parties, with a majority of voting Democrats opposing a majority of voting Republicans.

television and direct-mail campaigns, and through challenges in the courts. Political pressure groups can invariably find factions within the existing heterogeneous political parties willing to campaign for their causes, and this has been an important factor limiting the multiplication of competing parties. In such circumstances, politics in the United States has in many respects always resembled a complex pluralistic game of bargaining and compromise, as an attempt is made to balance the demands of diverse sectional groups. It is almost a business regulated by skilled, invariably legally trained, Congressmen and State officers. In this respect, American politics and its party system differ substantially from the disciplined and ideological model of Western Europe.

During recent years, fragmentation in politics has increased, although fragmentation in American society has arguably been reduced by the continuing development of television as a national medium and by the reduction in regional income differentials between North and South.[4] Political commentators now regularly write about the decline of the party system and the spread of individualism in American politics. This is not to say that the parties themselves have disappeared, but that public allegiances have weakened (with one-third of the electorate now viewing themselves as independents), that the control exerted by party bosses has been all but eroded and that party labels give no clear indication of a Congressman's beliefs or voting intentions. Candidates instead run as individual 'political entrepreneurs', using the party label and the residual machine as a convenience. One prominent factor behind this 'atomisation' has been social – the decline in traditional religious and ethnic loyalties as a result of continuing social and spatial mobility, and the usurping of the party's traditional 'brokerage' role by modern welfare agencies. The second factor has been the television revolution, which has enabled candidates to appeal directly to broad electorates.

The first contest to be affected by such changes was the presidential, which, with the spread of binding primaries, was rapidly thrown open to charismatic outsiders. This 'individualist revolution' has more recently affected contests for Congressional and gubernatorial offices, particularly following the 1971 and 1974 Federal Election Campaign Acts, which introduced the public funding of presidential contests and thus freed new resources for lower-level races. The cost of Congressional elections has, in consequence, spiralled astronomically during the last decade (rising from $73 million in 1974; $151 million in 1978; $289 million in 1982; $375 million in 1984; $450 million in 1986; to $458 million in 1988) and campaigns have become increasingly sophisticated, with computerised marketing and media consultants now essential appendages to a prospective Congressman's political team.

These changes have helped gradually to shift power away from party leaders towards individual Congressmen. However, the need for huge sums to fight campaigns – it now costs, on average, $3 million to fight a Senate race and $0.4 million for a House campaign – has also increased the power wielded by interest groups and particularly by single-issue groups. These bodies channel in funds through Political Action Committees (PACs). The number of PACs has multiplied from 608 in 1974 to 4268 in 1989 and they now contribute 31% of all the funds spent during Congressional contests (individuals, by contrast, contribute 64% of the resources and parties only 5%).[5] PACs also spend large sums on indirect campaigns aimed at moulding public opinion and can play a decisive role in tilting the balance in close contests. Once elected, a Congressman becomes difficult to oust – there is a supra-90% 'return rate' for Representatives, 75% for Senators – being able easily to attract PAC and interest group finance, as well as having access to free Congressional mailing facilities. In return, however, he/she needs to toe the interest group line and is thus rarely a truly free agent. Nevertheless, although American politics has become a hardnosed and often cynical business, ideology is never completely absent. This has been clearly demonstrated by the political and policy changes of the last decade and a half, which will be analysed in the pages that follow.

Part Two

POLITICAL DEVELOPMENTS: 1961–80

Chapter 2

BACKGROUND TO THE CARTER-REAGAN-BUSH ERA: 1961–76

The 1960s 'New Frontier' –
1970s Republican Realism

American politics in the 1960s was dominated by the Democrats and by the philosophy of liberalism. John F Kennedy (1917–63), despite an anti-Catholic electoral revolt in a number of States, narrowly defeated his Republican opponent Richard Nixon in the November 1960 presidential contest and entered the White House in January 1961 determined to open up a 'New Frontier' and press forward with social and civil rights reform after the passivity of the Eisenhower period. These policies fitted the changing temper of the times – a period of great hope, of technological change, of unprecedented affluence and of youth. However, Kennedy, assassinated in November 1963, did not live to see these cherished reforms come into effect. It was left to his successor, the Texan Lyndon B Johnson (1908–73), a man strongly influenced by the 'New Deal' policies of F D Roosevelt, to introduce the 'Great Society' programmes of this decade – these encompassed the Economic Opportunity Act and Civil Rights Act of 1964, the Medicare and Voting Rights Act of 1965, and the Housing, Higher Education and Equal Opportunity Acts. These measures extended the role of the Federal government in economic and social affairs and established a more comprehensive welfare state. Johnson, an ex-Senate Majority Leader, proved to be a particularly skilled manager of Congress and emerged as a strong and successful President, forcing through his own policy initiatives. He was aided by a large Democrat Congressional majority and by the rulings of an 'activist' Supreme Court.

Military misadventure in Vietnam ultimately brought about the downfall of Lyndon Johnson, and the divided Democrats, led by Hubert Humphrey (1911–78), narrowly lost the presidential contest of November 1968 to Richard Nixon, who pledged to bring about a rapid disengagement. Nixon's victory marked the onset of an era of revival for Republicanism and conservatism, as attempts were made to check the growth of the welfare state, the centralisation of government and over-liberalisation in social affairs. This revival was boosted by contemporary social changes and by shifts within the Supreme Court. The Republican Party thus made steady gains in the Congressional and gubernatorial elections of 1966–72 (gaining a majority of State governorships in 1969), and in November 1972, although still entangled in Vietnam, Richard Nixon won an overwhelming victory over the Democrat left-winger, George McGovern (1922–), to secure a second term in office.

Richard M Nixon was a bright and highly ambitious political technician from California. Born in January 1913 into a lower-middle-class Quaker family of Irish descent which had settled in the rural town of Yorba Linda, Nixon maintained a lifelong distrust of the eastern liberal establishment and a feeling of social inferiority. However, he shone as a lawyer, entered the House of Representatives in 1946 and became a national figure during the Hiss hearings (1948). He then moved into the Senate (1950), before serving for eight years as an aggressive Vice-President to General Dwight Eisenhower. Nixon tasted defeat in the 1960 presidential contest and the 1962 race for the governorship of California, but staged a dramatic recovery. He moved his family across to New York and built up an effective advisory and marketing team to mellow his public image for the 1968 presidential contest.

Nixon's political success derived from his ability to bridge the 'Main Street' and 'Wall Street' camps of Republican philosophy. In domestic affairs he was a conservative, opposed to Johnson's 'Great Society' welfarism and concerned to decentralise government; but he objected to attempts to turn the clock back sharply and refused to pander to crude racist sentiment. In economic matters, he favoured the competitive free-market economy, but

he tolerated temporary intervention and control when necessary. In foreign affairs, he was a strong, but constructive, anti-
communist, willing to negotiate from a position of strength.
Once in power, Nixon put together a powerful cabinet and
advisory team, which included Bill Rogers (State Department),
Mel Laird (Defense), John Connally (Treasury) and Henry
Kissinger (National Security Adviser – NSA). He soon, however, ran into difficulties in securing the passage of his domestic
packages through the Democrat-controlled Congress and became
more and more aloof and reclusive, surrounding himself with his
dedicated Californian personal aides, H R Haldeman (Chief-of-
Staff), John Ehrlichman and Chuck Colson, and concentrated
increasingly on foreign affairs. In his second term in office he
dreamt of introducing far-reaching administrative reforms and of
breaking the Democrats' dominance of Congress, the bureaucracy
and the media, and of establishing the Republicans as the new
majority party. These aspirations were, however, wrecked by the
Watergate crisis of 1973–4.

The direct complicity of President Nixon in the bungling
break-in of the Democrats' headquarters in Washington in June
1972 remains a matter of debate. Such an action was, however,
symptomatic of the increasingly paranoid attitude of the Nixon
administration during the early 1970s – a period of popular
protest orchestrated by anti-Vietnam War activists. Nixon, concerned to keep a lid on the affair during the 1972 election
campaign, rapidly became involved in an unsavoury 'cover-up'
which involved 'pay-offs', pressuring of the FBI and the erasure
of key conversation tapes. Matters were compounded by the dubi-
ous reputation already acquired by Nixon during a 1952 financial
scandal and by the enmity he had built up among the press. By
April 1973 his closest aides, Haldeman and Ehrlichman, had been
forced to resign, and although Nixon survived another sixteen
months, with impeachment by Congress pending, he was finally
forced to become the first US President to resign office on 8
August 1974.

The 'Watergate scandal', coming hard on the heels of America's
ignominious withdrawal from Vietnam and at a time of gathering
recession, was a sharp blow to national pride and the prestige of
the presidency. Further minor 'Watergates' and bribery scandals
were unearthed by zealous reporters during the following years.
Thus the public's distrust of politicians, already enshrined from
an early date in the American constitution's system of checks and

balances, plummeted to a low level between 1972 and 1975. It was left to Nixon's successor, Gerald R Ford, to attempt to restore confidence and to provide, in his own words, a 'period of healing'.

Gerald R Ford was a most unlikely new President and but for Watergate would never have reached this high office. His background was not, however, dissimilar from that of Richard Nixon. Only six months younger than Nixon, Gerald Ford also came from a fiercely religious, lower-middle-class family which had struggled through the 1920s. Born in Omaha, Nebraska in the Midwest, he moved to Grand Rapids (Michigan State) in 1915, worked his way through Yale and established himself as a lawyer, before entering the House of Representatives in 1948. Ford stood for similar political values to Nixon – economic conservatism at home, anti-isolationism abroad. He was, however, an unashamed moderate in social and racial matters, and close in these respects to the Republican Party's east coast establishment.

Ford enjoyed a career of steady progression up the House's committee hierarchy before being elected Republican Minority Leader in 1965. He lacked, however, the mental incisiveness or the political ruthlessness needed to reach the very top. He had planned to retire from politics in 1977 as a result of his wife's deteriorating health, but in October 1973 Vice-President Spiro Agnew was forced to resign on State corruption charges. President Nixon thus needed a malleable, loyal and unambitious new Vice-President who would quickly be ratified by Congress. Ford proved to be the perfect candidate and was approved in December 1973. Eight months later, the man whose previous ambition had been to become Speaker of the House of Representatives, succeeded to the US presidency.

Once installed in office, President Ford was determined to change the image of the presidency, conduct affairs in a frank and open manner and reduce the influence exerted by the inner cabal of personal advisers and aides. He rapidly ousted the remaining Nixon staffers and set about streamlining the White House Office, where the numbers employed had ballooned from 250 to 540 between 1969 and 1974. In addition, having served for more than 25 years in the House of Representatives, and having viewed the presidency from a Congressional angle, Ford was determined to forge closer links between Congress and the White House and to upgrade the role of the cabinet – his motto upon assuming office was 'communication, conciliation, compromise and co-operation'.

Ford partly inherited and partly constructed anew a strong cabinet, which included Henry Kissinger (State Department/NSA), James Schlesinger (Defense), Bill Simon (Treasury) and the seasoned 66-year-old New York liberal Republican, Nelson Rockefeller (1908–79), as an active Vice-President. He encouraged each departmental head to manage his own affairs and build up support among Congress and the media, leaving the President to determine broad national priorities. This shift was never fully realised. The new President gradually came to recognise the value of a powerful Chief-of-Staff and White House Office to sift correspondence and channel contacts. He thus gradually built up his own team of loyal aides (directed by Chiefs-of-Staff Don Rumsfeld and Richard Cheney) and created an informal, brainstorming 'kitchen cabinet', which included Mel Laird, Bill Scranton, Bryce Harlow, Bill White and David Packard. The Ford administration did nevertheless represent a significant departure from the sealed cliquedoms of the Nixon era. This change was not, however, reciprocated by an evolving Congress which in the immediate aftermath of Watergate was determined to curb the authority of the new President.

The 'New Congress' and President Ford

Congress changed in character during the early 1970s under pressure exerted by reformers within and by new public interest pressure groups without, most notably John Gardner's 'Common Cause', as well as a result of broader social changes outside. The 'Old Congress' of the 1950s had been a conservative gerontocracy dominated by a phalanx of southern Democrats (100 in the House, 22 in the Senate). Assured of their seats for life and aided by the 'seniority rule', these 'Dixie Democrats' captured more than 50% of the committee chairs (including those of the 'blue ribbon' Rules, Appropriations and Ways and Means) and held most of the leadership posts – producing such men as Sam Rayburn (House Speaker) and Lyndon Johnson (Senate Majority Leader). (See Appendix Table B4.) However, their dominance began to crumble during the 1960s as, first, economic development and the introduction of the Voting Rights Acts ended one-party control in the South and raised Congressional turnover rates; and as, secondly, younger liberal Democrats, disillusioned by Vietnam and enraged by Nixon's ready impoundments of funds allocated by Congress for welfare spending, sought to reform and democratise Congress and to regain some of the ground lost in recent decades to the presidency.

Congressional reform began first with the 1970 Legislative Reorganization Act and was continued with the passage in 1973 of the War Powers Resolution (placing restrictions on the President's deployment of troops overseas) and the Congressional Budget and Impoundment Control Act of 1974. The last act ended the President's ability to impound funds once an appropriation had been approved and involved Congress for the first time in the framing of broad budgetary targets and priorities – a new budget office and two budget committees being set up for this purpose. The pace of reform increased following the November 1974 'post-Watergate Election', which resulted in the Republicans' loss of many northern and suburban seats and brought in scores of young new Congressmen. Seventy-five Democrat freshmen packed the party's House caucus and forced through major rule changes which downgraded the importance of seniority in the selection of committee chairmen and extended the influence of House members. These changes led to the deposition of the southern chairmen of three important committees – Banking, Agriculture, Armed Services. The other chairmen who survived found their control weakened, as power was increasingly dispersed to the broader ranks of the sub-committee chairmen. Such changes failed to transform Congress into a more cohesive unit and radical new policy centre. Instead, Congress became more unpredictable and individualistic, with members fighting for their own local interest. It became, in addition, more assertive in its dealings with the President, seeking to block his policy initiatives and to put forward costly social spending schemes of its own.

President Ford was thus forced to battle constantly with the Democrat-controlled Congress in an attempt to steer measures in his chosen direction. He was frequently, however, unsuccessful – particularly in foreign affairs, where Congress checked military spending and further potential involvement in South-east Asia and Angola against the wishes of Kissinger and Ford. (See Appendix Table B7 for the 'Congressional Success Rate' of the Ford term.) In domestic affairs President Ford was forced to employ his veto an unusually large number of times to check Congressional profligacy – issuing 35 regular vetoes and 11 'pocket vetoes' of 'public bills' – but found himself overridden eight times by countervailing Congressional majorities.[1] The

President's decision to grant an unconditional pardon to Richard Nixon in September 1974 did not help these relations, so that by the end of his term in office this former proponent of Congressional power took a new and more chagrined view.

The Ford presidency was a period of confusion and despondency for the American public and political process. It was also a period of economic recession. Recovery recommenced slowly from 1975; however, the 'approval rating' of President Ford still amounted to only 39% in January 1976. Ford carried with him the stigma of being unelected and, though decent and well-meaning, lacked personal charisma or vision.

The 1976 Presidential Election Campaign

President Ford fought for re-election in November 1976 on a centrist conservative programme of retrenchment, deregulation and decentralisation. He did not, however, receive automatic endorsement as his party's nominee, having to fight instead a prolonged and costly campaign against the former film star and Governor of California, Ronald Reagan, the darling of the party's right wing.

Ford faced peculiar difficulties in his campaign for re-election. He lacked the experience and aura of an elected President; he had to assemble a campaign team at short notice; and he was faced by a most effective opponent. The 65-year-old Reagan was an outstanding speaker, who was able to put across simple and direct messages which appealed to the 'Main Street' grassroots of the party. He campaigned upon a radical tax-cutting, free-market domestic platform coupled with a staunch anti-communist foreign policy and succeeded in projecting himself as an outsider fighting the corrupt political élite. This captured the anti-Washington mood of the nation.

Reagan's battle for the party nomination was bruising and lasted more than six months. He won an unprecedented ten primaries (concentrated in the southern, midwestern and western States) against an incumbent President, but was in the end defeated by 1187:1070 votes at the Kansas National Convention on 19 August. The policy programme presented by Reagan was too dramatic for the nation in 1976. However, his determined candidature was of importance in, first, pushing the 'Ford ticket' towards the right – forcing the selection of Senator Robert Dole (1923–) of Kansas as running-mate in preference to Nelson

Rockefeller – and in, second, damaging the re-election prospects of President Ford. By the middle of August 1976 Gerald Ford lagged 20 points behind his Democrat challenger, who had gained a decisive Convention victory in July.

The contest for the Democrat nomination had at first been wide open, involving 13 challengers, and looked set to end in a deadlocked Convention at which an undeclared senior figure, such as Hubert Humphrey or George McGovern, would quietly emerge and once more steal the nomination. However, by March 1976 the field had narrowed down to five – Senator Henry 'Scoop' Jackson of Washington, Governor George Wallace of Alabama, Senator Frank Church of Idaho, Congressman Morris Udall of Arizona and the former Governor of Georgia, Jimmy Carter. Jimmy Carter emerged as the clear front-runner, gaining particularly strong support from the South and Midwest. Jerry Brown, the Governor of California, made a late entry into the contest in May 1976 and proved to be a strong vote-winner in the North-east and West, but his challenge was too late. By June 1976 Jimmy Carter had secured a huge lead in delegates and the influential figures of George Wallace, 'Scoop' Jackson and Richard Daley (Mayor of Chicago) had moved behind the Carter bandwagon, pledging him their delegates and support. Within days, the remaining challengers – Church, Udall and Brown – conceded the nomination to Carter, who triumphantly arrived at New York for the party Convention of 12–14 July at the head of a united and enthusiastic party.

Jimmy Carter was a surprise victor for the Democratic Party establishment, who at one stage in March 1976 had attempted to set up a 'Stop Carter' movement. Such was Carter's lack of a national profile that he gained the tag of 'Jimmy Who?', which proved to be an asset in the popular mood of 1976. Carter was born the son of an enterprising peanut farmer on the outskirts of the small town of Plains in Georgia in October 1924. Trained as an engineer at the Annapolis Academy in Maryland, he served in the navy for 11 years before returning to Plains in 1954 to take up the management of his late father's farm. He became involved in local school board, farming and charitable committees, and served as a deacon and Sunday School teacher in his local Baptist church, before winning a seat in the local State Senate in 1962 after his opponent had been found guilty of ballot-rigging. Carter became Governor of Georgia at the second attempt in 1970 after intensive campaigning by his skilled and devoted canvassing team.

From the summer of 1972 Carter began broadening his knowledge and expertise, researching and preparing for a presidential challenge. He worked as chairman of the Democrats' National Campaign Committee for the 1974 elections, building up contacts with middle-ranking State party figures, and began campaigning early after his term as Governor ended – bursting on the scene at the Iowa caucuses in January 1976 in what was to become a paradigm campaign for future contenders. Carter developed a political style and philosophy which placed a premium upon contact with the people, and exhibited a deep concern for the poor and unfortunate and an antipathy to the power exerted by pressure groups and big business. Deeply religious – a 'born again' teetotal Christian – Carter saw politics in moral terms and represented a new generation of southern leaders who were concerned with integrating the black community and bringing the 'New South' back into the political mainstream.

Jimmy Carter's appeal in 1976 was in many ways very similar to that of Ronald Reagan. He projected himself as an outsider drawn from the religious, rural heartland of the country, free from the corruption of the cities of the North-east with their sophisticated but cynical lawyer-politicians. He appealed to grassroots party activists above the head of the party bosses and was able to establish an early lead in the now crucial primary contests which created an unstoppable bandwagon.[2] Unlike Reagan, he projected a pacific image in foreign affairs and did not advocate dramatic restructuring at home. Unlike Ford, he promised novelty, optimism and a vision for the country's future. In Carter's eyes, America had been humiliated by Watergate and Vietnam, but it could be rebuilt economically, politically and morally. He pledged to break the control of the insider Washington clique, open up the government, bring in a new generation of younger, honest and accountable politicians, involve the people and inject a sense of ethics, justice and morality into decision-taking at home and abroad. Following such principles, America would be able to set an example to the world community and recover its sense of pride and authority to lead. Northern Democrats remained sceptical of this philosophy and were wary of the possible conservatism of this 'new southerner'. These worries were, however, assuaged, first by Carter's acceptance speech in New York on 14 July, when he spoke of the need for a national health system, cuts in the defence budget and policies designed to help the poor and boost employment, and then by his selection of Walter Mondale (Senator for Minnesota), an undiluted liberal with extensive Washington experience, as his running-mate.

TABLE 3 THE NOVEMBER 1976 PRESIDENTIAL ELECTION (TURNOUT 54.4%)

Candidate	Party	Pop- ular Vote (m)	As % of Total	Electoral College Votes	States Captured
Jimmy E Carter	D	40.83	50.4	297	23
Gerald R Ford	R	39.15	48.3	240	27
Eugene McCarthy*	Ind	0.76	0.9	0	0
Lester Maddox†	AIP	0.18	0.2	0	0
Others‡		0.17	0.2	1§	0
Total		81.09	100.0	538	50

* Eugene McCarthy, the former Democrat Senator for Minnesota who had unsuccessfully contested the party's presidential nomination in 1968, ran as an Independent and was named on the ballot of 29 States.
† Lester Maddox, the former ultra-conservative Democrat Governor of Georgia, stood as a candidate for the American Independent Party (AIP).
‡ Ten other candidates were entered on the ballot paper in a number of States across the Union.
§ One 'electoral college' vote from Washington State was cast for Ronald Reagan although he had failed to gain the Republican nomination.

Carter's energy, apparent youth – campaigning with his attractive wife Rosalynn and young daughter Amy – confidence, integrity and vision, attracted wide popular support. The incumbent President appeared by contrast dull, uninspiring and uncertain, offering second-rate leadership for what was threatening to become a second-ranking power. The gap between the two contenders narrowed in a low-key campaign, fought within new spending limits, which was punctuated by four important national television debates. On the election day of 2 November 1976 only 54.4% of those eligible turned out to vote, but Carter recorded a narrow, though still comfortable, victory. He brought together the southern and northern wings of the Democratic Party, winning all

the former Confederate territories except Virginia and most of
the populous industrial States of the North-east.[3] (See Figure 2.)
Carter captured in all 50.4% of the vote and gained an 'electoral
college' majority of 56. Ford trailed behind with 48.3% of the vote
and was the first incumbent President to be rejected for over 40
years. Nevertheless, he won 27 States and recorded almost a clean
sweep in the Centre and West of the nation. In the concurrent
Congressional elections the Democrats made a net gain of two
seats in the House of Representatives and the Republicans a net
gain of one seat in the Senate, leaving the Democrats with a handsome majority in both chambers. (See Appendix Table B3.)

TABLE 4 VOTING BY REGION FOR CARTER AND FORD IN 1976

	Turnout (m)	Carter (%)	Ford (%)
East	22.0	51	47
South	20.5	54	45
Midwest	24.0	48	50
West	14.6	46	51
Total	81.1	50	48

Figure 2   Map of 1976 Presidential Election

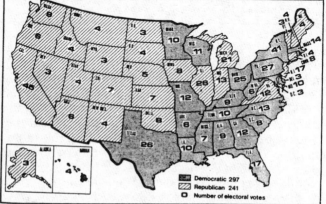

Source: *The Economist* 1 November 1980 p22

TABLE 5   THE CONGRESSIONAL AND GUBERNATORIAL ELECTIONS OF NOVEMBER 1976

	House Seats	Result	Senator- ships	Result	Governor- ships	Result
Total Contested	435		33*		14	
Democrat Victories	292	+2	21	0†	9	+1
Republican Victories	143	−2	11	+1	5	−1

* One Independent Senator, Harry Byrd (Va), was returned.
† The Democrats recorded a net loss of one seat to the Republicans, which was counterbalanced by the gain of a seat in New York from an independent Conservative-Republican.

29

Chapter 3

THE CARTER ERA

The Carter Administration: 1977–80

Jimmy Carter entered the White House in January 1977 on a wave of optimism that a new face with an open, populist approach to government would restore American self-respect after the humbling events of 1972–4. He was to leave office four years later harrowed and exhausted, having endured constant battles at home, major diplomatic reversals abroad and humiliating defeat at the hands of a veteran former movie star. Carter was unfortunate in assuming office during a period of economic transition and recession, of reassessment of America's world role, and of resurgence in the power of both Congress and the media. He thus shared the problems which had also overwhelmed his predecessor, and, despite his popular mandate, failed equally to overcome these difficulties, becoming castigated as an uncertain, vacuous leader.

Things were different in January 1977. Carter began his term in office keen to establish a more accessible style of presidency. The first example of this new style was the decision of the Carter family to stop the official limousine and walk the final mile down Pennsylvania Avenue to the White House during the 20 January Inauguration Day parade. This was followed by orders to abandon much of the pomp and ceremony and many of the costly perks which had surrounded the presidency. Instead, a more frugal, informal and open form of government was placed on show. White House staff were instructed to drive to work instead of using chauffeur-driven limousines; room temperatures were reduced to set an energy-saving example; press conferences became more frequent; and the President began to appear on television wearing cardigans instead of formal suits.

President Carter, like Ford before him, also sought to establish an effective and broad-based form of government and to foster close, co-operative ties with Congress. Lacking Federal experience, the new President had tremendous difficulties in selecting his initial cabinet and had to rely heavily on the advice of the Democrat National Committee and of Vice-President Mondale before personally interviewing candidates in Atlanta in December 1976. His final team represented an unusually varied mixture of academics, lawyers, businessmen and representatives of various ethnic and religious groups, but naturally contained a particularly strong southern element. (See Table 6.)

TABLE 6   THE CARTER CABINET OF JANUARY 1977

Secretaries	
State Dept	C Vance (New York, ex-Kennedy & Johnson admins)
Treasury	M Blumenthal (Michigan, business)
Defense	H Brown (California, academic physicist)
Interior	C Andrus (ex-Governor of Idaho)
Agriculture	B Bergland (Minnesota, ex-Congress)
Commerce	Dr Juanita Kreps (North Carolina, academic)
Labor	Dr R Marshall (Texas, academic)
Health, Education & Welfare (HEW)	J Califano (Columbia, lawyer & ex-Johnson aide)
Housing & Urban Development (HUD)	Mrs P Harris (Columbia, black lawyer/ambassador)
Transportation	B Adams (Washington, ex-Congress)
Attorney-General	G Bell (Georgia, ex-Carter legal adviser)
UN Representative	A Young (Georgia, black lawyer & ex-Congress)
Dir of OMB	B Lance (Georgia, banker & State administrator)
Asst for Energy	Dr J Schlesinger (Virginia, ex-Ford admin)
Chmn CEA	Dr C Schultze (Maryland, academic)
NSA	Dr Z Brzezinski (New York, academic)
Dir of CIA	S Turner (Admiral, ex-Annapolis)
Sp Trade Adviser	R Strauss (Texas, ex-Democratic Party chairman)

Jimmy Carter was supported, in addition, by a team of devoted and trusted personal advisers who had worked with him when Governor and during the presidential campaign. Chief among the group was the 32-year-old Hamilton Jordan, who had acted as Carter's campaign manager in 1970 and 1975–6 and as executive secretary in the Georgia administration. He became the co-ordinating Chief-of-Staff between 1976 and 1980. Next came Jody Powell, the new White House press secretary or 'Voice of Carter', who had first acted as a student driver during the 1969–70 gubernatorial campaign. Bert Lance, a banker from Calhoun who had served Carter in the Transport Department and advised on fiscal matters in Georgia, was the third powerful member of what became known as the 'Georgia mafia' and was appointed head of the crucial OMB. Other Georgians, including Stuart Eizenstat, Jack Watson, Frank Moore, Charles Kirbo, Gerald Rafshoon and members of the Carter family, provided additional support and advice, with his wife Rosalynn regularly attending cabinet meetings.

Despite this wealth of advice, the new President's team lacked direct experience of the workings of Washington. They had campaigned as 'outsiders' and this remained a problem throughout the next four years. President Carter faced two immediate problems – first, of controlling the executive machine and large cabinet, many of whom were completely new faces to the President; and second, of working with Congress.

Carter and his Cabinet   At the outset of the new administration President Carter sought to establish strong cabinet government with much discretion being left to departmental Secretaries while the President sat back and co-ordinated policies and his aides provided quiet administrative support. However, this proved to be impractical as the Carter team came to recognise the realities of American government. Such is the size of each department and the pressure exerted from the bureaucrats within and from pressure groups and Congressmen outside that Secretaries rapidly become submerged, unable to contribute meaningfully to broader policy debates, and become entangled in departmental alliances. Presidents have thus come to recognise the need to work through smaller specialist cabinet groupings, to make policy from the White House Office and to interfere increasingly in departmental affairs through their loyal aides. American cabinets have thus tended to move through cycles as an administration progresses – from a large 'great cabinet' at the outset through to smaller *ad hoc* specialist teams in its final years – and the influence of the President's White House aides has similarly tended to increase as the life of the administration has lengthened.

The Carter administration was not immune from such a cycle of evolution. In the first year of its life the full cabinet met 36 times and in the second year it met 23 times; in the final two years there were only nine and six meetings respectively. Instead, the smaller teams of Vance, Brzezinski, Brown and Turner, and Schultze, Blumenthal, Schlesinger, Strauss and Lance, began to meet frequently with Carter to discuss foreign affairs and economic matters, and Vice-President Mondale took an unusually active role in both foreign and domestic affairs. Carter and his Georgian aides also gradually began to meddle in more and more departmental matters. This partly resulted from their disaffection with the performance of individual Secretaries, for example the liberal Joseph Califano at HEW, who was viewed as disloyal and opposed to a number of Carter's policy goals, and Michael Blumenthal at the Treasury Department, who was seen as ineffective in dealing with Congress. It also resulted, however, from Carter's own concern to keep abreast of the conduct of each department – a concern which dated back to his days as a Senator in Georgia, when, having pledged that if elected he would read each document before voting, Carter embarked on a fast reading course and diligently ploughed through more than a thousand bills each year.

Power thus passed increasingly into the hands of the President and his 'Georgia mafia'. These loyal advisers were, however, extremely young and inexperienced and far stronger at campaigning and marketing than at governing and administrating. The most experienced and worldly member of Carter's Georgian advisory team was Bert Lance, who as head of the OMB was expected to prepare the budget and oversee the President's plans for administrative reorganisation. Unfortunately Lance became a victim of the critical post-Watergate press and of the high ethical standards set for public servants by Carter before he assumed office. Lance divested himself of shares in the Bank of Georgia, but, when journalists and Senate committees began to probe closely into his affairs, a question mark was raised over the propriety of his financial dealings. Subsequent investigation showed Lance to have acted properly; however, the attention attracted by his case during 1977 paralysed government affairs. The President was thus forced on 21 September 1977 to accept Lance's resignation and replace him with James McIntyre, a former budget director in Georgia. This loss was a grave blow to the new administration, denying it the services of its 'key' figure and the one most skilled at cementing ties inside and outside of Congress.

Carter and Congress   The resignation of Lance led to a greater role for Chief-of-Staff Hamilton Jordan, who, however, lacked the weight and respect enjoyed by Lance. It was thus left to Frank Moore, a professional management specialist from Georgia, to take on the brunt of liaising with Congress. This proved to be a difficult task as the resurgence of Congressional power and individualism noted between 1973 and 1976 gained pace.

In the House of Representatives the Speaker, Carl Albert (Oklahoma), retired in December 1976 and two influential southern committee chairmen – Wilbur Mills (Ways and Means) and Wayne Hays (Rules) – resigned following sex scandals. Another two southern chairmen – George Mahon (Appropriations) and Olin Teague (Science) retired in 1978.[1] In the Senate both the Majority Leader, Mike Mansfield (Montana), and the Minority Leader, Hugh Scott (Pennsylvania), retired in November 1976, and the deaths of Hubert Humphrey (Minnesota), James Allen (Alabama) and John McClellan (Arkansas) and the retirement in November 1978 of James Eastland (Mississippi – Chmn Judiciary Committee) and John Sparkman (Alabama – Chmn Foreign Relations Committee) served to weaken traditional bonds and create a new sense of uncertainty and flux. Chance factors and the work of nature contributed in large measure to these changes of personnel, but turnover rates were also temporarily raised as a result of the volatile post-Watergate mood of the electorate. For example, in the 96th Congress (1979–80) 20 Senators and 77 Representatives were freshmen and more than 30 other Senators had served less than a full term. The average age of Congressmen was thus falling – dipping to below 50 years in the case of the House and to 55 years in the Senate – and the new House Speaker, Tip O'Neill (Massachusetts), and Senate Majority Leader, Robert Byrd (West Virginia), had to fight to control two undisciplined and inexperienced chambers which increasingly became prey to the pressure of outside lobbyists.

The prospects of gaining strong and steady Congressional support were further diminished by the curiously unique philosophy, beliefs and programme supported by President Carter, a man who defied political labels.

In domestic affairs, President Carter was a conservative on economic matters but an earnest liberal on social issues. He opposed the free-spending policies of traditional northern Democrats, pledging instead to narrow the Federal budget deficit and eliminate it by 1981. However, Carter, as a committed Christian, was also determined to improve the conditions of the poor and deprived, and to reduce levels of unemployment. He was willing to tolerate some limited Keynesian fiscal dabbling, but sought primarily to provide funds for social programmes through the elimination of waste and inefficiency in government spending and through an improved targeting of scarce resources towards the most needy. He planned therefore to reorganise and stream-line the Federal administration (following the example he had set in Georgia[2]) and to reform the income tax and welfare system in the interests of lower income groups. Second, Carter was driven on by a populist desire to attack monopolies, deregulate businesses and remove professional perks. The President's other great domestic aim was to deal with the energy problem through the establishment of an integrated national programme which would encourage greater economy in fuel use in a planned and equitable fashion. In foreign affairs (see Part 6), he proposed a bold new policy based around a concern for justice, morality and human rights.

The policy programme pursued by the Carter administration lacked coherence and thus alternately engaged and enraged conservative and liberal opinion within Congress. This meant that the President could not rely on a stable bedrock of support and would have to construct varying alliances on specific issues and build up outside public support. President Carter frequently failed, however, in these tasks and found instead large and diverse coalitions building up to block or radically alter each initiative.

Policy Initiatives 1977–80

The President's performance in the first legislative session – usually a co-operative 'honeymoon period' – was particularly disappointing and the administration never fully recovered from this early setback. As Carter later recognised, he introduced a confusing rush of measures, many of which were controversial and painful, and provided little in the way of douceurs to coax along doubting members – vetoing, for example, the 'pork barrel' Public Works Bill which included 33 new water projects sought by western Congressmen. These actions immediately gained the President a clutch of Congressional enemies and although his reflationary tax-cutting budget package of 1977 was passed, the new administration ran into a minefield of opposition when its tax, health and welfare reforms were introduced. This opposition continued throughout Carter's period in office, as conservatives and interest groups (including the hospital and private insurance lobbies) ranged up on one side criticising the cost of Carter's proposed changes, and as traditional northern liberals argued conversely that these reforms were too limited. It was the new energy package – the centrepiece of its legislative programme – which became the exhausting battlefield for the Carter administration, and which highlighted the problems the President faced when dealing with the fragmented Congress of 1977–80.

The Carter Energy Bill Urgent action was clearly necessary to overcome the United States' mounting dependence on the importation of foreign oil, which had caused serious balance of payments problems as world oil prices had spiralled after 1973. The crux of the problem centred around the regulatory system which placed a low ceiling on American fuel prices, encouraging wasteful consumption which discouraged the exploration of new oil and gas fields. It was widely agreed by energy experts that these controls should be eased and American oil and gas allowed to float gradually towards world market levels; however, no President had previously shown sufficient determination to tackle the interest groups – producer and consumer lobbies – involved.

Things were different under President Carter. The energy question was given top priority and the framework for a coherent national policy was gradually established. On 18 April 1977 the new President addressed the nation and declared that the need to reduce energy consumption was, with the exception of preserving the peace, 'the greatest challenge our country will face during our lifetime' and unless tackled at once, it would gradually overwhelm the country. It was the 'moral equivalent of war'. A new Energy Department, bringing together more than 20 government agencies, was thus rapidly established, with Dr James Schlesinger at its head. Then on 20 April a detailed energy plan was unveiled. It envisaged halving by 1985 both the level of oil imports and the growth rate in US energy demand. This was to be achieved by raising energy prices with justice and with the minimum of economic disruption, and by promoting energy conservation. Penalties would be imposed on gas-guzzling automobiles; tax inducements would be granted to householders who invested in insulation and to factories which converted to coal; the revenue raised from higher energy prices would be returned to the public in the form of tax rebates; and prices would be equalised across the country.

However, this plan was necessarily large and complicated and impinged upon many diverse interests. A rift rapidly developed between the energy-rich States of the South and West and the energy-deficient North, with oil- and gas-producing and consuming lobbies ranging up on either side. President Carter's energy plan had most success in the House of Representatives, which treated the issue as a whole in an Omnibus Committee and had a bias towards the consumer interest. It faced fiercer opposition from the Senate, where the measure was divided between five committees and where Senators from the southern States fought for the recirculation of the increased taxes into oil and gas company coffers rather than into the pockets of the general public. The oil and gas industry naturally concentrated their lobbying campaign on the Senate.

The Carter Energy Bill was forced to endure months of endless scrutiny and gradually each of its main policy planks was removed by the Senate Finance Committee chaired by Russell Long of Louisiana. This forced the Carter administration to allow the dismembered motion to die without result in 1977 and to attempt a second legislative assault in 1978. During this second battle President Carter made frequent television appeals in defence of his bill and improved his Congressional lobbying skills, inducing thousands of supporters to pressurise Capitol Hill. The President still, however, faced great opposition from interest groups for what still appeared to be a distant crisis. His persistence, nevertheless, paid off in October 1978 when, following further Conference Committee wrangling, Congress, with its eye on impending midterm elections, finally approved the Energy Bill. The bill had been diluted, with two of its original main planks, the proposed oil and petrol taxes, being abandoned. However, it did herald a number of significant departures: first, it introduced financial incentives to encourage fuel efficiency on the road and in homes and new regulations to discourage oil-burning by industry, and, second, it legislated for the gradual de-regulation of gas prices. It thus represented an important first step in the battle to reverse the upward course in American energy consumption and to educate the public on the value of conservation.

This partial achievement was won at a great cost to the Carter presidency, both in time and in popular esteem, as the administration's battle with Congress and its frequent reversals during 1977 and 1978 rubbed away the glitter of November 1976. The President gained the image of a man unable to control his cabinet and

Congress and, from his handling of the economy and foreign affairs, as unpredictable – liable to make sudden changes in course and to cave in at times of pressure. By the end of June 1978 the popularity of President Carter had slumped dramatically with a bare 38% of those questioned approving of his conduct of affairs. (See Figure 3.) Only President Truman between 1946 and 1947 had experienced a similar nose-dive in support. Respected observers, for example James Reston of the *New York Times*, commented upon the administration's loss of direction and Carter's lack of decisive leadership qualities, noting that 'the main charge against him is not that he doesn't listen to anybody, but that he listens to everybody and cannot make up his mind – or maybe that he makes it up too often.'

Figure 3   President Carter's Gallup Poll Approval Rating 1977 – 1980

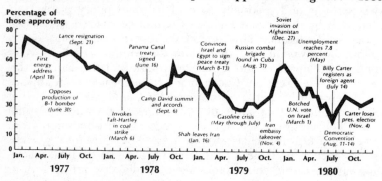

Source: President Carter: 1980 *Congressional Quarterly Inc* 1983 p3

Jimmy Carter was increasingly seen as a 'one-term President', certain to lose or even fail to obtain nomination in 1980, and this weakened his potential bargaining power and influence over Congress. However in the autumn of 1978 the President's fortunes were sharply revived by two dramatic initiatives overseas – the Camp David 'framework for peace' accord between Egypt and Israel and the agreement to resume diplomatic relations with China. (See Part 6.) Such an excursion into foreign affairs was a typical ploy for a President finding his policies blocked at home and it reaped temporary dividends for the Democratic Party. They emerged from the November 1978 Congressional and gubernatorial elections losing, in net, only three Senate seats, 16 House seats and six governorships (concentrated in the Mid-west and South-west). (See Table 7.) There was, nevertheless, a swing towards conservatism in the character of the Congressmen elected in November 1978 and in the popular mood. Right-wing single-issue campaigning bodies, for example the 'pro-life' (anti-abortion) movement, became more assertive, and a middle-class tax revolt spread from California after a public referendum (Proposition 13) in June had resulted in a vote in favour of a reduction in property taxes by 57%. Such changes promised to make it more difficult for President Carter to gain support for health and welfare spending and for his SALT-2 arms limitation initiative.

TABLE 7 THE CONGRESSIONAL AND GUBERNATORIAL ELECTIONS OF NOVEMBER 1978 (TURNOUT 34.9%)

	House Seats	Result	Senator-ships	Result	Governor-ships	Result
Total Contested	435		35		36	
Democrat Victories	276	−16	15	−3*	20	−6
Republican Victories	159	+16	20	+3	16	+6†

* Among the defeated Democrats were the ultra-liberal Dick Clark of Iowa, an expert on African affairs and strong supporter of Carter's foreign policy, Wendell Anderson of Minnesota, Floyd Haskell of Colorado, Thomas MacIntyre of New Hampshire and William Hathaway of Maine.

† Republican gains included the governorships of Texas, Pennsylvania and Minnesota.

President Carter, with his ear attuned to the popular mood and with his natural proclivity for restraint in economic affairs, adjusted to these changes and introduced a package of more cautious fiscal measures in the autumn of 1978 and spring of 1979 under the slogan a 'New Foundation'. These encompassed cuts in, and postponements of, public works programmes; a rise in defence spending (whose share of Federal outlays had fallen from supra-30% during the early 1970s to barely 23% by 1978); a policy of voluntary pay restraint; and the induction into the administration of Alfred Kahn – a Cornell economist who had recently deregulated the airline industry – as a special adviser on inflation. Unfortunately for the Carter administration, the economic indicators rapidly worsened during 1979 as oil prices spiralled in the wake of the Iranian revolution. Inflation rose to a post-war peak of 13% and the Carter administration was faced with the novel spectre of stagflation (high inflation combined with declining industrial growth). It was forced to frame new and more radical initiatives – a hospital costs containment bill, a 'real wage insurance' clause and a petrol-rationing scheme – but found these in turn blocked in Congress by interest group lobbies. Thus the economic situation continued to deteriorate, petrol shortages developed, and by the time the President returned home from the Tokyo Western Economic Summit in July 1979 he was faced with a gathering crisis of public confidence.

President Carter responded to this crisis by dramatically cancelling a planned nationwide energy appeal and withdrawing to his Camp David (Maryland) retreat. Here he set up meetings with small groups of more than 130 outside advisers – State Governors, Congressmen, businessmen, labour leaders, clerics and party activists – to reassess the position of the administration; its performance, policies and public perception. Sitting on a cushion on the floor, the President received a barrage of conflicting criticism and advice, with the majority calling for cabinet changes and the induction of more substantial and mature personnel into the White House Office. At the conclusion of this 'conference' President Carter made a number of unannounced visits to private homes near Pittsburgh and Martinsburg to talk with ordinary 'Middle Americans', before returning to the White House reinvigorated and catharsised.

On 15 July he delivered a major speech to the nation referring to these conversations and pinpointing a crisis in national confidence. The President reaffirmed his faith in the ability of both government and the people to overcome the mounting problems and launched a major new six-point energy programme. It was one of Carter's best speeches and was favourably received by a record 100 million viewers, but within two days its impact was lost by a bungling reshuffle. Instead of just replacing the five Secretaries who eventually left – Califano, Schlesinger, Blumenthal, Bell and Adams – President Carter, wishing to signal a decisive change in direction, called first for the resignation of his entire cabinet. This created confusion and uncertainty before the final details of this manoeuvre became clear and resulted in a loss of momentum for the new energy programme.[3]

President Carter had intended his Camp David 'conference' and cabinet reshuffle to signal a change of approach for the final year and a half of his presidency. As part of this strategy he brought fresh east coast blood into his own advisory and support team in the shape of Hedley Donovan (the former editor of *Time*) and Alonzo McDonald, who became the new staff director. In many respects, however, Carter's actions rekindled memories of Carter the outsider and populist campaigner of 1975–6. He had taken a step back, consulting with representatives of the public, before berating Congress and his own government departments for inertia and mismanagement and calling for a moral renewal in the nation at large. The impact of these actions proved, however, to be only short-lived. Significant progress was made on energy reform, with the oil companies finally being forced to accept the phased decontrol of oil prices and a modified windfall profit tax in March 1980. However, this achievement was overshadowed by a sharp nose-dive of the economy into recession – unemployment rising to 7.8% in May 1980 while inflation still exceeded 13% – and by the double shocks of the capture of American hostages in Teheran and the Soviet Union's invasion of Afghanistan in November and December 1979 respectively. The tight fiscal policies pursued after 1978 by the Carter administration were blamed for exacerbating the economic recession, while its lax foreign policies were blamed for encouraging Soviet and Iranian adventurism. Thus, while the Teheran and Afghanistan crises brought an initial rallying of support around the presidency, the administration's failure to resolve either crisis rapidly seriously diminished its public standing. This was to prove fatal in what was an election year.

The Campaign for the Presidency in 1980

Elected incumbent Presidents start out as overwhelming favourites in the campaign for re-election. They carry the prestige of office and the ability to grant favours to wavering regions. In such circumstances the challenge to an incumbent from within his party's ranks is invariably only muted and token, while the challenge for the presidential nomination within the opposing party is bitter and hard-fought. Events did not, however, follow this course in the troubled later 1970s. In 1980 President Carter, like his predecessor President Ford in 1976, faced a strong and

41

ideologically based challenge from a prominent section of his own party. By contrast his opponent, the Republican Ronald Reagan, had to contend with numerous minor challengers, but faced little major opposition and went on to unseat an elected President for the first time since 1932. Three factors contributed to this result – the growing divisions within the Democratic Party; the revival in conservatism as a populist ideology; and the unprecedentedly low public esteem endured by President Carter in the 'year of Teheran'.

The Divided Democrats Jimmy Carter's success in 1976 had shocked the Democratic Party's establishment. Their fears concerning the depths of the new President's liberalism were confirmed by the rightward drift of the administration after 1978. Priority was placed upon fighting inflation rather than on welfare and inner city programmes. This led first to a Congressional rebellion by north-eastern Democrats and then to an attempt – drawing in support from trade union leaders, feminists and black activists – to push forward an alternative liberal candidate for the party nomination. Early indications of such disaffection were to be seen at the party's midterm national convention in Memphis in December 1978 and by the summer of 1979 a full-blooded 'Dump Carter' campaign was underway. The favourite son of this liberal activist wing was Senator Edward Kennedy of Massachusetts, the heir to the popular but ill-fated Kennedy dynasty. Opinion polls during 1978 and 1979 regularly showed a clear voter preference for Senator Kennedy over President Carter and leftward-leaning groups began actively to push for a Kennedy candidacy. Two such groups were the Progressive Alliance (established in February 1979 by Douglas Fraser, president of the United Autoworkers union – UAW) and the 'draft Kennedy' movement, which, set up by Richard Nolan in Minnesota in June 1979, had spread to 25 more States by October 1979. Inside Congress, Edward Kennedy attacked the Carter administration's conservative fiscal programme, rejected the decontrol of oil prices and spoke out in favour of a comprehensive Federal health care system. He thus established himself as the guardian of the party's liberal tradition, before announcing his intention to contest the party nomination in November 1979.

Edward Kennedy came from the old school of urban north-eastern lawyer-politicians. Born in Boston in 1932, the fourth son of a wealthy Irish-American Catholic family, he passed through Harvard and entered the Senate at the earliest opportunity in

1962 – taking over the Massachusetts seat recently vacated by John F Kennedy. He lacked the keen intellectual and oratorical skills of his two elder brothers,[4] but, following their tragic assassinations in 1963 and 1968, found transferred to him much of their popular affection. Aided by a large, skilled and clever team of political advisers, Edward Kennedy rapidly established a reputation as a most able and diligent Senator with a strong affinity, despite being a millionaire, with the poor and underprivileged. He attracted strong support from traditional Democrat groups – blue-collar unionists, marginal farmers, blacks, Jews (attracted by his pro-Israeli stance) and Hispanics – and from the substantial Irish-American and Catholic communities. Support was weaker, as for his brother John, in the South and West of the country and in small-town, Protestant America.

Kennedy was viewed by many on the right of the American political spectrum as a dangerous big-spending 1960s-style liberal Democrat. However, while it is true that he remained committed to the establishment of a national health system and opposed attacks on welfare and urban spending, Edward Kennedy had by 1980 shifted ground to meet the circumstances of this less expansionary post-OPEC decade – supporting a number of President Carter's themes, for example transport deregulation and tax reform, and favouring wage and price controls. Although the gap between Kennedy and Carter remained significant, he managed to support the President on 84% of roll-call votes in the 96th Congress – a record exceeded by only three Senators. Edward Kennedy's moderation in economic matters increased as the battle for the 1980 Democrat nomination and for the 'floating voter' progressed.

Kennedy enjoyed many advantages in his quest for the Democratic Party nomination – the magic of his name in the age of 'media politics'; strong party and sectional support; solid financial backing; and the popular desire for a strong leader with a coherent policy programme and sense of style following the shambling drift of the Carter years. He remained, however, vulnerable on two counts. First, his moderation in foreign affairs and his welfare liberalism at home, while popular with radical Democrats, ran against the grain of the increasingly belligerent and conservative late 1970s and early 1980s. Second, a series of scandals and tragedies in Kennedy's private life continued to cast doubts as to his fitness for the highest office and his ability to deal with its associated pressures. These scandals commenced at

Harvard when Kennedy was sent down for cheating in a Spanish examination and they continued to bedevil him in 1979, with his wife's alcoholism, his own infidelities and his marriage on the verge of irretrievable breakdown. It was, however, the mysterious July 1969 'Chappaquiddick affair' – when he failed to report a late-night road accident which resulted in the death by drowning of a female passenger, Mary Jo Kopechne, after his car had careered over the side of a bridge – which hung like an albatross over Edward Kennedy and which was resurrected during the 1980 campaign.

A second, though less dangerous intra-party challenge to President Carter was provided by Jerry Brown, the austere but charismatic 42-year-old Zen Buddhist Governor of California who had pressed Carter late in 1976 – winning every primary he had contested. However, by 1980 Brown's political star was on the wane. A strong supporter of radical environmental and social issues during his first term as Governor, Brown alienated many of his early backers with a sudden and opportunistic shift to the right following his re-election in November 1978 – emerging, for example, as a converted advocate of a Federal balanced budget amendment. Brown was well financed and began campaigning early at the Iowa caucuses in January 1980; however, he lacked blue-collar support or a political base in the North-east or South and seemed certain to meet with defeat.[5]

It was Edward Kennedy who headed the field as favourite at the outset of the race for the Democrat nomination in November 1979. His campaign team, led by brother-in-law Stephen Smith, was strong and experienced and he rapidly gained the support of eight significant labour union leaders (including the Machinists and the Electricians) and the endorsement of Mayor Jane Byrne of Catholic Chicago. President Carter was able to counter the growing grassroots support for Edward Kennedy by winning over many party bosses and many of the remaining union leaders through offers of presidential largesse and patronage, and he retained a clear lead in the southern States. It was, however, the Teheran hostage crisis and the Russian invasion of Afghanistan which radically altered the whole complexion of the Democrat campaign and killed off the Kennedy challenge as a patriotic warmongering mood swept the nation, temporarily returning popular support to its beleaguered President.

President Carter dominated the early primaries, capturing 60% of the vote to Edward Kennedy's 30%. During April,

Kennedy's fortunes were briefly revived by victories in four northern industrial States, before being finally destroyed by 11 straight
Carter victories in May as the President left the White House
and began campaigning in person. However, although trailing
hopelessly, Edward Kennedy refused to retire graciously. He won
five of the last eight primaries on 3 June (including California and
New Jersey) and decided to take the fight to the New York National
Convention in August in the hope that a further deterioration
in the economy or setback abroad would persuade delegates to
move across to his camp. He was joined in this strategy by a
number of influential Democrats, including Hugh Carey (Governor of New York) and Patrick Moynihan (Senator for New York),
who, viewing President Carter as 'unelectable', sought an 'Open
Convention' or even the induction of Vice-President Mondale as a
compromise candidate. In the end, President Carter succeeded in
gaining a comfortable first ballot majority; however, the continuing Kennedy challenge served to exacerbate Democrat divisions
and to diminish their prospects of success in November 1980.[6]
The Republican Party had meanwhile united around its chosen
nominee, Ronald Reagan.

The Resurgent Republicans Conservatism and Republicanism,
checked by Watergate, had been steadily reviving since 1977,
drawing sustenance from a number of parallel economic, social
and philosophical movements.

Firstly, the rise in per-capita living standards and the movement of the population towards the suburbs witnessed during
the 1970s had begun to transform the American political map
and to change attitudes and outlooks. These changes created
a swathe of new suburban Republican seats and undermined
the Democratic Party's monopoly hold of the South. (See Part
5.) They led, in addition, to a shift in popular attitudes, as a
significant section of the voting public, having become satisfied
with the 'Great Society' welfare programmes established during
the 1960s, became determined to resist the cost of any further
growth. The Californian taxpayers' revolt of June 1978, the decision of 41 other States to slash taxes in 1979 and the growth of
the 'balanced budget movement' were all clear indications of this
changed public mood.[7] This shift in attitude was given intellectual
sustenance by the rebirth of monetarist and free-market economics under the aegis of the Chicago professor Milton Friedman
(1912–) and supply-side economics under the lead of Arthur
Laffer of the University of Southern California. It also drew

stimulus from the development of right-wing 'think tanks', most prominently the American Enterprise Institute (AEI) and the Heritage Foundation (established in 1973 by Paul Weyrich and Edwin Feulner) and such 'neo-conservative' journals as Irving Kristol's *Public Interest* and Norman Podhoretz's *Commentary*. Fiscal restraint, deregulation and decentralisation, derived from these works, became the new 'buzz words' for the early 1980s.

This austere, almost masochistic, philosophy fitted well with the changing social temper of the later 1970s and early 1980s: a period of self-doubt for America as its economy stagnated and its role in world affairs was put into question by the humiliation of Vietnam. There was, in consequence, an upsurge in interest in fundamentalist religious sects – the Southern Baptists, the Mormons and the Seventh Day Adventists – and in the new television and radio preachers who offered a message of simple, certain salvation and who preached a conservative philosophy of thrift, chastity and patriotism. By 1980 these 'born again' fundamentalists formed almost a third of the large American churchgoing population of 90 million and were well entrenched in the growing States of the South and West. One particularly vocal segment, led by the Rev Jerry Falwell of Virginia, optimistically proclaimed itself the 'Moral Majority' and began a series of well-funded single-issue campaigns – opposing abortion, the Equal Rights Amendment and pornography. It joined with conservative grassroots lobbying organisations, such as Terry Dolan's National Conservative Political Action Committee (NCPAC), Howard Phillips's 500 000-strong Conservative Caucus and Richard Viguerie's Direct Mail Organisation, to form the cutting edge for what became known as the 'New Right'.

The third force which welded together this new cross-class conservative coalition was a resurgent nationalism in reaction to events in Afghanistan and Iran and five years of creeping communism. The feeling spread from conservative to majority circles that the limit of tolerance had been reached and that the United States should put its foot down and rearm to halt and, if possible, reverse the Soviet advance.

In the circumstances of 1976 the custodian of the Democratic Party nomination appeared almost assured of success in the November presidential contest. In 1980 the positions were reversed, making the battle for the party nomination one of extreme importance. Not surprisingly then, 11 candidates lined up at the start of the contest, but three figures – George

Bush, Ronald Reagan and John Anderson – dominated the campaign.[8]

Ronald Reagan, the man who came within a whisker of unseating President Ford in 1976, started off the campaign as a clear favourite although he was now 69 years old. However, George Bush began campaigning at an early date and gained a surprise victory at the Iowa caucuses in January 1980. The 55-year-old Bush, born in Milton, Massachusetts, came from a wealthy 'Wall Street' Republican background. He was the son of a liberal Senator (for Connecticut) and married into a New York publishing family. However, after distinguished wartime service as a navy pilot and securing an economics degree from Yale, he moved to Texas in 1948. There he built up from scratch his own multi-million oil-drilling business and became during the early 1960s a fervent supporter of the right-wing ideologue, Barry Goldwater. Bush's views later moderated and, after serving in the House of Representatives during 1967–70, he was given a clutch of top-level posts by the Nixon and Ford administrations – becoming US Ambassador to the UN (1971–3), Republican Party chairman (1973–4), Special Envoy to China (1974–5) and Director of the CIA (1976–7). Bush's varied political pedigree thus made him an acceptable choice to both wings of the party and enabled him to build up a wide and influential collection of contacts. His campaign was well organised (being directed by his close Texan friend, James Baker, Ford's 1976 campaign deputy manager) and was liberally financed. However, it met with a jolting setback at the opening New Hampshire primary: Bush capturing only 23% of the vote and finishing a bad second behind Ronald Reagan despite a year of patient nursing. Bush went on to record a number of victories in northern liberal and industrial States, but he failed to make any headway in the South and West. He lacked the personality and charisma which now seemed essential in the age of media politics, and his political message appeared unclear and vacuous.

It was Ronald Reagan, a defeated challenger in 1968 and 1976, who finally captured the Republican nomination in 1980 with unusual ease. By the end of May his final challenger had conceded, leaving Reagan to move triumphantly towards the party's National Convention in Detroit in July. A year earlier, however, his candidature had been seen as suicidal for the party. Reagan was viewed as too far to the right and too regionally based (in the South and West) to be a successful presidential challenger.

Thus the Carter camp looked with glee to the prospect of his candidature, anticipating a crushing Goldwaterian defeat. Within the Republican Party many 'Wall Streeters' also viewed with dismay a Reagan challenge. Throughout the 1980 campaign there were recurrent, but in the end unsuccessful, attempts to 'draft' the former President, Gerald Ford, as a more palatable replacement, and such was the feeling against Reagan that John Anderson remained to fight on as an independent.

The background of Ronald Reagan was unconventional but not markedly dissimilar from that of the previous three Presidents. He was born in the small hamlet of Tampico in the midwestern State of Illinois in February 1911, the second son in a lower-middle- class first-generation Irish family. His father Jack, a hard-drinking Roman Catholic, was a salesman who became part owner of a store in 1920 but was later bankrupted during the Great Depression. His mother, Nelle, to whom he was closest, was a devout teetotal Protestant. Ronald Reagan gained an economics degree at Eureka College, Illinois, but his real ambition lay in acting – being signed up by Hollywood (Warner Brothers) in 1937, after several years working as a radio sportscaster in Des Moines, Iowa. During these years the Reagans were strong supporters of the 'New Deal' Democrats and were impressed by the style of F D Roosevelt. Ronald Reagan showed a growing interest in politics after he became president of the Screen Actors' Guild between 1947 and 1952, but he remained at first a moderate liberal, resisting McCarthyite attempts to blacklist suspected communist sympathisers. During the 1950s, however, his political outlook shifted rightwards as he became critical of the bureaucratic excesses of 'New Dealism' which he saw as stifling enterprise. His (second) marriage to the affluent actress Nancy Davis – a devout and conservative Presbyterian – in 1952 gave an added impulse to this political realignment.

The new conservative Ronald Reagan became increasingly evident during the later 1950s as he began promotional work for General Electric (GE) and as he finally switched to the Republican Party in 1962 and delivered a fervent national television appeal on behalf of Barry Goldwater in 1964. Reagan, with his midwestern roots, had always supported conservative social values and was a fervent believer in the free-enterprise, 'land of opportunity' spirit of traditional America and John Wayne patriotism. Now, during the early 1960s, he saw this society under threat from over-regulation, creeping welfarism and communism. Self-made businessmen friends led by the auto dealer Holmes Tuttle and the oil developer Henry Salvatori, recognising Reagan's communicative qualities, persuaded him to stand for the governorship of California and he surprisingly succeeded in ousting the Democrat, Pat Brown (the father of Jerry Brown) in 1966. Reagan held the governorship of this, America's most populous and expansionary, State for eight years, and this provided the platform for his assaults on the presidency in 1968, 1976 and 1980.

The strident, free-enterprise, small-government and anti-Soviet rhetoric of Ronald Reagan's speeches made him a darling of the 'Main Street' activist. He was a particularly impressive speaker, able to put across serious political points with an endearing simplicity and sincerity, often articulating previously unspoken popular anxieties. He was equally adept, following his work with GE, at delivering a rousing and inspirational campaign speech and in engaging in a quiet and reassuring television 'fire-side' chat studded with anecdotes and quips. Reagan became associated with a number of 'Moral Majority' and Fundamentalist causes during the 1970s and gained a reputation as a zealous right-winger. However, his record as Governor in California revealed him to be a more pragmatic and moderate politician than was outwardly apparent. State spending and taxes, instead of being reduced, were in fact raised during his period in office, and it was Governor Reagan who sanctioned the introduction of a comparatively liberal abortion bill. Nevertheless, despite such departures, the policy programme offered to the electorate by candidate Reagan in 1980 remained unusually extreme – the reduction of taxation at its upper levels; curbs on public spending; the decentralisation of many previously federally financed and administered activities; deregulation in the industrial, environmental and social spheres; and large-scale military rearmament.

Reagan, drawing upon the roots left from his 1976 campaign, was easily able to capture the Republican Party nomination after once more gaining strong support from the 'sunbelt' States. However, what gave Reagan a decisive boost in 1980 was the growing evidence of support from the traditionally hostile North and from blue-collar groups. Some of this support came from the new cross-class recruits who were being drawn into the Republican Party on the coat-tails of the 'Moral Majority' and Fundamentalist movement. Others were attracted by Reagan's message of economic rebirth through a return to free-market basics and by his tough, patriotic foreign policy stance.

The circumstances of 1980 were unusually conducive to a Reagan candidature. Four years previously the country, sickened by the experience of Vietnam, had voted for a smaller American role on the world stage and had remained content with the conservative Keynesianism which was producing a recovery from the 1973–5 recession. Now, however, with a deep new recession at hand and with the country having suffered further humiliation abroad, the public sought a renaissance in the nation's economic and military strength. President Carter attempted to move with this tide of opinion and became a tough new rearmer. He also flirted with the formulation of a radical new economic strategy based on the West German and Japanese model – involving a tripartite relationship between government, employers and workers and targeted state investment in potential growth industries of the future.[9] In general, however, Carter offered a depressing message of 'limits', reduced expectations and conservation, and he offered a record of four years of weak and indecisive leadership. Ronald Reagan projected, in contrast, a jaunty, optimistic demeanour founded upon the belief that America could recover its lost greatness and that the free-enterprise economy could revive and create new jobs and opportunities. He offered clear and decisive leadership with glamour and style.

Reagan began the final campaign in August 1980 with a substantial 25-point lead over the incumbent President. Nevertheless, the Carter campaign team, underrating the qualities of their opponent, expected to close this gap as they drew attention to Reagan's extremism, particularly in international affairs. However, the further deterioration in economic conditions – drummed home by the Reagan campaign slogan 'Are you better off now than in 1976?'; the failure to secure the release of the American hostages in Iran; and the irruption of the Billy Carter 'Libya scandal',[10] forced Carter on to the defensive. Ronald Reagan was supported by a largely united Republican team, which, under the direction of the party chairman Bill Brock, had significantly improved its grassroots organising skills, and this was backed up by the support of wealthy right-wing PACs and that of his own talented unit under the direction of the Mormon computer psephologist, Richard Wirthlin, and campaign troubleshooter, Stuart Spencer. President Carter was given the support of Democrat local bosses and labour leaders, but it was often grudging. The influence of these groups was in any case diminishing, as traditional political machines disintegrated and as unionisation levels declined.[11]

TABLE 8 THE NOVEMBER 1980 PRESIDENTIAL ELECTION (TURNOUT 52.6%)

Candidate	Party	Popular Vote (m)	As % of Total	Electoral College Vote	States Captured
Ronald W Reagan*	R	43.90	50.7	489	44
Jimmy E Carter*	D	35.48	41.0	49	6
John B Anderson*	Ind	5.72	6.6†	0	0
Ed Clark*	Lib	0.92	1.1	0	0
Barry Commoner	Cit	0.23	0.3	0	0
Others‡		0.25	0.3	0	0
Total		86.50	100.0	538	50

* These candidates collected the necessary 1.3 million signatures from petitions across the country to qualify to be on the ballot in all 50 States.

† Anderson surmounted the 5% 'electoral hurdle' needed to qualify for the post-election public financing of a portion of his campaign expenses. His total national campaign spending amounted to $15 million and he was later reimbursed $4.2 million by the state.

‡ More than 18 other minor party candidates were named on the ballot paper of a number of States. The most important of these were: Hall (Communist Party), 45 000 votes; Rarick (American Independent Party: AIP), 41 000; de Berry (Socialist Workers Party), 40 000; McCormack (Right to Life), 32 000; and Smith (Peace and Freedom), 18 000.

Ronald Reagan's relaxed, moderate and confident performance in the 28 October televised debate with President Carter allayed many of the lingering fears in the minds of undecided voters and on 4 November he secured a resounding victory, capturing 51% of the popular vote compared to President Carter's 41%. (See Table 8.) Reagan captured 44 States in all, including many former Democrat strongholds in the South and Northeast. (See Figure 4.) The margin of President Carter's defeat was made worse by the candidature of the moderate Republican Representative, John Anderson of Illinois, as an Independent. Portraying himself as the only liberal candidate of the three, Anderson captured 7% of the popular vote – much coming from former Democrats (particularly Jews). His vote tilted the balance in 14 States with a combined 'electoral college' vote of 158. These included the north-eastern States of New York (41 electoral votes) and Massachusetts (14). However, the principal factor behind the President's defeat was Carter's inability to hold together the traditional Democrat coalition. Blacks stayed with the party ticket, but many small farmers, blue-collar workers, Irish-Americans and Jews from the Midwest, North-east and South defected to the Reagan camp. (Compare Tables 4 and 9 and see Table 14.) Other traditional Democrat voters stayed at home, as the electoral turnout slumped to only 52.6%.[12] It is likely, from the evidence of the primaries, that if Edward Kennedy had captured the Democrat nomination he would, as a traditional liberal, have held on to many of the north-eastern States and that the margin of defeat would have been narrower. A Reagan victory would still, however, most probably have been achieved.

The Republican Party also made large gains in the Congressional and gubernatorial contests of November 1980, capturing in net four governorships (Arkansas, Missouri, North Dakota and Washington), 33 seats in the House of Representatives and 12 seats in the Senate. (See Table 10.) They also achieved an unexpected majority in the upper house for the first time since 1954. In the Senate, the swing to the Republican Party was exaggerated by the fact that almost half of the gains represented marginal seats captured by the Democrats in the landslide 'Post-Watergate Election' of November 1974. But the swing in the Congressional and gubernatorial contests remained marked, with a number of prominent liberal politicians, for example the experienced Senators George McGovern (South Dakota), Frank Church (Idaho – the former chairman of the Foreign Relations Committee), Birch Bayh (Indiana) and John Culver (Iowa) and Representatives John Brademas (Indiana – the former Majority Whip) and Al Ullman (Oregon – the former chairman of the Ways and Means Committee), being ousted following targeting by NCPAC. Republicans viewed the elections of November 1980 as heralding a watershed comparable to the election of 1932, in which a cross-class conservative coalition deposed the old Democrat 'New Deal – Great Society' coalition as the new political majority with its own coherent ideology.[13] However, while there had clearly been an important swing towards conservatism in the popular mood and in the broader economy and society, this shift was exaggerated by events in Iran and Afghanistan and by public contempt for President Carter.

TABLE 9   VOTING BY REGION FOR REAGAN, CARTER AND
ANDERSON IN NOVEMBER 1980

	Turnout (m)	Reagan (%)	Carter (%)	Anderson (%)
East	21.9	47	43	9
South	23.1	52	44	3
Midwest	25.2	51	41	7
West	16.3	54	34	9
Total	86.5	51	41	7

TABLE 10   THE CONGRESSIONAL AND GUBERNATORIAL
ELECTIONS OF NOVEMBER 1980

	House Seats	Result	Senatorships	Result	Governorships	Result
Total Contested	435		34		13	
Democrat Victories	243	– 33	12	– 12	6	– 4
Republican Victories	192	+33	22	+12	7	+4

Figure 4   Map of the 1980 Presidential Election

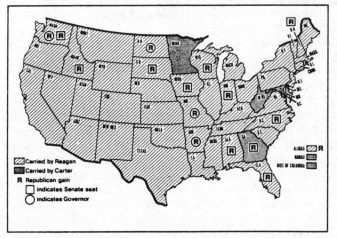

+ Source: 'The Economist', 8 November 1980, p.22'.

The Carter Administration: An Assessment

Jimmy Carter was the first of a new style of outsider politician who had devoted himself to the year-long slog of caucus and primary hustings and who had made full use of the television medium to capture his party's nomination over the heads of traditional Washington insiders. His skills lay in campaigning and in appealing to diverse groups of potential voters rather than in administration. These weaknesses became clearly apparent during his four years in office. President Carter failed to grasp the right levers or find sufficient allies to enable him to control Congress, and he failed to exert sufficient pressure from outside through personal appeals to the American public. On paper, President Carter's 'Congressional success rate' (the proportion of times when Congress supported the position taken by the President) was creditable – averaging 76.4% compared to rates of 57.7% and 67.0% recorded by his immediate predecessors, Presidents Ford and Nixon. (See Appendix Table B7.) However, this masked a number of significant defeats on key parts of his programme and forced concessions on other elements. Carter's greatest achievements were in the social, civil rights and environmental spheres, where he gained firm Congressional backing for an impressive clutch of liberal reforms and executive appointments.[14] However, many other planks of his domestic programme, for example, welfare and health care reforms, met with almost total failure.

Part of the reason for President Carter's disappointing legislative record stemmed from his inability to pursue one clear ideological course and his unique brand of 'ethical liberalism' which served to accumulate enemies of diverse hues. Part also derived from the President's stubborn, self-righteous refusal to compromise and 'horse-trade' over legislation and his imprudent neglect of the personal element in his dealings with members of Capitol Hill. However, it should be noted that Carter assumed the presidency at a difficult time – during a climacteric period of faltering economic growth and of general uncertainty. Carter tried to force the nation to face up to these economic difficulties by stressing the need for a 'New Realism' founded upon the canons of frugality and efficiency. The 1978 and 1980 energy bills represented a substantial step in this direction and the administration's planned administrative and welfare reforms were equally well-intentioned.[15] The Carter presidency was thus one of frankness and responsibility. However, its message of reduced expectations was not electorally appealing in 1980. The American public sought instead a revival in national dynamism and growth under the unlikely helmsmanship of its oldest elected President.

Part Three

REPUBLICANISM RAMPANT

Chapter 4

REAGAN IN POWER:
THE FIRST TERM, 1981–4

The Reagan Team and Administrative Style

Although Ronald Reagan was viewed as a torchbearer for 'Main Street' and the 'New Right', it still remained unclear in January 1981 whether he would inaugurate a new era of radical reform or whether he would be stronger on rhetoric than on action. His record as Governor of California and his willingness, during the 1980 presidential campaign, to move towards the centre and accept the need for state financial and tariff support for the ailing automobile and steel industries of the North-east, vexed a number of his radical colleagues. There was thus more than the usual interest in the composition of President Reagan's first cabinet.

Ronald Reagan had throughout his political career displayed a talent for collecting together unusually skilled and experienced teams of like-minded administrators and personal aides, whom he relied on to work out the policy details and the available options, before making the final decision himself. Reagan's first support and advisory team were the California-based 'millionaire backers' – Henry Salvatori (79), Theodore Cummings (72), Justin Dart (73), Earle Jorgensen (82), Holmes Tuttle (75), Jack Wrather (62) and William F Smith (62) – who began masterminding his political career from the mid 1960s. They helped select his cabinet in California, attracting into government service many of the successful no-nonsense entrepreneurs for whom Reagan, as a result both of his family background and his loathing for paper-pushing bureaucrats, had a particular respect. A somewhat different team of political strategists was built up by Reagan for his presidential campaigns of 1976 and 1980, involving marketing experts such as Clifton White (manager of Goldwater's 1964 campaign) and Bill Timmons. After gaining the party nomination in 1980 and selecting George Bush as his running-mate, a further group of advisers came in from the Republican establishment, leaving the new President a wide choice of personnel as he began deliberations at his Santa Barbara ranch in November 1980.

In deciding upon his cabinet and staff team, President Reagan was determined to avoid the mistakes made by his predecessor. He would not surround himself with a young and inexperienced clique of aides drawn from his State administration or select too diverse a group of cabinet Secretaries, whose bickerings and obstructions would smother progress. Reagan plumped instead for a team of accomplished and experienced 'staffers' and cabinet Secretaries who were in touch with his general political philosophy but who were by no means fervent 'New Right' hardliners or acolytes. He envisioned an extended role for the Vice-President and for an 'inner cabinet' of six or seven key Secretaries and aides, who would be expected to advise the President on policy matters right across the board rather than act as narrow departmental advocates. In addition, Reagan intended to delegate considerable authority to his departmental Secretaries. The President would sit back, like the head of a board of directors, and listen to policy proposals – presented verbally and in the form of short four-paragraph 'mini-memos' – sanctioning those which he approved. This was the style of government which Reagan had adopted with success in California and it contrasted with the stupefying love of detail exhibited by his predecessor Jimmy Carter. It was akin to that successfully pursued by the, so-called, "hidden hand" President, Dwight D Eisenhower and it suited a man who was a good listener – drilled in by years of listening to Hollywood movie directors – and was receptive to ideas, but who was not a great creative thinker. It enabled the President to keep his mind clear and remain fit and healthy, working only an eight-hour day, while at the same time enabling him to think ahead and map out the future course of policy programmes.

The team Reagan selected for this task was particularly strong (see Table 11) – including friends, businessmen, Republican troupers and academics from the favoured Hoover Institute

(Stanford, California) and Georgetown University (Washington). It was, however, white, male and Protestant-dominated and was centre-right in outlook. The key figures who formed the core for the 'inner cabinet' were the State and Defense Department Secretaries, Alexander Haig and Caspar Weinberger (see Part 6), and the Treasury Secretary, Donald Regan – a Wall Street entrepreneur and fiscal conservative who had built up Merrill Lynch into the country's largest security firm. The bridge between these Secretaries and the President was provided by Ed Meese, the cabinet co-ordinator, and by Richard Allen, David Stockman and Martin Anderson, policy advisers on foreign, economic and domestic affairs respectively. Stockman, a young two-term former Congressman from Michigan, and one-time personal adviser to John Anderson, emerged as an intelligent advocate of 'supply-side' economics. The more experienced Meese, who had already served as Reagan's Chief-of-Staff in California, became an efficient and influential liaiser. This inner staffer team was to increase its influence as the administration progressed, with Meese, Michael Deaver (a long-standing California aide and public relations expert) and James Baker emerging as a powerful troika. It was more worldly and experienced than Carter's 'Georgia mafia'. This was to prove advantageous in its relations with Congress.

TABLE 11   THE REAGAN CABINET OF JANUARY 1981

Secretaries

State Dept	Gen AM Haig (56, ex-Nixon admin)
Treasury	DT Regan (62, financier)
Defense	CW Weinberger (63, ex-California & Nixon admins)
Attorney-General	WF Smith (63, Reagan friend & lawyer)
Interior	JG Watt (42, Denver lawyer & ex-Ford admin)
Agriculture	JR Block (45, Illinois farmer & State Secretary)
Commerce	M Baldrige (58, Connecticut industrialist)
Labor	RJ Donovan (50, New Jersey labour relations adviser)
HUD	SR Pierce (58, black NY attorney, ex-Nixon admin)
Health	RS Schweiker (54, Pennsylvania, ex-Senator)
Energy	Dr JB Edwards (53, ex-South Carolina Governor)
Education	TH Bell (58, Utah, ex-Federal Educational Cmmr)
Transportation	AL Lewis (49, Pennsylvanian management consultant)
UN Representative	Dr Jeane J Kirkpatrick (53, Georgetown academic)
Sp Trade Repr	W Brock (50, ex-Party chairman & Tennessee Senator)

White House Posts

NSA	RV Allen (44, Georgetown & Hoover Institute)
Dir of OMB	DA Stockman (34, ex-Congressman)
Dir of CIA	WJ Casey (67, NY lawyer, 1980 campaign manager)
Dir of CEA	M Weidenbaum (53, ex-Ford admin)
Chief-of-Staff	J Baker (50, Texas lawyer & ex-Ford admin)
Sp Counselor	E Meese (49, former Chief-of-Staff in California)
Assistant Chief-of-Staff	MK Deaver (41, ex-California admin)

Reagan and Congress

Ronald Reagan, while lacking direct Washington experience, embarked upon his term as President in better preparedness than his predecessor. Jimmy Carter had, as Governor of Georgia, previously worked with only a part-time legislature and one which was dominated by representatives of his own party. Ronald Reagan had, by contrast, governed in California, where two-party politics was very much in evidence and where a strong Democrat-controlled legislature vied for dominance with the new Governor. This experience was to prove valuable as he became the first President since Woodrow Wilson in 1918 to find himself faced with a 'split' Congress.[1]

In California, Reagan's first two years were disastrous. He adopted a haughty and antagonistic attitude to the legislature, instead of searching for compromise and co-operation. Gradually, however, he came to learn to arrange bargains with the Speaker, Bob Moretti, and used his communicative skills to make television appeals to build up grassroots pressure on important measures. On assuming the presidency in January 1981 President Reagan employed the same twin tactics of backroom consultation and public appeals. In addition, he learned from the mistakes made by the Carter administration. He changed the style of the presidency, inviting Congressmen to lavish White House receptions, and sought out allies for each key vote, working through Max Friedersdorf (head of liaison) and personal Congressional friends, such as Senator Paul Laxalt of Nevada (Reagan's campaign director in 1976, 1980 and later 1984) and New York Representative, Jack Kemp. In addition, to ensure the beneficial fusion of public liaison and lobbying, a special Legislative Strategy Group (LSG) was set up under the stewardship of Chief-of-Staff James Baker.

Reagan was further aided by the sobriety and conservatism of the 97th (1981–2) Congress. The Senate was now in Republican hands under the leadership of the loyal and co-operative Howard Baker (Tennessee) and, following the defeat of many prominent liberals in November 1980, the general tenor of the chamber had changed. This was most strikingly illustrated by the capture of a number of important committee chairs – such as Judiciary (Strom Thurmond – South Carolina), Budget (Pete Domenici – New Mexico), Agriculture (Jesse Helms – North Carolina) and Intelligence (Barry Goldwater – Arizona) – by prominent 'Main Street' right-wingers. The House remained under Democrat control, but it had also become a more cautious and moderate-minded chamber. The Republicans acquired a larger share of committee and sub-committee seats and the balance of power was held by 47 conservative Southern 'Boll Weevil' Democrats. This group had previously frequently voted with the Republicans on economic and social issues and, after the careful targeting of public works and oil industry favours by the Reagan administration, did so again in 1981. This enabled the traditional 1950s to 1970s 'conservative coalition' to be reforged (see Appendix Table B11), giving the Reagan team temporary control over both chambers of Congress for the passage of controversial reforms.

The Reagan Reformation – Policy Achievements 1981–4

On assuming office in January 1981 President Reagan was presented with the huge 3000-page tome 'Mandate for Leadership' compiled by the Heritage Foundation, laying down 1270 recommendations for action, the distilled wisdom of contemporary radical conservatism. Other 'New Right' interest groups pressed for immediate action on a swathe of social issues. However, President Reagan, acutely aware of the lesson learned by the overly ambitious Carter administration of 1977, wisely decided not to introduce a mass of legislation in the first session of Congress. Instead, a set of priorities was decided upon, with economic reform and rejuvenation top of this list, and a strategy of working through and with Congress. This sensible, pragmatic, step-by-step approach threatened to alienate the President's more radical supporters. A series of symbolic acts and gestures were thus made to maintain their belief and fidelity – the immediate scrapping of oil and gas price controls (due to end in October), a freeze on Federal hiring and the invitation of anti-abortion leaders to the White House for talks.

The need for rapid economic renewal based around incentives and deregulation had been the constant theme in Ronald Reagan's election campaign. He came to power pledged to cut taxes by 30% in three years (the Kemp-Roth proposal), reduce Federal spending (excepting defence) and regulatory interference, lower the inflation rate and balance the budget by 1985. This strategy appeared inconsistent and doomed to failure. However, Reagan was convinced that this 'supply-side' approach would have a dynamic and liberating impact, thus expanding the economic cake and broadening the tax base. The President set about implementing his recovery package in February 1981. He told a joint session of Congress that the administration sought $50 billion of savings from the 1981–2 Federal budget to pay for $50 billion in tax cuts, which would leave a deficit of $45 billion. These spending cuts would not affect the original 'New Deal' welfare disbursements to the truly needy (Medicare, old age pensions, veterans and unemployment benefits), but would be concentrated on the more recent, and less popular, 'Great Society' public works programmes, subsidies (student loans, synfuel and farm subsidies, legal and overseas aid), and grants to the marginally poor (food stamps, Medicaid and AFDC payments).

These cuts threatened to stir up a hornets' nest of opposition from individual Congressmen and from interest groups as the budget was slowly worked through each sub-committee. Thus the Reagan administration skilfully succeeded in getting the budget and tax cuts considered as a whole in a combined and expedited omnibus ('Budget Reconciliation') bill. Inside Congress the President sought to appease potential opponents by moderating his stance on other issues (for example, by shelving plans immediately to disband the Education and Energy Departments and by extending loan guarantee aid to the ailing car giant Chrysler). Outside of Congress, Reagan, following the precedent he had set in California, embarked upon a determined media campaign of television speeches and advertising in support of the new initiatives. He was successful in these endeavours, being aided by the surge of popular affection which followed the return of the Teheran hostages on 20 January and an assassination attempt on 30 March, which left President Reagan with a bullet in his lung which was successfully removed following surgery. By the middle of May Congress had approved the major portion of Reagan's budget plan (with cuts of $36 billion). Two months later it had accepted a rolling 25% tax-cut scheme.[2]

President Reagan's ascendancy in Congress was unusually marked in 1981. He secured an 82% success rate on votes on which he took a clear stand, with the Democrat 'Boll Weevils' providing crucial support on many bipartisan votes. He had been successful in pushing through the major planks of the 'Reagan revolution' – the largest tax cuts and budget reductions in American history (which resulted in the loss of 300000 Federal jobs) and the biggest-ever peacetime defence build-up. Meanwhile, outside of Congress the new President had instructed his Interior, Energy, Commerce and Transport Secretaries to press forward with deregulation and to be less vigorous in their enforcement of existing controls. The *New York Times* commented that, taken together, the President's economic reforms of 1981 had brought about the most significant shift in the balance between the public and private sectors of the US economy since the introduction of Roosevelt's 'New Deal'.

However, while the 'Reagan revolution' was clearly under way, it failed to lead to a rapid economic upsurge. Instead, following OPEC's further quadrupling of oil prices, the country was plunged into its most serious post-war recession. Unemployment rose rapidly to 10.8% in December 1982 as the US economy was dramatically restructured, and the Reagan fiscal strategy was blown sharply off course by a shrunken tax revenue base and by an explosion in welfare demand. In January 1981 the President had envisaged annual growth of 4% and a Federal budget moving into surplus. Instead, industrial production declined by 2% and 9.5% respectively in 1981 and 1982 and record budget deficits of $98.5 and $110 billion were recorded. Meanwhile, the Federal Reserve Bank, under its monetarist chairman Paul Volcker (a 1979 Carter appointee), maintained a tight rein over the money supply and set high interest rates, discouraging industrial investment.

Faced with these mounting economic problems, dissent began to emerge within the administration, while inside Congress the President had to battle fiercely to achieve further spending cuts in the autumn of 1981 and in 1982. These cuts ate into the bone of the welfare programme and vexed liberal Democrats and northern 'Wall Street' Republicans, who, with their eyes fixed on forthcoming elections, began to press for slower growth in the defence programme and for the raising of new taxes to deal with the growing budget deficit. Outside of Congress, the public mood also changed, with labour, minority and welfare lobbies becoming increasingly vocal. Two examples of this changed mood were the September 1981 'March on Washington' by 250000 to protest against 'Reaganomics' and the development of the 'nuclear freeze' movement in 1982.[3] At the State level, the tax-cutting Proposition 13 campaign met with a growing number of reversals as voters became concerned with the deterioration in public services.

President Reagan, a 'conviction politician', remained convinced in his 'supply-side' strategy, but Congress became less willing to acquiesce in 1982. It overrode his veto on the $14.2 billion Supplementary Appropriations Bill, rejected his plan for a balanced budget amendment and forced some scaling-down of the defence budget and the introduction of a number of indirect taxes. The 'honeymoon period' for President Reagan was clearly over and he would need in future to battle hard to build up majorities for his domestic programme. A second rebuff to the 'Reagan reformation'was delivered by State Governors, who rejected the ambitious decentralising 'New Federalism' scheme introduced in January 1982. This reform had sought to streamline and simplify – returning 40 Federal programmes, including the AFDC and Food Stamps schemes to the State and local governments, while giving the Federal administration full responsibility for the Medicaid programme – but also to shift an increased proportion of the welfare burden to the State level.

Despite such opposition inside and outside Congress, the Reagan administration was still successful in achieving substantial cuts in the Federal programme while at the same time boosting defence spending. The administration was more cautious in its approach to social reforms (the prohibition of abortion, the ending of school 'busing' and the introduction of school prayers), recognising the lack of an overwhelming popular mandate for such controversial changes. This earned the President the opprobrium of the 'New Right', whose midterm report gave him a mark of only 'C–C minus'. However, the verdict of American voters in the Congressional and gubernatorial elections of November 1982 was more equivocal. (See Table 12.) They swung away from the Republican Party in the depressed industrial States of the Midwest and in the South, particularly in the gubernatorial contests, where the Democrats gained seven governorships. At the Congressional level, the Republicans (with only 12 seats to defend) kept their Senate majority intact, but in the House of Representatives they lost 26

Politics in the USA

seats – many being radical conservative freshmen who had entered Congress in the 'swing election' of November 1980. This could not be viewed as a decisive vote against the genial new President, but there were indications of growing antipathy to 'New Right' extremism.[4] This sent out a warning to President Reagan. In addition, this election brought to an end the slender House majority held in 1981 and 1982 by the 'Main Street-Boll Weevil' conservative coalition, which promised to make it increasingly difficult for the Reagan administration to push through unpalatable welfare cuts and seemed to rule out the possibility of the passage of radical social reforms.

TABLE 12 THE CONGRESSIONAL AND GUBERNATORIAL ELECTIONS OF NOVEMBER 1982 (TURNOUT 41%)

	House Seats	Result	Senator- ships	Result	Governor- ships	Result
Total Contested	435		33		36	
Democrat Victories	269	+26	20	–*	27	+7‡
Republican Victories	166	– 26	13	+1†	9	– 7

* Among Democrat missed opportunities in the Senatorial races was the failure of Jerry Brown to defeat Pete Wilson (Republican Mayor of San Diego) in the contest for an 'open' Senate seat in California.

† The Republicans captured one seat in Virginia (Paul Trible) which had previously been held by the Independent Harry Byrd, who had frequently voted with the Republicans on roll-call votes.

‡ The Democrats recaptured the governorships of Texas, Arkansas, Ohio, Michigan, Minnesota, Wisconsin, Nebraska, Nevada and Alaska, but lost control in New Hampshire and California.

This changed balance of forces became evident in the Congressional sessions of 1983 and 1984. Tip O'Neill, the 70-year-old Irish-American 'New Dealer' Speaker of the House of Representatives, had been unusually mute during the 97th Congress, finding it difficult to control his party colleagues. However, from the winter of 1982 he was reinvigorated and, assured of a dependable liberal House majority, emerged as a determined leader of Democrat opposition to the injustices of Reaganomics. O'Neill, in conjunction with his committee chairmen, began to press for defence programme cuts, for substantial public investment job-creation packages and for tax reform to benefit lower income groups. Such 'budget busting' schemes were, however, unacceptable to President Reagan, who was forced to make increasing use of his veto. In these circumstances relations between the President and Congress deteriorated. The President sustained repeated defeats in the House on social issues, immigration law reform and on his attempt to introduce a presidential 'line veto'; in the Senate, northern liberal 'Gypsy Moth' Republicans became less willing to toe the administration's line; and, in both chambers, budget negotiations dragged on endlessly without result.

Figure 5   President Reagan's Gallup Poll Approval Rating, 1981-1984

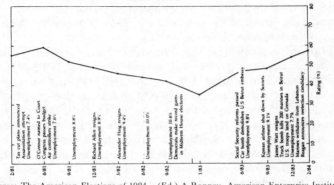

Source: The American Elections of 1984—(Ed.) A Ranney American Enterprise Institute: *Duke University Press* 1985 p17

Such Congressional rebuffs initially damaged the standing of the President (see Figure 5) during a period of continuing economic recession and of mounting concern over his policies in Central America and Lebanon. However, from the spring of 1983 the US economy began to revive with an unusual vigour, returning confidence. Real GNP grew by 3.3% in 1983 and by 8% during the first half of 1984, reducing unemployment to 7.5%, while inflation was brought down to 4%. This was the strongest recovery since the early 1950s. The three key factors behind this upturn were the Federal Reserve Bank's loosening of its monetarist grip from July 1982; the unintended growth in the Federal budget deficit (reaching $195 billion or 6% of GNP in 1983);[5] and the stimulus given to the defence sector. This was not, however, a simple Keynesian 'pump primed' recovery. A significant boost was also given to the private sector by the administration's staggered

65

tax cuts and by its 'supply-side' strategy of deregulation and waste elimination. On top of this, the President added a magical 'confidence factor'.

The strength of this economic recovery eased the pressure on the administration to cut the budget deficit and enabled the President to face with equanimity defeats in Congress. The Reagan administration gained an additional boost from the autumn of 1983 from two incidents overseas – the Soviet Union's shooting down on 1 September of an errant South Korean Boeing 747 passenger airliner; and America's overthrow of the new Marxist regime in Grenada in October. The first incident seemed to vindicate the Reagan administration's uncharitable interpretation of Soviet motives and ambitions. The second restored America's belief in its ability to play an influential role on the world stage and was the precursor to a wave of strident patriotism which was to grip the nation in 1984.

Thus, by November 1983, President Reagan, as he prepared for the forthcoming election, appeared strong both at home and abroad. The budget deficit remained high and vexing, but the economy continued to expand. Overseas, the country had re-established itself as a world power. The President himself remained unusually popular, able to shrug off Congressional setbacks and recurrent scandals within his administration. He managed to project a regal image, being viewed as somehow remote and above politics, while at the same time pressing forward with a substantial reformation of American government.

The First Reagan Administration: An Assessment

The principal attention of the first Reagan administration was necessarily focused upon reviving the American economy and rekindling its dynamic, risk-taking entrepreneurial spirit. The first two years of the Reagan administration were desolate as the nation was gripped by a severe recession, which was uneven both regionally and socially. However, the administration's new 'supply-side' package did in the end, both by accident and design, engender a buoyant, inflation-free recovery. At the same time it changed attitudes and the balance of government. Between 1980 and 1984 major cuts were made in social programmes and in Federal support to the States – with some schemes disappearing altogether and others being consolidated into 'block grants'[6] –

and the overall Federal tax burden fell by 8.5% in real terms. In addition, many 'Great Society' health, environmental and safety regulations were ignored in what became a new pro-business era.

These were substantial achievements for the conservative 'New Right'. Progress was less striking in the field of social reform. Here the Reagan administration was forced to concentrate upon a step-by-step institutional approach, geared towards changing the outlook of those working in the Federal administration, civil service and judiciary.

The Carter administration had been a fervent believer in 'affirmative action' (positive discrimination) and 'judicial activism' to advance minority interests, and this had been reflected in its appointment policies.[7] The Reagan administration, in contrast, viewed 'affirmative action' as a policy of reverse discrimination against whites and opposed activist measures designed to foster, what it viewed as, false equality (for example the Equal Rights Amendment movement). The President believed instead in the virtues of self-help and private initiative, and in individual rather than group rights. He appointed like-minded people to head the Federal Regulatory Commissions and attempted to bring critical independent bodies, for example the Civil Rights Commission, more closely under his tutelage. The Reagan administration thus gradually shifted the social climate in a 'New Right' direction through its executive actions – a more permissive attitude being adopted towards segregationist schools by the Justice Department, while support for 'affirmative action' and abortion programmes became more limited as Federal funding was scaled down.

This shift was buttressed by the increasingly cautious rulings of the Supreme Court of Chief Justice Burger. The Court continued to uphold its 1973 *Roe v Wade* decision, which permitted abortion during the first three months of pregnancy and gave qualified support to 'affirmative action' racial employment quotas in the cases of *Bakke* (July 1978) and *Weber* (July 1979). However, many more of its new rulings were conservative – extending in July 1976 the use of the death penalty[8] and controversially ruling in the *Chadha* case of June 1983 that Congress's use of the 'legislative veto' was unconstitutional.[9] The Attorney-General, William French Smith, supported by the 'New Right' Senate Republicans Strom Thurmond and Jesse Helms, attempted to accelerate such a movement towards 'judicial restraint' by legislating to bar

Federal courts from interfering with State laws. This measure foundered in Congress. The President did, however, succeed in swinging the balance on the Supreme Court further to the right when in July 1981 he was able to appoint Arizona's Sandra Day O'Connor (a 'States' rights' supporter) as the replacement for retiring Justice Potter Stewart.[10] This institutional movement towards conservatism was mirrored at the State level, where vocal 'New Right' single-issue lobbyists, under the direction of Phyllis Schlafly's Eagle Forum, succeeded in killing the Equal Rights Amendment in July 1982 and in persuading 37 States to re-introduce the death penalty and a similar number to ban the government financing of abortions.

However, while the first Reagan administration did see a significant transformation in the balance of the economy and in the handling of social questions, not all groups were satisfied with these changes, as its tax- and budget-cutting economic policy, although benefiting the rich, created pockets of new and deep poverty, particularly among the nation's black urban 'underclass'. Official surveys now showed the number of Americans living below the poverty line had increased by a fifth to 35 million (a number equivalent to 15% of the population) between 1980 and 1983, following two decades of amelioration, as rising levels of unemployment, coupled with Federal and State cutbacks in the AFDC and Food Stamp programmes, had dragged increasing numbers into abject poverty. Queues at charitable soup kitchens increased more than fivefold during these years and ramshackle tent cities were now erected, in scenes reminiscent of the 1930s 'Great Depression'. Others were antagonised by the new administration's social, deregulationary and defence policies – women over its attitude to abortion, equal pay and the Equal Rights Amendment; ethnic groups over its hands-off policy of 'negative action'; environmentalists over the free-rein given to coalmining in the western States and to offshore and on-shore oil drilling; and peace groups over the rearmament programme. This disenchantment stimulated the growth of radical peace, environmentalist, feminist and ethnic movements, fighting both positive and rearguard action as they attempted to stem the rising tide of conservatism.[11] It was to the support of these groups that a number in the Democratic Party now looked as they sought to establish a new and effective anti-Reagan coalition.

Chapter 5

THE 1984 PRESIDENTIAL ELECTION

The Democrat Challenge

The margin of the Democrats' 1980 defeat had led to talk of the emergence of a new Republican majority in the nation. However, while considerable progress had been made by the Republican Party since the mid 1970s, opinion polls and State and County elections still showed the Democrats holding a substantial national lead and remaining the clear majority party.[1] This lead was extended by the elections of November 1982, after which the Democrats held more than two-thirds of city mayorships and 34 governorships, and controlled the legislative houses in 34 States. It was in national presidential elections that the Democratic Party faced its greatest problems, finding it difficult to bridge the ideological gulf that existed between its southern and northern wings. The liberal southerners, Lyndon Johnson and Jimmy Carter, managed to unite the two wings in 1964 and 1976, but in 1968, 1972 and 1980 the South defected to a more conservative Republican. Within Congress, the rebellious voting actions of southern 'Boll Weevils' during the Carter and, particularly, Reagan presidencies served further to undermine the authority of the party's leadership.

These divisions continued to bedevil the Democrats in 1984. However, an attempt was made between 1980 and 1984 to carry out much-needed organisational reform and to develop a more attractive and coherent policy programme.

Party Reorganisation The Democrats lagged behind the Republican Party in the area of organisation terms during the 1970s. The Republicans, always strong in business support, pioneered the sophisticated use of computerised mailshots to draw in funds from the common voter. This paid off to such an extent that by 1982 the party was six times as rich as the Democrats and was able to pour substantial funds into Congressional and gubernatorial campaigns. The Democrats, chaired by the Californian businessman Charles Manatt, belatedly woke up to the need to revamp their organisational and marketing structure to cope with the new and costly needs of modern media-centred campaign politics and began after 1981 to establish their own direct mail networks and offshoot PACs, as well as a central 'think tank' (The Centre for Democratic Policy) and candidate coaching school.[2]

A second change for the Democrats centred around their election rules. The 1970s had witnessed a progressive democratisation of the selection process, with the spread of primaries, of proportional representation within contests and of ethnic and sex quotas for delegates attending the National Convention. However, after the experience of the outsider Carter presidency and the lengthy and damaging Carter-Kennedy contest of 1980, it was felt that reform had gone too far. In 1984 the party was faced with the prospect of an uncontested Republican ticket and a divisive Democrat battle. The Democrat National Committee thus decided in March 1982 to compress and 'frontload' the 1984 primary season: reducing the number of binding State primaries to (including the District of Columbia) 26; increasing the number of State caucuses to 25; switching several States from proportional to first-past-the-post delegate selection; and raising the proportion of official and unelected delegates sent to the Convention to 14%.[3] These changes, it was hoped, would lead to a brisk outcome – possibly by March – in the 1984 race and improve the prospects of an 'insider' nomination. In addition, it was hoped that the reforms, by allowing 60% of the Democrats' Representatives and Senators and several hundred senior party workers and State-level elected officeholders (including Governors and city Mayors) to attend the National Convention as voting 'superdelegates', would bring about a closer relationship between the party's Congressmen and officials and the successful candidate, which would prove of value during his ensuing term in office.

Policy Divisions However, while Democrat bosses immersed themselves in rule changes and the fine-tuning of the party's organisation, there still remained substantial differences over policies and strategy during the early 1980s. Excepting the 'Boll Weevils' and 'Defense Democrats', who supported significant elements of the new Republican administration's programme, the liberal ADA-orientated north-eastern and midwestern rump of the Democratic Party remained bitterly opposed to the 'Reagan Reformation'. They were joined in this conviction by the radical fringe and interest groups noted above and most significantly by the powerful American Federation of Labor-Congress of Industrial Organizations (AFL-CIO) labour union organisation.

This body, under its new leader Lane Kirkland, suspended its traditionally bipartisan approach to party politics during the Reagan presidency and came out firmly in support of the Democrats, providing it, through its COPE political arm, with 20% of its national funds. In return, the AFL-CIO gained an increased share of National Committee and National Convention seats and a powerful voice within the party's decision-making councils. The liberal factions within and aligned to the Democratic Party, while firmly opposed to Reaganism, found it difficult to agree, however, upon a common alternative strategy and programme for government, particularly in the economic sphere. Some dreamt of adopting a radical new social democratic tripartite platform and of relaunching an updated version of Roosevelt's Reconstruction Finance Corporation as a means of channelling investment funds into both ailing smokestack and promising new high-tech industries. Most, however, preferred to stick to a more modest and traditional investment package to be financed by increased taxes. As a consequence of such internal differences, the party's policy programme remained fudged and vague. This rendered the selection of a dynamic and persuasive presidential candidate for November 1984 a critical task.

The Battle for the Democrat Nomination

Senator Edward Kennedy remained the most popular Democrat politician during the early 1980s and received a rousing reception at the midterm Convention in Philadelphia in June 1982. He thus took the party by surprise when he declared in December 1982 that he would not contest the 1984 nomination. Kennedy ostensibly withdrew to protect his family's privacy and in order to concentrate on his work in the Senate. However, he probably also realised that, faced with a popular incumbent President, his chances of victory in 1984 were slim. This withdrawal left Walter Mondale, Vice-President during the Carter years, the overwhelming favourite to head the party ticket.

Mondale, the 56-year-old son of a Methodist preacher of Norwegian stock, came from the small town of Ceylon in Minnesota – the midwestern home of the radical, but now crumbling, Democratic Farmer-Labor Party (DFL). Affectionately nicknamed 'Fritz', Mondale was a modest and down-to-earth

71

man who displayed a strong antipathy towards what he termed modern 'theatre politics'. He concentrated instead on tradition-al committee room and backroom political activity, gaining the reputation as a 'machine politician', on good terms with party bosses, trade unions and interest groups, and was renowned at hammering out compromise deals in a broker fashion. Utilising this support, he was appointed State Attorney-General (1960–4) and Senator for Minnesota (serving in the position for 12 years between 1964 and 1976) and finally Vice-President in 1977. Mondale's wealth of experience at home and abroad[4] made him the Democrats' clear front-runner in 1984. His prospects were further improved by the party's March 1982 rule changes and by the early endorsements extended to his candidature in November 1983 by the influential AFL-CIO, the National Education Association (NEA) teachers' union and the National Organization for Women (NOW). However, Mondale's lack of charisma made him still vulnerable to challenge in this media age.

Seven candidates offered such a challenge, with two emerging as significant threats – the Rev Jesse Jackson (42) and Senator Gary Hart (47).[5]

Jesse Jackson was a controversial and flamboyant black activist leader, who stood, not to secure the party nomination, but to raise black political awareness and pride and to influence the subsequent party programme. Born illegitimately in Greenville, South Carolina, in October 1941, Jackson moved north on a football scholarship to the University of Illinois before entering a Chicago theological seminary. Working initially alongside Dr Martin Luther King (1929–68), he emerged as an influential Baptist preacher, established, in 1971, People United to Serve Humanity (PUSH) to promote black economic advancement and built up a powerful political machine which succeeded in capturing the mayorship of Chicago in April 1983. He was a magnetic and rhythmic speaker and a skilled publicist and campaigner. During the summer of 1983 Jackson embarked on a 'Southern Crusade' with the aim of registering three million new black voters by November 1984 and of drawing attention to the continued abuse of electoral laws in the Confederacy States. 'Voter registration' was to become the principal theme of his 1984 electoral campaign. A secondary theme was the need for the Democratic Party to open its doors and establish a new 'rainbow coalition', embracing downtrodden and discriminated groups and middle-class radicals – blacks, Hispanics, feminists, environmentalists, peace campaigners and homosexuals.

Jackson's candidature was doomed to failure, but it served to enliven an otherwise dull campaign and it brought to the public's notice a radical alternative programme, which included a call for urban renewal and the launch of a second 'war on poverty' coupled with a new even-handed, pacific and 'South-minded' foreign policy. The Jackson campaign, drawing away black and Hispanic support, was, however, a major blow to the hopes of a speedy Mondale victory. It was for this reason that many older and more conservative black leaders – including Mayors Andrew Young (Atlanta), Tom Bradley (Los Angeles), Wilson Goode (Philadelphia) and Marion Barry (Washington), the NAACP executive and the influential King family – refused to endorse the Jackson nomination, viewing Mondale, a committed 'New Deal' liberal with a fine civil rights record, as the most realistic candidate for the black interest.

A beneficiary of this split black vote was Gary Hart, who emerged as the most serious and unexpected challenger for the Democrat nomination. Born in the small midwestern town of Ottawa, Kansas, in November 1936, Hart later moved to New England to read divinity and law at Yale, where he became immersed in Democrat politics. He worked as a volunteer during John F Kennedy's successful 1960 campaign, assisted Robert Kennedy in 1968 and was the manager of George McGovern's ill-fated tilt at the presidency between 1970 and 1972.[6] During these years Hart was viewed as a radical liberal, but he went on to capture a Senate seat from a Republican in conservative Colorado in the 'Post-Watergate Election' of November 1974 and moved progressively towards the centre in the later 1970s. He established himself as a new-style 'neo-liberal' – committed to civil rights reform, the relief of poverty and environmentalism, but concerned to foster greater efficiency in government and to experiment with new policy approaches. These included the call for the creation of a computerised national job bank, workers' participation, a programme of investment in high-tech industries, compulsory military and non-military national service, and a shift of emphasis towards the strengthening and modernisation of conventional defence forces.

Hart sought to project himself as the spokesman for a 'New Generation' in the manner of John F Kennedy and as a more dynamic and idealistic leader than the staid Walter Mondale. As the Senator of a western State and as a candidate who enjoyed strong appeal amongst young urban professionals, he believed that he had a better chance of capturing the vital white-collar and suburban middle-class vote which would be required for a Democrat victory. Hart's major problem was his shortage of finance compared to the well-funded Walter Mondale. This was compounded by his refusal, on grounds of principle, to take money from PACs. Hart was served, however, by a dedicated team of young volunteers led by Patrick Caddell, a skilled pollster who had served on the 1972 McGovern and 1976 and 1980 Carter campaigns, and concentrated upon achieving early successes in the primaries to create a bandwagon effect. This, he hoped, would bring in funds and publicity following the pattern set by Jimmy Carter in 1976.

This strategy got off to a a remarkably successful start when, following weeks of personal door-to-door canvassing and factory visits, Hart shocked the Democratic Party establishment by topping the poll at the inaugural New Hampshire primary on 28 February, capturing 37% of the poll compared to Mondale's 28%. This State, with its young, predominantly middle-class, population and its high-tech bias, was fertile ground for the 'New Generation' Coloradan. Hart proceeded to follow up this success by winning the next three caucuses and six out of the 11 primary and caucus contests held on the 'Super Tuesday' of 13 March. However, Mondale, though stunned by his ominous defeat in New Hampshire – no candidate losing in New Hampshire had ever gone on to capture the presidency – began to fight back in March, removing his gloves for what proved to be a lengthy and bruising nomination contest.

During the following weeks Hart continued to record victories in New England and in western States, while Mondale prevailed in the South and in the heavily unionised North. However, Hart's early novelty value began to fade as he came under the microscope of close media attention. Questions were raised about his character,[7] personal life and inexperience, while his policy initiatives were criticised for appearing muddled and confused, prompting the ultimately wounding Mondale camp jibe, 'Where's the beef?' Mondale, by contrast, while failing to inspire, showed qualities of dogged determination and quiet competence. He gradually fought back and established a small but comfortable lead in the delegate race by the close of the primary season in early June. To these pledged votes he added, through his contacts and influence within the party, the vast majority of the 568 uncommitted official 'Super Delegates' and appeared certain of victory at the San Francisco National Convention in July. Party leaders, including Manatt and O'Neill, tried to persuade Hart to concede in the interests of unity. However, Hart persevered in the hope that unfavourable opinion polls might prompt a last-moment switch of delegate support.

These hopes proved to be forlorn as the Mondale team took decisive action – first gaining the endorsement of Senator Edward Kennedy on 25 June and then announcing on 12 July that Geraldine Ferraro, the 48-year-old three-term New York Representative, would be their choice as the country's first-ever major party female vice-presidential candidate.[8] This dramatic move added sparkle to the Mondale ticket and secured the support of the feminist, Catholic and Italian lobbies – Ferraro being the 'rags to riches' daughter of humble Italian immigrants, who had established herself as a wealthy and successful professional.[9] The Mondale team were thus able to capture the party nomination by acclamation in San Francisco on 18 July. A number of 'platform' concessions were then made to the Hart and Jackson camps in an attempt to restore unity, as the party hastily readdressed itself to the need to challenge and defeat President Reagan.[10]

The Mondale-Reagan Contest of November 1984

While the Democrats had become embroiled in a protracted struggle for the party nomination, President Reagan was able to proceed regally towards the Republican National Convention in Dallas on 20–23 August without challenge, spending time investigating his family roots in Ireland and visiting Europe to attend D-Day commemorations. The lack of an intra-party challenge was unusual, but it served to demonstrate the hold that the President exerted over his party and was a reflection of his growing national popularity. It enabled the Republican National Committee to concentrate finance and resources on preparations for the November contest, while Democrat funds were dissipated in internecine disputes.

By the start of August, President Reagan led Walter Mondale by more than ten points in national opinion polls. The economy continued to grow robustly and the withdrawal of US marines from Beirut in March 1984 had removed a key area of foreign policy criticism. The President's major continuing weakness lay in his apparent indifference to the poor and to blacks, Hispanics, environmentalists and feminists, and the stridency of his foreign policy. Recognising this, the Reagan team began to moderate its approach to social and environmental issues during 1984 and set about attempting to court community leaders. Little hope was extended to winning over the support of the black community, which had perennially voted Democrat by a huge margin. However, greater hopes surrounded the Hispanics, who shared the Republican belief in strong family ties and their antipathy towards communism (particularly in the case of 'Latino' Cuban refugees) and who had proved averse to supporting Jesse Jackson's 'Rainbow Coalition'. The administration also hoped to win back support from women who had been frightened in 1980 by Reagan's warmongering rhetoric and his promised attack on social programmes and had been repelled by his unyielding opposition to the Equal Rights Amendment. The Reagan team now pointed to the appointment of Sandra Day O'Connor as the first female justice to the Supreme Court and to the midterm induction of Elizabeth Dole (Transport) and Margaret Heckler (Health) into the cabinet team as evidence of the President's absence of chauvinism and his genuine concern for female advancement.

In foreign affairs the Reagan team was less willing to compromise. Instead, a virtue was made of the President's strong stance and the fact that during his term in office not one inch of soil had 'fallen under the Soviet yoke'. President Reagan proudly announced in his January 1984 State of the Union message that 'America is Back', as a wave of patriotism gripped the nation, reaching a crescendo during the August 1984 Los Angeles Olympic Games. However, the President did somewhat temper this forceful approach with the launch of the visionary and pacific Strategic Defense Initiative (SDI) in March 1983 and by agreeing, following a meeting with the Soviet foreign minister, Andrei Gromyko, in Washington in September 1984, to re-open East-West arms control negotiations in Geneva in March 1985.

Despite the growing popularity of President Reagan, the Democrats hoped to snatch victory in November 1984 by gaining the support of five crucial sets of voters: the ten million new freshmen electors; the liberals who had supported John Anderson in 1980;[11] Catholics and ethnic (Italian, Scandinavian,

German) European-Americans; and blacks, a record turnout from whom might tip the balance in the crucial southern States. This would be achieved, they hoped, through a concerted attack on the weaker areas of the Reagan administration's record – its Central American policy, the widening social divisions at home and the dangerously spiralling Federal budget deficit – and through the pronouncement of a detailed set of alternative policy prescriptions, the most prominent of which was Walter Mondale's solemn promise to slash the Federal deficit by two-thirds by 1989 through the implementation of a new tax-increase programme. This strategy of 'issues and realism' was, however, scuppered by the irruption in August 1984 of a damaging tax avoidance scandal involving Geraldine Ferraro's millionaire property-speculator husband, John Zaccaro, which served to paralyse the Democrat campaign.

This enabled President Reagan to concentrate on an image-based campaign of confidence, strength, success and optimism, which he contrasted with the 'pessimism, fear and limits' of the preceding Carter-Mondale administration. These themes were presented in a series of slick television adverts, paid for by both the Reagan team and by NCPAC, which, under the slogan 'It's morning again in America', struck a responsive chord. Thus on polling day, 6 November 1984, President Reagan achieved an overwhelming electoral victory, capturing both a record 54.5 million votes and a record 525 'electoral college' votes. (See Table 13 and Figure 6.) His proportionate share of the total votes cast – 58.8% – lagged 2% behind that achieved by Richard Nixon in 1972, Lyndon Johnson in 1964 and Franklin Roosevelt in 1936, but represented a comforting 8% advance on his result in 1980. His opponent, Walter Mondale, gathered 40.6% of the popular vote, a figure comparable to that of the defeated President Carter in 1980, but only topped the poll in his native Minnesota and in the predominantly black District of Columbia.

The Reagan victory of 1984 was a great populist landslide. It was founded upon the bedrock of support inherited from 1980 in the South, West and Midwest – among the white Protestant middle classes who had benefited from four years of tax-cutting Reaganism. In addition, the President retained the support of blue-collar workers and a 33% share of the Hispanic vote; he won over the 'second wave' of immigrants from Europe (Scandinavians, Irish, Poles, Germans, Slavs, Greeks and Italians); and, with his engaging personality and upbeat, 'go-getting' philosophy, he attracted a surprisingly large proportion of young freshmen and freshwomen electors. (See Table 14.) The Democrats did win increasing support from Jews (vexed by Reagan's Middle East policy and his fundamentalist social philosophy), blacks and the poor, but lost proportionate support from women and made little headway among Catholics, despite the efforts of Geraldine Ferraro. Most serious of all, the party failed to win over middle-income groups; captured a mere 34% of the white vote; and performed disastrously in the South.

TABLE 13   THE NOVEMBER 1984 PRESIDENTIAL ELECTION (TURNOUT 53.3%)

Candidate	Party	Popular Vote (m)	As % of Total	Electoral College Vote	States Captured
Ronald W Reagan*	Republican	54.45	58.77	525	49
Walter F Mondale*	Democrat	37.57	40.55	13	1
David Bergland†	Libertarian	0.23	0.25	0	0
Lyndon LaRouche‡	Ind Democrat	0.08	0.09	0	0
Sonia Johnson	Citizens	0.07	0.08	0	0
Bob Richards‡	Populist	0.06	0.06	0	0
Dennis Serrette	Ind Alliance	0.05	0.05	0	0
Gus Hall	Communist	0.04	0.04	0	0
Mel Mason	Socialist Workers	0.02	0.02	0	0
Others§		0.08	0.09	0	0
Total		92.65	100.00	538	50

* By the end of the campaign Reagan and Mondale had each spent in the region of $75 million, two-thirds of which came in the form of Federal funding grants.

† Bergland succeeded in securing his name on 41 State ballots. The other minor party candidates were named on only a few State ballots.

‡ These two candidates were based in the depressed Midwest farmbelt States and propounded a radical programme of protectionism with a racist undercurrent.

§ Five other candidates collected over 2000 votes apiece: Larry Holmes (Workers World), 15 220; Delmar Dennis (American Party), 13 150; Ed Winn (Workers League), 10 801; Earl Dodge (Prohibition Party), 4242; and Gavrielle Holmes (Workers World), 2718.

TABLE 14   VOTER PREFERENCES BY SOCIAL GROUPS (%) 1976–84

	(% of 1984 Voters)	1976 Carter (D)	1976 Ford (R)	1980 Carter (D)	1980 Reagan (R)	1980 Anderson (Ind)	1984 Mondale (D)	1984 Reagan (R)
Total	100	51	49	41	51	7	41	59
Men	47	52	48	36	55	7	37	61
Women	53	52	48	45	47	7	42	57
White	86	48	52	36	55	7	34	66
Blacks	10	83	17	85	11	3	90	9
Hispanics	3	—	—	59	33	6	65	33
Under 30s	24	56	44	44	43	11	41	58
30–49 years	44	52	48	37	54	8	41	58
Over 50s	32	48	52	40	54	5	38	61
Protestants	51	46	54	31	63	8	26	73
Catholics	26	55	45	42	49	7	44	55
Jewish	3	—	—	45	39	15	66	32
'Born Agains'	15	—	—	33	63	3	20	80
Union families	26	62	36	48	43	6	53	45
Family income								
Below $12 500	15	—	—	51	42	6	53	46
$12 500–25 000	27	—	—	46	44	8	42	57
Over $25 000	52	—	—	34	58	8	35	64
East US	24	51	47	42	47	9	47	52
Midwest	28	48	50	40	51	7	38	61
South	29	54	45	44	52	3	36	63
West	18	46	51	34	53	10	40	59

White apathy to the Mondale candidature was already clear in the South during the primary campaign. In November 1984, appalled by the untrammelled liberalism of the Mondale-Ferraro ticket, and shocked by the novelty of an inexperienced female running-mate and by the black registration drives of Jesse Jackson, this group now capitulated to the Reagan camp. Eighty per cent of southern whites voted for President Reagan, while the large black minority voted solidly for the Democrats. The early post-Civil War voting pattern of the region was thus starkly reversed. A better balance to the Democrat ticket, with, for example, a Southern 'Dixie Democrat' in the form of Senator Lloyd Bentsen of Texas, or Senator Dale Bumpers of Arkansas running as Vice-President designate, or the selection of Gary Hart, or the centrist John Glenn as presidential candidate would undoubtedly have eased this 'southern squeeze' and narrowed the margin of defeat for the Democrats in November 1984. However, the tendency for voting to divide starkly on racial lines was a clear warning to the party as it began to contemplate its future electoral strategy.

Figure 6   Map of the 1984 Presidential Election

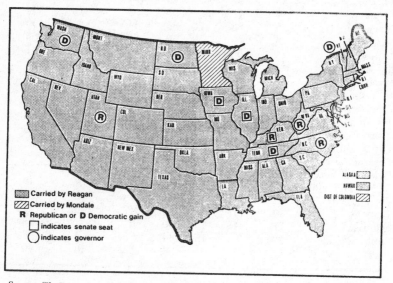

Source: *The Economist* 10 November 1984 p32

The Reagan landslide of November 1984 was not, however, replicated in the concurrent Congressional elections. This demonstrated to what extent there had been a personal vote for the President himself rather than an ideological vote for the Republican Party or for 'New Right' policy prescriptions and also highlighted the degree to which Congressional elections continued to be fought on local issues and personalities.[12] It also, in the opinion of a number of prominent Republicans, reflected unfavourably on the President, who had vainly spent his last hours campaigning in Minnesota in search of an historic clean sweep of

TABLE 15 THE CONGRESSIONAL AND GUBERNATORIAL
ELECTIONS OF NOVEMBER 1984

	House Seats	Result	Senator-ships	Result	Governor-ships	Result
Total Contested	435		33		13	
Democrat Victories	255	−14	16	+2*	5	−1†
Republican Victories	180	+14	17	−2	8	+1

* The Democrats gained the senatorships of Tennessee, where former Representative Albert Gore Jr filled the open seat vacated by the retirement of Senate Majority Leader Howard Baker; Illinois (Paul Simon); and Iowa (Tom Harkin), but lost Kentucky to the Republicans (Mitch McConnell). (The Democrats had earlier lost the senatorship of Washingon when, following the death of Henry 'Scoop' Jackson (1912–83), the Republican former State Governor, Dan Evans, defeated the Democrat Representative Mike Lowry in a special November 1983 head-to-head contest.)

† The Democrats made three gubernatorial gains – North Dakota (George Sinner), Vermont (Madeleine Kunin) and Washington (Booth Gardner) – and recorded four losses – North Carolina (James Martin), Rhode Island (Edward DiPrete), Utah (Norman Bangerter) and West Virginia (Arch Moore).

the 50 States and had failed to come to the aid of candidates fighting marginal seats. The Republicans did make a net gain of 14 seats in the House of Representatives, one governorship and 305 seats in the State legislatures, but in the Senate, defending 19 of the 33 seats being contested, they endured a net loss of two seats (see Table 15).[13] The Congressional results, with incumbent Representatives and Senators enjoying the unprecedentedly high 'return rates' of 95% and 90% respectively, reflected an overriding desire on the part of the electorate in 1984 for continuity rather than change. This mood contrasted sharply with that recorded in the 'swing elections' of 1976 and 1980. The Republicans retained their overall majority in, and control over, the Senate, but remained in a clear minority in the House of Representatives and had failed to recoup their losses of 1982. Trailing the Democrats by 75 seats in the House, the prospects of a successful reconstruction of the majority-wielding conservative Republican-'Boll Weevil' coalition of 1981 thus appeared to be remote.[14] This promised to present serious problems for the Reagan administration between 1985 and 1988.

Part Four

CONSOLIDATING THE REPUBLICAN HEGEMONY

Chapter 6

THE SECOND REAGAN ADMINISTRATION: 1985–8

Reassembling for the Second Term

President Reagan was only the third post-war President to be re-elected for a second term. Discussion thus revived on the restrictions placed by the Twenty-Second Amendment and on the likelihood that, unable to seek re-election again, he would become a powerless 'lame duck' whose priorities would shift to foreign affairs.

Reagan and his Cabinet The President himself, however, put such matters aside as he set about constructing a new cabinet for this second term. He decided to retain the core of his existing team, while reshuffling and bringing fresh blood into the second-tier departments. (See Table 16.) The most important departure was that of William Clark (Interior Secretary since October 1983), who returned home to California and was replaced by former Interior Deputy and Energy Secretary, Donald Hodel from Oregon. In the Justice Department, the President's close friend Ed Meese, after undergoing 13 months of rigorous inquiries by the Senate Judiciary Committee, gained belated approval as the new Attorney-General in February 1985. The third and most significant change involved the transfer of the skilled and ambitious Chief-of-Staff, James Baker, to the Treasury to replace the abrasive conservative, Donald Regan, who now became head of the White House Office.

TABLE 16 THE REAGAN CABINET IN JANUARY 1985*

Department Secretaries

State Dept	George P Shultz (64, New York, ex-Nixon admin)
Treasury	James A Baker (54, ex-Chief-of-Staff)
Defense	Caspar W Weinberger (67, ex-California & Nixon admins)
Attorney-General	Edwin Meese (53, ex-California admin)
Interior	Donald P Hodel (48, Energy Secretary since Nov 1982)
Agriculture	John R Block (49, ex-Illinois State Secretary)
Labor	Raymond J Donovan (54, New Jersey, labour adviser)
Commerce	Malcolm Baldrige (62, Connecticut industrialist)
Housing and Urban Development (HUD)	Samuel R Pierce (62, New York, former Nixon admin)
Energy	John S Herrington (44, Californian lawyer)
Health and Human Services	Margaret M Heckler (53, New York)
Education	William J Bennett (41, ex-Chmn National Humanities Foundation)
Transportation	Elizabeth H Dole (48, Kansas, former Nixon admin)
UN Representative	Gen Vernon Walters (67, ex-Deputy Director CIA)
Special Trade Representative	William E Brock (54, former Trade Representative)
Dir of CIA	William J Casey (71, New York lawyer & ex-Californian admin)

White House Advisers

Chief-of-Staff	Donald T Regan (66, ex-Treasury Secretary)
National Security Adviser	Robert McFarlane (48, ex-Deputy NSA)
Dir of OMB	James C Miller (42, ex-Chmn Federal Trade Commission)
Chmn of CEA	Beryl Sprinkel (41, ex-Treasury Under-Secretary)
Dir of Communs	Patrick Buchanan (46, ex-Nixon aide)
Press Secretary	Larry Speakes (46, Mississippi, ex-Ford aide)

* UN Representative Jeane Kirkpatrick and Education Secretary Terrel Bell resigned in January 1985. CEA chairman (since July 1982) Martin Feldstein, a critic of high budget deficits, resigned in May 1984 to return to Harvard.

This move, which had been made at the mutual request of the two men involved, pleased Republican right-wingers, who had always viewed Baker as a dangerous moderating influence on the

President.[1] Donald Regan, being a self-made millionaire from a poor Massachusetts Irish working-class background,[2] had become a very close friend of President Reagan and was to emerge during 1985–6 as a most powerful Chief-of-Staff, wielding the authority of an unofficial prime minister. He re-organised and stream-lined the White House along corporate lines, reducing the seven existing domestic policy cabinet councils (which had dealt with commerce and trade; economic affairs; food and agriculture; human resources; legal policy; management and administration; and natural resources and the environment) into two (economic policy, headed by James Baker, and domestic policy, headed by Ed Meese), leaving the foreign policy councils untouched. Sec-ond, following this centralising trend, Regan came to monopolise access to the President and rooted out dissenting voices from the advisory councils. This persuaded a string of influential aides to resign during 1985 – Michael Deaver in May, David Stockman in July, and Max Friedersdorf and Robert McFarlane (NSA) in December.[3] They were to be replaced by quieter and more obedient servants. Thus, although Baker and Meese retained considerable influence in the domestic sphere and Shultz and Weinberger over foreign affairs, it was Regan who clearly domi-nated the administration during the first half of this second term, emerging as a new Sherman Adams. This was displayed graphically in July 1985 when the President was forced to enter hospital for a colon operation. It was Regan who tested the President's mental alertness and ability to resume control after Vice-President Bush's brief nine-hour tenure as chief executive and it was he who was to be left in effective day-to-day charge of the nation during the President's ensuing convalescence period.

Reagan and Congress　During his first term in office President Reagan had been able to recover some of the power of the presi-dency which had been conceded to Congress during the Ford and Carter eras. He had used his skilful control of the television medium[4] and his personal ascendancy in the nation to press home controversial policy packages and he had found his authority fur-ther augmented by the Supreme Court's legislative veto ruling. However, Congress still remained powerful and resistant to many aspects of the President's policy programme. Shifts in the balance of party power and changes among its personnel promised to make the 99th Congress of 1985–6 particularly troublesome.

In the Senate, the conciliatory Majority Leader, Howard Baker, retired in November 1984 and was replaced by Robert Dole of

Kansas (previously chairman of the Senate Finance Committee). Dole was an ambitious centrist-conservative politician who, with his eye on the party's 1988 nomination, wished to make a rapid and significant impact. He presided, however, over a wafer-thin Republican majority, with 22 of his colleagues facing re-election in November 1986. Many of these were freshmen who had entered the Senate in the 'swing election' of November 1980 and who represented southern or midwestern seats. They were concerned with high interest rates and with the cutbacks in Federal support which had led to a severe credit crisis in the farmbelt. They thus sought to strike out independent lines and distance themselves from the administration during the next two years. This made the Senate an increasingly difficult chamber to control. The House of Representatives, with Tip O'Neil due to retire as Speaker in November 1986, was also to become increasingly anarchic, as Democrats geared themselves up for a succession struggle.

Policy Initiatives in the Second Term

In 1985 the overriding domestic problem facing the new administration was the huge and growing Federal budget deficit. This deficit fell 5% to $185 billion during 1984 following 18 months of rapid economic growth, but at 5.2% of GNP was still at an uncommonly high level. It had forced up interest rates and the dollar exchange rate, thus discouraging industrial investment and encouraging imports. In the short term, this had been advantageous for American consumers, but from the autumn of 1984 the pace of American economic growth suddenly slowed, as did the precipitate decline in the unemployment rate.[5] The budget deficit clearly needed to be reduced, but instead, with faltering growth, it moved remorselessly upwards, threatening in 1985 to overshoot the $210 billion mark and thus turn the United States into a net debtor nation for the first time since 1914.

President Reagan had remained coy about how he would deal with the deficit problem during his 1984 campaign, but on his return to office in January 1985 he presented a two-pronged scheme. He rejected Democrat calls for defence cuts, tax increases and protectionist tariffs, and concentrated instead on a growth-orientated 'supply-side' approach which combined further substantial reductions in social spending with radical tax reform. The administration thus put forward in February 1985 a budget which envisaged increasing defence spending by 6% in real terms and (following an election pledge) raising pensions in line with inflation, but which would at the same time lower the budget deficit to $144 billion (2.9% of GNP) by 1988 through savage cuts in the remainder of the Federal programme. Three months later the President unveiled a radical new tax reform package, which anticipated reducing the existing 14 tax bands (at between 11 and 50%) to only three (at 12, 25 and 35%) and removing many of the existing dodges and shelters which had served to distort investment decisions and unduly discriminate in favour of the very rich. This 'flat-tax' scheme, it was hoped, would raise incentives and would lead to a small decrease in the overall tax burden to be paid for out of administrative savings.[6] These two reform packages were radical, recalling those of 1981. They were, however, to find themselves buffeted by a welter of Congressional opposition during the months ahead.

The President's new budget package, introduced in February 1985, was a non-starter from the very beginning. House Democrats simply refused to countenance a scheme which put all the burden for economies on the social programmes for the poor which had already been savagely cut back during the previous four years, while leaving the Defense Department inviolate. Many moderate Senate Republicans concurred, seeing the need for greater flexibility in the defence budget. Both chambers thus introduced between March and July 1985 packages which were designed to reduce sharply the budget deficit, but which placed the onus for savings on areas contradictory to the President's programme.[7] The new tax reform plan found itself savaged by an even broader coalition, which included the swathe of business and consumer interest groups who stood to lose from the removal of diverse tax privileges. The President attempted to outflank these opponents by conducting a determined national campaign in support of this reform, addressing public meetings in Miami, Oklahoma, Pennsylvania, Atlanta and New Jersey in May and June 1985. However, much ground was lost by the President's enforced seclusion in July and by the resignation of David Stockman, and many potential supporters were alienated by the inept and abrasive lobbying tactics of Donald Regan. By the time the President recommended campaigning for these measures in August 1985, the initiative for reform had passed to Congress.

In the House of Representatives, the Ways and Means Committee chairman, Dan Rostenkowski (Chicago), devised an alternative tax reform package which gained broad Democrat support. This safeguarded existing Federal tax deductions for local taxes – thus placating residents of the highly State-taxed North-east – and raised the tax burden for businesses. In the Senate, the radical Gramm-Rudman-Hollings (GRH) bill was passed on 9 October with the aim of balancing the budget in stages by 1991 through forcing statutory cuts in years when voluntary agreement was absent. The President was loath to accept either of these reform measures until December 1985, when, with no progress having been made on his own schemes, he was left with little alternative. The President thus grudgingly gave his consent to the balanced budget bill passed by Congress on 11 December and pressured Republican colleagues into voting for the Democrat tax reform bill in the House on 18 December.

Thus, by the close of 1985, the President had failed to push through his own budget and tax reform measures, but had at least forced Congress to address the issues and devise their own alternatives. These were, however, controversial, particularly the GRH balanced budget act, which promised to have major constitutional and political implications. It prescribed broad percentage cuts in non-exempt programmes (pensions, food stamps and Medicaid were exempt, Medicare was partially protected, but defence was non-exempt) during non-recessionary years when the budget deficit appeared certain to overshoot the statutory target by more than $10 billion. It thus stripped Congress and the President of their powers to decide on revenue allocation and seriously imperilled the Pentagon's defence build-up. The bill was accepted, however, as a necessary deterrent, acting as a gun at the heads of Congress and the President in the expectation that it would in future force compromise within a rigid timetable. It was thus an indication of the absence of voluntary consensus in the 99th Congress and of the inability of the existing political system to deal responsibly with budgetary matters.

Thus during 1985, although President Reagan remained an unusually popular figure – recording a public approval rating in excess of 65% – he was unable to dominate policy-making. He did win a number of key votes in the foreign policy field, for example on the resumption of aid to the Nicaraguan Contra rebels (June 1985). Overall, however, his 'Congressional success rating' plunged from a first-term average figure of 71.9% to a Ford-like level of below 60% in 1985. (See Appendix Table B7.) In the economic sphere, in particular, President Reagan suffered significant defeats over such vital issues as protection to the textile industry and the balance of cuts in the Federal budget. His policy prescription of lower taxes, higher defence spending and social services economies was no longer believed or supported. Instead, a new Congressional consensus was emerging which sought to restrain defence spending, protect the remnant social budget, and which was willing to tolerate elements of protectionism and higher indirect taxation.

This became clear in 1986 when President Reagan presented his new budget for fiscal 1987 (1 October 1986 – 30 September 1987). It sought once more to avoid tax increases and to raise defence spending by 3% in real terms while at the same time reducing the Federal deficit (in line with GRH) to $144 billion through cutbacks in the social programme and selective privatisation. Both chambers of Congress, however, immediately rejected these proposals and agreed instead, in June 1986, on a compromise package, scaling down the defence budget and protecting the social programme. They acted with unusual alacrity, partly as a result of the pressure of the new GRH budget-cutting timetable.[8] They were also impelled by a gathering crisis in the American economy caused by the still-widening trade deficit and by the sudden halving of world oil prices between January and May 1986.[9] The latter event brought slump conditions to the oil-rich states of Texas, Louisiana, Oklahoma and Alaska, while elsewhere growth in the manufacturing sector stalled, creating new pockets of distress.

With midterm elections due in November 1986, Congressmen were anxious to be seen to be taking a lead in economic affairs and did so in the budget negotiations, significantly restricting growth of the bloated defence programme.[10] Congress, secondly, achieved startling success in its efforts at tax reform during 1986. A radical reform package was agreed upon by the Senate Finance Committee chaired by Robert Packwood (R – Oregon), removing the forest of tax shelters and reducing Federal taxation to a dual rate of 15% and 27%. It was approved by the overwhelming margin of 97–3 in the Senate in June. The measure was then sent on to a joint House-Senate Conference Committee chaired by Dan Rostenkowski and a compromise bill drafted in August which was rapidly approved by both chambers and signed into law by President Reagan on 22 October. The act represented the most sweeping and populist reform of the Federal tax system for more than 40 years, favouring private individuals at the expense of companies, freeing millions from the tax net and dealing a deathly blow to the burgeoning chain of tax advisory intermediaries.[11]

On both the measures of budget deficit reduction and tax reform, not only did Congress rather than the President take the lead during 1986, but, in addition, Democrat Representatives and Senators, rather than Republicans, played the most decisive and innovative roles. The tax reform bill, for example, was in large measure drafted in the House by Richard Gephardt (D – Missouri) and in the Senate by Bill Bradley (D – New Jersey) and would certainly have failed if Democrat leaders in the House of Representatives had withheld their backing. On other measures, including trade, environmental and foreign affairs, Democrats, particularly in the House, similarly played a pioneering role. This reflected a returning self-confidence and growing assertiveness among Democrats as they geared themselves up for November 1986 and for the 1988 'post-Reagan' presidential contest, as well as a sharpening in inter-party rivalry. Thus, during both 1985 and 1986 voting within Congress became unusually polarised along party lines, the 99th Congress recording the highest 'party unity' scores (see Table 2) seen in three decades. As a consequence of such partisanship, President Reagan's 'Congressional success rate' slumped to its lowest annual figure, 56.5%, in 1986. (Only Gerald Ford in 1976, Richard Nixon in 1973 and Dwight Eisenhower in 1959, among post-war Presidents, had endured lower annual totals – see Appendix Table B7.) In the Senate the President's 'success rate' remained respectably high at 81%, but in the House of Representatives it plummeted to a new low of 34%, a figure less than half that recorded in 1981.[12]

The End of the Reagan Revolution? The 'Social Agenda' in 1985–6

The sharp drop in Congressional support for President Reagan during 1985–6, his failure to force through many elements of his proposed reform programme[13] and his defeat and compelled reversal on a number of key issues – for example sanctions against South Africa (September 1985 and August–September 1986, with, on the latter occasion, his veto being overridden), environmental protection and appropriations for new public works projects – led a number of observers to view the President, at the midterm stage of his second term, as a 'spent force' and to suggest that the era of radical reform had reached its end. This view was shared by many of the President's former supporters from the 'New Right', who felt disenchanted and betrayed by what they saw as the limited changes brought about by the 'Reagan reformation' and the weak-willed pragmatism of their chosen torchbearer. Such an interpretation was, however, unfair and only partially tenable. It failed to take account of, first, the realities of diffused and divided power in the American system of government, a problem which was exacerbated during 1985–6 by the sharp party political cleavage that existed within Congress, and secondly, the lack of clear public support that existed for many of the President's more controversial 'New Right' policy proposals. However, while President Reagan's ability to push through radical reform had been progressively reduced since 1981, he had, on occasion, been able to record a number of striking victories, and continued slowly to shift the policy debate and political 'agenda' in a new and more conservative direction. This remained the case during 1985–6.

In the sphere of foreign affairs, President Reagan, having established a new consensus for a policy of containment during his first term,[14] gained support in 1985 and 1986 for moves to increase covert aid to Nicaraguan, Afghan and Angolan anti-communist rebels, following intense personal lobbying. At home, he successfully withstood pressure to raise taxes and introduce tariff protection, Congress failing in August 1986 to override his veto on the textile bill. The President also continued to reduce the level of central participation in economic and welfare programmes and pressed on with deregulation.[15] Such trends towards a 'small government' hands-off approach appeared likely to gain momentum during 1987–8 as pressure to reduce the budget deficit forced further cuts to be made in the non-protected Federal programme and to privatise a number of the activities and organisations under government control.

More disappointing for the 'New Right' was the previously limited progress achieved by the Reagan administration in the implementation of reforms on the controversial 'social agenda' during 1985–6. With the installation of 'New Right' supporters Ed Meese and William Bennett as Attorney-General and Education Secretary respectively, much was expected on the key 'touch-stone' issues of the scrapping of Federal employment quotas, the outlawing of abortion and the reintroduction of school prayers. Partial progress was made on the first issue when, in August 1985, a radical draft executive order was prepared by the Justice Department with the aim of repealing the existing requirements that Federal contractors should set 'affirmative action' hiring quotas by race. The measure was subsequently diluted and shelved, however, as a result of the opposition of the HUD, Transportation and Health Secretaries. The administration was more successful in piloting through Congress conservative new legislation directed against drug-taking (involving the statutory drug-testing of categories of Federal employees) and illegal immigration. It succeeded, in addition, in opening up a major new national debate on the questions of pornography (a special 'Meese Commission' being established to inquire into this issue during 1985–6) and the introduction of greater choice (the 'voucher system') into public education. However, when the more controversial issues of halting abortion and introducing school prayers were debated in Congress, they were, once more, heavily defeated. President Reagan was thus forced, as during his first term, to attempt to remould social policy in an indirect manner through the character of his administrative and, particularly, judicial appointments, rather than through legislation. Opportunities presented themselves during 1985–6 to render this course unusually productive.

The decision of Chief Justice Warren Burger (78) to retire in June 1986, so as to concentrate on his work as chairman of the commission planning the celebrations for the 200th anniversary of the US constitution, opened up a vacancy within the Supreme Court and, in addition, gave President Reagan the opportunity of choosing the new Chief Justice. He duly selected the conservative Catholic, Antonin Scalia (50), formerly a Regional Appeals Court judge in the District of Columbia, as the Court's new ninth member and he controversially promoted the assertive ultra-conservative William Rehnquist (61) to the post of Chief Justice.[16] These two changes, while not significantly altering the voting balance on the Court[17] – Warren Burger having usually (although not on the abortion issue) been a member of its conservative wing – did give the right, as a result of the special powers enjoyed by the Chief Justice, greater control over case selection and judicial assignments. At the District Court and Court of Appeals level, the changeover of personnel was even more sweeping and consequential. President Reagan had, during his first term in office, appointed 165 Federal judges, a figure which represented

17% of the total 959 such posts. A further 122 places were filled between 1985 and 1986 as a consequence of retirements and resignations. With a similar number of vacancies expected to arise during 1987–8, President Reagan appeared set to play the pre-eminent role in the appointment of almost half the nation's Federal judges by the time his second term in office expired. The majority of the new Federal judges promoted during 1981–6 were supporters of 'judicial restraint' and 'States' rights' and were sympathetic towards 'New Right' attitudes on the questions of abortion, school prayers and 'affirmative action'.[18] This, coupled with the unusually low 'qualifications ratings' assigned to many of the nominees by the American Bar Association (ABA), meant that considerable opposition to the new appointments emerged among Senate Democrats. This antagonism resulted in June 1986 in the Senate Judiciary Committee rejecting by a 10:8 margin, the nomination of the allegedly racist Jefferson Beauregard Sessions III for the district judgeship of Mobile in Alabama in what represented only the second such 'judicial veto' imposed by Congress since 1938. However, with the remainder of the new nominees being accepted, President Reagan appeared, by the autumn of 1986, to be on course towards creating a powerful legacy of judicial conservatism that would endure in the 1990s and beyond.

Thus, in executive and legislative terms, the 'Reagan reformation' in the economic, political and social spheres had, by the autumn of 1986, been considerable but not complete. While the President had wished, in many respects, to return the nation back to the strong defence, small government, low inflation, buoyant growth conditions of the 1950s and to restore traditional Christian and family-orientated public morality, he was unable to turn the clock back fully. The President had instead to operate in the circumstances of the 1980s, an era characterised by powerful Congressional, extra-Congressional (public opinion and the post-Nader civic interest lobbies) and judicial checks which continuously constrained executive actions both at home and abroad. He was necessarily forced to act in a pragmatic, step-by-step manner. Considered against such a backdrop, the achievements of President Reagan in changing outlooks and framing a new 'political agenda' between 1981 and 1986 had been impressive. However, as the Republicans prepared to face the electorate in the crucial midterm Congressional elections of November 1986 defending a slim and precarious Senate majority, it remained to be seen whether the incremental advances achieved for the right by the Reagan administration would endure and be safeguarded during the President's final two years in office or whether a new Democrat counter-assault against economic and social conservatism would be mounted.

Reaganism Halted? The Midterm Elections of November 1986

During 1986 President Reagan, despite enduring a series of embarrassing defeats and policy reversals within Congress, retained a public approval rating well in excess of 60%. He continued to cultivate a mood of national optimism and vigour, aided by his decisive, and domestically popular, action in ordering an air-strike on Tripoli (April 1986) and by the public celebrations which surrounded the centenary of the Statue of Liberty (June 1986). In addition, the President claimed substantial credit for the passage of the populist Rostenkowski-Packwood tax reform bill in October 1986 and, during the same month, on the very eve of the Congressional elections, he visited Reykjavik (Iceland) for a well-publicised 'mini-summit' meeting with the Soviet leader, Mikhail Gorbachev, in which considerable progress was made towards agreement on an 'historic' arms reduction treaty between the two superpowers. However, despite the popularity of President Reagan during the autumn of 1986, the Republican Party was unusually apprehensive about the outcome of the forthcoming Congressional contest, since elections held during the sixth year of a presidency – for example 1938, 1958, 1966 and 1974 during the Roosevelt, Eisenhower, Kennedy-Johnson and Nixon-Ford presidencies – had traditionally been disastrous for the party of the incumbent. For the Republicans in 1986, they did not face the special Vietnam War and 'Watergate' circumstances of 1966 and 1974, but, in the Senate, they were defending 22 seats to the Democrats' 12, amongst which were 14 'freshmen seats' captured during the 'anti-Democrats' landslide election of November 1980 and ten seats situated in the depressed Midwest cornbelt and southern oil and textile manufacturing States. In addition, in three other States, Maryland, Arizona and Nevada, longstanding incumbents (Charles Mathias, Barry Goldwater and Paul Laxalt) had retired, creating dangerous 'open contests' liable to swing in the direction of either party. In such circumstances, the Republican Party entertained genuine fears of losing their Senate majority, leaving President Reagan to face a hostile and unified Capitol Hill during his remaining two years in office.

Anxious to avert such a loss of its Senate majority, the Republican Party National Committee poured substantial resources into key races and mounted a $10 million nationwide 'get-out-the-vote' campaign, while the National Republican Senatorial Committee (the fund-raising body for upper chamber Republicans) lavishly outspent its opposition Democrat counterpart by an 8:1 margin. Their activities were bolstered by the vigorous efforts of President Reagan, who, in his final national campaign, set aside between two and four days each week during September and October 1986 to visit 22 key 'marginal' States. The President, attempting to turn the election into a referendum on his six years in office, called on voters to provide him with the tools to carry out further reforms during his final two years in power and appealed to Republican 'converts' from 1980 to continue to stand by the party ticket. Despite such efforts, however, on the part of the White House and the central Republican Party organisation, when electors finally cast their votes on 4 November it was on local issues and local personalities that the Congressional contests revolved. The Democrats, fielding a clutch of unusually able candidates and campaigning in a more down-to-earth grassroots manner than their Republican opponents, benefited both from this narrow focus and from regional difficulties and recorded startling gains in the Senate races. They ousted six of the Republican freshmen and freshwomen of November 1980, swept the board cleanly in the southern Confederacy States (recapturing four seats from Republican control), captured two farmbelt seats in the Dakotas and triumphed in the two 'open contests' in Maryland and Nevada. In total, the Democrats recorded a net gain of eight senatorships (see Table 17), the party's largest advance since 1958, and thus comfortably recaptured control of the upper chamber of Congress, holding now a 55:45 seats Senate majority margin.

The Republicans' performance in the Senate elections was disastrous and far worse than anticipated. In the House elections, however, the party endured a net slippage of only three seats, while in the contemporaneous gubernatorial races, with 27 Democrat-held offices being contested against only nine Republican, it reversed the trend and made a striking net gain of eight governorships.[19] The latter advances included three governorships in the South, one in neighbouring oil-dependent Oklahoma and three in the Midwest. The results of the November 1986 elections were thus confusing and in many respects contradictory. The relatively small Democrat advance in the House of Representatives was in some measure due to the fact that the party had 'held the fort' well in 1984 and thus had few seats to 'recapture' in 1986. In contrast, the Democrats' dire gubernatorial performance could be ascribed in part to its unusually strong showing in the anti-Reagan year of 1982 (the Democrats losing three governorships which they had captured during that year – Nebraska, Texas and Wisconsin) and to internal party divisions in a number of States (for example Alabama and Arizona). Overall, however, the general mood of the Statewide contests in 1986 was one, in contrast to that of 1984, of concern with contemporary economic conditions, with electors voting in many cases for a change in personnel and policy approach. Thus, more than a quarter of Senate incumbents were defeated in November 1986, while 50% of Senate 'open contests' and 63% of 'open governorships' swung in the direction of the challenging party.[20]

TABLE 17   THE CONGRESSIONAL AND GUBERNATORIAL
ELECTIONS OF NOVEMBER 1986 (TURNOUT 37.3%)*

	House Seats	Result	Senatorships	Result	Governorships	Result
Total Contested	435		34		36	
Democrat Victories	258	+3	20	+8[†]	19	−8
Republican Victories	177	−3	14	−8	17	+8[‡]

* Turnout ranged from a low of 24.6% in Kentucky to a high of 58.3% in North Dakota.
† The Democrats made gains in Alabama (Richard Shelby), Florida (Robert Graham), Georgia (Wyche Fowler), Maryland (Barbara Mikulski), Nevada (Harry Reid), North Carolina (Terry Sanford), North Dakota (Kent Conrad), South Dakota (Thomas Daschle) and Washington (Brock Adams). The Republicans recorded a gain in Missouri (Christopher Bond). In 13 States the margin of victory was unusually narrow, the victor capturing only 50–53% of the total vote.
‡ The Republicans made gains in Alabama (Guy Hunt), Arizona (Evan Mecham), Florida (Bob Martinez), Kansas (John Hayden), Maine (John McKernen), Nebraska (Kay Orr), New Mexico (Garrey Carruthers), Oklahoma (Henry Bellmon), South Carolina (Caroll Campbell), Texas (William Clements) and Wisconsin (Tommy Thompson). The Democrats recorded gains in Oregon (Neil Goldschmidt), Pennsylvania (Robert Casey) and Tennessee (Ned McWherter).

Democrat leaders moved swiftly to 'organise' Congress after the November 1986 elections. The party's House and Senate caucuses held elections to leadership posts and committee chairs from which Robert Byrd (West Virginia) emerged as the Senate Majority Leader and Jim Wright (Texas) as the new House Speaker.[21] Byrd and Wright, who shared a similar centrist policy outlook, sought to work in closer union than the Democrat leaders of the O'Neill era 95th–99th Congress. In addition, they began, following consultations with committee chairmen, to outline a new programme for the 100th Congress geared towards seizing the legislative initiative from President Reagan and effecting a significant change in the national policy direction. At the top of the Democrats' new agenda were plans to introduce a trade bill which would encourage exports and curtail imports and an agricultural package aimed at raising the price supports granted to the troubled farming community. Second, with two northern liberals chairing the Senate's Judiciary and Labour and Human Resources Committees, Joseph Biden (Delaware) and Edward Kennedy (Massachusetts), the party's leaders vowed to block the promotion of further far-right judicial nominees, introduce legislation designed at improving education, training and health care provision, and raise the statutory minimum wage. In the defence and foreign policy spheres, the Democrats pressed for firmer sanctions against South Africa, a less interventionist policy in Central America, greater progress in arms reduction negotiations with the Soviet Union, adherence to the limits of the SALT-2 treaty and for greater economies on the part of the Defense Department. However, on the final and most pressing issue of the budget deficit which, under the terms of GRH, was supposed to be sharply reduced to a level of only $108 billion in fiscal 1988, the Democrats' new leaders were less certain in their approach. House Speaker Jim Wright privately believed that the only way to make significant inroads into the size of the budget deficit, without resorting to major cutbacks in welfare 'entitlement programmes', would be temporarily to shelve the proposed income tax reductions of 1987–8, or at least the planned reductions at upper levels. However, like his predecessor Tip O'Neill, Wright was unwilling for the Democrats to be the initiator of such an unpopular measure without first gaining prior presidential approval. Since the President remained adamantly opposed to tax increases, threatening to veto any proposed measure, Wright and Byrd thus chose instead what was termed a strategy of 'flexibility', using the GRH targets as figures to be strived for and worked towards rather than slavishly and statutorily adhered to.

The Democrats' leaders on Capitol Hill were anxious to make a success of the 1987–8 Congressional session in order to convince the public of their party's ability to govern prudently and efficiently, and thus its fitness to resume control at the presidential level in 1989. However, lacking majorities in either chamber substantial enough to override presidential vetoes on controversial legislation, Byrd and Wright would need to adopt a less partisan stance in the 100th Congress than had been the case in the 99th and would need to build consensual, vote-securing, bipartisan bridges to their Republican counterparts, Robert Dole and Robert Michel. Much thus depended on the attitude adopted by the Republican Congressional leaders during 1987–8. One of these members, Robert Dole, entertained strong presidential ambitions for November 1988. Much also rested on the attitude and approach of the White House. Buttressed by his powers of veto, President Reagan, if satisfied with the achievements of 1981–6, could decide to retreat into the seclusion of the Oval Office and resort to blocking tactics in the manner of his Republican predecessors, Nixon and Ford. Alternatively, President Reagan could choose, as he had successfully done in Sacramento during 1969–74, to bargain and trade with the leaders of the opposition-dominated legislature as a means of securing the passage of further cherished programmes at the cost of concession on unpopular measures.

The initial indications after 4 November suggested that the Senate Minority Leader Robert Dole, following remarks made during a joint election-night television appearance with Robert Byrd, would be willing to join the Democrats in the framing of a moderate, compromise trade bill that would not be unduly protectionist and would seek to achieve further progress in deficit reduction. The Reagan administration, while possessing a hardline minority, grouped around Communications Director Patrick Buchanan (which favoured the adoption of a starkly confrontational approach in defence of 'New Right' principles), also appeared willing to adapt to the new conditions and bargain, within limits, in a realistic manner. However, within days of the 4 November elections, the administration was to find itself rocked by the most serious political scandal since 'Watergate', a scandal which paralysed its actions, sharply reduced the standing and credibility of its leader and forced sweeping personnel changes that effectively created a radically restructured and reorientated new presidency.

The Shattering of Illusions: President Reagan and the 'Irangate Scandal'

Ronald Reagan had been swept to power in November 1980 in large measure as a result of public discontent with the inability of President Carter to secure the release of the 52 American hostages held ransom in the US Embassy in Teheran by Islamic fundamentalists. During the 1980 presidential election campaign Reagan, chiding his Democrat opponent for the impotent weakness of a foreign policy that had led to the nation's humiliation at the hands of a medium-ranking power, had vowed, if elected, to prevent such actions in the future through the adoption of a resolute new defence and anti-terrorism strategy. This new policy was based around three tenets: a categorical refusal to negotiate with terrorist leaders; the imposition of diplomatic and economic sanctions against terrorist-sponsoring nations; and the resort to Israeli-style military retribution against offending countries as a means of dissuading further actions. The prime target of this strategy became Libya and its leader Colonel Gaddafy, who, enjoying close links with the Palestine Liberation Organisation (PLO), on three occasions experienced the force of American retribution. First, in August 1981 two Libyan fighter planes that had attacked US military aircraft over the Libyan Gulf of Sirte were shot down. Then in October 1985 US naval planes intercepted and diverted to Italy an Egyptian aircraft carrying four Libyan-linked PLO terrorists who had hijacked an Italian cruise ship, the *Achille Lauro*, and murdered one American passenger. Third, and most controversially, during March and April 1986, as a reprisal against alleged Libyan involvement in a series of 1985–6 terrorist explosions against American targets across Western Europe, American A-6 and F-111 bombers were unleashed upon Tripoli, resulting in the death of more than 100 civilians.[22]

The Reagan administration's new anti-terrorism strategy was extremely popular with the American public. However, it was less successful in reducing the level of terrorist incidents, which continued to increase during 1981–6. It proved to be politically unenforceable against the two largest and most powerful sponsors of Middle Eastern-based terrorism, Soviet-linked Syria and fundamentalist Iran, and failed to persuade captors to release the rising number of hostages held in the anarchic city of Beirut (Lebanon). By the summer of 1985 nine American citizens, including the director of the CIA's regional bureau, William Buckley, were being held captive by radical Islamic groups in the Lebanon. The plight of the victims and their families was given widespread television coverage and threatened to develop into a debilitating Teheran-like sore for the Reagan presidency as the Congressional elections of November 1986 approached. Fortunately for the administration, however, three of the most prominent hostages, the Rev Benjamin Weir (September 1985), the Rev Lawrence Jenco (July 1986) and David Jacobsen (November 1986), were released in a staggered fashion during the autumn of 1985 and summer and autumn of 1986, as a result, it appeared, of the humanitarian intervention of the British Church envoy, Terry Waite. The release of these figures transformed the public mood and served to give the impression that the plight of the remaining hostages was by no means hopeless. These national illusions were, however, to be rudely shattered during November 1986.

On 3 November 1986, an astonishing story was published in Beirut in the pro-Syrian magazine *Al Shiraa* which, drawing, it claimed, upon informed Middle Eastern sources, painted a sharply differing picture of the reasons for the hostages' release. *Al Shiraa* claimed that there had been a secret despatch of American arms to Iran (which, having been engaged in a bitter war of attrition with its neighbour Iraq since September 1980, desperately required new spares for its old American-purchased tanks and planes) via the conduit of Israel in return for Iranian help in using their influence over the Beirut-based 'Islamic Jihad' terrorist group to secure the release of Weir, Jenco and Jacobsen.

The authenticity of this story was immediately refuted by the Reagan administration press corps. Gradually, however, further details of contacts between the US government and Iran were uncovered by investigative journalists in America and the Middle East which gave credence to these claims. A picture emerged of the National Security Council (NSC), under the direction of first Robert 'Bud' McFarlane and then (from December 1985) Vice-Admiral John Poindexter (1936–), engaging, during an 18-month period and despite the protestations of the State and Defense Departments, in clandestine meetings with Iranian leaders which ended in the covert shipment of more than $600 million of sensitive military hardware and spare parts. Eventually, on 12 and 13 November, in briefings to Congressional party leaders and during a national television broadcast, President Reagan admitted that such contacts had taken place and that arms shipments to the arch enemy of Iran had been secretly sanctioned in a presidential directive. He stated, however, that there had not been a 'trade-off' for hostages, but rather that the motive had been strategic and geopolitical, arms being sent to Iran as a goodwill gesture directed towards the re-establishment of dialogue with moderate elements within Iran in readiness to be able to influence the outcome of the succession struggle that would follow the death of the nation's supposedly ailing ruler, the Ayatollah Khomeini.[23]

The President's admission of his sanctioning of such arms transfers to a nation with which the United States had broken off all official links in 1979 and against which it had sought to impose a broad arms embargo during the succeeding years, was damaging to the nation's international credibility and respect. (Indeed one Reagan appointee commented colourfully, 'It's like suddenly learning that John Wayne had secretly been selling liquor and firearms to the Indians.') It laid the administration open to charges of illegality (breaching the Arms Export Control Act) and of failing to inform Congressional elders of such covert actions, as required under the National Security Act and the 1980 Intelligence Oversight Act. If taken for lofty, forward-looking geopolitical reasons, the decision may have been subject to immediate sharp criticism for naïve wrong-headedness, but may have been tolerated at the possible cost of an NSC head. However, the 'Iran affair' refused to go away as evidence began to mount of the close correlation between the timing of arms shipments and the subsequent releases of Weir, Jenco and Jacobsen, which strongly suggested that the primary motivating factor behind the transfers of arms had been to secure the release of hostages rather than a strategic one. Thus, with opinion polls showing that less than two-thirds of the American public believed the White House's version of events, popular support for President Reagan slumped by an unprecedented 21% to a level of 46% during November 1986 and pressure mounted for the dismissal of not only National Security Adviser Vice-Admiral John Poindexter but also of Chief-of-Staff Donald Regan and State Department Secretary George Shultz.

From 21 November the House and Senate Intelligence and Foreign Relations Committees commenced investigative proceedings into the 'Iran affair', with Democrat members, scenting blood, playing a vigorous role. However, the crisis seriously worsened for the administration on 25 November when the Attorney-General, Ed Meese, having carried out an internal preliminary inquiry into the arms dealings, revealed to an incredulous press a damaging new aspect to the scandal. Meese's report found that not only had there been covert arms transfers to Iran but that $16 million profits from the deals had been deposited in numbered Swiss bank accounts and used to finance Contra Nicaraguan rebels, thus illegally circumventing the fiscal 1985 Congressional ban (Boland Amendment) on such funding. The 'laundering operation' had been carried out by a small group of zealots within the NSC, under the leadership of special aide Lt-Col Oliver North (1943–). North was a highly decorated former Marine platoon leader during the Vietnam War who had served during the Reagan administration as chief of special operations, playing a key role in organising the invasion of Grenada in October 1983 and the *Achille Lauro* and Tripoli actions during 1985–6. He had also acted as planning supremo for the Contra forces in Central America. Lt-Col North and his superior, Vice-Admiral Poindexter, having supposedly acted on their own without presidential sanction in this diversionary operation, immediately resigned their posts on 25 November. A day later it was announced that a special three-member commission comprising Lieutenant General Brent Scowcroft (NSA during the Ford administration) and Edmund Muskie (State Department Secretary during the Carter administration) and chaired by the former Republican Senator from Texas, John Tower (ex-chairman of the Senate Armed Services Committee), would be established to investigate and report swiftly on the role and workings of the NSC and its actions in relation to what was now termed the 'Iran-Contragate' or 'Irangate' Affair.

The Meese revelation served to undermine further the public standing of President Reagan, disbelief being registered to the assertion that the President had been hoodwinked on the 'Contra Connection' by a small group of aides and kept thoroughly in the dark until 24 November. The President's renowned personal interest in the Nicaraguan issue, his close contacts with prominent Contra leaders and fund-raisers and the fact that Lt-Col North had been seconded to and specifically retained within the NSC on the President's personal request made it almost inconceivable that he had not been informed of this operation and led to countervailing charges from Senate Majority Leader Robert

Byrd that if the President had not been informed on such a consequential matter then 'something is profoundly wrong'. In addition, the Meese report, taken in conjunction with further press revelations, aroused strong suspicions that the CIA, anxious to secure the release of its Beirut station chief, William Buckley, who had been abducted as early as March 1984,[24] had played a key role in the arms transfer and money-laundering operations (the Swiss bank accounts in question, for example, having been used on earlier occasions by the CIA).

During the closing days of November 1986 President Reagan came under increasing pressure from both Republican colleagues and Democrat opponents to 'come clean' on the whole 'Iran-Contragate' affair, admit that serious errors of judgment had been made, appoint a Special Prosecutor[25] to investigate the affair thoroughly and clean out from his staff team figures, including Regan, Casey and Shultz, who had had any involvement with the policy decisions. Without such actions, they believed, the trustworthiness and credibility of the administration would remain in doubt, paralysing its actions at home and abroad. President Reagan, however, noted for his intense loyalty to staff colleagues and for his sense of outward pride, refused to entertain the suggestion of dismissals and felt unable to admit publicly that the Iran policy had been misconceived. In an interview in *Time* magazine on 1 December he declared his belief that 'as the truth comes out, people will see that what we were doing was right' and he bitterly criticised the press for the tone of their reporting of the affair. The President did, however, effect a number of conciliatory moves directed at Congress on 2 December, announcing his acceptance of the need for an independent investigation by a Special Prosecutor and appointing the popular and experienced Frank Carlucci as the new National Security Adviser. In addition, he called upon his staff to 'co-operate fully' with the inquiries being made by the Congressional committees.

As the Congressional investigations moved under way, it emerged from evidence given by former NSA Robert McFarlane that other senior administration officials had been aware of fund diversions to support the Nicaraguan Contras and that Afghan and Angolan rebels had also drawn upon the 'slush funds' created by the arms sales to Iran. McFarlane admitted, in addition, that, although the shipment of arms to Iran had initially been instigated for stategic reasons, by the autumn of 1985 the primary motivation had become that of securing the release of American hostages from Beirut. The other principal functionaries at the centre of the 'Irangate' affair proved to be less forthcoming during their Congressional committee appearances during December 1986. Lt-Col North and Vice-Admiral Poindexter, seeking to secure offers of immunity from prosecution, remained determinedly tight-lipped, pleading the Fifth Amendment. The CIA's Director William Casey testified to the Senate Intelligence Committee behind closed doors but mumbled incoherently and was subsequently admitted into hospital following a cerebral seizure. He was later diagnosed as having a malignant brain tumour and was hospitalised in a paralysed condition.[26]

In early January 1987 President Reagan also briefly entered hospital himself, undergoing routine checks on his colon and an operation on his prostate gland. Before entering hospital he announced that he had appointed the experienced retiring US Ambassador to NATO, David Abshire, to a special new cabinet-ranking post charged with overseeing and co-ordinating the White House's dealings with Congress over the 'Irangate' affair. When the new, Democrat-dominated, 100th Congress convened on 6 January two new special Watergate-style investigative select committees were established to take over formally the 'Irangate' inquiries. The Senate Select Committee consisted of 11 members and was chaired by a 'Watergate' veteran, Daniel Inouye (62: D) of Hawaii. The House Select Committee consisted of 15 members and was chaired by Indiana Representative Lee Hamilton (55: D), the experienced chairman of the House Intelligence Committee. The Special Prosecutor, Judge Lawrence Walsh of Oklahoma (74: a former Deputy Attorney-General during the Eisenhower administration and president of the American Bar Association), also commenced a broad-based investigation into the affair, seeking to establish specific cases of criminal wrong-doing.

Both the Senate and House Select Committees and the Special Prosecutor's inquiries were hampered by the refusal of the key witnesses, North and Poindexter, to testify and also by North's document-shredding activities during his final days in office. However, the Tower Commission, investigating the NSC's role in 'Irangate', unexpectedly unearthed vital new evidence in the form of NSC computer messages sent by North and Poindexter. They were, in addition, granted access to the President's personal hand-written notes and diary and were allowed to interview President Reagan in person on two occasions during January and February 1987.

The Reagan team sought to regain the initiative that had been lost to Congress during November and December 1986 and to re-establish a clear sense of policy direction during the President's annual State of the Union address on 27 January 1987. However, internal divisions within the White House over the tone and content of the address, coupled with the diminished health, vigour and confidence of the President himself, resulted in a disappointing and lacklustre performance. President Reagan did admit in the address that 'serious mistakes' had been made during the 'Irangate' affair, but refused to state by whom and continued to maintain that the dealings with Iran had not been ill-conceived. The President attempted, instead, to divert Congress's and the nation's attention to other domestic issues. He failed, however, to unearth a new theme or sense of purpose for his remaining two years in office. With polls continuing to show that almost 60% of the nation still believed that the President had not been frank and truthful on the 'Irangate' issue and with his 'approval rating' standing at below 50%, the American public's six-year love affair with Ronald Reagan had seemingly been brought to a sudden and humbling end. Four weeks later, on 26 February, the Tower Commission delivered its much-awaited report on the NSC and 'Irangate' affair. It condemned the secret arms dealings with Iran and Nicaragua as 'clearly an aberration' in the conduct of foreign policy, sharply criticised the advice and role of the President's closest aides and directly rebuked the President for failing to keep a close check on the actions of his staff as his position as chief executive required.

The scathing Tower Report proved to be a deeply embarrassing document for President Reagan, depicting him as indolent, hazy in both mind and memory, lacking control over his cabinet and staff team colleagues and proving incapable of making sensible strategic decisions. The report, however, reserved some of its strongest criticism for the actions of Chief-of-Staff Donald Regan both before and following the outbreak of the scandal. It portrayed the impatient Regan as having been a firm supporter of the NSC 'arms to Iran' initiative as a corner-cutting means of satisfying the President's wish to secure the speedy release of the Beirut hostages and as subsequently having acted to 'freeze-out' State and Defense Department Secretaries Shultz and Weinberger from discussions on the progress of the Iran operations. Once the scandal had broken, Regan had attempted to set in train a 'cover-up' and damage-limitation operation which had been confused and ineffective, and, in the process, had allowed the policy work of the White House Office to become paralysed and chaotic.[27] Faced with this damning evidence and with a further slump in his public approval rating to a post-1982 low of 40%, President Reagan was compelled to take decisive action in an effort to retrieve his crumbling position. Thus, on the advice of his increasingly influential wife Nancy, his close friend Paul Laxalt, and Treasury Secretary James Baker, he finally decided on 27 February that the time had come to part with the services of Donald Regan. Then, in a skilled, though in many respects desperate, move, the President announced that Howard Baker, the moderate former Senate Majority Leader and a prospective presidential candidate for 1988, had agreed to serve as his new Chief-of-Staff.[28]

Baker's appointment, which proved to be particularly popular with Congress, was rapidly followed on 4 March by an effective and moving television address to the nation in which President Reagan accepted 'full responsibility' for everything that had gone wrong and finally admitted that the Iran operation had, as a result of his concern and compassion for the hostages in Lebanon, descended into an arms 'trade-off'. He agreed that, with hindsight, the 'trade-off' had been 'a mistake', but stated that lessons had been learned. He vowed that in future he would function as a more active 'hands-on' chief executive and promised that the NSC and administration would engage in no further such covert actions without first receiving Congressional approval.

Reagan's selection of Howard Baker as the new Chief-of-Staff and his contrite, but dignified, television address, with its call to learn from the past, change and 'go forward', was well received, leading to an immediate six-point rise in the President's national approval rating. With Baker immediately making his presence felt through changes in personnel (see below), style and policy priorities, talk began to emerge of the commencement of a Reagan 'third term', with the 'Teflon President' emerging phoenix-like from the ashes of despair. However, although the Tower Report effectively ended the damaging first stage of the 'Iran-Contragate' affair and allowed a new, freshly orientated and staffed administration to assume control for the final two years of the Reagan presidency, the 'Irangate' scandal had by no means ended. The investigations of the Senate and House Select Committees continued and began to extend their net, following up the trail of funds sent from Iran and examining closely the activities of ultra-conservative groupings linked directly and indirectly with the Nicaraguan Contra cause. These inquiries began to uncover a complex network of clandestine anti-communist activities (codenamed 'Operation Democracy'), over-seen by Lt-Col Oliver North at the NSC, which involved a colour-ful grouping of former CIA and military officers, mercenaries, international arms traders and wealthy domestic and overseas financiers. They revealed, second, the deep personal involvement of President Reagan with fund-raising activity on behalf of many of the far-right pro-Contra groups – granting for example, special 'audiences' at the Oval Office to wealthy benefactors – who pro-vided finance for Lt-Col North's covert adventures. In addition, the Special Prosecutor Lawrence Walsh, following similar leads, began to institute criminal proceedings against law-breakers in the affair, commencing in April 1987 with the successful charging of Carl 'Spitz' Channell, head of the far-right National Endowment for the Preservation of Liberty, with the offence of utilising funds granted a charitable status for the illegal purchase of Contra arms.

Further revelations of such funding activities appeared during the summer of 1987 when North and Poindexter testified before joint hearings of the Senate and House 'Irangate' Select Commit-tee.

In his televised appearances before this Joint Committee, the emotional, uniform-clad Lt-Col North struck a popular patriotic chord. He insisted that his actions had been solely motivated by a concern to check communism in Central America and, further-more, he declared that 'I never carried out a single act . . . in which I did not have authority from my superiors.' It was, however, the subsequent testimony delivered in July 1987 by the calm bespecta-cled Vice-Admiral Poindexter which proved the most crucial. Poindexter asserted that, although he had informed President Reagan in a 'general way' that the NSC were working to assist the Contras, he had never told him the money derived from the sale of arms to Iran was being diverted for that purpose. Indeed, Poindexter specifically stated that, although personally convinced that 'the President would approve if asked, I made a very deliber-ate decision not to ask the President so that I could insulate him from the decision and provide some future deniability for the President if it ever leaked out.' He went on to conclude: 'On this whole issue, the buck stops with me.'

Poindexter's acceptance of full personal responsibility for the 'Iran-Contra' imbroglio effectively brought to an end the investi-gative phase of the 'Irangate' affair and, moreover, ensured the Reagan presidency's survival. Later, in November 1987, the Congressional Joint Investigative Committee published its damning report on the proceedings[29] and during 1988–90 a number of the leading actors in the drama were brought to justice by Special Prosecutor Walsh.[30] Already before this time, however, it had become possible to entertain preliminary reflections on the lessons, significance and consequences of the 'Iran-Contragate' affair both for the American political system and the Reagan presidency.

The first and most striking feature of the 'Irangate' crisis had once more been the ability, as in 'Watergate', of both the American press (the 'fifth estate') and Congressional committees to play a robust and vital investigative role in unmasking misdeeds by the executive and bringing law-breakers to book. These actions contrasted with the relative weakness of such similar watchdog institutions in France and Britain during the *Rainbow Warrior*, 'Westland' and MI5 affairs during 1985–7. Whispers and leaks from warring factions within the administration opposed to the NSC's line helped the 'Irangate' investigators. In addition, the subpoena- and record-demanding powers enjoyed by the Special Prosecutor and US Congressional Select Committees, coupled with the freedom of publication granted to the press under the First Amendment, served to prevent an effective smoke-screen 'cover-up' by the executive.

However, while the 'Irangate' affair highlighted once again the strength of the checks deliberately built into the American constitution, the crisis itself displayed the problems of executive control that exist within the American system of government. The mistakes made by the administration in connection with Iran and Nicaragua resulted primarily from two factors. First, it was the inability of President Reagan to gain Congressional support for his cherished ambition to aid the Contras in their efforts to defeat the leftist Nicaraguan Sandinista government during 1983–5, which forced the administration to function in a covert manner to maintain military support through 'private channels'. The chosen arm for these actions was the NSC, a special body which includes the Director of the CIA and State and Defense Department Secretaries as ex-officio members, but which is primarily staffed by personal appointees of the President who do not require Congressional approval. The NSC had been established by President Truman in 1947 as a means of circumventing Congressional opposition to elements of his activist anti-communist foreign policy and, although supposedly charged with concentrating on an advisory and co-ordinating role in foreign affairs, has been frequently used for secret presidential 'pet projects' in a covert, short-cutting manner. During the Reagan administration, under the leadership of the swashbuckling former marines McFarlane, Poindexter and North, the extent of these activities escalated. Matters moved out of control during 1985–6 as a result of the unusually detached, delegatory style of management adopted by President Reagan,[31] which was compounded by the deterioration of the President's health and his enforced seclusion at his Santa Barbara ranch during the summer of 1985. In such circumstances, presidential aides began to frame policy on their own in accordance with what they saw as the general wishes and aspirations of President Reagan with regard to the American hostages in Beirut and the Contra cause. A secret administration within an administration thus emerged during 1985–6 which, cut off from the advice of the experienced diplomats of the State Department, committed the most serious error in American foreign policy judgment since the May 1960 U-2 incident during the Eisenhower administration.

The 'Irangate' affair, involving the existence of a clandestine foreign policy network acting in breach of Congress and also possibly the President's own wishes, was, in many respects, of greater constitutional consequence than the 'Watergate' scandal of 1972–4. However, the popularity enjoyed by President Reagan prior to the irruption of the scandal and the lack of stomach that existed within Congress to humiliate the President to the point of impeachment proceedings meant that President Reagan was able to survive and see out his final two years in office. The scandal, however, radically altered the balance of power between Congress and the President during this 'third term' period, strengthening the hold of Congress and forcing the Reagan team on to the political defensive.

The 1987–8 Reagan 'Third Term': 'Lame Duck' or Consensus Builder?

The position of President Reagan, which had already been seriously weakened by the Congressional elections of November 1986, threatened to be fatally undermined by the 'Iran-Contragate Scandal', turning the President into an irrelevant 'lame duck' figurehead ruler whose views would be ignored by an increasingly assertive Congress. This appeared to be the case during December 1986 and January 1987 when the work of the administration was paralysed by the contempt in which Chief-of-Staff Donald Regan was held by Capitol Hill leaders and by the flight of upper- and middle-level cabinet personnel into more lucrative posts as they deserted what they viewed as a sinking ship. The reception given to the budgetary and new policy proposals in President Reagan's 27 January State of the Union address by Congress's Democrat majority was cool and derisory, while matters were compounded by the President's decision to impose a string of vetoes during the same month on new environmental and spending packages.

However, with the appointment of Howard Baker (61) as the new Chief-of-Staff on 27 February matters changed dramatically and talk of a new phase of consensual compromise between the White House and Capitol Hill began to emerge. Baker, in stark contrast to his predecessor Donald Regan, was a highly experienced political operator and Washington insider with a fine grasp of policy practicalities both at home and abroad. He had served first as Minority Leader and then as Majority Leader in the Senate for eight years between 1977 and 1984, working as a particularly effective bridge-builder between the White House and Congress during the Reagan first term. He enjoyed a warm relationship with both Republican and Democrat leaders on Capitol Hill and, as a result of his witty, self-deprecating manner, equally cordial relations with the press. Baker proceeded to build on the initially favourable 'goodwill response' to his appointment by instituting a series of key personnel changes (see Table 18), included in which was the transfer of the respected, highly principled and apolitical figure of William Webster (63), from the directorship of the FBI to become the new head of the CIA.[32]

The most crucial need for the new Baker-Reagan administration was to find a new policy theme for its final two years in office and rapidly to establish grounds for a new working consensus with Congress. In his 27 January 1987 State of the Union address President Reagan had unrealistically asked once more for the familiar shopping-list of 'New Right' measures – a balanced budget amendment, a line item veto and the reintroduction of school prayers – as well as increased military funding for the Strategic Defense Initiative and Nicaraguan Contras. In addition,

TABLE 18   THE REAGAN CABINET IN MARCH 1987*

Secretaries

State Dept	George Shultz (66, New York, ex-Nixon admin)
Treasury	James Baker (56, Texas, ex-Ford admin)
Defense	Caspar Weinberger (69, ex-California & Nixon admins)
Attorney-General	Edwin Meese (55, ex-California admin)
Interior	Donald Hodel (50, Oregon, former Energy Secretary)
Agriculture	Richard Lyng (68, ex-agr secr in California admin)
Commerce	Malcolm Baldrige (64, Connecticut industrialist)
Labor	William Brock (55, Tennessee, former Trade Repr)
HUD	Samuel Pierce (64, black NY attorney, ex-Nixon admin)
Energy	John Herrington (46, California lawyer)
Health	Otis Bowen (69, former doctor & Indiana Governor)
Education	William Bennett (43, ex-Chmn National Humanities Fdn)
Transportation	Elizabeth Dole (50, Kansas, ex-Nixon admin)
UN Representative	Gen Vernon Walters (69, ex-Deputy Director of CIA)
Sp Trade Repr	Clayton Yeutter (56, ex-Chicago Exchange Director)
Special Counselor	David Abshire (60, ex-US Ambassador to NATO)
Dir of CIA	William Webster (63, ex-FBI Director)

White House Advisers

Chief-of-Staff	Howard Baker (61, ex-Tennessee Senator)
Deputy Chief-of-Staff	Kenneth Duberstein (42, previously a White House aide)
NSA	Frank Carlucci (56, Pennsylvania, ex-Deputy Defence Secretary)
Dir of OMB	James Miller (44, ex-Chmn Federal Trades Commission)
Chmn of CEA	Beryl Sprinkel (43, ex-Treasury Under-Secretary)
Press Secretary	Marlin Fitzwater (44, Kansas, ex-Press Secretary to Vice-President Bush)
Domestic Policy Adviser	Gary Bauer (40, ex-under Secretary of Education)

* Bowen had taken over as Health Secretary in 1985 and Brock had moved to the Department of Labor (from the position of Special Trade Representative) in the same year after Raymond Donovan had become the first ever member of a presidential cabinet to be indicted on criminal charges. Lyng had become Agriculture Secretary in 1986 and Fitzwater had replaced Larry Speakes (who took up a lucrative post at Merrill Lynch) as Press Secretary in January 1987.

he had proposed, yet again, a Federal budget for fiscal 1988 which included a rise in the level of defence spending by 3% in real terms, to be financed through further social economies and privatisation. This package was pronounced 'dead on arrival' by the Democrat-controlled Congress, whose leaders began to frame an alternative new legislative agenda based around defence economies, a measure of protectionism and the introduction of a 'catastrophic illness' health care initiative for the elderly, increased investment in education and new welfare schemes for single parents. This opposition programme gained momentum during April 1987 with the passage of a special 'open market' amendment by Representative Richard Gephardt (D – Missouri) designed at eliminating trade imbalances with individual nations.

The Baker-Reagan administration responded to these Democrat moves by adopting a more forceful attitude in trade negotiations – special new tariffs being imposed on selected Japanese electrical items on 17 April 1987 – by moderating its defence budget demands and by framing its own health care reform plans.

A sudden, record one-day 23% slump in Wall Street share values on 19 October 1987 – as a result of recent bank interest rate hikes and worsening trade and Federal budget deficit figures[33] – gave urgent additional momentum to the reformulation of the administration's economic strategy. With fears being entertained that this 'Black Monday' stock market crash might be followed, as in October 1929, by a disastrous downward spiral into deep general economic recession, the new chairman of the Federal Reserve Board, Alan Greenspan – a former chairman of President Ford's CEA who had replaced the retiring Paul Volcker in August 1987 – moved swiftly to lower interest rates and pump liquidity into the overstretched market. President Reagan, meanwhile, organised in late October 1987 a special four-week-long 'economic summit' meeting between White House and Congressional leaders to discuss means of securing deeper cuts in the Federal programme. As a result of these negotiations, on 20 November 1987 a bipartisan agreement was reached for the reduction of the budget deficit by $76 billion over a two-year period, both by means of introducing $23 billion of new taxes (primarily targeted against the rich and businesses) and $13 billion of defence cuts – these constituted major concessions on the behalf of the President – and by securing $10 billion in economies in Federal benefit programmes, excluding social security (old age pensions).

The White House's accession to this compromise deficit-cutting compact, which, during 1988, was to prove to be of great value in helping to avert an economic recession, was indicative of a mellowing of the Reagan presidency as it moved into its final year. Once more, in the 25 January 1988 State of the Union address, President Reagan made demands upon Congress to pass a line-item veto, balanced budget and school prayer constitutional amendments, an act to outlaw the Federal funding of abortion and to furnish military aid to the 'freedom fighting' Contras, but they continued to fall upon deaf ears. They were demands of a ritualistic character and they were to be overshadowed by more dramatic and substantive events in the diplomatic sphere. Here, with Chief-of-Staff Baker, NSA (and later, from November 1987 – following Weinberger's departure – Defense Secretary) Carlucci and State Department Secretary Shultz acting in an unusually united fashion, and with Nancy Reagan giving full encouragement to the process, a popular policy theme for the closing reels of the 'Reagan story' was decided upon, that of full-scale detente with the Soviet Union. Aided by the flexibility displayed by the Soviet leader, Mikhail Gorbachev, new impetus was given to the arms reduction talks with the USSR on-going in Geneva. This bore fruit, at the Soviet-American summit in Washington DC on 7–10 December 1987, in the signing of a treaty accord to eliminate Intermediate Nuclear Forces (INF) in Europe and, at the follow-up summit held in Moscow in May–June 1988, in considerable progress being made towards reaching an agreement on a Strategic Arms Reduction Treaty.

This 'new detente' initiative, which served dramatically to transform Reagan, the one-time hardline scourge of the Soviets' 'evil empire', into an historic peacemaker, went some way towards rehabilitating the President's reputation and public standing following the damage inflicted by the 'Irangate' scandal. It also helped provide additional justification for the softening of the administration's budgetary stance with respect to defence spending. President Reagan proved unable, however, during 1987–8 to fully recoup his pre-Irangate popular esteem or the grudging respect once accorded to him by Congress. He remained a wounded leader and was forced to endure two most taxing Congressional sessions in 1987 and 1988 in which his 'Congressional Success Rating' slumped to the unprecedentedly low levels of barely 43.5% and 47.4% respectively: ratings below even those registered by Presidents Nixon and Ford during the dark Watergate days of 1973–6 (see Appendix Table B7). In the House of Representatives, now under the activist leadership of the pugnacious Jim Wright, the President was victorious, in this 100th

Congress, on only a third of the roll-call votes on which he staked his position: a proportion even lower than that in 1986. In the case of the now Democrat-controlled Senate, his 'success rate' slumped to barely 56% and 65% in 1987 and 1988 respectively: the lowest figures of the Reagan presidency. This was reflective of the almost complete retreat of the once influential and Reagan-supportive Republican and Democrat 'Boll Weevil' 'conservative coalition', which, during the 100th Congress, appeared on barely 8–9% of recorded Congressional votes: another record low (see Appendix Table B11). It was also reflective of a continuance of the high levels of voting partisanship in both chambers, particularly in the House. This partisanship, which had been evident ever since 1983, had been heightened by the outcome of the Congressional elections of November 1986 and reached record levels in 1987 (see Table 2).

The waning Congressional influence of the increasingly 'lame duck' Reagan presidency during 1987–8 was also exhibited by Congress's overriding of three (38%) of the eight regular vetoes imposed by President Reagan on bills of which he disapproved.[34] Even more striking than this, however, was the Senate's rejection in October 1987, by 58 votes to 42, of the President's controversial nomination of Judge Robert Bork (60), of the Federal Appeals Court for the District of Columbia circuit, as his choice to replace the 'swing-voting' Lewis Powell who retired as justice of the Supreme Court in June 1987. Bork, depicted by Democrats as an ultra-conservative 'interpretivist' jurist who opposed abortion and moves towards greater sex equality and who sought to turn the clock back on two decades of progress in the civil rights sphere, was the first Supreme Court nominee to be rejected by the Senate since Harold Carswell in 1970, while his margin of defeat was the largest in the history of Supreme Court nominations. President Reagan had hoped that 'Boll Weevil' Democrats would join with Republicans to provide a narrow majority in favour of Bork's confirmation. In practice, however, southern Democrat Senators, who were unwilling to reopen old civil rights wounds, particularly the more liberal-minded 'New South' Senators who had recently been elected with strong black support in November 1986, overwhelmingly sided with their Northern Democrat colleagues: only two, David Boren (Okla) and Ernest Hollings (SC), supported Bork's confirmation. This was despite pro-Bork lobbying expenditure of more than $1 million by NCPAC. The President's embarrassment over this judicial confirmation defeat was further compounded in November 1987 when his second choice, the almost equally conservative Douglas Ginsburg (41), a protégé of Bork also from the District of Columbia Court of Appeals, was forced to withdraw his name from consideration following revelations that he had smoked marijuana during the 1960s and 1970s. Not until February 1988 was the vacant justiceship filled, when Judge Anthony Kennedy (51), a more 'convention-al' conservative from the Court of Appeals for California whose nomination had been strongly touted by Chief-of-Staff Baker (against the wishes of Attorney-General Meese), was unanimously confirmed by the Senate.

The Bork and Ginsburg nomination fiascos of 1987 were indicative of a presidency, despite its success in the diplomatic sphere and its new-found realism on the economic front, in a state of terminal decay. The irrepressibly optimistic President Reagan, despite the damage that had been inflicted by 'Irangate', still remained personally a surprisingly popular figure with the American public, being accorded an approval rating in excess of 50%, but he was now more a figurehead monarchical ruler rather than an effective political operator. The legislative initiative had clearly passed to Congress, who passed, in the surprisingly busy and successful 1988 session, important bills which revamped the welfare system (by encouraging a greater resort to education and training to help mothers find jobs so as to be able to escape from the welfare dependency trap), rewrote US trade law and provided catastrophic health insurance for the elderly and disabled, though the last measure was, following lobbying pressure, subsequently repealed in 1989. In addition, as 1987–8 progressed, there was a continuous outflow of personnel from the President's cabinet, as Secretaries sought more lucrative posts in the private sector or joined the campaign teams of presidential hopefuls for November 1988.[35] This served further to accentuate the administration's 'lame duck' profile. By 1988 the 'Reagan Reformation' had clearly come to an end and political commentators' attention began to turn to the framing of obituary reviews of its principal achievements and upon attempting to assess the relative permanence of the changes effected.

Such assessments of the 'Reagan Reformation' have already substantially been made above with respect to the progress secured up to the eve of the November 1986 Congressional elections. Two years on, and with additional perspective, the achievements remained broadly similar. Domestically, the most striking successes had been recorded in the taxation sphere, with the 1981 and 1986 Federal tax reduction and reform bills standing out as prominent testaments to populist supply-side Reaganism. Overall, indeed, the burden of Federal taxation had fallen from 20.1% of GNP in 1981 to 18.1% in 1983, although by 1987 it had begun to edge up to 19.4%. The Reagan presidency had proved to be less successful in securing its goal of effecting sweeping general domestic expenditure economies and in reducing government outlays as a proportion of GNP. Here, Congressional and interest group opposition had proved too formidable and, as a consequence, the Federal budget deficit problem was born.[36] Nevertheless, such had become the scale of this deficit problem by the mid 1980s that a sea-change in Congressional attitudes had effectively been forced and, from GRH onwards, on both sides of Congress, a much more sober and 'realistic' attitude towards 'appropriations' had become evident: the doctrines of fiscal conservatism and government 'limits' had spread from minority to majority circles.

The other notable, and least satisfactory, feature of domestic 'Reaganomics' had been the skewed character of the benefits that had been derived. Thus, between 1980 and 1988, national statistics showed that while the top 20% of American households had enjoyed an inflation-adjusted advance in their overall incomes of more than 15%, the real incomes of the poorest 20% had fallen, with the tax burden imposed upon them actually having increased. The gap between rich and poor had widened substantially and both the absolute number and the proportion of the population that lived below the official poverty line, despite falling back from their 1983 highs, increased between 1980 and 1987 from 29 to 33 million and from 13.0% to 13.6% of the population respectively. In particular, with Federal funds for low-income housing being slashed by 70% and social and welfare programmes for the poor also being sharply reduced, the plight of the country's urban underclass significantly deteriorated, with the numbers of the homeless climbing to more than 0.5 million, on the most conservative of estimates, and with drug addiction and crime rates also soaring.

In contrast, externally, the Reagan Presidency had proved, for the US, to be a period of notable success and enhanced influence in most regions of the world, with the exceptions of Central America, the Middle East and Southern Africa. Having almost doubled the defence budget to $290 billion and raising it as a share of

GNP from 5.3% to 6.4%, America was indubitably 'back', with its might restored on the world stage, and, in 1987–8, from a position of strength, sensible rapprochement with the East had at last begun.

Finally, despite the Supreme Court nomination embarrassments of 1987–8, the Reagan administration's most enduring legacy had clearly been judicial. By the close of his presidency, Reagan had made 360 lifetime appointments to the bench. These included three Supreme Court justices and the Chief Justice, as well as 48% of the 160 full-time Federal appeals court judges and 49% of the 556 full-time district court judges. In the case of the Supreme Court, with the replacement in 1988 of Justice Powell with Anthony Kennedy, a new conservative judicial majority had finally been established. This was made plain in July 1989 when Kennedy aligned himself with Chief Justice Rehnquist, the Reagan appointees O'Connor and Scalia and Justice White to provide the majority in the 5–4 ruling in the important case of *Webster v. Reproduction Health Services*. This majority ruling, which upheld a Missouri law which sharply restricted the availability of publicly funded abortion services and which required doctors to test for the viability of a foetus at 20 weeks, served to undermine substantially the 1973 *Roe v. Wade* landmark verdict on abortion. Additional rulings during the Court's 1988–9 session on the death penalty – whose reach was extended to embrace potentially both teenagers and the mentally retarded – and on 'affirmative action' and civil rights – whose scope was narrowed – gave added confirmation that a rightward shift had indeed taken place.

In the short to medium term, this Reaganite judicial legacy would appear to be irreversible, since the aging justices who are most likely to be replaced in the near future, Blackmun (81), Brennan (83), Marshall (81), are all occupants of the Court's liberal wing. However, whether other aspects of the 'Reagan Reformation' would prove to be equally enduring appeared to very much depend upon the outcome of the November 1988 presidential contest. This election – the first 'open' presidential contest not involving an incumbent for two decades – assumed critical significance as both parties, the Republicans and Democrats, sought confirmation of their dominance as the nation's 'majority coalition' and sought to establish decisive control over the country's political agenda for the new decade ahead.

Chapter 7

THE 1988 PRESIDENTIAL ELECTION

Party and Presidential Prospects on the Eve of 1988: A Republican Realignment or Democrat Recovery?

Ronald Reagan's victory in the presidential election of November 1984 had represented the Republican Party's fourth success in the last five contests. During this period the Republicans, having captured 216 million votes to the Democrats' 174 million and 77% of the total 'electoral college' votes, had emerged as the pre-eminent presidential party. They appeared favourites, before the outbreak of the 'Irangate' scandal, to record a further victory in November 1988 under the leadership of George Bush, Robert Dole, Jack Kemp, Paul Laxalt or Howard Baker. The party had built up a strong base of support among the white middle classes and had promulgated a free-market, strong defence policy programme which had come to dominate the national agenda. The gap which had once separated the two national parties in terms of popular allegiance had been sharply narrowed – in June 1984, 45% of the public viewed themselves as Republicans, 48% as Democrats – and the Republicans had begun to make substantial breakthroughs in State-wide senatorial and gubernatorial contests. In the House of Representatives and in local Statehouses, Democrat gerrymandering had served to stymie the party's progress between 1980 and 1984.[1] The Republicans thus launched a major State-level 'Operation Open Door' recruitment and promotion drive during 1985–6,[2] which provided the basis for a number of heartening lower-tier successes during the elections of November 1986 which served to broaden and deepen the party's base. Outside the political chambers, the Republicans found increasing support from among the ranks of the State and Federal bureaucrats, universities, the media and the judiciary during the early 1980s. Talk thus mounted that a conservative ideological realignment was under way, promising to replace the post-1933 'New Deal – Great Society' liberalism consensus.

117

The Democrats, alarmed by the margin of their defeat in November 1984 and vexed by discussions of a political re-alignment, launched an introspective inquiry into the ills of their party during 1985. The inquest concluded in a grave and sombre tone that the party had reached a critical organisational and ideological crossroads. A swathe of diverse ethnic, religious, socio-economic and ideological interest groups had, during the 1960s and 1970s, affixed themselves around the party's traditional middle-class core and had begun to influence the Democrats' policy programme in a manner which proved to be advantageous at the city and local level, but detrimental in national and many State-wide contests. The most vocal of these minority groups, the black and Hispanic sections, pressed for high-spending anti-poverty, urban renewal and 'affirmative action' programmes, feeling that the 'Great Society' reforms of the 1960s and early 1970s had been insufficient and ineffective. This 'big government' approach was, however, increasingly opposed by America's white middle-class majority, who believed that equality of opportunity now existed.

The Democratic Party needed to choose, therefore, whether to give continued prominence to minority issues or to take a more centrist and conservative course. Radicals, led by Jesse Jackson, urged the former course, arguing that the fast-growing black and Hispanic communities would increase in electoral significance during the coming decades. However, the majority saw it as essential for the party to adopt a more centrist defence and growth-orientated programme and to reduce the power wielded by minority factions. Such a shift in emphasis took place from February 1985 following the election of Paul Kirk (a former Kennedy aide and party treasurer) to the post of National Committee chairman vacated by the retiring Charles Manatt. Kirk proceeded to withdraw the special standing that had recently been granted to black, feminist and homosexual groups in the party's ruling committees. He encouraged unions not to interfere in primaries by endorsing candidates at an early stage and he cancelled the party's activist-dominated midterm Convention. He also revamped the party's fund-raising structure, more than doubling the inflow of funds between 1984 and 1988. Finally, he established a clutch of powerful new Policy Commissions, many of the key chairs on which were granted to moderate-minded western and southern Democrats. These changes surprised conservative Democrats, who, having viewed Kirk as an unreconstructed liberal, had set up their own ideas and policy-framing Democratic Leadership Council (DLC) and had appeared alarmingly secessionist.[3] This shift in approach during 1985–6 heralded the emergence of a new realism among Democrats and was buttressed by additional reforms geared towards recapturing the support of targeted groups, including young voters and the older ethnic communities.[4]

The Democrats thus, while retaining their concern for social justice and reduced inequality, clearly shifted towards the centre-right during the years immediately following the November 1984 election in response to broader changes in the political environment. The 'neo-liberal' 71-page policy document, 'New Choices in a Changing America', adopted by the party's leadership in September 1986, which supported a firmer, anti-Soviet defence strategy and set aside discussion of the contentious issues of abortion and homosexual rights, successfully encapsulated this new approach. These changes in style and substance were a factor behind the party's heartening performance in the crucial November 1986 Senate, House and State legislature elections, which served both temporarily to halt the conservatives' national advance and to provide the Democrats' leaders with the legislative means of checking and beginning to reverse the Reagan economic and social 'counter-revolution'.

However, the longer-term success of the Democrats in reversing the conservative tide that has been evident in American politics since the later 1970s appeared very much to depend upon the party's ability to capture the presidency in November 1988 and to maintain its precarious Senate majority.[5] The 'Irangate' scandal of 1986–7 had considerably improved the Democrats' prospects in 1988 through damaging the succession hopes of the Republican front-runner Vice-President George Bush, who had been indirectly implicated in 'Irangate' as a result of his membership of the NSC and his close contacts with CIA officers involved in the Contra deals. Concurrent scandals concerning the fraudulent and amoral activities of a number of fundamentalist television preachers had, in addition, served to tarnish the image of the religious 'New Right', one of whose leaders, the Rev Pat Robertson, had commenced on a Jackson-like struggle for the Republican nomination, anxious to place conservative issues at the top of the party's 1988 agenda. The Republicans, in contrast to 1980 and 1984, thus lacked a clearly obvious and strongly supported candidate for the presidency in 1988. They appeared set to endure a lengthy, divisive and ideologically grounded contest for the party's presidential nomination similar to that of 1976 between figures from the ultra-radical 'New Right' (Robertson and Kemp), the 'Main Street' right wing (Laxalt and Bush) and from the more moderate 'Wall Street' centre-right (Dole, Du Pont, Haig and possibly Howard Baker). Buoyed by the successful legislative record of its Congressional leaders during the 100th Congress, the Democrats' prospects of presidential success thus appeared, in 1988, to be the most promising since 1976. Much still depended, however, on their selection of a nominee who would be both in tune with the dominant ideological currents of the fiscally more conservative later 1980s, but who also possessed sufficient personal charisma to draw together the traditional cross-class North-South Democrat coalition in the manner of Kennedy, Johnson and the early Carter.

The Democrat Nomination Race: The Battle of the 'Seven Dwarfs'

In 1986, when initial preparations for the 1988 nomination contest were being made, the Democrats appeared to possess such an electorally appealing frontrunner in the form of the challenger who had come so close to defeating Walter Mondale, the insider candidate of 1984, Senator Gary Hart of Colorado. Hart enjoyed national name recognition, following his 1984 exploits, and had used the years since to 'flesh out' extensive new policy programmes so as to be able to counteract any continuing 'Where's the beef?' jibes of political vacuity. In 1986 he had established, with his sister-in-law (a former Congressional Representative), the Centre for a New Democracy as both a think-tank and a fund-raising institution and he recruited to his campaign team Paul Tully, a close former adviser to Edward Kennedy. To exhibit further the seriousness of his 1988 presidential bid, he stepped down as Senator for Colorado in November 1986 and concentrated full-time on campaigning activity. Propounding a new, more internationally-minded foreign policy programme, dubbed 'enlightened engagement', and 'neo-liberal', small-business-orientated retraining and investment programmes in the economic sphere, Hart appeared uniquely attuned to the 'New Times' and rapidly gained the endorsement of a clutch of Democrat Congressmen and Congresswomen. Indeed, by the spring of 1987 Hart led declared and undeclared Democratic presidential challengers by a substantial margin. Suddenly, however, in the space of several dramatic weeks during April–May 1987 Hart's campaign self-destructed and, with it, the race to head the Democrat presidential ticket was thrown wide open.

For years gossip-column stories had circulated concerning alleged 'womanising' on the part of the ruggedly handsome Hart. These had, however, been given limited coverage by the serious press and television media, until in April–May 1987 the Republican-leaning *Miami Herald* published a series of headline stories in which it was revealed, with supporting photographic evidence, that Donna Rice, a 29-year-old Miami model, had spent several days in Hart's company, first on a boat called *Monkey Business* off Florida and then overnight at Hart's Washington home. Hart, supported firmly by his wife Lee, asserted that the relationship had been an innocent one and, initially, tried to brush the incident aside. However, opinion poll support for his candidature collapsed and, amid tales of further earlier infidelities during his 29-year marriage, a crestfallen Hart was forced, on 8 May 1987, to announce his withdrawal from the presidential nomination race. Later, in December 1987, Hart, concerned to place 'his issues' on the national agenda, surprisingly returned to the fray. However, lacking both credibility and funding, he was to finish last, with barely 4% of the poll, at the inaugural New Hampshire primary on 16 February 1988. A month later, after garnering less than 2% of the vote on 'Super Tuesday', he withdrew from the Democrat race for good.

The self-destruction of the Hart candidacy during 1987 left the field wide open for the Democrat nomination as 1988 approached. In the absence of Hart, as well as the retirement from politics of the party's disillusioned torchbearers of 1984, Walter Mondale and Geraldine Ferraro, the party's four best known figures electorally were: the two northern 'Great Society' liberals, Senator Edward Kennedy (56) of Massachusetts and Governor Mario Cuomo (56) of New York; the fiscally conservative new wave 'neo liberal', Senator Bill Bradley (45) of New Jersey; and the conservative southern Democrat, Senator Sam Nunn (50) of Georgia. For a variety of personal reasons, however, none of these popular 'heavyweight' figures proved willing to subject themselves to the gruelling year-long, media-intrusive campaign that had now become essential for prospective presidential hopefuls. Instead, the party faithful was left to choose between seven relatively young and inexperienced 'second tier' representatives drawn from the evolving 'New Democratic Party': a grouping which was cruelly dubbed, by the disrespectful press, the 'Seven Dwarfs'.

These seven officially declared presidential aspirants – former Arizona Governor Bruce Babbitt (50); Senator Joe Biden (45) of Delaware; Massachusetts Governor Michael Dukakis (54); Missouri Representative Richard Gephardt (47); Senator Albert Gore Jr (40) of Tennessee; the Rev Jesse Jackson (46); and Senator Paul Simon (59) of Illinois – were drawn from a broad range of geographical regions and represented a wide diversity of ideological outlooks, spanning the radical left (Jackson), the tradition of north-eastern liberalism (Biden and Simon), the newer breed of 'neo-liberalism' (Babbitt and Dukakis), small-town populism (Gephardt) and a reformed version of 'southern conservatism' (Gore). Two of the candidates, Babbitt and Simon, despite running the most intellectually challenging and courageous of the campaigns – Babbitt actually proposing, as Mondale had done in 1984, the raising of taxes to reduce the level of the Federal budget deficit – were to prove to be too ill-funded and untelegenic to make an effective impact and were to pull out at an early stage of the race: Babbitt after the New Hampshire primary and Simon after the 5 April Wisconsin primary. A third candidate, Biden, a liberal-minded Catholic and powerful platform orator who was well funded and enjoyed support from the 'Kennedy clan' and the talented pollster Patrick Caddell, had appeared to be more strongly positioned. However, his campaign, like Hart's, self-destructed following revelations of incorrigible plagiarism in his speeches. In particular, in a debate at the Iowa State fair in August 1987 he included rhetorical passages concerning his humble family background and the 'life chances' which had been provided to him by the 'platform' of the Democratic Party which had been crudely 'lifted' from a recent powerful general election address made by Britain's Labour Party leader, Neil Kinnock. As soon as these similarities were brought to the media's attention in September 1987, by means of a special video tape released by the Dukakis campaign team, Biden was forced to withdraw formally from the nomination contest.

In such circumstances, and despite the continued threat (up to September 1987) of an additional intervention by Representative Patricia Schroeder (46) of Colorado – whom the press dubbed 'Snow White' – the Democratic presidential race swiftly descended into a four-man contest between Richard Gephardt, Albert Gore, Michael Dukakis and Jesse Jackson.

Richard Gephardt was, in many respects, the most experienced and Washington-wise of these four candidates. The Baptist son of a St Louis milk-truck driver turned property dealer, he had been a Congressional Representative for his native city since 1977 and had gained national exposure during 1986 as the key mover within the House behind tax reform and in 1987 as sponsor of a semi-protectionist trade amendment. In addition, as a founder member of the DLC in 1985 and as House Caucus leader since 1987 he enjoyed growing influence within Democrat leadership circles. However, despite this 'insider' status, Gephardt chose, in 1987–8, to challenge for the party's presidential nomination as a populist, anti-establishment 'outsider' in the manner of Carter in 1976 and Hart in 1984, coining the slogan, 'It's your fight too'. He announced his candidacy as early as February 1987 at the very railway station where the Missouri-born President Harry Truman had claimed victory after the election of 1948. Thereafter, he travelled extensively across the Midwest States, championing the farm and blue-collar industrial interests, in an effort to secure a strong showing at the Iowa caucuses on 8 February 1988, which would attract in campaign funds in a bandwagon manner.

In marked contrast, Albert Gore, a diligent Kennedyesque freshman Senator from a wealthy establishment background (his father had preceded him as a Senator) and the youngest candidate from either party in the race, gambled on a radically different strategy of delayed entry into the race. As the only Democrat contestant from a southern State, he concentrated his resources on a 'media blitz' just prior to the new 'Super Tuesday' of 8 March, hoping to sweep the board in the ten southern and four bordering States which were due to hold co-ordinated primaries on this day and which embraced 30% of the 4162 National Convention delegates which were to be selected before July.

Meanwhile, Michael Dukakis, the Greek-American Governor of the thriving State of Massachusetts, determined on a more conventional campaigning approach. His plans were centred upon performing strongly at the inaugural 16 February primary in neighbouring New Hampshire and then, boosted by media attention, securing a respectable overall showing on 'Super Tuesday', before stepping up the pace of his challenge as the primary trail swung northwards to the industrialised 'rust belt' States later during March and April. This 'long haul' strategy was buttressed by the assembly of a particularly effective and the best funded campaign team headed, until their resignation on 29 September 1987 over the 'Biden tapes' issue, by John Sasso (42), a former 'field organiser' for Edward Kennedy in 1980 who had also managed Ferraro's 1984 vice-presidential campaign, and Paul Tully, drawn from the crumbling Hart campaign.

The fourth aspirant for the Democrat nomination, Jesse Jackson, in the wake of his 1984 bid, was the 'veteran' of the field and had the highest national profile. Since 1984, he had established himself as the unchallenged national leader and spokesman for the black movement and had successfully led extra-Congressional campaigns to force the introduction of a special holiday to commemorate the life of Dr Martin Luther King and to pressurise business and Federal, State and local governments to 'disinvest' in South Africa. In addition, Jackson had also worked hard to broaden the electoral appeal of his 'National Rainbow Coalition' (estd 1986) movement, attracting to its ranks white farmers concerned with low crop prices and homestead-dispossessions, unemployed blue-collar workers and an additional swathe of white middle-class radicals and populists. This was achieved through the promulgation of a populist economic programme, akin to Gephardt's; through the moderation of his defence policy stance, backing, for example, SDI research; through making the issue of combating drug abuse – an issue which was of great concern to whites – a central theme of his campaign; and through a general professionalisation of his organisational and media marketing techniques, with Willie Brown, speaker of the California Assembly, being persuaded to serve as campaign chairman and Gerald Austin, a talented white political consultant, as campaign manager. Bert Lance, Jimmy Carter's former budget director, and John C White, a former chairman of the Democratic National Committee, also provided strategy advice in the southern States.

At the opening test of Democrat opinion, the Iowa caucuses of 8 February, Richard Gephardt secured his planned-for victory. However, his margin of success, after 150 days of campaigning in the State, was somewhat disappointing: Gephardt capturing barely 31% of the vote to Simon's 27%, Dukakis's 22%, Jackson's 9% and Babbitt's 6%. A week later, in the New Hampshire primary, Dukakis headed the pack by a much more decisive margin, defeating Gephardt by a 37% to 20% margin. Gephardt did strike back with victory in the South Dakota primary on 23 February, but, on the same day, disappointingly trailed in fifth, with only 7% of the vote, in the more important Minnesota caucus, which was won by Dukakis (34%), with Jackson coming in a surprisingly strong second, securing 20% of the primary vote in a State which had a black population of less than 1%.

Dukakis followed up his Minnesota triumph with decisive victories in the Maine caucus on 28 February and Vermont primary on 1 March, and on 'Super Tuesday' on 8 March not only topped the poll in the northern and western primaries and caucuses in Hawaii, Idaho, Massachusetts, Maryland, Rhode Island and Washington State, but also finished first in the large, specially targeted, southern States of Florida and Texas, being helped by his strong, Spanish-speaking, rapport with the Hispanic and, through his wife Kitty, Jewish communities. In contrast, the candidacy of the less well funded, midwestern-orientated Gephardt – as well as Simon – was effectively killed on 'Super Tuesday': Gephardt finished first in only one State, his native Missouri, and, overall, secured only 13% of the Democrat vote. Instead, the two principal victors in the novel co-ordinated contests of 8 March 1988 were, as had been hoped, the white southern Democrat, Albert Gore, and, as had not been anticipated by the party's elders, the black southerner, Jesse Jackson. Gore, who also narrowly won the preceding Wyoming caucus on 5 March, finished first in five southern region primaries – Arkansas, Kentucky, North Carolina, Oklahoma and Tennessee – as well as in the caucus in Nevada. He was also second in five southern States and, in all, captured 27% of the Democrat votes cast. Jackson, receiving 96% of the votes of blacks and between 5 and 10% of white votes, similarly topped the poll in five southern primaries – in Alabama, Georgia, Louisiana, Mississippi and Virginia – and gained a 26% share of the overall poll: the same proportion as Michael Dukakis.

The split outcome of 'Super Tuesday' effectively left the Democrat nomination race a three-cornered contest, involving Jackson, the torchbearer for the party's radical left wing and Gore, the representative of the moderate right, with Dukakis positioned in between as a consensual centrist figure. By this time, 47% of the 3518 delegates (excluding the 644 appointed 'super-delegates') who were due to be selected for the party's National Convention in Atlanta in mid July had already been chosen. Of these, Dukakis had secured 455 (28%), Jackson 397 (24%), Gore 346 (21%), Gephardt 143 (9%) and Simon 36 (2%), with 260 (16%) remaining uncommitted. This left all of the leading contenders well short of the 2082-delegate margin required for automatic nomination, prompting prognoses within senior party circles that no one candidate would be able to break clear decisively and that, in such circumstances, the Atlanta Convention would degenerate into a divisive 'brokered' meeting.

Such fears were ultimately to prove ill grounded as the primary trail swung north and westwards in late March and April 1988 towards States which had been well cultivated by the Dukakis campaign team. Initially, however, the post 'Super Tuesday' initiative in the Democrat contest was surprisingly assumed by Jesse Jackson. He topped the poll in the party's Alaska and South Carolina caucuses on 10 and 12 March respectively and finished a strong second behind Simon, with 31% of the vote to 43%, in the traditionally important Illinois primary on 15 March. Then, most surprising of all, he secured a crushing victory, by 55% to 28%, over Dukakis in the 26 March Michigan caucus. This victory, which, secured in a State with a black population of only 13%, was the first ever for a black candidate in the industrialised north, left Jackson briefly in the lead in terms of overall pledged delegates.

As March 1988 drew to a close the Democrat nomination contest began, finally, to narrow down to a two-man head-to-head struggle: between Jackson and Dukakis. Gephardt, whose campaign had been fatally undermined by charges of opportunistic policy 'flip-flopping' and by Jackson's – and, in Michigan, Dukakis's and even Gore's – wresting of the populist mantle, announced his formal withdrawal from the nomination struggle on 28 March after securing only 13% of the vote in make-or-break Michigan. Simon, having accumulated 170 delegates, also announced a 'suspension' of his campaign a week later. Gore, meanwhile, continued in the race up to the New York State primary on 19 April, securing the endorsement of New York Mayor Ed Koch in this contest, but, after capturing only 10% of the State's vote and having accumulated a debt of $1.5 million, also announced the 'suspension' of his campaign. He had failed to broaden his appeal beyond the southern 'Super Tuesday' States, but still retained potentially valuable control over 426 delegates.

In the immediate wake of the Michigan caucus, political commentators and Democratic Party elders began to focus attention seriously upon the possibility that, having proved able to broaden his appeal, Jesse Jackson might in fact now create such an unstoppable bandwagon that he would win the party's nomination. Reflecting these changed perceptions, a series of detailed in-depth profiles of Jackson's past career began to be published in news magazines and, on 30 March, he was invited to Washington DC for a cordial 'power-breakfast' with Democrat elders, including Clark Clifford (81) and Frank Mankiewicz. These media profiles were by no means flattering, with grave doubts, for example, being cast upon the veracity of a televised claim made by Jackson in 1968 that he had held the dying Martin Luther King in his arms. Jackson was also indirectly accused of past 'womanising'; his record as administrator of the heavily indebted PUSH was strongly criticised; and his judgment questioned in the light of his past support of the Black Muslim leader Louis Farrakhan and sympathy exhibited towards both the PLO and the Cuban leader, Fidel Castro. However, despite such flaws in his résumé, Jackson continued to remain a serious contender for the Democrat nomination as a result of his charismatic and unparalleled speech-making ability. These were qualities which starkly differentiated him from his principal rival, Michael Dukakis.

Dukakis, born in the Boston suburb of Brookline – also the birthplace of John F Kennedy – in November 1933, the second son of a hard-working, 'high-achieving' Greek immigrant family, had acquired the reputation of being a highly intelligent and efficient managerial technocrat, but also, less favourably, of being an austere, passionless politician. He had excelled at the rigorous Quaker university of Swarthmore (Pa), where he secured a degree in political science, and, following military service in Korea (1955–7), graduated from the Harvard Law School in 1960. He then concentrated on a political career, setting for himself the goal of becoming Governor of Massachusetts. This ambition was achieved in 1974, being preceded by four terms of public service as an earnest elected representative of the Massachusetts State legislature (1963–71), three years in the media working as the presenter of the current affairs television programme, *The Advocates* (1971–3) and two political defeats, in 1966 and 1970, in the races for the positions of State Attorney-General and Lieutenant-Governor.

During his initial term as Massachusetts' Governor, Dukakis disastrously alienated the local Democrat machine through his stubbornly self-righteous refusal to grant post-election favours. He also forfeited broader popular support by over-zealously slashing the welfare budget in an effort to bring the State budget back to balance while at the same time not reneging on his campaign pledge that he would not raise taxes. As a consequence, he failed to secure re-election for a second term, being defeated in the Democrat primary in 1978 by Ed King, a 'Reagan Democrat'. He fought back, however, from this wounding blow and, from his new position as lecturer in intergovernmental studies at Harvard's JFK School of Government, began to reassess his past career, mistakes and leadership style. Taking on board the lessons learned, Dukakis, under the shrewd direction, from 1981 onwards, of his campaign strategist John Sasso, began to remould his image and political approach. In particular, like Governor Reagan in Sacramento from 1969 onwards, he came to recognise the vital importance of consensual coalition-building to secure the passage of his cherished programmes and of exhibiting greater humility. He also evolved a new economic strategy for the State's rejuvenation. This was founded upon, in the revenue sphere, a clampdown on unpaid taxes (the Revenue Enhancement and Protection, REAP, Program) and, on the supply-side, increased public investment in a special Employment and Training (ET) Choices Program in an effort to wean away welfare recipients, as well as the encouragement of a closer partnership between the state and private enterprise.

The 'new' Dukakis, popularly dubbed 'Duke II', proved electorally appealing and, in 1982, after defeating King in the Democrat primary, he was elected Governor again. Helped by favourable extra-local factors, in particular the sharp rise that took place in Federal defence spending from 1980 onwards, which helped stimulate local high-tech industries, this revitalisation strategy proved remarkably successful. The unemployment rate, which had reached nearly 13% in 1975, fell sharply to below 3% in 1987, less than half the national average, and Dukakis, with the State's coffers bulging, was able to make four successive tax cuts while at the same time continuing to boost the social welfare budgets. Indeed, such was the rapid pace of the upturn in the State's economic fortunes from 1983 onward that the term 'Massachusetts Miracle' was coined. In March 1986 Dukakis secured the rating as the nation's 'most effective Governor' in a *Newsweek* poll of his colleagues and seven months later he was re-elected by a landslide for a third term by Massachusetts' electors.

Dukakis's interest in running for national office was stimulated by John Sasso, who was drafted by the Mondale team to take charge of Geraldine Ferraro's vice-presidential campaign during July–November 1984. Unimpressed by the quality of the possible alternatives, Sasso came increasingly to view Dukakis, with his credibility in the economic sphere, as a viable Democrat presidential candidate for 1988. Dukakis, who had secured some national-level experience as head of the economic policy grouping of the Democratic Policy Commission set up by DNC chairman Paul Kirk in 1985 and as co-chair of the National Governors' Association and chairman of the Democratic Governors' Association during 1986–7, finally decided to commit himself to a presidential bid once his fellow north-eastern liberals, Edward Kennedy and Mario Cuomo, publicly announced, in December 1985 and February 1987 respectively, that they would not contest the party's nomination in 1988. In the early spring of 1987, he made a number of exploratory trips to Iowa, New Hampshire, North Carolina, Louisiana and Washington DC and held private discussions with a number of former candidates, including Walter Mondale, John Glenn and Jimmy Carter. He received a positive feedback from these talks and formally announced his candidature on 29 April 1987. An experienced campaign team was assembled which was directed, initially, by Sasso and then, from September 1987, by Susan Estrich (35), an energetic young Harvard Law School professor who had been an aide to Edward Kennedy in 1980 and to Mondale and Ferraro in 1984, and a Democrat record was set in the amount of funds, $16 million, that was raised by February 1988: the figure was more than double that, $7 million, raised by his nearest rival, Gephardt.

In the wake of the 'Irangate' scandal and the burgeoning of the Federal deficit, the chief theme stressed in the Dukakis campaign was the 'hands on' administrative competence and integrity of their candidate, particularly in the economic sphere, with Dukakis pledging to put into practice the lessons learned in his home State and to reproduce the 'Massachusetts miracle' on a national scale. In addition, much was made of Dukakis's ethnic and immigrant roots, with his successful 'rags-to-riches' family being presented as an exemplar of the 'American dream'. White middle-class suburbanites and the older ethnic communities of the North-east were thus specially targeted for support. In addition, the growing Hispanic communities of the South and West were viewed as potential Dukakis 'vote banks'. The campaign suffered early shocks when Dukakis's wife, Kitty, was forced to reveal, in July 1987, that she had been addicted to amphetamine diet pills for 26 years between 1956 and 1982 and when Sasso and Tully were found implicated in the 'Biden tapes' incident of September 1987. It soon recovered, however, and by the spring of 1988 had established itself as the most efficiently organised in the Democrat race. However, the Dukakis campaign was notably cautious and lacked a sense of either excitement or dynamism. For this reason, primary and caucus support for Dukakis was grudging and somewhat shallow. Following his New Hampshire and 'Super Tuesday' successes, Dukakis should really have begun to sweep the board as the nomination race moved north towards 'liberal territory' and by late March he might have expected to have built up for himself a commanding lead. This failed to occur and was to be an ominous sign for the subsequent presidential election in November.

Ultimately, the Dukakis team were to succeed in grinding out a nomination victory. This occurred only, however, after the choice for the Democrats became, from mid March, a stark one between Jesse Jackson, who was conventionally seen as 'unelectable' at the national level, and the centrist Massachusetts Governor. Dukakis strung together victories in the Kansas caucus and Connecticut primary of 18 and 29 March respectively to restore his lead in the national tally of convention delegates. Then on 4–5 April he secured crucial defeats of Jackson in the Colorado caucus and Wisconsin primary. The latter victory, by a 48% to 28% margin, effectively brought to a halt the Jackson bandwagon and was to be confirmed by further Dukakis successes in the Arizona caucus on 16 April and, following a racially tinged campaign (stoked up by Gore and Mayor Koch, but from which Dukakis remained aloof), in New York on 19 April. In this contest, Dukakis outpolled Jackson by 51% to 37%, with Gore trailing in a poor third with 10% support, in what was his last contest of the 1988 campaign. Jackson secured 93% of the black community's vote and 61% of the Hispanic's; Dukakis captured 69% of white, including much of the Jewish, and 38% of the Hispanic support.

The New York primary proved, in retrospect, to be the last knife-edged contest of the Democrat nomination race. Thereafter, as the race narrowed to a two-man battle, Dukakis's superior organisation and lock upon the white vote proved sufficient to enable him to defeat Jackson in all but one – the District of Columbia (on 3 May) – of the remaining 14 State primaries and caucuses which were held between 25 April and 7 June 1988. In the immediate wake of the New York primary, Dukakis had accumulated 1065 pledged delegates to Jackson's 859, with the remaining 1038 being either uncommitted or controlled by candidates who had 'suspended' their campaigns. By the close of the California, Montana, New Jersey and New Mexico primaries on 7

June, Dukakis, having attracted to his ranks sufficient numbers of the uncommitted and formally unpledged 'Superdelegates', had comfortably surpassed the 2082 delegate count hurdle required for nomination.

By the close of the primary season, Dukakis, boosted by favourable press coverage and by his remorseless post-New York delegate 'surge' past Jackson, had at last begun to establish himself on the national political stage and held a commanding lead over his Republican rival for the presidency in November. This lead was increased further, to a 17-points margin, by the Democrats' successfully stage-managed National Convention which was held in Atlanta (Ga), between 18 and 21 July 1988. At the Convention, Dukakis was formally endorsed on the first ballot, by 2876 delegate votes to 1218 for Jackson,[6] as the party's presidential nominee. He then proceeded to select, in what was seen as an astute move, the experienced Texas Senator, Lloyd Bentsen (67),[7] as his vice-presidential running-mate. This choice served to add a conservative 'southern balance' to the party's November ticket, as well as rekindle memories of the earlier, successful Boston-Austin partnership of 1960. Jesse Jackson's supporters were naturally disappointed that their candidate, who had earlier publicly stated that he would accept the vice-presidential nomination if offered, was not on the ticket. However, the Jackson camp were assuaged by Dukakis's soliciting of their participation in the drawing up of the party's policy platform for November – a brief 4000-word document (a ninth the size of that adopted in 1984) being finally agreed upon – by the adding of new seats to the DNC for Jackson supporters and by the provision of finance to enable Jackson and his existing campaign staff to play a supporting role in Dukakis's fall campaign. These gestures succeeded in their goal of uniting the party and both Jackson and Dukakis swapped mutual tributes in their warmly received televised addresses to the convention on 19 and 21 July.

The Republican Nomination Race:
The Bush-Dole-Robertson Contest

The election of 1987–8 witnessed the first serious Republican presidential nomination contest in eight years. For this reason, the party's contenders were significantly older than the 'Democrat Seven'. By the close of 1987, six men had formally declared themselves as candidates: Pierre ('Pete') du Pont IV (52), the scion of a wealthy chemical industrial family who had served as a radical tax- and budget-cutting Governor of Delaware during 1977–84; General Alexander Haig (63), the former NATO Supreme Allied Commander during 1974–9 and Reagan administration State Department Secretary between 1981 and 1982; Jack Kemp (52), a New Right 'supply-side' Representative for New York State since 1970; the Rev Pat Robertson (57), a fundamentalist television evangelist; Senator Robert Dole (64) of Kansas, the Senate Minority Leader; and Vice-President George Bush (63). Four other men, former Nevada Senator Paul Laxalt (65), former Reagan administration ultra-conservative Communications Director Patrick Buchanan (48), and the former Ford and Reagan administration Chiefs-of-Staff Donald Rumsfeld (55) and Howard Baker (63), and one woman, the 'neo-conservative' former UN Ambassador Jeane Kirkpatrick (61), had also contemplated running, but failed, in the end, to cast their hats into the ring.

The clear early favourite for the Republican nomination was Vice-President George Bush, the loyal lieutenant to President Reagan who had been carefully preparing for this bid ever since 1980. Bush was the best financed candidate; enjoyed the highest national, and international, profile; could draw on a wealth of political IOUs; and proved able to attract to his banner a talented and experienced team of campaign strategists. At the latter's head was an aggressive southerner, Lee Atwater (36), who had previously worked on Senate races in South Carolina and as deputy manager of President Reagan's 1984 re-election campaign. Also included, as media adviser, was Roger Ailes (47), the man who had successfully sold Richard Nixon to America's voters in 1968, and, as Chief-of-Staff, Craig Fuller, a former assistant to Ed Meese. The team's strategist, Atwater, who had been recruited as early as December 1984, having recognised both that the ideological centre of gravity in the now-Reaganised Republican Party had, since 1980, shifted significantly rightwards and that, as a result of 'Super Tuesday', a strong showing in the South would be the key to securing the nomination (as well as victory in the subsequent presidential contest), devised a two-pronged campaign/marketing strategy. First, a concerted effort was made, from 1985 onwards, to 'toughen out' Bush's policy stance and to project a more hardened and populist personal image – through 'photo-opportunities' and voice training – so as to counteract the prevailing 'wimpish', 'silver spoon' picture of Bush projected by the media. In support of this, Bush, during Reagan's second term, began to align himself with the forces of the 'moral right', emerging as a staunch opponent of abortion and the ERA and developing warm relations with the Rev Jerry Falwell. Second, campaign funds were specially set aside for the targeting of southern States; close ties developed with influential legislators, Governors and Mayors of the region; and the Vice-President's personal links with the South were increasingly played up, with Texas being chosen as his 'adopted home'.

This nomination strategy was a sensible one. However, it remained vulnerable to charges of opportunism by 'New Right' opponents who viewed the Vice-President's 'conversion' to Reaganite conservatism as purely cosmetic, while the remoulding of public perceptions of Bush's character was to prove to be a protracted process. Even more serious for the Vice-President was the unexpected irruption, during 1986–7, of the 'Irangate' scandal, in which, because of his past service as director of the CIA, his participation in Reagan administration NSC meetings and his overseeing of its special anti-terrorism unit, Bush seemed likely, from the outside, to have been closely involved. During the 1987 Congressional hearings on the affair, it was, indeed, established that Bush had known of the arms shipments to Iran. It remained unclear whether he also knew either of the hostage link or diversion of funds to the Contras. However, there were constant fears in the Republican camp throughout 1987–8 that 'something damaging' might emerge from the continuing inquiries that were being undertaken. For this reason, although during spring of 1987 the Vice-President easily led the field of potential Republican contenders for the party nomination by a wide margin, his support appeared to be unusually 'soft'.

Of the five formally declared challengers to Bush, two, Haig and du Pont, enjoyed little real party support and were to depart from the contest at an early date, on 12 and 18 February 1988 respectively, following the Iowa caucuses and New Hampshire primary. A third contestant, Representative Jack Kemp, supposedly the torchbearer for the party's populist 'economic right' and the hawkish 'spiritual heir' to President Reagan, was initially viewed as a much more serious challenger. Born in Los Angeles, California, in July 1935, Kemp, a successful former quarter-back in American football (he won two championships with the Buffalo Bills), a campaign helper for Ronald Reagan during the 1960s and a committed 'born-again' Presbyterian, was believed to enjoy a strong support base among both blue-collar workers and among adherents to the 'religious right'. He was well funded, boasted Ed Rollins as campaign chairman and was particularly well organised in New Hampshire, where, during 1987, he succeeded in winning the backing of more than half of the Republican Party's county chairmen. His campaign was also brimming with ideas: in the economic sphere, support for further tax reductions, free-trade and a new system of fixed exchange rates; in the social sphere, opposition to abortion but advocacy of school prayer, increased civil rights and the preferment of women; and in the defence sphere, fervent support for Contra aid and the SDI initiative. Unfortunately, however, for Kemp, with the Federal budget deficit increasing, support for an intensification of the tax-cutting 'supply-side revolution' and of the defence build-up had, by 1987–8, begun to wane. Moreover, in his quest for support from the 'moral right' he faced competition from the Rev Pat Robertson. For these reasons, the Kemp campaign failed to 'take off' and, following disappointing showings in Iowa and New Hampshire in February 1988, where he secured only 11% and 13% of the Republican vote respectively, and on 'Super Tuesday' on 8 March, when he won barely 5% of the votes cast and only 4 of the 735 delegates which were at stake, a downcast Kemp withdrew from the contest on 10 March and also announced his intention not to seek re-election to Congress.

It was instead the Senate Minority Leader Robert Dole and the evangelist, the Rev Pat Robertson, who were to prove the most serious intra-party rivals to Vice-President Bush.

Dole, the former running-mate of President Ford in 1976 who had also briefly run for the presidency in 1980, was the most experienced and Washington-wise of either party's nomination race candidates in 1987–8. Born in Russell, Kansas, in July 1923, the son of a Methodist mechanic and cream and eggs stall-holder, he had been severely wounded during the Second World War when leading an assault on a hilltop in Italy, permanently losing the use of his right arm. After the war, he had trained as a lawyer and was elected to the House of Representatives in 1960 and to the Senate in 1968. He had gained a national profile during 1971–3 as chairman of the Republican Party's National Committee and as Senate Majority Leader between 1985 and 1986 and, although originally viewed as a hardline conservative, had begun to moderate his policy outlook, particularly in the social sphere, following the marriage to his second wife, the high-flying Elizabeth Hanford (1936–   ), in 1975. By the spring of 1987, Dole had established himself, in opinion polls, as the strongest rival to Vice-President Bush for the Republican nomination, boasting a 20% rating to Bush's 38% and an appeal which crossed party boundaries. As the year progressed, he had set about assembling a powerful campaign team, headed by the former Labor Secretary William Brock (Tenn) and which included Dole's southern-born wife Elizabeth (NC), as well as the renowned pollster Richard Wirthlin. This team devised a campaign strategy which laid stress upon the decisive, hands-on leadership qualities and humble small-town origins of their candidate, contrasting them with the allegedly weak, indecisive and deferential leadership approach of the privileged Bush, the perennial appointee who had 'started at the top and stayed there'. In addition, they decided to concentrate their resources on the northern farm and industrial States in the hope of securing sufficiently strong early showings in Iowa and New Hampshire so as to undermine decisively the Bush campaign and provide enough momentum to see Dole through what would be a difficult 'Super Tuesday'.

Bush's other principal rival, the Rev Pat Robertson, was very much an unknown quantity, though one with great 'spoiling' potential. The son of a wealthy conservative Senator for Virginia, Robertson had built up a reputation as a charismatic, miracle-generating southern Baptist television preacher. His Christian Broadcasting Network (CBN), which he had established in 1960, boasted more than 30 million subscribers and had an annual revenue of $200 million, while his own '700 Club' programme was viewed by 440000 households. He had also later established the Freedom Council as a political pressure group, championing a return to 'traditional' Christian moral values, conservative fiscal policies and a strong, anti-Soviet defence strategy. Immediately prior to announcing formally his 'divinely ordained' candidacy in October 1987, Robertson had resigned his Church ministry and stood down from the CBN. However, despite these actions, his campaign was to draw strongly upon these earlier links and was to be the best funded and most enthusiastically staffed on the Republican side.[8]

The Republican's nomination race began unusually early with precinct-delegate caucuses in Michigan State in August 1986. Vice-President Bush, after spending more than $1.5 million in contesting these unofficial contests, emerged the victor, although the results were challenged by the supporters of Robertson. More than a year later, however, with the effects of 'Irangate' being felt, Bush's opinion poll lead over his chief rivals had significantly narrowed and at the Iowa caucuses of 8 February 1988 the Vice-President, who had won the State in his earlier 1980 nomination challenge, suffered a humiliating rebuff, being beaten into third place, behind Dole (37%) and Robertson (25%), with only a 19% share of the vote. In the immediate wake of this defeat, Bush's support threatened to evaporate and fears began to mount in his camp that Dole, who was warmly endorsed by the retiring candidate General Haig and who was gathering the momentum of a 'fast freight train', would be able to secure a follow-up success the next week in New Hampshire. The Bush campaign team thus worked frantically to remould their candidate's image. Dressed casually in a blue parka and wearing a baseball cap, the Vice-President was photographed variously at the controls of a lumberyard forklift and 18-wheeler, while a series of 'negative' television adverts, codenamed 'Straddle', were broadcast, which, focusing upon Dole's supposed ambivalence about tax-raising and defence matters, were designed to undermine their opponent's reputation and integrity. These 'attack ads', to which the Dole team fatally failed to respond, proved remarkably successful, enabling Bush, on 16 February, to secure a comfortable (38% to 29%) victory and thus save his foundering campaign. The Vice-President's cause was further improved by Dole's bitter televised reaction to his defeat, acerbically calling upon the Bush team to 'Stop lying about my record'.

Dole briefly rebounded by securing dual victories in the Minnesota caucus and South Dakota primary on 23 February 1988. However, he received little publicity for these wins since Bush had chosen not to campaign formally in these small farm-belt States. Bush, likewise, finished first in the Maine caucus and Vermont primary on 28 February–1 March against little competition. Instead, the resources of all camps were concentrated on the decisive cluster of contests to be held on 'Super Tuesday' on 8 March. In these contests, the Robertson camp, with its Virginia base and 'bible belt'-orientated message, hoped to perform strongly. Unfortunately, however, Robertson was fighting at a time when, following the revelation, in February 1988, that the Rev Jimmy Swaggart, a highly popular Louisiana-based television evangelist of the Pentecostalist Assemblies of God (PAG) who had recently endorsed Robertson's candidacy, had a recent history of sexual involvement with New Orleans' prostitutes, the fundamentalist cause was at a low ebb. The Swaggart case – Swaggart was subsequently defrocked in April 1988 – had come hard on the heels of the uncovering of other sex and financial scandals involving tele-evangelists, including the Rev Marvin Gorman, also of the PAG (who was defrocked in 1987), and the Rev Jim Bakker of the South Carolina-based Praise the Lord (PTL) television ministry (who was defrocked in May 1987 and subsequently, in 1989, sentenced to 45 years' imprisonment for defrauding his ministry). Robertson attempted to distance himself from these damaging cases, but was to find his own reputation tarnished by the revelation, in October 1987, that his first child had been conceived out of wedlock and by the assertion made in February 1988 by the former Republican Congressman, Peter McCloskey, that Robertson's father had pulled strings to keep him out of combat zone duty during the Korean War.

In the light of these events, Robertson was to do well to secure a pre-'Super Tuesday' victory in the caucus in Alaska on 28 February. On 'Super Tuesday', however, his much vaunted 'silent army' of supporters failed to materialise and he finished a disappointing third behind both Bush and Dole, polling only 13% of the Republican vote and capturing only nine delegates. Indeed, while 39% of the Republicans' primary voters on 'Super Tuesday' identified themselves as born-again Christians, fewer than half of them voted for the fundamentalist preacher. Only in the activist-dominated caucus contest of Washington State did Robertson secure a victory. Robert Dole also, similarly, had a disastrous 'Super Tuesday', scoring only 24% support and collecting only 103 delegates. His campaign proved to be inadequately funded and chaotically organised in the southern States and was not helped, moreover, by the development of a serious rift between Dole and his team's senior strategists, including Brock. This enabled the well-oiled and prepared Bush machine, which gambled vast resources on an 8 March 'wipe-out' of its opponents, to achieve a landslide victory. Indeed, such was the scale of this victory that their candidate captured 57% of the votes cast, 619 delegates (being helped by the prevalence of the winner-takes-all system) and finished first in all 16 of the primaries held on 'Super Tuesday', as well as in the immediately preceding trendsetting, 5 March, South Carolina primary.

This crushing 'Super Tuesday' victory by Vice-President Bush, which was secured by attracting to his banner the very voters who had supported Ronald Reagan in the South in 1980 and 1984, effectively brought to an end the Republican Party's nomination campaign. Jack Kemp immediately withdrew from the race and by 12 March, with 1139 delegates being needed to secure the nomination formally, Bush had already secured 702 (73%) of the 959 delegates that had thus far been chosen. Dole trailed way behind with only 165 delegates (17%), Robertson with 17 (2%) and the remaining 75 (8%) were either uncommitted or were pledged to candidates who had since withdrawn. Dole effectively conceded defeat, when, on 12 March, with his financial reserves nearly depleted, he decided to dismiss half his paid campaign staff and cancel much of his pre-booked television time. Advised to fight on by former President Richard Nixon, he formally remained in the race up to the end of March. However, following a crushing defeat in the make-or-break Illinois primary on 15 March and in the Connecticut primary on 29 March, Dole finally withdrew from the race, turning to concentrate on his demanding Senate duties. Robertson, his coffers similarly exhausted, also ceased to campaign actively following his decisive defeat in the Colorado caucus on 4 April. However, despite Bush having passed the delegate winning-post at the Pennsylvania primary on 26 April – in what was the quickest victory achieved by a non-incumbent candidate since Richard Nixon in 1968 – Robertson did not formally withdraw from the contest until 16 May 1988, returning then to Virginia to try to rescue the financially faltering CBN.

'Fighting Dirty': The Bush-Dukakis Presidential Campaign

George Bush's surprisingly comfortable victory in the Republican nomination race of 1987–8 represented a great triumph of planning and organisation. In the presidential contest of August–November 1988, the campaigning acumen of the Bush team was again to come to the fore. In this race, however, the Vice-President was to begin his challenge from behind, forcing him to begin his attacks on his opponent at an early date.

In May–June 1988 national opinion polls had shown Dukakis to be holding a lead of around ten points (49% to 39%) over the already effectively nominated George Bush. Immediately after the Democrats' unusually successful Atlanta Convention this lead extended to 17 points (50% to 33%) and an unusually high proportion, 40%, of registered voters declared that they held the

Republican nominee in positive disfavour: Bush's 'dissatisfaction rating' being even higher than that which had been accorded to Goldwater and McGovern at comparable stages of their doomed 1964 and 1972 campaigns. Dukakis benefited from the fact that from late March 1988 onwards, with the Republican nomination clearly 'in the bag', the media spotlight had been monopolised by the Democrats for four long months. During this period, Dukakis had performed coolly, professionally and honourably while under fire, impressing on-looking potential voters.

Such was the lead held by Dukakis in late July, that Democrat activists left Atlanta in an unusually confident mood, an ABC News poll showing that 93% of the Convention's delegates expected a Democrat victory in the fall contest. This figure was way ahead of the 53% 'confidence rating' exhibited when a similar poll was taken at the end of the 1984 San Francisco Convention. Despite the nation's continuing 'peace and prosperity' and despite the public's waning interest in the, for Republicans, potentially damaging 'Irangate' affair, Democrats firmly believed that 1988 would, politically, be 'their year'. They had in Dukakis, they felt, a candidate of a centrist hue and of proven executive expertise who was well attuned to the 'consolidator' administrative needs of the post-Reagan era. Moreover, their opponent, George Bush, they believed, was an 'easy' target: a man prone to verbal blunders who had not been elected to public office for two decades and who lacked natural public rapport. In these judgments, however, subsequent events were to show the Democrats as having been mistakenly complacent. Instead, as the fall campaign unfolded, the party's strategists were to be totally outmanoeuvred and the tables overturned by a Republican team which had devised a shrewd campaign 'game plan' months in advance and was to execute it ruthlessly.

This Republican team, which was still headed by Lee Atwater and still included Ailes as image-maker, was boosted by the addition, in August 1988, of James Baker, a veteran of the 1980 and 1984 presidential campaigns, as its co-ordinating chairman. Recognising that both Dukakis and Bush were presenting broadly similar policy programmes, particularly in the economic sphere,[9] and were seeking to appeal to similar middle-ground, 'crossover' voters, the Bush team determined on a strategy designed, first, to accentuate any differences that did exist between the two candidates on policy matters; second, to challenge Dukakis's claims of managerial acumen and, third, to make personal 'values' a key issue. At the core of this campaign strategy was a belief, held by Atwater, that during the course of the 1980s a new national consensus had been established in favour of Reaganite 'populist conservatism', the philosophical creed which embraced the domestic tenets of low taxes, 'small government' and traditional Christian 'family values' and, overseas, staunch anti-communism. He determined to project Bush as the natural guardian of this new 'conservative consensus', while presenting Dukakis as sharply at variance, being, in their view, a carefully disguised old-fashioned Massachusetts-liberal who was 'soft on crime', equivocal on anti-communist intervention overseas and who viewed increased government spending as the solution to all society's ills. In support of this strategy, Jim Pinkerton, head of Opposition Research, was specially hired, being furnished with a $1 million war-chest and team of several dozen 'negative researchers', and given the brief of meticulously investigating Dukakis's Massachusetts record. Every past public statement and vote cast by the Governor was computer-catalogued in an effort to 'dig dirt' and provide vital ammunition for future campaign ads and debates.

The Bush team became convinced that this 'negative defining' strategy had great prospects of success when, on 26 May 1988 in Paramus, New Jersey, a test was made of the emotional reactions of 30 Roman Catholic, middle-class, Democrat 'swing-voters' to an assortment of anti-Dukakis 'attack ads' and Bush speeches using a sophisticated system of computerised hand-held 'galvanic response meters' which had first been employed in the Reagan campaign of 1984. The commercials, which included one concerning a convicted black murderer, Willie Horton, who had raped a young woman and tortured her fiancé after absconding to Maryland whilst on weekend leave from a Massachusetts prison, another concerning Governor Dukakis's veto of legislation requiring teachers to lead their classes in the pledge of allegiance and a third concerning the polluted state of Boston harbour, had a powerful, instant impact upon their target audience, persuading, by the end of the evening, half of the Paramus 'guinea pigs' to switch sides and declare their support for Bush. They were subsequently to be aired on television during the fall campaign with telling effect, as the public's perception of Dukakis, a man who had been tagged, by his opponents, as an unalloyed moderate during the Democrat nomination race,[10] was progressively remoulded.

The Republicans' concerted attack upon Dukakis's policy stance, character and leadership abilities commenced in earnest in late July 1988, soon after the Atlanta Convention. Mudslinging rumours were spread, initially by followers of Lyndon LaRouche, that Dukakis had been treated for severe mental depression following, first, the death of his elder brother Stelian, in a hit-and-run accident, in 1973 and, again, after his election defeat in 1978. Similarly unsubstantiated accusations were also made to the effect that Dukakis's wife Kitty had publicly burned a US flag during a 1960s anti-Vietnam War demonstration. These personal attacks were to be followed at the Republicans' New Orleans Convention, held between 15 and 18 August 1988, by the launching of an all-out ideological onslaught against both the Democratic Party and, more specifically, the Dukakis-Bentsen ticket. The first shots were fired on the Convention's opening day by President Reagan who denounced the current Democratic leadership for avoiding the 'L word' and castigated them as 'liberal, liberal, liberal'. The following day, the keynote speaker, Governor Thomas Kean (NJ), ridiculed the Democrats' newly adopted 'pastel patriotism' and depicted Dukakis as, in essence, a closet tax-raiser and disarmer. Further speakers were to reiterate this carefully orchestrated refrain, including the Rev Pat Robertson who denounced Dukakis for being a 'card-carrying member' of the ACLU.

These proceedings were to receive a temporary setback when Bush announced, on 16 August, that his choice for vice-presidential running-mate was to be James Danforth (Dan) Quayle, a junior Senator from Indiana.[11] The name of Quayle, a little-known 41-year-old, had not appeared on any of the pre-Convention lists of 'possibles': Kemp, the Doles and Senators Alan Simpson (Wy) and Pete Domenici (NM) had been the most widely touted names. However, he had been recommended by pollster Robert Teeter (49), who believed that Quayle might attract to the party's ticket young, postwar, 'baby boom' voters, as well as, with his Redfordesque 'good looks', female electors. The Indiana Senator was, moreover, a staunch Reaganite conservative, hawkish on defence issues and a firm opponent of abortion and supporter of school prayer. Quayle's selection, it was thus hoped, would also appease the party's still restless 'New Right' wing. Finally, he had a reputation of being a loyal team-player. This made Quayle's selection appealing to Bush who sought a partner who, unlike Dole, for example, would not be difficult to work with and who would, moreover, not threaten to overshadow the head of the party's ticket.

Almost immediately that Quayle's name was announced, questions began to be raised whether his political experience was sufficient for such a key prospective position. Then, even more seriously, on 17 August, damaging press assertions were made that, as a result of 'string-pulling' by his influential father, Quayle had avoided possible combat action during the Vietnam War between 1969 and 1975 by 'queue-jumping' his way into the Indiana National Guard. In the furore that ensued there were fears, for a time, that Bush might be forced to follow George McGovern's precedent, in the case of Thomas Eagleton, in 1972 and abandon Quayle and select an alternative running-mate. It was decided, however, to brazen through the commotion. Quayle was sent into purdah and assigned for 'coaching' to the former Reagan campaign aide, Stu Spencer, while a valiant attempt was made to turn the tables on the media who were accused of vilification. These actions helped limit the damage inflicted to the Bush candidacy by Quayle's selection. However, throughout the campaign the 'qualifications' and 'heartbeat away' issue was to remain an important sub-theme.

Bush's own personal standing was restored on 18 August at New Orleans when, in an acceptance address which had been scripted by the former Reagan speechwriter Peggy Noonan (36), he delivered one of the most effective speeches of his career. In it he promised to build upon the achievements of the Reagan presidency and to work to improve the 'quality of life', environmental and social, painting the vision of a 'drug-free America' characterised by a 'new harmony among the races', in essence 'a kinder, gentler nation'. At the same time, he questioned the patriotism of his opponent, whom he castigated as a liberal, and declared the forthcoming election to be about 'beliefs . . . values . . . and principles' and not just, as Dukakis had asserted in Atlanta, 'competence'. Significantly, for the campaign that followed, Bush concluded his address by leading the Convention in the recitation of the Pledge of Allegiance.

Despite the continuing ructions of the 'Quayle affair', national opinion polls taken soon after the New Orleans speech showed Bush ahead of Dukakis (by 46% to 40%) for the first time since April. The month-long series of attacks that had been launched against the Democrat ticket had begun to pay dividends, being helped by the failure of the Dukakis team to respond either with counterblasts of their own or to establish clearly an alternative campaign agenda. Instead, Dukakis, already drained by his primary battles, had decided, immediately after Atlanta, to return to Massachusetts to resume his gubernatorial duties and, in particular, to tackle a politically embarrassing budgetary shortfall of $200 million that had recently arisen.

By Labor Day on 5 September 1988, the official opening date of the campaign, Bush's opinion poll lead over Dukakis had stretched to 12 points (47% to 39%). The mounting concern of the Dukakis camp with this state of affairs was made clear by the decision that was now made to recall John Sasso to assume charge of their floundering campaign. However, despite Sasso's return, Dukakis's fortunes continued to ebb. The gap between the two candidates briefly closed to two points (45% to 43%) in the immediate wake of the first televised presidential debate in Winston-Salem (NC) on 25 September, a contest in which Dukakis performed strongly. Ten days later, on 5 October, Lloyd Bentsen even more convincingly outperformed the uncertain Quayle in the vice-presidential debate held in Omaha (Neb), Bentsen effectively disparaging his opponent's attempt to compare himself with John F Kennedy with the crushing rejoinder: 'Senator, I served with Jack Kennedy. I knew Jack Kennedy. Jack Kennedy was a friend of mine. Senator, you're no Jack Kennedy.' However, in the second, and final, presidential debate, held in Los Angeles on 13 October, Dukakis performed poorly and may well have sealed his electoral fate with his unemotional response to the opening question put by the moderator, Bernard Shaw of CNN : 'Governor, if Kitty Dukakis were raped and murdered, would you favour an irrevocable death penalty for the killer?'

By the close of October, Bush's lead in the opinion polls had widened to a commanding and apparently unassailable 13 points (51% to 38%). The Bush team began to tone down their personalised attacks on their opponent and, with the 'revolving-door' Horton prison furlough commercials, the verging-on-racist core theme of their campaign and instead began to concentrate upon projecting a 'warmer' and more 'statesmanlike' image for their candidate. Dukakis, meanwhile, finally began to remove his

143

gloves, adopting, despite his inherent abhorrence of rhetoric, a more energetic, impassioned and partisan campaigning style. While on the stump in California he castigated the Bush team for pursuing a campaign based on 'lies, fear and smear'. Also, more significantly, for the first time since his nomination he openly accepted the 'L word' label, asserting that, yes indeed, he was a liberal, but a liberal 'in the tradition of Franklin D Roosevelt and Harry S Truman'. The Dukakis team, in the light of their private poll soundings, decided to concentrate in the final week of the campaign upon a group of 18 marginal states in New England, the Midwest and West (California, Oregon and Washington), it having been decided to write off, as irretrievably lost, Texas and Florida, as well as the rest of the South and interior. Resources and personal appearances were targeted upon these regions. In addition, in the hope of repeating the famous 'victory from behind' achieved by Truman over Dewey in 1948, Dukakis began to propound a new 'populist', economic-nationalist message, frenetically racing from State to State by train and plane to deliver the shirt-sleeved refrain, 'I'm on your side'. His efforts were supported by those of Jesse Jackson, who, at the prompting of Sasso, was persuaded now to convert his earlier August–October black voter registration drive into a committed and specific endorsement of the Dukakis-Bentsen ticket.

This new approach helped to galvanise the Democrat faithful and attract to the party's banner many of the disgruntled northern State farmers and blue-collar workers. Indeed, with two days to go before voting formally commenced, opinion polls showed that Dukakis, in the wake of his proud and fiery assertion of Democrat values, had succeeded in narrowing Bush's national lead to between 5 and 12 points, with the gap being even narrower in the targeted marginal States. This persuaded Dukakis, in a desperate last-ditch victory bid, to embark on a lightning 8500-mile whistle-stop 'swing' through 11 States, continuing his campaign, both by plane and by satellite television, up to the morning of election day itself. However, as the early 'projected results' began to be relayed on television, it soon became apparent that this 'final kick' had come too late. With three of Dukakis's 'must-win States', Missouri, Connecticut and Maryland, falling early to Bush, the '18 State Strategy' was in tatters and defeat was certain. Thereafter, the list of States captured by the Bush-Quayle ticket began to mount steadily, turning national television monitors Republican red, and, as soon as the polling booths closed on the west coast, Dukakis telephoned Bush formally to concede defeat.

The Outcome of the 1988 Presidential and Congressional Elections

When all the votes cast on 8 November 1988 had finally been counted, the Bush-Quayle ticket's margin of victory over Dukakis-Bentsen was established at 7.8%. However, in the Electoral College, the Republican tally was a sweeping 426 seats to the Democrats' 112 (see Table 19). Bush enjoyed the distinction of being only the third ever Vice-President to have been elected to the presidency at the conclusion of his vice-presidential term and the first since Martin Van Buren (D) in 1836. He was elected following the most expensive ever presidential campaign,[12] but on a voter turnout which, at 50% of the voting-age population, was the lowest since 1924[13] (the first contest following female enfranchisement). Turnout among registered voters was, however, as usual, much higher, reaching nearly 80%.

Bush's margin of victory, at 7.8%, was well below the landslide 18.2% margin achieved by Ronald Reagan in November 1984, as well as the margin of 9.7% secured by Reagan in 1980. Like-wise, Bush's Electoral College winning margin of 314 seats was substantially down on the 512- and 440-seat margins secured by Reagan in those years. Nevertheless, Bush's triumph remained a convincing one. At the time of the summer Conventions, political pundits had anticipated a knife-edged contest similar to those of 1968 and 1976 and, in particular, 1960. Indeed, speculation had mounted that, with the regionally skewed, State-based winner-takes-all Electoral College selection system still in force, 1988 might result, as had previously occurred in 1824, 1876 and 1888, in the election of a candidate who had attracted fewer popular votes than his opponent. These fears were to be removed by Bush's steady advance in the opinion polls from August onwards and, in the end, his victory, in terms of his share of the popular vote, was to be a clear one. However, Bush's victory in terms of Electoral College seats was somewhat deceptive. In 12 States – California, Colorado, Connecticut, Illinois, Maryland, Michigan, Missouri, Montana, New Mexico, Pennsylvania, South Dakota and Vermont – he secured only between 2 and 8% more of the popular vote than Dukakis and it can be calculated that if in 11 of these 'marginal States' (Colorado being excluded) there had

TABLE 19: THE NOVEMBER 1988 PRESIDENTIAL ELECTION (TURNOUT 50.1%)

Candidate	Party	Popular Vote (m)	As % of Total	Electoral College Vote	States Captured
George HW Bush	Republican	48.88	53.37	426	40
Michael S Dukakis	Democratic	41.81	45.65	111	10
Dr Ron Paul*	Libertarian	0.43	0.47	0	0
Lenora B Fulani*	New Alliance	0.22	0.24	0	0
David E Duke*	Populist	0.05	0.05	0	0
Eugene J McCarthy*	Consumer	0.03	0.03	0	0
James C Griffin*	Independent	0.03	0.03	0	0
Lyndon H LaRouche*	Independent	0.03	0.03	0	0
William A Marra*	Right-to-Life	0.02	0.02	0	0
Others†		0.08	0.11	1‡	0
Total		91.58	100.00	538‡	50

* The name of Paul, a former Republican Congressmen from Texas, was on the ballot of 46 States, plus DC; that of Fulani, a New York psychologist, on all 50, plus DC (the first black and first woman to achieve this distinction); that of Duke, a white supremacist, on 12; that of McCarthy, the former Democrat Senator for Minnesota, on 4; that of Griffin on 1: that of LaRouche, the cranky anti-Russian conspiracy-theorist, on 12, plus DC; and that of Marra on 1. Fulani also received $0.94 million in State funds in support of her campaign and LaRouche, who originally contested for the Democrat nomination, $0.83 million.

† Eight other candidates collected over 2000 votes apiece: Ed Winn (Workers League), 18662; James Warren (Socialist Workers), 15603; Herbert Lewin (Peace and Freedom), 10370; Earl Dodge (Prohibition), 8000; Larry Holmes (Workers World), 7846; Willa Kenoyer (Socialist), the other woman to head a ticket, 3878; and Delmar Dennis (American), 3476. In every State, the voter was presented with a choice of at least three presidential candidates, with, in Minnesota and New Jersey, the number reaching 11. However, for the first time since 1964 the Communist Party presented no candidate.

‡ One elector from West Virginia actually cast his ballot for Dukakis's running-mate, Bentsen, when the second stage of voting took place at the State capitals on 19 December 1988.

been a 'perfectly executed' shift of 0.563 million votes from the winning to the losing ticket then a Dukakis-Bentsen Electoral College victory, by 272 to 266 seats, might have been achieved, though on a minority share (by 46% to 53%) of the national vote.

Figure 7   Map of the 1988 Presidential Election

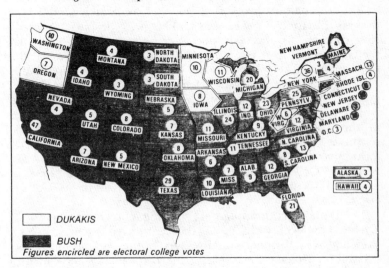

The 1988 Presidential Election Result:
A Regional and Social Analysis

As is exhibited in Figure 7, Bush's presidential election victory in November 1988 was founded upon his sweeping the Republican heartland States of the Centre and West of the country – losing only Washington and Oregon in the North-west to Dukakis – as well as the South and its fringe States of Kentucky and Oklahoma. In the former region, Bush captured 105 (86%) of the 122 seats available, while in the latter he secured all 155 seats, including his 'adopted State' of Texas, despite Bentsen

147

being on the Democrat ticket, and Louisiana, notwithstanding the State's depressed economic condition. Indeed, almost
two-thirds of the Republicans' plurality of 7.1 million votes
over the Democrats in November 1988 was secured in the
South and in this region Bush's lead over Dukakis was a
massive 17 points, 58% to 41%. This compared with a
lead of only four points elsewhere in the country. In New
England, Bush's ancestral home – he was born in Milton,
Massachusetts, brought up in Greenwich, Connecticut, and
owned a summer holiday home in Kennebunkport, Maine
– the Republicans won four of the six States and 19 of
the 36 Electoral College seats. This was despite unusually
close-calls in Connecticut and Vermont and the fact that
the more firmly New England-based Dukakis headed the
opposition's ticket. Even more surprisingly, the Republicans
finished well ahead of the Democrats in the crucial battle-
ground States of the industrialised Frostbelt-Rustbowl of the
North and southern Great Lakes region. Of the 14 States
in this broad zone, which stretches from Missouri in the
south-west to New York in the north-east and embraces,
including the solidly Democrat District of Columbia, 218
Electoral College seats, the Republicans finished first in
nine and secured, overall, two-thirds, or 144, of its College
electors.

   The Democrats' disappointing showing in its traditional northern heartland – notwithstanding the victories it did achieve in New
York and West Virginia – was presaged by the low level of support
evinced for Dukakis in the party's March primaries and caucuses
in Illinois and Michigan. In addition, Dukakis's decision to select
Lloyd Bentsen as his running-mate in preference to the widely
touted and highly respected Senator John Glenn may have denied
the party Ohio's 23 Electoral College seats, as well, possibly, as
a further 45 seats from the highly marginal adjoining States
of Michigan and Pennsylvania. The more fundamental reason,
however, why Dukakis failed to carry the industrial Frostbelt
States in 1988 was that, while the major urban centres of this
region remained firm in their support for the Democrat ticket,
the turnout, particularly among blacks in such cities as Baltimore
(Md), Chicago (Ill) and Philadelphia (Pa) was disappointingly low,
while, most crucial of all, the party failed to achieve its hoped-for
inroads in the expanding and predominantly pro-Republican
suburbs.

TABLE 20:   VOTER PREFERENCES BY SOCIAL GROUPS
IN 1988

	% of 1988 Voters	Bush (R) %	Dukakis (D) %
Total	100	53	46
Men	48	57	41
Women	52	50	49
(Married Men)	(34)	(60)	(39)
(Unmarried Men)	(14)	(51)	(47)
(Married Women)	(35)	(54)	(46)
(Unmarried Women)	(17)	(42)	(57)
Whites	85	59	40
Blacks	10	12	86
Hispanics	3	30	69
Under 30s	20	52	47
30–44 years	35	54	45
45–59 years	22	57	42
Over 60s	22	50	49
White Protestants	48	66	33
Catholics	28	52	47
Jewish	4	35	64
White Fundamentalists	9	81	18
Union Familes	25	42	57
Family Income			
Below $12 500	12	37	62
$12 500–25 000	20	49	50
Over $25 000	64	58	41
($25 000–50 000)	(40)	(56)	(43)
(Over $50 000)	(24)	(62)	(37)
East US	25	50	49
Midwest	28	52	47
South	28	58	41
West	19	52	46
Large Cities	12	40	58
Suburbs/Small Cities	55	54	44
Rural/Towns	33	56	42
1984 Reagan Democrats	9	48	51

It was, instead, in the States of the West and South-west where
the Dukakis-Bentsen ticket polled most promisingly. In this huge,

but relatively sparsely peopled, region, which is bounded by Montana in the north-east and New Mexico in the south-east and by the Pacific Ocean in the west, the Democrats were, it is true, victorious in only two of the 11 States and captured only 17 of the 104 available Electoral College seats and 46% of the 18 million votes cast to the Republicans' 52%. Nevertheless, overall Dukakis polled as strongly here as Carter had in his victory year of 1976, while in Oregon and Washington, where the timber industry was ailing, the Democrats actually achieved their best results since 1964 and first successes since 1964 and 1968 respectively. In Colorado and Montana, Dukakis also garnered a higher proportion of the vote than any Democrat presidential nominee since Johnson in 1964, while in California the Republicans' victory margin was narrowed from its 1984 level of 16 points to less than four. In this western Pacific Coast region, environmental concerns were uppermost in voters' minds in 1988 and the Democrats benefited from the strong stance taken by Dukakis in opposition to offshore oil drilling. Furthermore, anti-Washington feeling was also notably greater in the far West than elsewhere, with the possible exception of the three politically progressivist and economically troubled drought-hit farmbelt States of Iowa, Minnesota and Wisconsin, as well as adjoining Kansas, Missouri, Nebraska and the Dakotas. Here, also, the Democrats polled strongly in November 1988, with Iowa falling to the party for the first time since 1964, and by a comfortable margin.

The data concerning voting by social categories which is presented in Table 20 shows, when compared with that in Table 14, that while, in 1988, the Democrats gained some ground among white electors, they slipped back slightly among blacks — among whom turnout levels also fell — and Jews, although both these voting blocks remained strongly pro-Democrat. Most notable, however, of the trends in race voting was the Democrats' advance among Hispanics. This community, despite Bush's pre-election pledge that he would include an Hispanic in his presidential cabinet and the Republicans' investment in a community-targeted $2.5 million television and radio blitz in the South-west, were attracted by Dukakis's ability to campaign in Spanish and by his successful courting of the influential Hispanic leader, Willie Velasquez. Unfortunately for the Democrats Velasquez, who had agreed to act as a deputy manager of the Dukakis campaign, died in July 1988. Nevertheless, the support that was subsequently given to the Dukakis campaign by Velasquez's aides did help to boost significantly the Democrat vote in California, New Mexico, Texas and Colorado.

Other notable 'voting blocks' who were attracted to the Democrat ticket in 1988, primarily as a result of the party's social and welfare policies, were pensioners and women, especially unmarried. Indeed, a particularly striking feature of November 1988 was the continuance, and indeed strengthening, of the marked 'gender gap' in party voting patterns that had become apparent in 1980. Thus, while Bush led Dukakis by 16 points among men (21 points among married men), support for the two candidates was split evenly among female voters. In 1988, there was also a significant swing of support away from the Republicans among the young (18–29 years) – although the majority in this age group continued to vote Republican – as well as among those with no college education, blue-collar union families, small farmers and those on low incomes. Republican support remained firm, in contrast, among the middle-aged, those on middle (but not higher) incomes and among white-collar and professional/managerial workers, while it actually increased among white fundamentalist Christians.

Overall, indeed, a comparison of presidential voting by social groups in 1988 with that in 1984 and 1980, points to a heightening of the class distinction between the two parties' voter bases. This occurred despite Dukakis running, until the final week, a centrist campaign specifically directed towards attracting back into the Democrat fold many of the white, suburban, middle-class and middle-aged voters who had 'defected' to the Republicans since the later 1960s. Dukakis did lure back more than half of the so-called 'Reagan Democrats', that is voters who had previously considered themselves Democrats but who chose in 1984 to vote for President Reagan. Many of these were blue-collar workers. He failed, however, to draw to his banner the longer lost suburban voters or 'culturally conservative' southern 'rednecks'.

Explanations of the Bush Victory

From an extended perspective, the performance of Michael Dukakis in November 1988 was well above the recent Democrat presidential election par. His 46% share of the popular vote was, with the exception of Carter's 50% in 1976, the best showing

151

by a Democrat nominee since Johnson in 1964: although, of course, Dukakis did not face a strong 'third party' challenge as Humphrey and Carter had in 1968 and 1980. Dukakis's Electoral College score of 11 seats was also the second highest secured by a Democrat since 1968, while the 800 counties he carried (to Bush's 2300) exceeded by more than 100 Humphrey's tally in 1968. Nevertheless, despite these crumbs of comfort, Democrat insiders viewed November 1988 as a 'lost opportunity', as an election which they could have won, but which, instead, had been thrown away as a result both of the relative weakness of their selected candidate and of the inept strategy of his campaign team.

For the first three months of the presidential campaign, the Dukakis team, dominated by a 'Harvard intelligentsia' who were both ill-attuned to the nation's popular pulse and who lacked experience of national-level election fighting, had been thoroughly out-thought and outfoxed by their seasoned, grassroots-conscious opponents. They had allowed Bush's handlers to swing the campaign debate away from such potentially damaging issues as the Federal budget and trade deficits, ethics in government, 'Irangate', the 'Quayle issue' and Bush's alleged past links with the drug-smuggling Panamanian strongman General Noriega and, instead, set their own agenda of relative values and ideologies. In projecting this 'Republican agenda', the Bush team skilfully pressed symbolic 'hot buttons', most notably the American flag, family and country, brought into play their traditionally strong defence and law and order 'cards' and relentlessly worked to denigrate and redefine their Democrat opponent in an unchallenged manner. The bulk of the blame for these campaign mistakes rested ultimately with Dukakis himself, who, unlike Bush, interfered constantly in the details of his campaign and images projected, vetoing a series of what he viewed as 'unfair', 'attack adverts' and over-emotionally scripted speeches at the last minute. He failed, additionally, to provide his campaign with a coherent alternative vision, his dual themes of 'goods jobs and effective government' and 'the best America is yet to come' being notably vacuous. Finally, the overall image he projected was unappealingly parochial, cerebral and cold.

In marked contrast, Bush 'rose to the occasion', emerging almost as a transformed figure once nominated in August and freed from the shadow of President Reagan. As the campaign progressed, he held up well under pressure, producing none of the expected verbal gaffes, and, helped by his voice coaching by Ailes and the arrangement of evocative 'sound-bite' backdrops, he succeeded in projecting a forceful presidentialist image. This was evidenced by election night opinion polls which suggested that of the 40% of voters who proffered the characteristics of 'experience' and 'competence' as an 'important reason' for backing a particular candidate, 90% of them chose Bush in preference to Dukakis.

However, while the comparative competence of the two campaigns was clearly of great importance in determining the outcome on 8 November, additional, both shorter- and longer-term, factors lay behind Bush's triumph.

One was the resurgent popularity of President Reagan whose public job approval rating had risen from a figure of 50% in late July 1988 to 60% in mid October (and was subsequently to reach the record end-of-term level of 68% in January 1989). The close correspondence that existed between the fluctuations in public support for the President and George Bush's own national opinion poll standings during this same period strongly suggested that the presidential election of 1988 was, in many respects, a referendum on Reaganism, with a significant measure of support being transferred to Bush, Reagan's 'Crown Prince' who campaigned on a 'stay the course' message. This was especially the case in the South, a region in which the 'Reagan Coalition' held unusually firm.

However, the most important short-term influences behind Bush's victory in 1988 were the state of the economy – no out-of-power Democrat having been elected to the presidency this century without the 'aid' of a recent economic contraction – and international scene. The former, despite the budget and trade deficit worries, was booming, with both the 'misery indexes' of unemployment and inflation at unusually low levels, while consumer spending was rising at a real annual rate of almost 4%. Indeed, having enjoyed 70 months of continual expansion, the country stood in the midst of its longest peacetime expansion of the century. Externally, the country was at peace and in a strengthened position vis-à-vis its great enemy, the Soviet Union, with its national spirit rekindled. As in 1984, this dual theme of 'peace and prosperity' proved to be compelling. Opinion poll surveys showed that 60% of voters believed that the economy was in a better condition than

153

it had been in 1980 and 80% were very or fairly well satisfied with their personal financial circumstances. Three-quarters of the voters who viewed the economy as in an improving state backed the Bush ticket: conversely two-thirds of those who judged it to be deteriorating supported Dukakis. Most significantly, the voters in 1988 believed, by a 27-point margin, that the Republicans would manage the economy in the future better than the Democrats and would be more likely to be able to avert a recession. Despite his much vaunted expertise in the economic sphere, Dukakis, the manager of the 'Massachusetts miracle', had clearly failed to convince the electorate that his policy prescriptions were viable and transferable to the national stage.

The longer-term contextual background against which the Bush success of 1988 needs also to be set is that of continuing party realignment, at the presidential level at least. The results of 1988 confirmed the 'lock' that had been established over the 21, predominantly central and south-western, States with a combined Electoral College tally of 187 seats which had voted Republican in all six of the presidential elections since 1964.[14] They also re-confirmed the Republicans' ascendancy over the 11 States of the South (with 138 Electoral College votes) which, since 1968, had only defected to the Democrat camp when a popular southerner headed the latter's ticket. With these two bedrock zones of support, the Republicans had, since 1968, been able to boast a 'base' level of support which, aggregating 313 votes and spread across 31 States with a combined population of 131 million (58% of the national total), had proved sufficient to provide comfortable, regular Electoral College majorities. A further six States – Delaware, Kentucky, Maine, Michigan, Missouri and Ohio – outside of the South and with 70 Electoral College votes had also voted Republican in five of these presidential contests.

George Bush's success in November 1988, which constituted the Republicans' third successive presidential victory, something the party had last achieved in 1928, was a confirmation of this recently established executive-level hegemony, a hegemony derived both from a secular 'swing-to-the-right' in popular consciousness and from the fracturing of the traditional Democrat coalition. The results of the elections of November 1988 at the Congressional, gubernatorial and Statehouse levels, however, indicated that this party realignment still remained partial.

154

The Congressional and Gubernatorial Elections of November 1988

Most unusually, George Bush's presidential success of November 1988 was not accompanied by any net Republican gains in either chamber of Congress or, even, at the gubernatorial or Statehouse levels. Instead, 'presidential coat-tails' were completely absent and, for the first time since 1960, the party which won the presidency actually lost ground in Congress. This provided further evidence of the increased prevalence of split-ticket voting that has been evident during recent decades, with electors, apparently, appearing to favour conferring control of the national executive branch of government to the Republicans, while entrusting to the Democrats a counterbalancing, ombudsman charge over legislative matters, both at the national and State levels. In the opinion of a number of commentators, this voter preference for a 'split outcome' constituted 'a desirable informal addition to the constitutional scheme of checks and balances' and was reflective of a 'divided national mind', split between support for both 'ideological conservatism' and, in the spheres of health, education and civil rights, 'operational liberalism'.

TABLE 21: THE CONGRESSIONAL AND GUBERNATORIAL ELECTIONS OF NOVEMBER 1988

	House Seats	Result*	Senatorships	Result*	Governorships	Result*
Total Contested	435†		33		12	
Democrat Victories	260	+3	19	+1	5	+1
Republican Victories	175	−3	14	−1	7	−1

* From the position that pertained immediately prior to the election.
† Turnout was 44.6% in the House elections, 81.6 million votes being cast.

As Table 21 exhibits, the Republicans endured a net loss of three seats in the House of Representatives, with the Democrat majority in this chamber attaining its greatest margin since the midterm election of November 1982. This loss occurred despite the fact that the Republicans' share of the aggregate national vote cast in House elections was, at 46%, up 1% on its 1986 level (its share of House seats was 40% and 41% respectively). In this election the 'return rate' for incumbents reached the record figure of almost 99%, with 402 of the 408 incumbents who stood for re-election being returned and 96% of these romping home by a margin of ten points or more over their challenger. Indeed, a fifth (81) of these incumbents faced no major party opposition at all.

Looking more closely at these House results, of the six incumbent Representatives who lost in November 1988, four of them (two from each party) had been either under formal investigation for ethical improprieties or had been subject to newspaper charges, while the other two had been Republicans with two terms or less under their belts. Of the remaining 27 'open seats', the Democrats secured victories in two of the 15 which had previously been GOP-held, while the Republicans captured one of the 12 formerly Democrat-held constituencies. Overall, more than $260 million had been expended by candidates fighting House races in 1988, with 40% of these funds being furnished by PACs. Incumbent Representatives outspent their challengers by a 4–1 margin and received ten times the amount of funds that had been furnished to challengers by PACs. As a consequence, the 101st Congress boasted the smallest House 'freshman class' of the 1980s, comprising only 33 members (17 Democrat and 16 Republican): see Appendix Table B9.

In the case of the Senate elections, 18 of the 33 contested seats had been defended by the Democrats and 15 by the Republicans, with incumbents standing in 27 races. Overall, the Democrats achieved a slight net gain of one Senatorship, restoring their majority in the upper chamber to a 55–45 margin. Most strikingly, however, 85% of incumbent Senators managed to secure re-election, the third highest proportion since 1966 (see Appendix Table B9). This, as in the case of the House elections, reflected the funding advantages enjoyed by incumbents, who in the 1987–8 'election cycle' (in which $200 million was spent) were able to outspend their challengers by a 2–1 margin and who were favoured by PAC donors by a 4–1 margin. It also reflected the general mood of 'cautious continuity' that characterised the national- and State-level elections held in 1988.

Of the four incumbent Senators who were defeated in November, three were Republicans. One, Lowell Weicker of Connecticut, a three-term Senator, was a maverick liberal Republican highly rated by the ADA who, as a result of his stance on such issues as abortion and civil rights, had actually been endorsed by the AFL-CIO in 1988. This had persuaded disaffected Republican voters to support his more conservative Democrat opponent, Joseph Lieberman. The two other Republican incumbents who also narrowly lost in November 1988, Chic Hecht of Nevada and David Karnes of Nebraska, had both been freshmen – Karnes indeed being an unelected appointee – who found themselves faced by highly popular, high-profile challengers: an incumbent Governor, Richard Bryan, in the case of Nevada and a former State Governor and highly decorated Vietnam veteran and marathon-running amputee, Bob Kerrey, in the case of Nebraska.

The one Democrat incumbent who was defeated in November 1988 was John 'Doc' Melcher of Montana, a lacklustre two-term Senator who had failed to respond to a successful campaign of 'negative ads' launched by his opponent, the popular farm broadcaster Conrad Burns, who became the State's first Republican Senator for 42 years. The remaining 14 Democrat incumbent Senators who stood for re-election in 1988 were successful. They included Lloyd Bentsen, who carried Texas by a 60-40 margin despite the State falling to Bush (by 56% to 43%) in the presidential election.

In the six 'open' Senate contests, however, the Republicans enjoyed a clear edge, winning four overall, including two seats in the South, Florida (Connie Mack, by a margin of barely 0.8%) and Mississippi (Trent Lott), which had previously been Democrat-held and in which, with Bush sweeping these States by margins of more than 20 points, the 'presidential coat-tails' may have had some effect. In contrast, only one formerly Republican-held Senate seat, that of Virginia, which was won by the convincing margin of 71–29 by Charles 'Chuck' Robb, the immensely popular son-in-law of Lyndon Johnson and the former Governor of the State, changed party hands.

The concurrent State-level elections of November 1988 were of unusual importance since, in many cases, those elected were subsequently to be in a position of overseeing the ten-yearly process of Congressional and State 'redistricting' once the results of the 1990 national census had been collated.

Prior to November 1988, the Democrats had held 27 State governorships, controlled both chambers of 28 State legislatures to the Republicans' nine, and had boasted, overall, 4446 State legislature seats to their opponents' 2923. The changes that occurred in these figures after the new elections were limited but were, uniformly, to the Democrats' advantage. In the 12 gubernatorial contests, the Democrats, defending four governorships, gained two States, Indiana and West Virginia, from the Republicans, who, in turn, wrested control of one State, Montana, from their opponents. Elsewhere, eight of the nine incumbent Governors who sought re-election in 1988 were successful, only Arch Moore (R), the three-term Governor of economically ailing West Virginia, being defeated (by Gaston Caperton, a wealthy, pro-business Democrat). In the Statehouse races, the Democrats succeeded in increasing their seat total to 4477 (compared to the Republicans' 2925), retaining charge, following the elections, of both legislative chambers in 28 States. A tied House result in Indiana, however, reduced the Republicans' control of both chambers to only eight States.[15]

Chapter 8

THE BUSH PRESIDENCY, 1989–

The Assembling of the Bush Cabinet Team

With the election of Bush to the presidency in November 1988, the country was to experience its first formal 'transition' within one party since Calvin Coolidge handed over the reins of Federal power to Herbert Hoover in 1929. Unlike Hoover, however, who had merely been the Secretary of Commerce under President Coolidge, Bush, as Vice-President, had been intimately tied to the preceding administration and had fought the presidential election substantially on its record. For these reasons, the new Bush administration had many of the characteristics of a 'Reagan Third Term'. The sudden changes of course and sweeping shake-outs of both senior and junior Federal government personnel that had been prominent features of the Carter and Reagan transitions of 1976–7 and 1980–1 were to be substantially absent in 1988–9. Instead, the transition was to a 'friendly takeover' in which both the outgoing and incoming heads of state worked in an unusually close and co-operative manner.

In overseeing this process, Bush had the benefit of eight years of insider-experience of the 'White House system'. This promised to make the handover of 1988–9 a smooth one. However, in deciding upon his new executive team he was confronted with the problem of arriving at a satisfactory balance between retaining Reagan era 'old hands' and inducting, without unduly ruffling the feathers of those replaced, sufficient enough of his own appointees for a distinctive 'Bush personality' to be stamped upon the new administration. To help Bush in this task, President Reagan, immediately the presidential election of November 1988 was concluded, called upon his own cabinet team to submit their resignations formally, along with more than a thousand of his most senior political appointees. This cleared the way for the President-elect to commence the reconstruction process.

The first to be appointed to the new Bush team was campaign chairman James Baker. who replaced George Shultz as State Department Secretary. The unusually early announcement (on 9 November) of Baker's elevation to this key position was clearly intended to indicate the influential role that Baker would play in the new administration, with a number of commentators suggesting that the new Secretary of State, who was viewed almost as a 'younger brother' to Bush, would serve as an 'unofficial prime minister' or 'deputy president'.

Gradually, as the 'transition' progressed, further positions were filled, resulting, eventually, in the cabinet and White House staff team which is presented in Table 22. It comprised, in all, ten effective 'holdovers' from the Reagan administration, equivalent to more than 40% of the total. The most prominent of these were Nicholas Brady, Dick Thornburgh and William Webster at the heads of the Treasury, Justice Department and CIA respectively. Brady, much of whose career had been spent at the Wall Street investment banking firm of Dillon, Read & Co., was an old tennis-playing friend of both Bush and Baker who, educated at Yale and Harvard Business School and himself the scion of a Irish financial dynasty, was a fellow member of the WASP patriciate. Thornburgh, a former 'Rockefeller Republican' assistant Attorney-General under President Ford in 1976, and a fiscally conservative, but socially liberal, Governor of Pennsylvania between 1979 and 1986, although highly regarded in legal circles as a determined corruption fighter, was not personally close to the new President. His retention as Attorney-General thus marked a break from the practice followed by many recent presidents in appointing political intimates to this position. Similarly, the retention of Webster at the head of the CIA was unusual, most previous President's having similarly chosen to install their 'own man' in this sensitive post. Bush acted, in this regard, against the advice of both conservative Republicans and intelligence insiders who, concerned at the downgrading of external covert operations since 1987, urged the appointment of a more activist director. However, Bush determined upon retaining Webster, for the short term at least, so as to make the point, which in the light of his own sacking on the assumption of the presidency by Carter in 1977 was a peculiarly sensitive and personal one, that CIA directors should not automatically be changed with each new President.

TABLE 22: THE BUSH CABINET IN JUNE 1989

Secretaries

State Dept*	James Baker (59, Texas, ex-Ford and Reagan admins)
Treasury*	Nicholas Brady (59, New York banker, ex-Reagan admin)
Defense*	Dick Cheney (48, Wyoming, ex-Ford admin & Congress)
Attorney-General*	Dick Thornburgh (56, Pennsylvania, ex-Reagan admin)
Interior*	Manuel Lujan (61, New Mexico, ex-Representative 1969–88)
Agriculture*	Clayton Yeutter (58, Nebraska, ex-Reagan admin)
Commerce*	Robert Mosbacher (62, Houston oilman & Bush intimate)
Labor*	Elizabeth Dole (52, North Carolina, ex-Reagan admin)
HUD*	Jack Kemp (53, California & New York, ex-Congress)
Energy*	James Watkins (62, California, ex-naval commander)
Health & Human Services*	Dr Louis Sullivan (55, Georgia, black haematologist)
Education*	Lauro Cavazos (62, Texan Hispanic, ex-Reagan admin)
Transportation*	Samuel Skinner (51, Illinois, head of NE Illinois Regional Transportation Authority since 1984)
Sp Trade Repr*	Carla Hills (55, California-born Washington lawyer, former HUD Secretary in Ford admin 1975–7)
Veterans' Affairs*	Edward Derwinski (62, Illinois, ex-Congress 1959–83)

White House Advisers

Chief-of-Staff	John Sununu (50, ex-Governor of New Hampshire 1982–8)
Dir of OMB*	Richard Darman (46, North Carolina, ex-Reagan admin)
Chmn of CEA*	Michael Boskin (43, Stanford economics professor)
NSA	Lt Gen Brent Scowcroft (64, Utah, ex-Ford admin NSA)
Domestic Policy Adviser	Roger Porter (43, Harvard academic)
Press Secretary	Marlin Fitzwater (46, Kansas, ex-Reagan admin)
National Drug Controller	William Bennett (45, New York, ex-Reagan admin)

Other Senior Officials

Dir of CIA	William Webster (65, ex-Reagan admin & FBI dir)
UN Representative	Thomas Pickering (58, ex-ambassador to Israel)
Head of Environmental Protection Agency (EPA)	William Reilly (49, Illinois, president of the Conservation Foundation since 1973)

* Members of the full cabinet.

All three of these senior officeholders had been in their posts for less than two years, having been appointed, in the wake of 'Irangate', to serve as consensual members of the 'third term' Reagan-Baker administration. Two of them, indeed, Brady and Thornburgh, had only entered the Reagan cabinet in August

1988, during its dying months, and, it is understood, only accepted the posts on the understanding that they would be automatically reappointed if Bush secured the presidency. The same, apparently, was true in the case of Education Secretary Lauro Cavazos, a Texan cattle ranch foreman's son who, with a PhD in physiology, had risen to become dean of Tufts University (Mass) and president of Texas Tech before being inducted into President Reagan's cabinet in September 1988.

The only other 'holdover' from the outgoing Reagan administration who was to retain fully his position following the inauguration of President Bush on 20 January 1989 was press secretary Marlin Fitzwater who, prior to 1987, had been press spokesman for Vice-President Bush since 1985. The other four former Reagan administration 'veterans' were to find their assignments switched: Clayton Yeutter, the owner of a 2500-acre Nebraska farm and the holder of a PhD in agricultural economics, being moved from trade to agriculture and entrusted with the unpopular brief of effecting budget-saving cutbacks in the farm subsidies' programme and of fighting hard to reduce international trade barriers imposed on American farm exports; Elizabeth Dole, despite her husband's evident disappointment at not having been chosen as Bush's vice-presidential running-mate, being attracted back into the cabinet as the new Labor Secretary; Richard Darman, James Baker's former deputy at the Treasury, being given the key brief of director of the OMB; and the forceful neo-conservative William Bennett being selected, instead of, as had been promised during the election campaign, Vice-President Quayle, to fill the special new high-profile co-ordinating post of 'National Drug Czar'.

The remaining places in Bush's first cabinet were distributed almost equally between an inner core of highly experienced Washington insiders and an imaginative assortment of 'freshmen'.

Most prominent among the 'old hands' was the retired air-force Lt-General Brent Scowcroft, a low-profile veteran of Washington's defence and foreign policy establishment who returned to the position of NSA which he had filled with distinction a decade earlier during the last year of the Ford presidency. Scowcroft, a pragmatic conservative, had close links with Henry Kissinger, having recently been vice-chairman of the latter's lucrative, private, New York-based strategic affairs consultancy firm, Kissinger Associates Inc.

Bush had also sought to appoint the equally experienced 'Tower Commission' chairman and acknowledged weapons expert, former Senator John Tower (63), as Defense Secretary. However, the unwavering support given by Tower, when chairman of the Senate's Armed Services Committee between 1981 and 1985, to the Reagan arms build-up and his unduly close recent links, between 1986 and 1988, as a paid consultant to defence contracting firms, bred Congressional doubts as to Tower's future likely impartiality and suitability for the defence portfolio at a time of a 'levelling off' in the department's budget. When to these doubts were added concerns, voiced by both conservative Republicans, including the 'New Right' activist Paul Weyrich, now head of the Free Congress Foundation, and, from the religious right, Pat Robertson, and Democrats, over the personal lifestyle of the twice-divorced Tower – in particular, his excessive fondness for alcohol and alleged 'womanising' – an unstoppable tide of opposition began to mount within the Senate. Despite Tower being 'cleared' in an FBI report and he himself, on 26 February 1989, making a formal pledge of future alcohol abstinence and despite Bush's courting of southern Democrat support (winning Lloyd Bentsen over to his side), such was the strength of Senate feeling that, on 9 March 1989, the President was forced to endure the indignity of witnessing the formal rejection, by 53 votes to 47, of Tower's nomination. This was the first Senate 'veto' of a Federal cabinet appointee since that of Lewis Strauss, Eisenhower's nominee as Commerce Secretary, in 1959, and only the ninth ever.

Bush moved swiftly to repair the damage caused to his standing by Tower's rejection by immediately proposing Dick Cheney, who had served as White House Chief-of-Staff to President Ford between 1975 and 1976 and had been a Congressional Representative for Wyoming since 1979 and the Republican Party's minority whip since January 1989, to take Tower's place as Defense Secretary. Despite Cheney's conservative views on such issues as support for the Nicaraguan Contra guerrillas and for the SDI programme, he secured unanimous Senate endorsement within a week.

The other experienced member of the new Bush cabinet was Jack Kemp, Bush's 1988 nomination contest rival, who was placed at the head of the Housing and Urban Development (HUD) department. A supporter, during the Reagan years, of the deep cuts that were made in the HUD budget, Kemp, who had represented a working-class Buffalo suburb for 18 years, was also known as a 'progressive conservative with a heart' who enjoyed warm relations with the black community and was committed to improving the lot of the inner-city poor. He favoured replacing many government programmes with public-private partnerships and, in particular, was anxious to encourage the sale of public housing to tenants and of providing tax-break inducements to businesses which decide to relocate themselves in new urban 'enterprise zones'.

Among the less experienced new members of the new executive team, perhaps the most controversial choice was that of John Sununu as White House Chief-of-Staff. It had been expected that Bush's campaign Chief-of-Staff Craig Fuller, who had been given charge of the 'transition', would be appointed to this key position. Instead, in a bold move, Bush went outside his 'inner circle'. Sununu, who had been born in Cuba of part Lebanese stock and had been raised in New York, held an MIT doctorate in mechanical engineering and had taught as a professor at Tufts University before becoming Governor of New Hampshire in 1982. As Governor, he had guided his State to prosperity through pursuing a deregulatory, tax-cutting programme. Despite lacking direct Washington experience, Sununu was selected as Chief-of-Staff partly as a 'pay-off' for the tireless and crucial support that he had accorded to Bush's campaign prior to and after the crucial New Hampshire primary in February 1988. His selection was also intended to assuage the party's conservative wing. Early worries were voiced, however, over Sununu's selection to such a sensitive organisational and presentational post because his record in New Hampshire exhibited him to be an unduly assertive figure, with a brusque manner reminiscent in many respects of that of Donald Regan. A Texan, Fred McClure, who also lacked Washington experience, was appointed to work closely with Sununu, serving, as head of legislative affairs, as his bridge with Congress, while the New Englander, Andrew Card, was selected to serve as Sununu's approachable deputy.

Another 'freshman' to the cabinet, Dr Louis Sullivan, the new Health and Human Services Secretary, was a controversial choice among Republican right-wingers as a result of his recently expressed support for a woman's right to have an abortion. He was, however, a personal friend of the Bush family, having worked closely with the President's wife, Barbara, on the board of the Morehouse School of Medicine, of which he was president. Three of the other 'freshman' cabinet members, Transportation Secretary Skinner, who had headed Bush's presidential campaign in Illinois during 1988, Commerce Secretary Mosbacher, a longstanding Texan yachting friend of the President who had been in charge of the campaign's fund-raising (as he had also done in 1980 and, for Ford, in 1976), and Edward Derwinksi, the Secretary of the Veterans' Affairs department, which was upgraded, from March 1989, to cabinet rank, who had been a colleague of Bush's in the House of Representatives during the late 1960s, also owed their appointments to personal ties.

In its overall profile, the new Bush executive team was a notably experienced one, almost two-thirds of its members having recent direct Washington executive experience, and the cabinet's average age, 57 years, was three years above that of Reagan's cabinets of 1981 and 1985. In its social complexion, it was strikingly patrician, being dominated by members of the country's traditional, Ivy League-educated WASP landed and monied élite, in marked contrast to the self-made millionaire parvenus who had been so prominent during the early Reagan years. Finally, geographically, it was, by the standards at least of the preceding early Carter and Reagan administrations, unusually broadly based. These attributes were reflective of Bush's much expressed determination that, once elected, he would fill his government not, as his predecessors had, to a considerable extent, done with members drawn from his campaign team, but with 'professionals' with specialist administrative skills, pledging to bring into government, in Bush's words, 'the best people'. The absence of a strong regional clique in the early cabinet – although, of course, a strong Texan element was evident – was, moreover, reflective of the fact that, unlike Carter and Reagan, Bush came to the presidency without prior experience of governing at the State level and and had thus not had the opportunity of building up his own ready-made administrative team. To this extent, the Bush presidency constituted a partial return to the pre-Carter era.

In its political hue, the Bush cabinet, being dominated by policy pragmatists in such key positions as the State Department, NSA, Defense, Treasury and OMB, had a distinct mainstream Republican, centre-right, bias. The inclusion of only a sprinkling of conservatives, in the form of Bennett, Kemp and Sununu, as well as Vice-President Quayle, was to lead to the early alienation of many 'New Right' Republicans, who were to denounce the new cabinet as an 'establishment team' dominated by 'Wall Street' Rockefeller Republicans.

Domestically, in the economic and fiscal affairs spheres, the key policy-framing strategists in the new administration were to be Treasury Secretary Brady, OMB Director Darman and CEA Chairman Boskin. However, it was also made clear that State Department Secretary Baker would continue to provide advice on international monetary and commercial issues. In the social policy sphere, HUD Secretary Kemp, 'Drug Czar' Bennett and Education Secretary Cavazos, were to be the most prominent actors, with Chief-of-Staff Sununu also taking a special interest in this area and additional input being provided by Domestic Policy Adviser Roger Porter, a long-time tennis partner of the President and former Harvard professor of government who was the author of the work, *Presidential Decision-Making*. For more general strategy advice, Bush was to rely on an 'inner cabinet' of trusted friends and advisers which embraced Baker, Brady and Mosbacher. In addition, from the summer of 1989 onwards, Bennett, Darman, Kemp, Quayle and Sununu (the 'forward strategy group') began to hold special biweekly working breakfasts together. Here, long-term policy goals were charted.

Leadership Changes in the New 101st Congress

The newly elected 101st Congress with which the new President needed to work differed little in personnel from the outgoing 100th, containing, as it did, a record low for the postwar period of only 44 freshmen/women and being the most senior, in terms of average age (see Appendix Table D4) since 1971. Nevertheless, despite this broad continuity, the retirement of several senior Congressmen, coupled, subsequently, during the early months of 1989 by the irruption of a series of ethics scandals which were to force the resignation of prominent Democrats, contributed to a significant reshuffling of the pack of those holding party leadership and committee chair positions.

In the case of the Senate, an early notable change in Democrat leadership ranks was made necessary by the decision of Robert Byrd to step down from his long-held position as Majority Leader in order, instead, to take over the two influential positions of President Pro Tempore and chairman of the Appropriations Committee which had been made available through the recent retirement of John Stennis, the veteran former Senator for Mississippi (1947–89). Byrd's relinquishment of the party's Senate leadership opened the way for a three-way succession struggle between Daniel Inouye (Hawaii), J Bennett Johnston (La) and George Mitchell (Me), in what was the first formally contested election for this position since 1937 (previously selection had been through private consensus, with the party's committee chairmen meeting as a 'College of Cardinals').

Inouye (64), a liberal veteran of the Watergate and 'Irangate' investigative committees, was the most senior and experienced of the three contestants, having been first elected to the chamber in 1962. Mitchell (55), a protégé of Edmund Muskie who had entered the Senate as recently as 1980, was the most junior. In between stood Johnston (56), a centrist southerner chairman of the Energy and Natural Resources Committee, who had been first elected in 1970 and was the most conservative in outlook. Being supported by the overwhelming majority of his 14 fellow southern Senators, including Bentsen, Gore and Nunn, he was also viewed as the clear favourite to succeed Byrd.

Surprisingly, however, in the secret caucus which was held on 29 November 1988, it was Mitchell who was comfortably elected by 27 votes compared to 14 for each of his two rivals. He had impressed his colleagues with both his work on the committees dealing with tax reform and 'Irangate' during 1986–7[1] and with his fund-raising and campaigning abilities, as chairman of the Democratic Senatorial Campaign Committee, during the 1986 midterm election and proved able to attract to his banner a broad coalition of northern centrists (including Bradley and Glenn) and liberals (including Kennedy and Simon), 'New South' reformists (Fowler, Graham, Robb and Sanford of Georgia, Florida, Virginia and North Carolina respectively), western environmentalists (as a result of his concern with the issue of acid rain) and most of the young freshmen/women intake of 1986 and 1988.

Mitchell's selection provided the Democrats with a Senate leader who, potentially, promised to be a far more televisually skilled communicator and more policy-orientated principal than the, hesitant, traditionalist, proceduralist Byrd. In addition, in political terms, his accession promised to herald a slight leftward shift in the Democrat leadership's ideological balance, Mitchell boasting ADA (liberal) and ACU (conservative) ratings in the 1988 session of the Senate of 95% and 8% respectively to Byrd's 70% and 23%.

Immediately upon his election, Mitchell magnanimously broke with precedent and announced that, unlike his immediate predecessors, Byrd, Mansfield and Johnson, he would not also assume the post of chairman of the Democrat Steering Committee, the body which is responsible for assigning Democrats to committees, but, instead, would confer it upon Inouye. Mitchell also decided to break with tradition and share leadership of the agenda-setting Democratic Policy Committee with Thomas Daschle (SD), one of his supporters in the November leadership contest. Inouye's promotion automatically opened a vacancy for the position of Secretary of the Democratic Conference. This was filled, following an unsuccessful election challenge by Patrick Leahy (Vt), by David Pryor (Ark), a centrist southerner. The change meant that, of the Democrats' top five leadership posts in the Senate, only the occupant of that of Majority Whip remained unchanged, this position being filled, for a record seventh term, by Alan Cranston (Calif). In marked contrast, the Republicans returned a Senate leadership which, headed by Minority Leader Robert Dole (Kan) and Minority Whip Alan Simpson (Wy) was (see Appendix Table D1) identical to that of the preceding Congress.

In the House of Representatives, changes in the Democrats' leadership ranks were, initially at least, far more limited than in the Senate. The party's three most senior officeholders, House Speaker Jim Wright (Tex), Majority Floor Leader Thomas Foley (Wash) and Majority Whip Tony Coelho (Calif) were each comfortably re-elected and it was at the leadership rung below, that of Chairman of the Democratic Conference, that change was evident, with the black Baptist minister William Gray (Pa) replacing Richard Gephardt (Mo) in this position, Gephardt being debarred from standing for re-election due to a two-term limit that had been set on this post by party rules. For the Republicans, the turnover in leadership positions was greater. Robert Michel (Ill) remained in place for a fifth term as Minority Leader, but, following the successful election of Trent Lott (Miss) to the Senate, a vacancy was opened for the post of Minority Whip. This, in January 1989, was filled by Dick Cheney (Wy). However, in March 1989 Cheney left to become Defense Secretary and Newt Gingrich, a controversial ultra-conservative Representative from Georgia, was narrowly elected as his successor. The other top-level Republican House leadership change was in the Chair of the Republican Conference, which, having been vacated by Jack Kemp, was filled by Jerry Lewis of California following a close, 85–82 vote, election contest with Lynn Martin (Ill).

At the standing committee level, 6 of the House's 22 chairs (see Appendix Table D6) also changed hands as a result, variously of the retirement, death or switch of position of the incumbents. The three most significant changes were the replacement of the retired Peter Rodino (NJ) with Jack Brooks (Tex), of William Gray (Pa) by Leon Panetta (Calif), and of Claude Pepper (Fla), who died in June 1989, by Joe Moakley (Mass), at the head of the Judiciary, Budget and Rules committees respectively. Panetta's promotion raised to eight the number of standing and select committees that the Democrats' 27 Representatives from the State of California chaired.

The most dramatic change in House leadership ranks was to occur, however, midway through Congress's 1989 session when, unexpectedly, on 26 and 31 May respectively, Majority Whip Coelho and House Speaker Wright tendered their resignations as a result of ethics scandals.

Concern over Wright's ethical conduct had been longstanding, the House Speaker having been under investigation for almost a year by a 12-member bipartisan Committee on Standards of Official Conduct (CSOC), headed by a specially hired outside attorney, following allegations that, over a ten-year period, he had derived more than $400000 in undeclared cash and gifts, including the rent-free use of a Fort Worth flat and an $18000 per annum 'no show' job for his wife Betty, from George Mallick, a property-developer friend, despite having a direct interest in related legislation that was before the House. Wright was also accused of having infringed Congressional rules by using bulk sales, both at political rallies and to lobbyists at the unusually high royalty rate of 55%, of his autobiography, *Reflections of a Public Man*, to circumvent limits that had been placed on the receipt of income from supporters and friends. During 1988–9, Republicans, smarting from 'Irangate' and the Deaver and Meese 'sleaze scandals', had sought to make hay out of the charges made against Wright. However, the Speaker proved able to successfully brush them aside until, on 17 April 1989, the CSOC voted unanimously that grounds existed for the bringing of charges against Wright on the count of 69 apparent violations of House rules on personal finances. With the party's national standing being seriously damaged by the affair, Wright finally decided at the end of May to bow to the inevitable and formally tender his resignation from Congress. He was, historically, the fourth Speaker to resign from his position, but the first-ever to be forced out as a result of charges of alleged misconduct.[2]

With Republicans, led zealously by Newt Gingrich, baying for additional blood and seeking retribution for their party's Tower nomination humiliation, Wright's young high-flying six-term colleague and PAC fund-raising mastermind, Tony Coelho, similarly fell victim to the new ethical 'high moralism' that, in the wake of the Hart, Biden, Ginsburg and Tower affairs, appeared, politically, to be sweeping the nation during 1988–9. Accused of illegally securing, through access to 'inside information', a $6800 profit from $100000 of 'junk bonds' bought for him by a friend who stood to benefit from legislation that was before the House, Coelho was threatened with a similar Ethics Committee investigation to that which Wright had undergone. Unwilling to endure such an inquiry, he chose, instead, to resign from Congress, terminating a promising career.

The dual resignations of the combative Wright and Coelho were an obvious blow to the Democrats. However, the damage was surprisingly swiftly repaired. In the special caucus elections held on 6 June 1989 the highly respected Thomas Foley was promoted to the position of Speaker, while William Gray and Steny Hoyer (Md) both also moved up a rung to become Majority Whip and chairman of the Democratic Conference respectively. Completing the new leadership team, the unsuccessful presidential contender Richard Gephardt moved to second position in the party's House hierarchy, being comfortably elected to succeed Foley as the new Majority Floor Leader.

Bush's Relations with Congress

George Bush was the first newly elected President since Richard Nixon in 1969, and only the second ever, to be faced with a Congress in which both chambers were under opposition control. On paper, moreover, Bush's position was considerably less favourable than Nixon's both in terms of the size of the Democrats' respective House majorities (51 seats in 1969 and 85 in 1989) and the fact that whereas the Republican Party had made advances in the Congressional elections of November 1968, it actually lost ground in November 1988. This had left Bush with the weakest aggregate base of party support in Congress of any new administration in American history. When added to this was the general anger felt by Democrats at the negative manner in which Bush's 1988 presidential campaign had been conducted, it was not surprising that many observers predicted that the new President would find it unusually difficult to forge good working relations with and support from Congress for his future legislative proposals and that, instead, lacking a genuine 'mandate', he would be forced to battle with Capitol Hill for control over the national legislative agenda.

Bush's own concern at the possible difficulties in working with Congress that lay ahead were made readily apparent in his post-election address of 9 November 1988. In it, he appealed for a slate-cleaning 'healing' of relations and made clear his desire to seek to forge a 'constructive partnership' with Congress, declaring that: 'The American people are wonderful at understanding that when a campaign ends business begins.' He followed this up by moving swiftly to try to mend broken fences in a series of early meetings with Congressional leaders from both parties, including Senate Minority Leader Dole, who had been enraged by the lack of support that the Bush campaign had accorded to Republican candidates fighting marginal seats in November. In his inauguration address in January 1989, Bush again repeated his call for co-operation, particularly in the budgetary sphere. Declaring that, 'the American people didn't send us here to bicker', he set as his goal a resumption of 'the old bipartisanship' which had characterised American politics during the two decades prior to the Vietnam War.

This dream of bipartisanship seemed far-fetched during the early months of 1989 as Congress became starkly divided down party lines over the Tower nomination and Wright and Coelho ethics issues. However, the moderate tone of the cabinet team that was appointed by Bush and the fact that it included several renowned liaisers, most notably Baker and Darman, and four recent former Congressmen, Cheney, Kemp, Lujan and Derwinski, held out the promise that, once the initial post-election party point-scoring battles had been concluded, a more constructive working partnership than had been apparent during the Reagan presidency might potentially be established. Such hopes gained further sustenance from the elevation, in June 1989, of Thomas Foley to the Speaker's chair: Foley, a more consensus-minded politician than his predecessor Wright, being anxious to bring an end to the 'mindless cannibalism' of the 'ethics war' of the spring of 1989 and to improve the lines of communication with his Republican opponents.

Bush's Governing Style

During both the transition period and the first year of his presidency, Bush worked assiduously to cultivate his own distinctive style of leadership. It was to be a style which differed significantly from that of his two immediate predecessors.

In contrast to President Reagan, Bush sought to project an image of vigorous 'hands on' leadership. During the transition, 'media events' were specifically arranged to exhibit the President-elect as a 'man of action', jogging, fishing, shooting, sailing, swimming, pitching horseshoes and playing tennis and golf with close colleagues, almost in the manner of a pentathlete. Once in power, the new President, in contrast to his carefully scheduled 9-to-5 predecessor, made the point of beginning his working day far earlier, commencing around 7 a.m. with a special CIA briefing and hour-long 'action items' meeting with Sununu and running on late into the evening, to 7 p.m. or beyond. Described, like Carter, as a 'sponge for detail', particularly with respect to foreign affairs, Bush called for a replacement of the 'mini-memo' briefing papers used during the Reagan presidency with 'backgrounders' of up to five pages in length, and sometimes more; encouraged aides and cabinet Secretaries, instead of separately lobbying for their preferred options, to 'think out' the pros and cons of contentious issues in staged open debates during which he would take copious notes and intervene with pertinent questions; and, finally, on occasions, the President would, without informing the interested cabinet Secretary, unilaterally reach down into the Federal bureaucracy to pick the brains of lesser staffers on specific items.

As well as being a much more active leader, Bush also differed from his predecessor Reagan in his projection of a spontaneously open and accessible public image. A small early indication of this was the promotion of the President's self-deprecating, matronly wife, Barbara (1925–   ), as a far more down-to-earth First Lady than her fashion-conscious predecessor, Nancy Reagan. More substantively, the new President accorded greater access to the media than his cocooned predecessor, holding, for example, 33 official press conferences during his first year in office compared with the mere five that had been granted by Reagan in 1981. In these press conferences, moreover, Bush, evidently possessed of a firmer grasp of the subjects in hand, also proved willing to depart from his brief and make additional off-the-cuff comments to questions put. Bush was less adept at scripted, staged speeches or at delivering the weekly Saturday afternoon radio broadcast to the nation that had been distinctive features of the Reagan presidency. These were now to be largely discontinued. Under the direction of White House image-meister Steve Studdert, Bush, instead, made a deliberate effort to develop close personal relations with individual journalists, flattering them with invitations to off-the-record dinners and calling them by their first names at press conferences. Similarly, he maintained regular close personal telephone contact with an extensive private network of political and business friends, Congressmen and overseas allies. Through such means, the President hoped to establish the aura of an engaging, as well as an engaged, chief executive.

In many of these respects, the new administration represented a return to the greater openness and informality that had characterised the Ford and Carter presidencies, while Bush's personal press diplomacy and grant of privileged access to new stories revived memories of the Kennedy and Johnson eras. However, concealed from public view, there also existed within the outwardly open Bush presidency an intensely secretive and manipulative 'inner presidency', the existence of which became increasingly apparent as Bush's first year in office progressed. This 'secret presidency' had, perhaps, its closest parallel in the reclusive Nixon presidency and was in keeping with the known character and past executive (CIA) experience of the new President. In particular, Bush, who had been appalled by the cabinet 'leaks' and publicised rifts between competitive colleagues that had characterised the Carter and Reagan presidencies, came to office determined to run a 'tight ship' and in constructing his executive team had made personal loyalty and team-playing qualities key criteria. Once appointed, he proceeded to work with his advisers and departmental Secretaries in small, compartmentalised teams, with oaths of secrecy being taken over key decisions made. Through such means, Bush was able to ensure that he retained firm top-down personal control over major executive initiatives and that, also, an element of surprise – as seen most clearly in the invasion of Panama in December 1989 – was maintained.

Policy Initiatives During Bush's First Year

On assuming the presidency in January 1989, Bush, like his predecessor in 1981, was presented by the Heritage Foundation with a new, updated version of 'Mandate for Leadership', setting out in clear policy form the conservative agenda which the 'New Right' wished to see implemented. However, to a far greater degree than Reagan in 1981, Bush made a deliberate choice effectively to ignore such partisan policy prescriptions and, instead, set his sights upon laying the ground for a pragmatic, consensual administration which, whilst seeking to consolidate and build upon achievements of the Reagan years and, on occasions, willing to make symbolic supportive gestures to the 'moral right', would also seek to remedy some of the most obvious defects and casualties in the economic and social spheres of the Reagan decade. The new President lacked an overarching vision of the new society which he wished to help mould. Instead, he set for himself the more modest dual goals of good 'reactive government', dealing competently with problems in both the domestic and foreign affairs spheres as they suddenly and unexpectedly arose, and, in a more general, medium-term manner, of pursuing a policy course of 'Reaganism with a heart', setting for himself, in his inauguration address of January 1989, a dutiful goal: 'It is to make kinder the face of our nation and gentler the face of the world.'

As a 'reactive' chief executive, the new President exhibited an impressive, and unexpected, streak of decisiveness. This was particularly evident in his handling of crises overseas, the two most striking during 1989 being the US military interventions in the Philippines and Panama ('Operation Just Cause') in December 1989 (see Part 6). Domestically, the new President proved much slower to react to the pollution disaster, the worst ever of its kind, along 350 miles of Alaska's coastline caused by a major oil spill from the grounded supertanker *Exxon Valdez* in March–April 1989. However, his Treasury Secretary Brady did move quickly in February 1989 to put together a $50 billion bail-out package to rescue the country's ailing savings and loans (building societies/thrifts) institutions, which, with many overextended, had been threatened with a calamitous collapse.

However, the most important immediate domestic problem which faced the new President was, as had been the case for Reagan since 1984, that of the continued dangerously great size of both the national trade and, in particular, the Federal budget deficits. In attempting to tackle the latter, which had served to paralyse seriously decision-making both by the White House and Capitol Hill, Bush was encumbered by daunting constraints imposed both by the rhetoric of his campaign and by the realities of power in Washington. This rendered a speedy solution a remote prospect.

Bush and the Federal Budget Deficit in 1989

The November 1987 two-year bipartisan agreement between the White House and Congress on spending economies had bought a temporary respite to the Federal budget deficit crisis and had enabled the meat-cleaver of GRH, which had been invoked in 1986 to impose cross-board cuts of $11.7 billion, to be averted during 1987 and 1988. However, by the autumn of 1988 it had become apparent once more that any improvement that had occurred in the Federal budget situation during these two years was, at best, minimal and, at worst, illusory, owing more both to unexpectedly buoyant economic growth and to the skilful manipulation of the loopholes that existed in GRH than to the achievement of real budgetary economies. This was made clear by the budget record of fiscal 1989 (1 October 1988 – 30 September 1989). For this year, the OMB had forecast a deficit of $145 billion, which was within the accepted +$10 billion overshoot range of the GRH target of $136 billion for that period. The necessity for statutory cuts was thus averted. In reality, however, as other outside analysts, including the non-partisan CBO, had foreseen, the true deficit for fiscal 1989 was actually to reach $165 billion: a figure 6% above the previous year's total.

George Bush's election to the presidency in November 1988 was, despite his pro-business background, treated with deep unease by the financial markets who feared, both because of his oft-repeated campaign pledge, 'Read my lips. No new taxes', and his lack of a Congressional majority, that the deficit crisis might well worsen, with the increasingly exacting GRH deficit targets of $100 billion in fiscal 1990, $64 billion in fiscal 1991, $28 billion in fiscal 1992 and a balanced budget in fiscal 1993 failing to be attained. Reflecting this sense of foreboding, during November and December 1988 Wall Street endured the sharpest post-election slump in share values since the election of Truman in

1948. The currency market was also affected, forcing Greenspan, at the head of the Federal Reserve, to raise interest rates.

During his presidential campaign, Bush had set out his strategy for reaching such deficit targets, while at the same time upholding his other campaign pledges of reducing the level of the capital gains tax from 28% to 15%, of not raising the level of other taxes and of increasing social expenditure in several specially targeted areas, most notably education, child care provision, AIDS research and the campaign against drug addiction. This grand strategy, termed the 'flexible freeze', had been devised by CEA chairman Michael Boskin. It entailed the offsetting of increased spending on specially targeted social programmes by the securing of compensating economies elsewhere in the domestic budget, with cutbacks in the agricultural support, social security and Medicare programmes, combined with receipts from privatisations, being the preferred options. In the case of spending in other budgetary areas, such as defence, the 'Boskin Plan' envisaged a status quo freeze. On the revenue side, the plan also, crucially, anticipated a steady rise in receipts based on the assumption that GNP growth would continue at an annual rate of more than 3%, economic activity being stimulated, it was hoped, by concomitant reductions in the level of interest rates.

On paper, this 'flexible freeze' strategy promised a relatively painless solution to the nation's budgetary problems and one which allowed the new President to remain true to his campaign pledges. However, it was a strategy which relied on forecasts of economic growth which, in the opinion of most 'mainstream economists', were unduly optimistic and whose proposed balance of budgetary economies was likely to be fiercely contested by the Democrat-controlled Congress. For both these reasons, the 'flexible freeze', in its pristine form, appeared, to most sober analysts, to be unrealistic as a practical solution to the deficit crisis. Nevertheless, with its mix of spending increases in a number of social programmes combined with defence outlay restraint, it constituted, for congressional Democrats, some advance, at least, on the highly partisan budgetary proposals that had been proffered by the Reagan administration since 1984. Moreover, as President Bush stressed, when, on 9 February 1989, he presented his first draft budget request for fiscal 1990 to Congress, it represented a basis for debate, bargaining and negotiation, constituting, he hoped, the starting point for the framing of a compromise bipartisan agreement.

176

This initial draft budget projected, on the basis of a bullish economic forecast, a Federal budget deficit of $94.8 billion for fiscal 1990, one which was well within the GRH limit. It envisaged new spending of $7.5 billion on child care, drug control, education, homeless and nuclear safety programmes, to be more than counterbalanced by proposed cuts of $9.1 billion in the Medicare and Federal health benefits programme and of $10.5 billion in the Agriculture Department's budget. In addition, defence expenditure was to be frozen in real terms, instead of rising by 2% as the departing Reagan administration had demanded. However, the Democrats in Congress, while reacting warmly to the conciliatory tone of Bush's budget address, voiced concern that the President's targeted social spending increases were inadequate, being over-reliant on tax-induced private initiatives, as well as strong opposition to his proposals to lower the capital gains tax and to cut the Medicare budget. Democrats were, secondly, suspicious as to the lack of specificity in the draft budget with respect to economies, fearing that, while seeking to monopolise credit for his education, child care and drugs initiatives, the President sought to transfer to Congress blame for the less popular cutbacks. In addition, more fundamentally, a number of traditional liberal Democrats, led by House Ways and Means Committee chairman Dan Rostenkowski, viewed Bush's 'flexible freeze' as a fatally flawed scheme, viewing the administration's agreement to some form of tax increase, whether direct or indirect, as ultimately essential if the budget problem was to be truly tackled and domestic social programmes 'saved'.

During the spring of 1989, both sides, the administration and Congress, remained, in public, firm in their stances of entrenched opposition to, for the former, new taxes and, for the latter, retrenchment in the social budget. However, behind the scenes an air of compromise was evident, with OMB Director Darman, who, it was asserted, nurtured dreams of effecting a far-reaching, consensual, deficit-solving 'Grand Agreement' in 1989 or at latest 1990, declaring his willingness to negotiate flexibly with Congressional budget leaders in talks in which all issues, including that of tax increases, would be 'on the table'. These negotiations, which commenced on 13 February 1989, bore initial early fruit in April 1989 when, ahead of schedule, both sides accepted the broad outlines of a bipartisan budget agreement for fiscal 1990. The major concession made in this compact on the part of the administration was a $10 billion cut in the defence budget in fiscal 1990, forming part of a broader five-year cost-cutting programme in this sphere. In exchange, Congress agreed not to press for any specific new tax increases and accepted some small economies in the Medicare budget.

In the summer and early autumn of 1989 work commenced on turning this budget accord into a formal omnibus budget-reconciliation bill. However, in these new negotiations the bipartisanship that had been evident during the spring foundered over the issue of reduction of the capital gains tax (whose level had been raised as part of the 1986 tax reform bill) to which the administration was committed. Republican and conservative, especially southern, Democrat Congressmen supported such a move as likely to encourage business investment. However, centrist and liberal Democrats, under the populist lead of House Majority Floor Leader Gephardt, implacably opposed it as a class-biased measure, promising as it did to transfer further resources to the already most privileged in society. On 28 September 1989, the Bush administration secured a significant House victory when 64 Democrats, headed by Ed Jenkins (Ga), after rejecting a Foley-Gephardt-sponsored amendment which had sought instead to raise the level of taxes paid by the nation's top 600000 earners, switched sides to provide the necessary victory margin for the approval of a temporary two-year cut in the capital gains tax rate from 28% to 19.6%. This tax cut was then duly included in a budget reconciliation bill which was passed by 333 votes to 91 on 5 October. In the Senate, however, the budget reconciliation bill, which was passed by a voice vote, after bipartisan agreement on 13 October, included no such provision for a capital gains tax reduction since Majority Leader Mitchell had promised to filibuster any such measure. A mammoth 332-member Congressional conference committee was immediately established to attempt to reconcile the obvious differences between the House and Senate bills. However, it failed to reach an agreement before the annual budget deadline of 16 October was reached. As a consequence, the GRH cleaver mechanism was automatically triggered and statutory across-the-board cuts of $16.1 million, half in the defence budget and half in the 'non-exempt' domestic programme, were ordered.

Eventually, on 22 November 1989, immediately prior to its Christmas adjournment, Congress passed, and the President approved, a compromise $14.7 billion deficit reduction bill which provided for a budget deficit for fiscal 1990 of $105 billion, a figure below the GRH ceiling. This compromise settlement was achieved following a decision by the President, on 2 November, to abandon his insistence that a capital gains tax reduction should be included. In return, Congress gave ground by agreeing not to demand the imposition of any new taxes or 'user fees' and also to accept some small cutbacks in the Medicare and agricultural support payments programmes. However, the bulk of the budget 'economies' that were achieved in the 1989 budget deal were illusory or mere paper entities, being derived, as in 1988, from creative accounting devices and from the OMB's adoption of a typically sanguine growth forecast. For the latter reason, outside unofficial forecasting bodies predicted that, despite US GNP continuing to increase by 2.9% during 1989 and the unemployment level remaining as low as 5.4%, the true deficit for fiscal 1990 was likely to exceed $140 billion.

With the passage of this compromise deficit reduction bill in late November 1989, Congress and the administration were able to secure the lifting, in February 1990, of the automatic GRH cuts that had been triggered in October 1989 ($4.6 billion of cuts were, in fact, however, kept and included in the final deficit reduction bill). Both parties had secured another escape from the act's unpalatable clutches for a further year without a serious loss of face or credibility. For this reason, the Bush administration was pleased with the outcome of their first year of budget negotiations, terming the finally agreed budget reconciliation bill an 'excellent' package. However, with the deficit limits set by GRH becoming progressively narrower between fiscal 1991 and 1993, it appeared that both sides were beginning to run out of 'easy options' for the achievement of its targets. In the ensuing years, the budget battle promised to intensify, with pressure for 'real solutions' likely to mount and, in particular, for the administration, notwithstanding further proposed defence economies, to give ground with respect to its stance on the issue of 'revenue enhancement'.

'A Kinder, Gentler Nation': Social and Environmental Initiatives in 1989

Outside the budget arena, Bush's other chief domestic priorities during 1989, in keeping with his goal of fostering a 'kinder, gentler nation', were in the social and environmental spheres, with new initiatives being launched to improve the standard of education and provision of child care facilities, and to combat drug addiction, the rising level of crime, the 'national shame' of homelessness, particularly the young homeless, and environmental pollution.

Having voiced a desire to establish himself as the 'education President', Bush convened, in September 1989, a special two-day summit with the nation's 50 State Governors, only the third such meeting of its kind in US history, at the University of Virginia at which broad nationwide targets for literacy, scientific and mathematical knowledge and for reducing dropout rates were agreed upon. In his budget plan, he had also earlier sanctioned the grant of special cash 'merit' awards to effective schools and teachers. Second, Bush, also in September 1989, unveiled, in a national television address, the outlines of a New National Drug Control Strategy which entailed the spending of $7.9 billion on combating drugs trafficking, constructing new prisons and expanding drugs education and treatment programmes with the goal of curbing US drug consumption by 50% within ten years. Third, in a policy address to Congress on 12 June 1989, he launched his ambitious anti-pollution campaign. This involved, at the cost of $14–19 billion – which was to be shared by industry and consumers – a fundamental revision and tightening up of the provisions of the 1970 Clean-Air Act, with the aim, during the course of the 1990s, of slashing by 40–50% the hydrocarbon and acid-rain-producing sulphur-dioxide emissions of motor-vehicles and power stations. In addition, he made clear his intention to upgrade, during 1990, the EPA into a new cabinet-ranking department.

Other more reactive initiatives were also taken by Bush during 1989 to deal with the issues, raised by the Deaver, Meese, Tower and Wright affairs, of ethics in government – the rules for lobbying by former Federal officials being tightened and honoria speaking engagement payments to Congressmen being phased out – and election campaign finance and, following Secretary Kemp's uncovering of an unseemly web of mismanagement, embezzlement and corruption during the Reagan presidency (involving the loss to the taxpayer of between $4 and 8 billion), to improve the operational efficiency of the HUD.

However, in many of these areas Bush was faced with a Democrat-controlled Congress which was also interested in these subjects – indeed, saw them as its own – and which favoured alternative conflicting or more extensive, and expensive, solutions. For this reason, a number of Bush's initiatives, as was the case with that of campaign finance reform, foundered, while other decisions, including those on clean air, housing and child care, had to be shelved until 1990 as a result of a shortage of time in a Congressional session that had been unduly preoccupied with internal scandals, confirmation hearings and budgetary wranglings. The President was, however, able to counter such challenges by Congress by successfully vetoing a number of cherished measures which figured highly on the Democrats' 1989 legislative agenda, most notably a proposed bill to raise the national minimum wage from $3.35 (a level at which it had been frozen since 1981) to $4.55 per hour which Bush publicly vetoed on 13 June 1989, while aboard Air Force One. (Later in the year a compromise rise to $4.25 per hour was enacted). Bush followed up this, his first, veto, by also subsequently striking down a series of appropriations bills (HUD, Washington DC and Foreign Aid) during October and November 1989 which included within them provision for the use of Federal funds for abortions in circumstances other than those of maternal risk. These actions were symbolic, being designed in the wake of the Supreme Court's July 1989 *Webster v. Reproductive Health Services* verdict (see above p. 116) to exhibit his personal support for the New Right's anti-abortion cause. In attempting to assuage his sceptical conservative supporters, Bush also announced, in May 1989, that in future the first Thursday in May would be annually celebrated as a 'National Day of Prayer' – it had previously been only periodically recognised as such since its first proclamation in 1775 – and pressed, between July and October 1989, though unsuccessfully, for Congress to support a constitutional amendment which would outlaw desecration of the US flag.

An Assessment of Bush's First Year in Office

Bush's first year as President commenced in a surprisingly uncertain manner considering the fact that the 'presidential transition' of 1988–9 had been only a partial one, involving the retention in office of several key departmental Secretaries, including the Treasury and Justice, and that Bush himself had had many years to prepare for this power handover. However, instead of 'hitting the ground running' and unveiling his key legislative priorities during his first 100 'honeymoon' days in office, as Reagan had successfully done in 1981, Bush's initial three months in office were enveloped in the embarrassing wrangling with Congress over the, ultimately unsuccessful, Tower nomination, with dealing with the ad hoc thrifts' crisis issue and with the launching of a 'grand review' of defence and foreign policy strategy (see Part 6) which effectively prevented the administration from responding positively to developments overseas until the summer of 1989.

However, despite this inauspicious beginning and the partisan passions that were to be inflamed in Congress by, first, the Tower and then the Wright-Coelho affairs, by the close of his first year in office, Bush had established a reputation for surprisingly effective, decisive and popular leadership, boasting a public approval rating at the year's end which, at almost 80%, was between 17 and 25% in excess of that recorded for either President Carter or President Reagan at the corresponding period and even in excess of the ratings recorded by Presidents Truman, Kennedy and Johnson. Much of this popularity, however, was derived from the President's initiatives in the external sphere, rather than at home, and, moreover, much of his success abroad derived from favourable external developments – the collapse of communism – over which Washington had limited real influence. Bush did, however, work sensibly with such outside developments, pledging, for example – though under Congressional urging – the provision of substantial amounts of American economic aid to help sustain the process of liberalisation in Poland and Hungary, and unveiling imaginative plans, in July 1989 and February 1990, for substantial cutbacks in the conventional forces' strength of NATO. Moreover, in his actions in the Philippines and Panama in December 1989 Bush exhibited a decisiveness in his willingness to deploy US military might which appeared to be even greater than that of his strong-minded predecessor.

Bush's predilection for initiatives overseas was partly influenced by his own special interest and expertise in this policy sphere. It was also, however, reflective of the fact that success appeared easier to achieve in this area than at home, where, because of the budget deficit and balance of Congressional forces, many of the problems appeared intractable. Indeed, prior to the presidential election of 1988 Bush had remarked to one of his aides that, in the light of such domestic difficulties, 'I think I'm going to be the foreign policy president'. This prediction, although intended as a joke, proved remarkably accurate for 1989 at least.

However, even domestically, Bush's first year in office, while it was by no means striking, was, considering the Congressional odds he faced and fiscal difficulties, not as unsuccessful as might have been anticipated in the immediate wake of the acrimonious presidential campaign of August–November 1988. The wounds opened during that campaign, and during the subsequent Tower, Wright and Coelho struggles, were surprisingly swiftly healed once the Democrats' new House leadership was installed in June 1989, with a sense of consensual give-and-take being evident on the part of both sides in the ensuing budget battle. This enabled a compromise, though fudged, deficit-cutting reconciliation bill to be eventually approved in November 1989.

In its general approach to domestic, economic and social issues, the new Bush administration, much to the chagrin of New Right conservative activists, was to be characterised by a studied pragmatism and belief in the efficacy of a more activist government. This contrasted starkly with the rhetoric of the Reagan era for whom, in the words of the President's 1981 inaugural address, 'Government is not the solution to our problem: government is the problem.' In its management of the economy, mainstream conservatism had triumphed over supply-side radicalism – except with regard to the capital gains tax – and untrammelled deregulation, with, for example, new life being breathed into the Occupational Safety and Health Administration (OSHA) which had been deliberately neglected during the Reagan presidency, with fatal consequences. Similarly, in the social and environmental spheres, the new President had promoted special spending initiatives which, with the goal of creating a 'kinder, gentler nation', constituted notable departures from hard-nosed Reaganism. Elsewhere, however, the Bush administration continued to espouse support for the moral right's social agenda of the 1980s, with both the President and, more surprisingly, the Attorney-General Thornburgh adopting a firm stance in opposition to abortion, as well as on such issues as school prayer and desecration of the flag. This coupled, with the increasing conservatism of the rulings of the new, post-Justice Powell, Supreme Court, suggested that the conservative social agenda gains of the 1980s would, despite State-level indications of an emergent pro-choice liberal counter-offensive on the abortion issue, remain securely in place during the early 1990s, at least, and might, indeed, be further extended.

Less certain, however, appeared to be the general position of President Bush who, following a benign, indeed fortuitous, year during 1989, both in terms of domestic economic performance and developments overseas, faced a potentially much more trying period during 1990–2 as the economy, at last, began to show clear indications of a slowdown in activity – US industrial production actually declining during the fourth quarter of 1989 – and as the political situation in Eastern Europe became increasingly unstable. The first development, in particular, promised to make much more difficult the achievement of substantive reductions in the budget deficit,[3] while the latter rendered uncertain the nation's defence strategy. Bush's prospects for re-election to a second term in November 1992 would very much depend, of course, on his response to and handling of such changed circumstances. Much appeared also to rest, however, as Presidents Ford and Carter had experienced before, on forces, economic and external, outside his direct control.

Onward Towards 1992: Party Fortunes in the Wake of November 1988

The Democrats' defeat in the 1988 presidential election came as a profound blow to the party's leadership which was only partially cushioned by the more heartening results of the concurrent Congressional and Statehouse elections. As after November 1980 and 1984, an internal inquest was immediately launched as to what had gone wrong and, while much of the blame for the failure was placed squarely upon the shoulders of Governor Dukakis, his organisation and his campaign tactics, some voiced concern, most prominently Bruce Babbitt, that the problem went deeper. Repeating the findings of the earlier 1985 intra-party inquiry, such conservative and 'neo-liberal' voices called upon Democrats to make a determined effort to escape from the time-warp of the 1960s and from their fatal over-identification with the poor and blacks and, instead, address the aspirations of contemporary 'mainstream', middle-class voters on such issues as economic growth (vis-à-vis redistribution), gun control, capital punishment and the use of military force overseas. Others, however, both from the traditional liberal party establishment and from the pro-Jackson 'New Left', countered that Dukakis

had failed in 1988 because he had been too weak in his defence
of 'Great Society' liberal values, failing to mobilise sufficiently the
party's regular 'voting blocks' and that, for example, if the black
community had been persuaded to turn out in higher numbers
in November 1988 victory could have been achieved.

Such differences in interpretation of both the reasons for the
Democrats' presidential failure in November 1988 and the way
forward were indicative of the existence of strong, and potentially
explosive, ideological, regional and race-based factional divisions
within the party's ranks. These divisions were brought into
particulary sharp focus between December 1988 and February
1989 when, following the decision of the DNC's chairman, Paul
Kirk, to resign and concentrate on a legal career, the way was
paved for a strongly contested succession contest. In this contest,
the most articulate and best qualified of the potential candidates
was Ron Brown (47), a partner in the Washington lobbying firm
of Patton, Boggs and Blow and former staff aide to Edward
Kennedy who, with AFL-CIO backing, was the torchbearer for
the party's northern liberal wing. The Haarlem-born Brown was
also, however, black and in July 1988 had served as Jesse Jackson's
Convention manager. His candidacy was thus fiercely opposed by
conservative southern Democrats who feared that, with Brown at
the party's helm, it would be perceived that Jackson had secured
ascendancy and that this would precipitate a mass of desertions of
party members in the southern States. A 'Stop Brown' campaign
was thus belatedly launched, with James Jones of Oklahoma,
a former chairman of the House of Representatives' Budget
Committee, and Richard Wiener, the Democrats' Michigan State
chairman, being put forward as more palatable centrist alternatives. This movement failed, however, to take off and, with Brown
enjoying the strong public backing of such moderates as Senator
Bill Bradley, his rivals eventually stepped aside, enabling Brown,
on 10 February 1989, to be unanimously elected the party's new
chairman by the 404-member DNC.

Brown's election left a number of conservatives deeply concerned for the party's electoral future, one anonymous leading
southern Democrat being quoted as terming the move 'a disaster in the making'. Others, however, were hopeful that, as had
been the case with his predecessor Kirk, the new chairman would
turn out to be much more accommodating to the sensitivities
of centrists and moderate conservatives than initially expected.
These hopes gained strength when, in his acceptance speech,

Brown made clear that it was his goal to 'be a unifying force, [and] to help craft a message to attract voters who deserted us in the last several election cycles' (i.e. 'Reagan Democrats'). Some even depicted Brown's choice as an inspired one, viewing him as the one possible figure within the party who might be able to stand up to Jesse Jackson successfully and even become a rallying point for more moderate black Democrat opinion.

In the immediate wake of the selection of Brown as party chief, while two southern Democrat Representatives did switch party sides, Bill Grant (Fla) and Tommy Robinson (Ark), the mass of defections that had been predicted failed to materialise. Instead, during 1989 the party, despite the damage inflicted by the Wright and Coelho scandals, appeared to gain in strength locally, securing several notable victories (and a net gain of one seat) in the eight House by-elections which were held during the course of the year, as well as in the mayoral and gubernatorial races of November 1989. Indeed, in the latter, a number of moderate black candidates achieved particularly notable breakthroughs in several cities and States: Douglas Wilder (Va), the grandson of slaves, becoming the nation's first elected black Governor and David Dinkins (New York), Norman Rice (Seattle), John Daniels (New Haven) and Chester Jenkins (Durham) achieving similar mayoral 'firsts'. In these contests, the Democrats drew in notably increased levels of support from younger voters, particularly women. They were attracted by the party's tolerant stance on abortion, which, following the Supreme Court's *Webster v. Reproduction Health Services* ruling and the subsequent attempt by several State Governors, including Florida, Louisiana and Pennsylvania, to introduce more restrictive regulations, had emerged as the country's most emotive political issue. This was indicated during the autumn of 1989 when a remarkably popular and effective counter-offensive against the Moral Right was launched by 'pro-choice' activists, culminating, on 12 November, with the holding of 1,000 co-ordinated abortion rights rallies in more than 150 towns and cities, including one attended by 300 000 in Washington DC.

The electoral success of the Democrats and the popular support that was shown for the 'pro-choice' movement during 1989 was indicative that, despite the Republicans' success at the presidential level during the 1980s, a realignment of national values had, in the social sphere at least, by no means been achieved and, indeed, instead, as DNC chairman Brown jubilantly claimed in November

1989, the ideological 'pendulum' may even have begun 'swinging back'. Furthermore, in a range of other domestic policy areas, Harris poll surveys taken during 1989 showed growing support (51% in favour, against proportions of 30% and 41% in 1982 and 1986 respectively) for the Democrats' belief in the need for a more activist government to tackle such problems as drug abuse, illiteracy, homelessness and environmental pollution, and a realisation that increased public funding was needed for this. This was underlined by the fact that throughout 1989, while President Bush consistently boasted an approval rating of supra-70% for his handling of foreign policy, when it came to domestic matters his level of support wavered between only 30 and 50%.

These poll findings fortified the Democrats' liberal and centrist wings who believed that if they stood firmly by the party principles enunciated in 1988, while improving their organisation and presentation and selecting a more appealing leader, victory could be achieved at the presidential level in November 1992. Some optimists even went so far as to suggest that, in retrospect, the election of 1988 might come to be viewed, like that of 1928, as a harbinger of an era of Democrat dominance. In 1928, despite enduring a third successive defeat, the party, led by New York Governor Alfred Smith – the first Roman Catholic to run for the presidency – began to attract to its ranks the north-eastern urban ethnic voters who were to form a crucial component of the subsequent 'Roosevelt coalition'. In 1988, while no new such ethnic 'voting block' had emerged, the Democrats had broken notable new ground in the traditionally liberal Republican States of the West and Centre-west, holding out the promise of a broad-based 'western advance' during the 1990s.

However, even if such an advance is achieved, the mathematics of the Electoral College and recent regional voting patterns are such that the Democrats will still need to surmount tremendous hurdles if they are to break the Republicans' post-1968 presidential reapportionment due before this election, the barrier will be raised even further as a result of the transfer of between 15 to 18 House, and thus Electoral College, seats from 11 northern Frostbelt-Rustbowl States – Illinois (–2), Iowa (–1), Kansas (–1), Massachusetts (0 or –1), Michigan (–2), Montana (0 or –1), New York (–2 or –3), Pennsylvania (–2 or –3), Ohio (–2), West Virginia (–1) and Wisconsin (0 or –1) – four of which voted for Dukakis in 1988, to six sunbelt States of the South and South-west – Arizona

(+1 or +2), California (+4 to +6), Florida (+3), Georgia (+1 or +2), North Carolina (0 or +1) and Texas (+3 or +4) – none of which voted Democrat in 1988.

Two alternative strategic approaches appear possible for the party in its assault on the presidency. The first, as long advocated by southern Democrats since 1984, would be for the party to make one last attempt to reunite its northern and southern wings and repeat its success of 1976 by selecting a centrist southerner, for example Senator Gore or Senator Robb, at the head of the party's ticket, balanced by a somewhat more liberal northern or western running-mate. However, within such an option there exists the danger that even such a figure might not be sufficiently ideologically conservative for the South to be fully carried in the face of a challenge led, as appears likely in 1992, if Bush seeks re-election, by a Republican with southern credentials of his own. If, instead however, a more conservative southern Democrat, for example, Senator Nunn, were to be selected, the support of northern liberals could by no means be taken for granted and the likelihood of a strong third party independent Democrat challenge would be considerable.

For such a 'southern strategy' to succeed, the South would need to unearth an unusually compelling and charismatic presidential candidate who would be able first to secure nomination in a selection process which, following rule changes conceded to the Jackson camp in July 1988, is still likely to favour a liberal or 'neo-liberal'. In the absence of such a candidate, the alternative for the party would appear to be, at the presidential level, to write off, as irretrievably lost, the Deep South and concentrate upon constructing a new winning 'northern tier' Electoral College coalition embracing the States of the industrial North-east and Midwest and the promising new pastures of the West. To unite such regions, the new breed of 'neo-liberal' Democrat, in the image of Gary Hart, but without his character flaws, would appear to be the ideal candidate, with Senator Bradley of New Jersey the most obvious current 'possible'.[4] Much of the party's chances in the presidential election will also undoubtedly rest upon more general trends in the economy – a recession being likely to enhance the electoral prospects of either a 'populist' candidate, such as Gephardt, or a traditional liberal Democrat, such as Cuomo – and upon the governing success of President Bush. The other imponderable factor will be the decision taken by Jesse Jackson whether or not to contest for the nomination again

– or instead, following the Barry cocaine scandal, seek the mayor-ship of Washington DC – and, if he does, whether he proves able to build upon the remarkable advance in support he achieved in 1988.[5]

In contrast to the Democrats, for the Republicans success at the presidential level has become accepted, since the late 1960s, as the norm and in 1992, with an incumbent President likely to seek re-election and, barring either a serious economic downturn – the 'Hoover scenario' – or period of misgovern-ment, be re-nominated with little serious challenge, the party's prospects of securing a fourth successive presidential election victory appear to be unusually strong. At the national level, indeed, the Republicans, following the Reagan presidency, have succeeded in shaking off their traditional image, derived during the 1920s, as the party of depression and unemployment and, instead, have become associated with economic growth at home and with strength and peace abroad. The party has attracted to it a significant block of younger and 'young middle-aged' voters during the course of the 1980s, as well as many former Democrats. As a consequence, the Republicans now stand, according to a July 1989 Gallup Poll survey, nationally only four percentage points behind the Democrats in terms of the proportion of the voting public who describe themselves as party supporters. In 1980, the gap was 22 points.

Still, however, at the Congressional and State levels the party remains a clear junior partner and in terms of the number of seats and leadership posts under its control has made no real advance over the course of the 1980s. At the start of the decade, the party's hierarchy devised a '1991 Plan' which, with its eye on post-1990 redistricting, sets as its target a State-level drive to build up its grassroots branch and Statehouse strength so as eventually, by the close of the decade, to be in a position to take over control of many previously Democrat-held legislatures. This plan appeared to be well on course during the early 1980s, with the Republicans picking up more that 300 State legislature seats in each of the elections of 1980 and 1984, while the Governorships under the party's control climbed to 34. Thereafter, however, this strategy disintegrated, the Democrats regaining 95 Statehouse seats in the 1982–3 elec-tions, 147 in 1986–7 and 13 in 1988, while the number of republican governorships had slumped to only 21 by the start of the new decade.

The Republicans variously ascribed the failure of their grand '1991 Plan' to both Democrat gerrymandering and to the advantages of incumbency and in 1989–90, with their last chance to make a breakthrough before reapportionment beckoning, the Republican National Committee (RNC), with, from January 1989, Lee Atwater at its head and working in tandem with the new pugnacious House Whip Newt Gingrich, embarked on an aggressive 'take no prisoners' ethics smear campaign designed to denigrate and ultimately force the retirement of incumbent Democrat Congressmen so as to create 'open contests' which could be specially targeted by the RNC and their opponents blitzed with 'attack ads'. Speaker Wright and House Majority Whip Coelho were notable early scalps from this campaign and even the new House Speaker Thomas Foley found himself a target in June 1989, being briefly smeared with the totally unfounded suggestion that he had 'homosexual leanings'. The Republicans' justly disappointing showing during 1989 in the House by-elections that were created by this 'ethics war', however, suggested that the financing of aggressive 'negative advertising' was not sufficient alone to guarantee success in 'open contests' and in some cases the reliance on out-of-state power brokers and finance proved to be positively detrimental. Instead, the House, gubernatorial and mayoral elections of 1989, for which parochial issues dominated, indicated that the Democrats remained a firmly entrenched local and State level force, able to recruit popular candidates, drawn from the local community and determined to articulate and defend their interests. Clearly the Republicans, identified more as a party with a national orientation and with a more shifting suburban socio-economic base, faced a much longer haul if it wished to achieve its goal of fundamental realignment.

Part Five

ECONOMIC AND SOCIAL FOUNDATIONS

Chapter 9

ECONOMIC AND SOCIAL CHANGE IN CONTEMPORARY AMERICA

This section examines the American economy and society during the last two decades and focuses upon a number of movements of political significance: the effects of differential regional growth; the rise of ethnic and feminist politics; and the decline of the old labour unions.

Economic Change: The Era of Restructuring, Recession and Differential Recovery, 1976–90

OPEC's quadrupling of world oil prices in 1973–4 and 1979–80 plunged the world economy into a decade of mounting inflation and industrial recession after two decades of robust growth, improving living standards and increased government spending. (See Table 23.) The onset of recession encouraged a shift in political philosophy away from the welfare interventionism of the 1960s towards a new politics of scarcity and frugalism which emerged during the Ford, Carter and Reagan presidencies and which was replicated at the State level. This was also a period of enforced restructuring in response to the competition of the low-wage 'Newly Industrialised Countries' (NICs) of South-east Asia and Latin America and to the spread of micro-technology and factory automation which caused the demise of many older 'Fordist' industries and resulted in an occupational movement towards the white-collar service sector.

This movement was regionally based. It was the steel and automobile industries of the States of the North-east and Midwest (Pennsylvania, Michigan, Ohio, Indiana, Illinois, New York and Missouri) which bore the sharpest brunt of the recession and of foreign competition. US steel production was halved to 56 million tonnes between 1970 and 1982 and huge losses were recorded by its under-utilised private firms. The American automobile industry was plunged into a similar crisis as the 1970s oil price rises forced it to reorientate production away from its huge gas-guzzling Cadillacs towards new, small, fuel-efficient family saloons. During this period foreign penetration of the car market doubled to 30% and hundreds of thousands of automobile, rubber, plastics, glass and engineering workers were laid off. Unemployment rates in the region thus doubled to over 12% in 1982, and in some localities, such as Detroit, Pittsburgh and Youngstown, exceeded 25%.

TABLE 23 ECONOMIC INDICATORS, 1978–89

	1978	1979	1980	1981	1982	1983	1984	1985	1986	1987	1988	1989
Ind Prod (%)	+7.5	+0.5	−3.0	−2.0	−9.5	+14.1	+6.6	+1.4	+1.1	+5.4	+5.0	+1.1
Inflation (%)	7.6	11.5	13.5	10.2	6.0	2.9	4.2	3.6	1.4	3.5	4.0	4.4
Unemployment (%)	6.1	5.8	7.1	7.6	9.7	9.6	7.4	7.1	7.0	6.3	5.6	5.3
Fed Deficit (bn)	$49	$28	$60	$58	$111	$195	$185	$210	$221	$150	$155	$165

This was a Democrat stronghold region and enjoyed the highest unionisation, wage and taxation rates and fuel costs in the country. It was thus ripe to be undermined by competition from lower-cost regions at home and abroad. It did not begin to bounce back from recession until 1983. This recovery was aided by import quota protection, but was mainly due to the realistic co-operation of the region's workforce and the initiative of its managers, who, learning from Japan, invested heavily in new technology. Labour productivity was significantly raised; new models and products were designed; and marketing became more aggressive. In places such as Minneapolis (Minnesota) and Columbus (Ohio) change was particularly striking, with new high-tech industries now developing. Elsewhere, older industries, such as cars and steel, were re-organised and returned to profitability, though with slimmed-down, skilled and often white-collared workforces. (Employment fell by 30% in the steel industry and by 25% in the automobile industry between 1980 and 1984.) This transition, though dramatic, has nevertheless left behind pockets of stark poverty and depression, particularly in the decaying black inner cities which have been bypassed by the new technologies. Between 1987 and 1990, faced with still high interest and exchange rates, with rising levels of manufactured imports, and, following two successive years of drought, with a quarter of its farm population threatened with bankruptcy, a further buffeting was endured by parts of the North-east and Midwest.

The other regions to be afflicted with high levels of unemployment during the 1974–6 and 1979–83 recessions were the North-west, the East-Central Appalachian States and parts of the 'Old South', as Figure 8 makes clear.

Figure 8   Regional Unemployment Rates in 1982

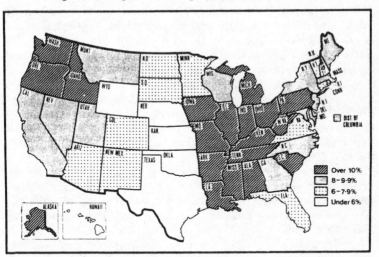

Source: *The Economist* 10 April 1982 p45

The north-western region (Washington, Oregon and Idaho), which depended upon the timber industry and Boeing of Seattle, suffered during these years from slack demand in the construction and aviation industries and from competition from southern pinewood. The East-Central Appalachian States of West Virginia, Kentucky and Tennessee, centres for the deep-mined coal industry, were badly affected by the post-1979 slump in energy demand and by the shift in US production towards the non-unionised opencast mines of the western States.

The States of the 'Old South' exhibited, by contrast, a unique mixture of both growth and decline. These previously poor and rural backwaters recorded growth rates above the national average during the 1960s and 1970s as textile, clothing, shoe and automobile parts industries were attracted by the beguiling combination of cheap, non-unionised labour and fuel supplies, low taxation rates and a pro-business political environment. The region was transformed as blacks moved out of the increasingly mechanised agricultural sector into small-town industrial employment. The region's population boomed, with in-migration beginning to exceed out-migration, and although average incomes remained the lowest in the country (15% below the national average in 1980), and poverty acute, differentials began to close. The recessions of 1974–6 and 1979–83 thus came as a shock to the 'New South'. Its steel, shoe and particularly its textile industries became unable to face up to the competition of even lower-cost NICs during a period of currency inflation, so that closures and lay-offs became imperative. High-tech industries were established in a number of centres, such as Atlanta (Georgia) and Raleigh (N Carolina), and the oil and gas industry continued to boom until 1981. Elsewhere, however, particularly in the small-town and agricultural hinterland, the picture became one of severe depression, until a recovery at last began to be mounted from the mid 1980s.

However, while the regions above, particularly the 'Rustbowl-Frostbelt', endured a period of severe recession during the later 1970s and early 1980s, several regions continued to grow rapidly – Alaska, Florida, New England and particularly the 'Sunbelt' West and South-west.

Alaska and Florida represented two unusual new 'frontier regions' – the former, an energy-rich Arctic Klondike filled with onshore and offshore oil and gas: the latter, a sun-drenched tourist and retirement centre for the urban middle classes of the North-east and Midwest, which also developed as a Mecca for Caribbean and Latin American trade and investment and as a centre for the defence industry. New England (Connecticut, Maine, Massachusetts, New Hampshire, Rhode Island, and Vermont) represented, by contrast, an old-established industrial region which, drawing upon its attractive physical environment, plentiful financial resources and fine educational infrastructure, rapidly developed as a centre for high-tech industries. Computer firms, such as Wang, Digital Equipment, Data General, Prime and Lotus, developed along Route 128 leading north from Boston, helping to create more than 300 000 jobs each year. The boom continued in this region until 1988. Thereafter, in the wake of the Wall Street crash of October 1987 and the announcement of cutbacks in the Federal defence budget, a sharp downturn commenced. However, this promised to be only a temporary setback.

Growth in the above three regions was unusually specialised. In the West and South-western 'Sunbelt' (comprising the States of Oklahoma, Arizona, Texas, New Mexico, Colorado, Utah, Nevada and California), which recorded a growth rate double the national average during the years between 1974 and 1985, the base for growth was broader and more varied. There was first an energy-prospecting and production boom as the rise in energy prices gave a fresh stimulus to the development of the vast onshore and offshore oil, gas and coal reserves of this region. Second, this underpopulated and relatively remote region was the site for numerous defence, aeronautical and space research stations (including Hughes, Lockheed, MDD and Rockwell in California alone). Like Florida and New England, it was thus to benefit substantially from the sharp rise in defence spending between 1978 and 1988 and was also well placed to develop spin-off high-technology industries. During the mid 1970s the Santa Clara valley near San Francisco ('Silicon Valley') became the centre for the world's new micro-electronics industry, bringing together a winning combination of enterprising venture-capitalists and talented technicians in more than 3000 new firms. This industry has rapidly expanded in size and spread to other university- or research station-served centres in the West and South-west, including Los Angeles, San Diego, Phoenix, Denver, Albuquerque, Austin and Dallas, and has become the leading growth sector. A third, though less spectacular, growth sector has centred around the area's Mexican-American and Asian immigrants who have provided cheap non-unionised labour for lower-tech factories, farms and for the tourist industry. This immigrant influx has helped maintain the restless, risk-taking, youthful, innovative and competitive environment which has epitomised this region ever since the gold rush of 1849.

195

The differential economic trends noted above have been matched by corresponding demographic movements as workers have been drawn away from the North-east and Midwest 'sunset' industry belt towards the southern and western 'sunrise' region, and out of traditional manufacturing and agriculture into the service and high-technology sector.

Between 1970 and 1987 the US population increased by 20% to 243.3 million, but expansion was concentrated in the States of the South and West. The population of the 12 States of the West and South-west, for example, increased by 48%, with the small State of Nevada (106%) topping the growth table but with Arizona (91%), Colorado (49%), Texas (49%) and California (38%) making the most significant contribution. The population of Florida and Georgia in the South-east rose by 67% and 36% respectively.[1] Population growth stagnated, by contrast, in the North-east and Midwest. Immigration from both the North-east and Midwest States and from overseas (particularly Central America and South-east Asia) were the principal factors governing growth in the West and South-east and resulted in population structures with an unusually low age bias (excepting Florida which has a retired population of 17% compared to the national average of 11%) and a high rate of natural increase. This has eased the dependency ratio (the proportion of old people supported by the working population), enabling tax rates to be kept low, and has maintained a downward pressure on wage rates, thus providing further boons for the development of the region. Such a trend highlights the continuing high degree of mobility in the American labour market, which has resulted from cultural as well as institutional factors (welfare and housing systems). This has played an important role in enabling the country to create 20 million new jobs during the decade 1974–84 at a time when Western Europe was losing an aggregate of more than two million jobs. A further 15 million new jobs were created between 1985 and 1990

A second demographic trend of the last two decades has been the movement, particularly of the white middle classes, away from city centres towards both the suburbs and towards smaller rural towns and villages, which have become new commuter centres. This has reflected a new concern for the 'quality of life' and has had important political consequences for the inner city shells left behind. A third important trend has been an occupation shift toward the service and high-technology white-collar 'post-industrial' sector. In 1960 7% of the American labour force was employed in agriculture, 36% in manufacturing and 57% in services: by 1980 the share held by agriculture and manufacturing had fallen to 2% and 32% respectively, while that held by services had risen substantially to 66%, the highest in the OECD.[2] A significant portion of the old manufacturing jobs lost had been held by highly paid white male manual workers. By contrast, many of the new service and office jobs have been filled on low wages by immigrant workers or by women, who have captured two-thirds of the new jobs created during the last decade and who now hold 60% of posts in the service sector. This occupational shift has served to squeeze the middle-income strata in American society – the proportion of families in the middle-income groups (earning salaries, in 1987 US dollars, of around $20000–50000) falling from 51% of the total in 1973 to only 47% in 1986 – and has further widened income differentials.

The Political Consequences of Economic and Demographic Change

Politics in the 'New South' and West

The most striking effect of the southward and westward movement of America's economy and society has been to increase this region's influence on national politics. The 'Old South' left its stamp on national affairs during the 1950s and early 1960s through its control of Congressional committee chairs. Today, the influence exerted by the 'New South' and the emergent West is more subtle, with the region's attitudes and interests gaining a practical and intellectual ascendancy at the Federal level. There has firstly been a 'Californiaisation' of politics, with the sophisticated use of media technologies, the spread of computerised campaigning, the weakening hold of party machines, and an increased emphasis on personalities. Second, there has been a conservative swing away from 'New Deal' northeastern liberalism towards a low-tax, laissez-faire approach to economic matters, a strong Protestant, often fundamentalist, approach to social issues, and a shift in overseas interests away from Europe and the Atlantic towards Latin America, Asia and the Pacific zone – the growth area for US overseas trade and investment. The increasing political muscle of the western and southern States has been reflected by the fact that, accepting Texas as George Bush's adopted home, each of the country's last five elected Presidents has been drawn from this region, and by the region's gain of 17 seats in the House of Representatives (and Electoral College) in the reapportionment which followed the 1980 census.[3] As has been noted above (see pages 187–8), it is likely to gain a similar number of seats in 1991.

Reapportionment and the demographic movement towards the commuter suburbs was a boon to the Republican Party, although Democrat State legislatures worked hard to minimise these losses through imaginative gerrymandering when the boundaries for the new electoral districts came to be drawn. Economic growth in the South and the resulting social changes that were set in motion were of even greater consequence, promising, as they did, to undermine Democrat dominance and introduce a competitive two-party system into a crucial 'hinge region'.

The Democrats' hold in the Southern States first showed indications of weakening during the late 1960s and early 1970s in the wake of the 1965 Voting Rights Act. This effectively enfranchised the region's 20% black minority and forced a new generation of liberal-minded Democrat Governors – Askew (Florida), Carter (Georgia), Bumpers (Arkansas), Edwards (Louisiana) – to seek out accommodation between the two communities. However, these efforts split the traditional white 'redneck' vote, the more racist of whom began to cast their ballot for conservative Republicans in, first, national and then State-level contests. The rapid growth of the South's leading cities during the 1970s, attracting in a swathe of northern middle-class professionals, created a second wellspring of potential Republican support. This encouraged the party to launch a determined 'Southern Campaign' with the aim of establishing firm State-level bases.

Unfortunately for the Republicans, the results of this campaign have been patchy and chequered. (See Table 24.) The party has achieved its greatest success in the States on the fringe of old Dixieland, particularly in Virginia, North Carolina, Florida, Texas and Tennessee, where its candidates have frequently captured gubernatorial and Congressional posts. In Virginia, which today is socio-economically almost a mid Atlantic State, the party was helped by the defections of the Democrat Senators Harry Byrd (in 1970) and William Scott (in 1974), and in North Carolina by the quixotic leader of the far-right Congressional Club, Jesse Helms (a declared Republican since 1970). In Florida and Texas, the Republicans have gained support from the strong white middle-class immigrant communities established in the suburbs of their burgeoning new high-tech cities and from anti-communist Cuban refugees. In Tennessee, the Republicans have become well entrenched in the east, a region which sided with the Union in 1861.

TABLE 24   PARTY STRENGTH IN THE SOUTHERN STATES, 1977–90*

| | Congress | | | | Governorships | |
	Senate		House			
1977–78	D–16	R–6	D–81	R–27	D–8	R–3
1979–80	D–15	R–7	D–77	R–31	D–7	R–4
1981–82	D–11	R–11	D–68	R–40	D–6	R–5
1983–84	D–11	R–11	D–80	R–34	D–9	R–2
1985–86	D–12	R–10	D–73	R–43	D–9	R–2
1987–88	D–16	R–6	D–77	R–39	D–6	R–5
1989–90	D–15	R–7	D–77	R–39	D–6	R–5

* Alabama, Arkansas, Florida, Georgia, Louisiana, Mississippi, N Carolina, S Carolina, Tennessee, Texas and Virginia.

The Republicans have made a number of spectacular advances in the South, capturing for example the governorship of Texas between 1979 and 1982 and even a senatorship in Mississippi when a black candidate divided the Democrat vote in 1978. They have, however, been less successful at the local and State level, holding in 1990 only 25% of the 1785 seats in the State legislatures compared to the Democrats' 75%. (See Table 25.) In the November 1986 Congressional and State elections the Republicans achieved a net gain of three governorships, including the recapture of Texas, and, for the first time since Reconstruction, Alabama, but lost four Senate and four House seats. In the November 1988 election round they made a net gain of a further Senate seat, securing two victories in Florida and Mississippi against one defeat in Virginia. However, they made only limited progress elsewhere; perhaps the most heartening trend for the party being the 9% advance achieved in their State legislator numbers, raising the total to 452.

TABLE 25   PARTY STRENGTH BY STATE IN THE SOUTH IN JANUARY 1990

State	House Seats		Senate Seats		Governor-ships	Share of State Legislature Seats (%)	
	D	R	D	R		D	R
Alabama	5	2	2	0	R	85	15
Arkansas	2*	2*	2	0	D	89	11
Florida	8*	11*	1	1	R	60	40
Georgia	9	1	2	0	D	80	20
Louisiana	4	4	2	0	D	84	16
Mississippi	5*	0*	0	2	D	91	9
N Carolina	8	3	1	1	R	62	38
S Carolina	4	2	1	1	R	72	28
Tennessee	6	3	2	0	D	62	38
Texas	19	8	1	1	R	64	36
Virginia	5	5	1	1	D	69	31
Total	75*	41*	15	7	D–6 R–5	75	25

* Following by-elections and defections during 1989.

The Republican breakthrough in the South thus remains incomplete, although Republican voter registration is rising and a two-party system is clearly beginning to emerge. This is taking place along ideological lines in some States, for example North Carolina and Texas, with liberal Democrat wings orientating themselves towards black and Hispanic voters and with the Republicans seeking out the white 'redneck' and suburban conservative vote. Such changes have already shattered the cohesion of the southern voting block in Congress (although a significant 'Boll Weevil' faction does still exist), as divisions along party, ideological and racial lines have broadened. In this connection, it is of particular note that of the six new southern Democrats who have been elected to the Senate since 1980 only two, John Breaux (La) and Richard Shelby (Ala), have regularly aligned themselves with the

'Conservative Coalition' when voting in Congress. Changes in the political complexion of the southern States seem set to accelerate in the decade ahead as the strong Democrat machines established in the Dixieland heartland of Alabama, Arkansas, Georgia, Louisiana and Mississippi are further transformed by economic and social change.[4]

Elsewhere in the growth areas of the country, the south-western States and New England, the Republican Party is well established and has made further gains during the last decade, for example, George Deukmejian capturing the governorship of California in 1982. In the few Democratic Party bastions remaining in these regions, for example Massachusetts in New England, there has been a swing away from traditional liberalism towards more cautious 'neo-liberalism' and even, on occasions, conservatism among the latter party's State-wide officeholders.

Ethnic Politics: Black and Hispanic Political Success

During the last two decades the political influence wielded by blacks (or, as they have been referred to since 1989, African-Americans) and Hispanics has increased significantly as a result of three important demographic trends – the growing disparity between ethnic birth rates; the flight of the white middle classes from the inner cities; and the steep rise in immigration from Latin America as the economies of this region have begun to collapse under a burden of mounting debt and unemployment.[5] Although blacks and Hispanics still remain a clear minority at the national level and although many remain politically apathetic, they have become a significant factor in a number of States and at the urban level.

The Hispanic community is concentrated in the States of the South-west, where it forms 12–20% of the local population (reaching 37% in New Mexico), although a smaller diaspora has settled in the industrial cities of the North-east and Midwest. (See Appendix Table A3.) With the exception of the much smaller Asian community, it is the fastest growing ethnic minority: its numbers having risen by 34% (to 19.4 million) during 1980–8. Sixty per cent of the community are Mexican-Americans and they have remained unusually introspective, clinging tenaciously to their indigenous culture and abjuring the politics of the surrounding 'anglos'. However, recently, following the extension

201

of the Voting Rights Act to the south-western States in 1975, they
have begun to make advances in local and urban elections.[6] They
have captured the mayorships of the important cities of Denver,
Miami, San Antonio, Santa Fe and Tampa, have temporarily held
the governorships of Arizona, Florida and New Mexico and can
now boast ten (all Democrats) full-voting Congressmen, two of
whom chair House standing committees. The community votes
Democrat by a 2:1 majority, and their vote has been critical in
State and national elections, particularly in November 1976 when
they gave Jimmy Carter a crucial knife-edge victory in the Texas
presidential race.

The black community is far more numerous than the Hispanic,
totalling 30 million (12% of the national population) in 1988, but
has found it difficult to match Hispanic successes at the State-wide
level.[7] However, it has made significant advances in urban contests. This has been achieved through the so-called 'doughnut
effect' – the flight of the white middle and working classes from
the decaying inner cities, which has left blacks as the new majority. In 1972 there were 86 black Mayors, but these were returned
predominantly by small towns, with Newark (NJ) standing out as
a notable exception. (Black mayors had also earlier been elected
in 1967 in Cleveland, Ohio, and Gary, Ind, but the former gain
did not stick.) During the two decades since 1970, however, blacks
have managed to secure control of five of the country's six leading
cities – Los Angeles (1973–), Detroit (1973–), Chicago (1983–9),
Philadelphia (1983–) and New York (1989–) – as well as Atlanta
(1973–), Washington DC (1974–), New Orleans (1978–), Baltimore (1987–) and Seattle (1989–), so that by 1990 they boasted
a total of 310 mayorships. Success has not been based solely upon
the black vote; support from Hispanics (who have been crucial in
Los Angeles) and white liberals (as in Seattle, which is only 10%
black) has also been needed. The majority of black Mayors have
thus been forced to adopt a studiously moderate stance.

Black political success has been more limited within Congress.
There were only 23 (all Democrats) full-voting blacks in the
House of Representatives after the November 1988 elections,
an advance of 17 on the 1967 total but of only seven on the
1976 figure, and there were no Senators. Progress has been
most disappointing in the southern States where blacks have
been thwarted by large multi-member primary constituencies.[8]
Within the House of Representatives, however, blacks, despite
constituting only 5% of the chamber's membership, do chair a

quarter of all its standing and select committees. Indeed, one of the community's members, William Gray III (D – Philadelphia, Pa) chaired the influential Budget Committee between 1985 and 1989 and in June 1989 was elected Majority Whip, the Democrats' third highest ranking House leadership post. Outside Congress, there has, since President Johnson's appointment of Dr Robert Weaver as HUD Secretary in 1966, at first, intermittently and since 1977 regularly, been at least one black representative in the Federal cabinet, with either the HUD or HEW/Education portfolios being most usually accorded. The community, despite being poorly represented on the Federal judicial benches, with only 44 out of a total of 752 judges (a 6% share) in 1989, has also had, in the form of Thurgood Marshall, a justice sitting on the Supreme Court since 1967.

Only very recently have black candidates shown signs of making advances in State-wide and national electoral contests for which cross-community coalition building is required. The first such State-wide success was achieved in November 1985 when Douglas Wilder (D), a moderate black lawyer and loyal party machine politician who had served in the State's Senate since 1970, was elected Lt Governor of traditionally conservative Virginia. A year later, in November 1986, two blacks, Tom Bradley (D) and William Lucas (R), won their respective party's nomination to contest the California and Michigan gubernatorial elections. Lucas was heavily defeated, but Bradley polled respectably against a popular and successful incumbent.[9] Two years later, in the November 1988 Congressional elections, two black Republicans, Alan Keyes of Maryland and Maurice Dawkins of Virginia, contested for the Senate, but were trounced by popular white Democrat opponents. Finally, however, in November 1989, a top-level State-wide victory was achieved when Douglas Wilder, by a wafer-thin 0.5% margin, narrowly secured election as Governor of Virginia, capturing in the process 40% of the white vote in a State in which less than 20% of the electorate was black. During the same year, Ron Brown became the first black to head a major national political party, being elected chairman of the Democratic National Committee.

Politically, during recent years, the Congressional Black Caucus (estd 1971), allied to activist groups outside, has achieved a number of notable legislative victories, persuading Congress, in 1983, to establish a Federal holiday (in January of each year) to commemorate the achievements of Dr Martin Luther King

(1929–68) and, in 1985–6, to force through tough sanctions packages directed against apartheid in South Africa.

However, while blacks and Hispanics have made a number of important political advances during the last decade, their economic advancement has been far slower. They have progressed in terms of educational attainment and a small, but sizeable, black middle class has emerged, which now includes the new political power brokers. Some of the black middle classes have followed whites into the suburbs – the black suburban population rising from 2.8 million to 6.2 million (23% of the total black community) between 1960 and 1980 – and have recently begun to espouse the Reaganite self-help and personal advancement philosophy. The bulk of the black community, however, remain desperately poor and find themselves at the wrong end of the indexes of income, poverty, unemployment and house ownership levels.[10] In recent years, since 1980 in particular, the relative position of blacks has seriously deteriorated, as economic growth has faltered. The contraction of employment in traditional northern blue-collar industries and in southern agriculture and textile factories has hit blacks hardest; they remain ill-equipped for the new white-collar service and high-technology jobs of the 1980s. The reduction in the level of Federal urban renewal and welfare support programmes and the contemporary rise in the number of divorces and the proportion of single parent families (now 55% of the total) has exacerbated this situation. Black discontent remains simmering under the surface, as the 1980 and 1989 Miami riots and the growing support for the radical black Muslim, Louis Farrakhan, have graphically demonstrated, but the increased political power now being wielded by black officials in urban areas and at the county level (where they now hold 7000 out of the 490000 elective posts) has done much to defuse a potentially explosive situation.

The Silent Majority: Female Advances in Politics

The civil rights struggle of the 1960s, coupled with contemporary economic and occupational changes, brought into being a powerful feminist movement seeking equal rights, pay and representation. The National Organization for Women (NOW – which presently boasts a membership of 200000 and a fundraising capability of $3 million per annum) was set up in 1966 and began campaigning for an Equal Rights Amendment to the US constitution. This Amendment has ultimately failed to gain ratification at the Federal level, but it has been incorporated into the constitution of 16 States.[11] The movement it spawned has, however, served to activise politically hundreds of thousands of women and has given an added thrust to the drive to increase the share of women in State and Federal legislatures.

Significant obstacles remain in the path of female political candidates, particularly the unwillingness of businesses and PACs to provide campaign finance. Women have thus made their most striking advances at the State level – their share of State legislature offices rising from 5% of the total to 17% (1270 out of 7467) between 1971 and 1989. Progress at the Congressional level has been more disappointing. For example, between 1976 and 1989 the number of women in the House of Representatives rose by only six to 25 (D–14; R–11), a figure which is equivalent to less than 6% of the chamber's membership. This is despite the fact that 53% of the registered voting age population is female. Moreover, within the House itself, because of both the split party character of the Congresswomen's Caucus and the low seniority of its members, Patricia Schoeder (D – Col), who was first elected in November 1972, currently constituting the Congresswoman with the longest record of service, female Representatives have occupied very few positions of authority, there being, for example no standing or select committee chairwomen in the 101st Congress. Female representation in the Senate has been even more disappointing, only three women, two Republicans, Nancy Landon Kassebaum (Kansas: 1979–), the daughter of former Governor and unsuccessful 1936 presidential challenger Alfred Landon, and Paula Hawkins (Florida: 1981–6), and one Democrat, Barbara Mikulski (Maryland: 1987–), having secured election to the chamber during the course of the 1980s. Six women did win their party's nomination to contest the final stage of the Senatorial races of November 1986 and 1988, but they were unsuccessful.

However, outside Congress there have been a number of notable female advances at the gubernatorial, mayoral, cabinet and judicial levels during the last decade. Within the States, Ella Grasso (D – Connecticut) became, in 1974, the first woman to be elected Governor without first following her husband into office. Her success has subsequently been replicated by two other Democrats, Martha Layne Collins (Kentucky) and Madeleine Kunin

(Vermont) in 1983 and 1984 respectively, and by one Republican, Kay Orr (Nebraska) in 1986, while another Democrat, Rose Mofford, the Arizona Secretary of State, was appointed Acting Governor in April 1988 when Evan Meecham (R) was removed from office following an impeachment trial.[12] This brought to three (6% of the total) the number of female Governors in 1990. Advances at the mayoral level have been even more striking, with, currently, as Appendix Table A4 exhibits, five of the nation's top 25 cities – Columbus, Dallas, Houston, San Antonio and San Diego – boasting female Mayors (and 16 of the top 100). During the course of the decade two other top-ranking cities, Chicago (Jane Byrne – D) and San Francisco (Dianne Feinstein – D), have had women, intermittently, at their political helm. Since 1975, when Carla Hills was appointed HUD Secretary by President Ford, at least one woman has also been regularly included in the Federal cabinet, the number rising to two at times during the Carter, Reagan (between 1983–5) and Bush administrations. The appointment in 1981 of Sandra O'Connor as the Supreme Court's first female justice, Geraldine Ferraro in 1984 as the Democrats' Vice-Presidential nominee and the placement of women at the head of eight Federal agencies during the Reagan presidency have constituted additional advances for the feminist movement.

Further political advances appear imminent as, in the wake of the Supreme Court's July 1989 abortion ruling, the movement became energised by a new wave of committed 'pro-choice' activists. Membership of both the National Abortion Rights Action League (NARAL) and NOW, which had been waning since the mid 1980s, are on the increase again and pressure for the re-introduction of the ERA or, instead, for a fundamental modification and updating of the Bill of Rights, so as to guarantee sex equality and the freedom to choose abortion, has mounted in tandem. The radical new leader of NOW, Molly Yard, has even floated the idea, in a speech delivered to the body's July 1989 Cincinatti Convention, of the formation of a new political party dedicated entirely to women's issues.

An Endangered Species: The Decline of American Labor Unions

The marked rise in blue-collar support for the Republican Ronald Reagan in 1980 and 1984, despite AFL-CIO endorsement of the Democrat ticket, has been one indication among many that the power of America's trade union (labor union) leaders has recently been on the wane. This diminishing authority has been a consequence of plummeting membership rolls and the hardening attitude of government and management.

Membership of trade unions has never been widespread in America. At the inception of the AFL-CIO federation in 1955 34% of the American labour force belonged to trade unions. This compared to a unionisation rate of 42% in Great Britain. During subsequent years American union membership has slumped, in relative, if not absolute, terms, falling to 29% of the total workforce in 1973, to 23% in 1980 and to barely 17% in 1988. This 'de-unionisation' has been caused by three factors – the decline of traditional industries in the Midwest and North-east and their movement towards the States of the South and West; the new emphasis upon the white-collar service and high-technology small firms sectors; and the spread of 'union busting' campaigns.

The States of the Midwest and North-east had been the heartland for American trade unionism, embracing, for example, the United Auto Workers (UAW), the United Steel Workers of America (USWA) and the United Mine Workers of America (UMWA). These unions were badly weakened by the 1979–83 recession – membership of the UAW falling by more than 33% and that of the USWA by 25%. However, it might have been expected that other unions would have sprung up in compensation in the growth regions of the West and South and in the new service and high-technology sectors. This has not, however, been the case.[13] The new growth States enjoyed an unsavoury anti-union reputation and all manner of obstacles were created by management, police and local politicians to thwart organising efforts. Skilful union prevention and 'union busting' campaigns were instituted by professional management consultants; anti-closed shop 'Right to Work' amendments were adopted by State legislatures; and employment contracts were carefully tailored to wean employees away from the unions. The natural conservatism and submissiveness of the workers of the southern and western States gave sustenance to these efforts.

The decline in union membership levels and unionisation rates has seriously reduced the bargaining power of labour at both the Federal and workplace level. During the final years of the Carter administration the relationship between unions and the Federal government had remained close – a national accord on pay restraint being signed in September 1979 – and unions had still been able to use their muscle in industrial disputes to gain preferential pay rises. By 1981, however, the unions were clearly on the defensive. Doors at the centre were rapidly closed by the pro-business Reagan administration and workers in general were cowed by the August 1981 sacking of 11 345 illegally striking air traffic controllers and by the mounting level of unemployment.

Union leaders were thus forced to rethink their strategy in this changed and hostile environment. The lead was given by Douglas Fraser, head of the 1.2 million-strong UAW, who, placing the emphasis on job security rather than on wages, began to offer major pay-cut concessions and work practice reforms, in an effort to keep troubled plants in operation. This 'new realism' spread across the union movement in 1982 and 1983, with more than 50% of union workers, including the UAW and USWA, fore-going wage increases in the new pay round, and was supported by the new progressivist AFL-CIO leader Lane Kirkland.[14] It has been continued during recent years as the strong US dollar has exacerbated overseas competition. This has forced many unions to accept new 'two tier' wage agreements (allowing companies to take on new workers on unusually low pay scales) and to accept German- and Japanese-style 'worker participation' in new auto-mated plants – enabling workers to suggest changes in production processes, removing traditional demarcation barriers and bring-ing workers on to the board of companies such as Chrysler. Taken together these concessions have led to a radical re-drawing of the role of American labour unions, moving them away from their overriding concern with wages to a more constructive involve-ment in company affairs. The unions have made a number of gains, for example, forcing Ford and General Motors to set up a $1.3 million 'jobs bank' to retrain unemployed workers. The price has, however, been high – with union wage increases lagging behind those of non-unionised workers during the years between 1980 and 1984.

During this period of industrial realism the AFL-CIO leadership sought, paradoxically, to raise the political profile of the union movement. Labour union ties with the Democratic Party were made closer, and the AFL-CIO took a lead in the opposition to Reaganomics, organising, for example, the September 1981 protest march on Washington. However, these initiatives failed lamentably to influence the outcome of the 1984 presidential elec-tion. Since 1984 the Democratic Party, anxious to demonstrate that it is not a captive of special interest groups, has determinedly maintained more distant relations with the union movement. This was most apparent during the 1988 Democrat nomination race, with the AFL-CIO being asked to maintain a low profile and not to endorse any candidate specifically. Only in August 1988, after the party's National Convention had chosen its presidential nominee, did the AFL-CIO formally come out in support of Michael Dukakis, opening, for his benefit, its $2.5 million COPE campaign war chest.

Since 1987 there has been some improvement in the economic and political environment within which labor unions operate. Of particular importance has been the return of lower unemployment levels which are comparable to those of the early 1970s. This has potentially improved unions' bargaining strength, although during 1987 and 1988 the number of strikes dipped to a 40-year low, unions now preferring to rely more on lobbying, on investment in slick anti-employer 'corporate campaigns' and on arbitration rather than on a swift resort to direct action. Politically, the last two years of the Reagan presidency were characterised by a softening in attitude on the part of the executive branch and a resurgence of Democrat power at the Congressional level. Indicative of the former trend was the appointment in January 1988 of James Stephens, a respected consensual figure, to replace Donald Dotson, who was perceived as anti-union, as chairman of the National Labor Relations Board (NLRB), the agency which, by law, supervises and protects labor union activities. Indicative of the latter was Congress's approval and the President's countersigning, in July 1988, of a bill which required companies employing 100 workers or more to give at least 60 days' advance warning of major layoffs or plant closures. This political 'thawing' seems set to continue and gain pace during the Bush presidency. During 1989 union-government relations were, it is true, somewhat marred by the tough stance that was adopted by the Bush administration during the course of a prolonged strike by machinists on Eastern Airlines. However, they were put back on track in November 1989 when President Bush approved a Congressional bill providing for the first increase in the national minimum wage since 1981.

Nevertheless, despite these more heartening recent developments, the future for the union movement as a powerful corporate interest body remains uncertain. The steep decline in membership levels that characterised the late 1970s and early 1980s appears, barring a fresh recession, to have been arrested, with many of the country's traditional industries now returning to profitability in a restructured and automated form after 1983. In an effort to attract new members, particularly from the female-dominated service sector, AFL-CIO unions have begun to offer an attractive new package of special benefits, such as low-cost credit cards, travel discounts and legal aid, to their members and have taken a greater interest in such 'quality of life' issues as health-care and child-care, rather than concentrating merely upon pay bargaining. However, notwithstanding such initiatives, it is unlikely that the unionisation levels of the 1960s or early 1970s will ever be regained. Instead, unions will continue as just one of many small interest groups and, at the workplace level, individual unions will need increasingly to compete with paternalist managements in terms of facilities and benefits provided in an effort to maintain their membership levels and forestall decertification.[15]

Part Six

EXTERNAL RELATIONS

Chapter 10

FOREIGN POLICY UNDER CARTER, REAGAN AND BUSH

Presidents are principally elected or re-elected on the basis of their domestic policy records and, in particular, their handling of economic affairs. However, as head of a global superpower, a substantial portion of a President's time in office is spent immersed in foreign affairs. In so doing the President must both respond to sudden and unexpected crises overseas as well as present a steady and coherent vision of America's world role. The President will seek to use his successful conduct of foreign affairs to advance his domestic reputation.

Much discretion has traditionally been left to the presidency in the field of foreign affairs. However, lobbyists, Congress and the bureaucracy do impose a number of constraints. Business and ethnic interest groups (blacks, Jews, Greeks, Irish, Italians and Poles) seek to influence armaments programmes and regional policies. Congress influences the administration's actions through its control of the defence and aid budgets; through its (the Senate's) ability to veto treaties and diplomatic appointments; and through the powers entrusted by the 1973 War Powers Resolution to force troop disengagements overseas after a period of 60 days. Finally, within the administration itself, there are conflicts of approach between the professional and moderate-minded diplomats of the State Department, the small and dynamic NSC, and the bullish Defense Department. The importance of these constraints has been clearly evident during the Carter, Reagan and Bush eras.

The 'New Foreign Policy' of the Carter Administration

President Carter acceded to power at a time when the public and Congressional mood remained unusually introspective. The nation had been soured by the Vietnam War, which had dragged on for more than eight years and had resulted in the death of 58000 and the wounding of more than 150000 American soldiers. The war had been instituted by the Johnson administration and was continued by President Nixon. It was fought in defence of the Trumanite foreign policy consensus which viewed communist expansionism as the overriding danger and sought to resist Soviet and Chinese advances in the developing world through the military and economic support of pro-Western regional allies. During the early 1970s, as Congress became less willing to expand the defence budget, this containment policy was subtly modified by Nixon's talented National Security Adviser (NSA), and later State Department Secretary, Henry Kissinger as the policy of detente was launched. This attempted to gain a breathing-space during a period of growing pacifism in the United States by, first, checking the Soviet military build-up through negotiating a series of arms limitations treaties (commencing in 1972 with SALT-1 and the ABM Treaty) and by, second, improving relations with China, to both vex Russia and reduce America's strategic anxieties. The policy proved to be a success during the early 1970s, but was challenged between 1974 and 1976 by the collapse of America's Cambodian (Kampuchean) and South Vietnamese allies in South-east Asia and by growing communist incursions into Africa (Angola and Mozambique) which followed the collapse of the Portuguese empire in 1974. Elsewhere, in Central and South America, Africa and Asia, economic modernisation or economic depression alternately served to destabilise incumbent regimes.

Conservatives, as well as former Democrat 'neo-conservatives', ascribed America's foreign policy problems of the mid 1970s to a weakening of resolve – the failure to stand up to the Soviet Union, match its increase in defence spending (which, averaging 11–18% of its GNP compared to America's 5%, overtook the US total in 1971 and exceeded it by almost 50% in 1980) and to intervene, covertly, if not overtly, in countries threatened by communist takeover. However they remained at first isolated voices. Broad national support for an interventionist policy was lacking before

1979. The country had turned instead to President Carter, who offered a laudable 'bold new course' in foreign policy.

President Carter's 'new foreign policy' was liberal and pacific, endeavouring to reduce military spending and to curb the proliferation of nuclear weapons. It was also, however, heavily influenced by the President's deep Christian beliefs, seeking to inject ethics and morality into international relations. The President believed that the country's 'inordinate fear' of communism during the Nixon era had led to it embracing all manner of inhuman dictatorships as useful pawns on a vast geopolitical chessboard. President Carter wished instead to begin on a new footing and refused to support brutal authoritarian regimes – curbing the sale of arms and the provision of economic aid to Argentina, Uruguay and Ethiopia. He wanted America to stand as an example for emulation by the international community. His administration thus renounced the commercial sale of plutonium, called for nuclear arms reduction, muzzled the CIA, sought out friendships with emergent democracies in the developing world, and embarked on an unusually frank and open conduct of foreign relations.

The President himself lacked extensive overseas experience, but still played a prominent role in the detailed execution of this policy. He was aided by the State Department Secretary, Cyrus Vance (59) – a seasoned former deputy Defense Secretary in the Johnson administration who became a close family friend of the Carters – and by the black UN Representative, Andrew Young (44), both of whom were committed supporters of his new liberal approach. The most significant input was, however, provided by the Polish-born Columbia University academic Zbigniew Brzezinski (48), who had served as an adviser to Jimmy Carter since 1973 and who became National Security Adviser in 1977. Brzezinski was a confident and bewitching theoretician who favoured a more traditional and hawkish geopolitical approach to foreign affairs in the manner of Henry Kissinger. He emerged as the dominating influence on policy formation and increasingly clashed with the more cautious Cyrus Vance.

The Carter administration recorded a number of diplomatic and Congressional triumphs during its first two years. Most striking were its peace initiatives in the Middle East. Here the Carter administration, recognising an earnest desire for peace on the part of the Egyptian President Anwar Sadat (1918–81), acted as middleman between Egypt and Israel. President Carter, courting disapproval from the vociferous Jewish community in America, applied pressure on the Israeli government to return territory in the Sinai peninsula occupied during 1967 and persuaded Congress, in May 1978, to approve a controversial and novel arms sale package to Egypt and Saudi Arabia. This was followed by an imaginative invitation to President Sadat and the Israeli Prime Minister Menachem Begin to attend an informal and open-ended 12-day summit at Carter's Camp David retreat in September 1978. This was a success and was climaxed by an agreement on a 'framework for peace' and the signature in March 1979 of an Egypt-Israeli peace treaty. The treaty itself failed to resolve the broader issue of a Palestinian homeland, but it did at last establish solid and pacific relations between the two most powerful states in the region. The second great success story for the Carter administration was its agreement (at the price of distancing itself from Taiwan) to a full 'normalisation' of relations with China in January 1979 – an agreement cemented by the inaugural visit of the Chinese Deputy Premier Deng Xiaoping to Washington.

In both these areas the Carter administration was working in favourable environments – with Egyptian and Chinese governments willing to take radical and flexible new initiatives. Elsewhere, the Carter administration's 'new foreign policy' met with more limited success and, in the case of relations with the Soviet Union, with bitter failure.

In Africa, Asia and Central America, the crucial testing-grounds for the Carter administration's new 'South-minded' policy accommodation with the developing democracies, there were two notable achievements. First, America, in combination with the British government, played an important role in pushing the white Rhodesian government towards majority rule and independence (achieved under the designation Zimbabwe, in April 1980) by its support of economic sanctions against the Smith regime. Second, US relations with Panama were significantly improved by the new September 1977 treaty which returned full control of the canal and canal zone to the Panamanian government by the year 2000 (Congress ratified the treaty, despite conservative Republican opposition, in April 1978). Elsewhere the Carter administration was stridently critical of many of the authoritarian and anti-democratic regimes which America had previously supported – South Africa, Chile, Argentina, Peru – and actively encouraged the resignation of the Somoza and Romero dictatorships in Nicaragua and El Salvador in 1979. However, such actions failed to win new allies, but led instead to pro-Soviet coups and Cuban-aided revolutions in destabilised Ethiopia, South Yemen and Afghanistan in 1978 and in Nicaragua in 1979; to the establishment of totalitarian regimes in newly independent Angola, Mozambique and Zimbabwe; to Islamic revolution in oil-rich Iran; and to the Vietnamese *anschluss* of Laos and Cambodia. Thus by 1979 the United States had lost considerable ground in Africa and West Asia; was confronted with a civil war on its doorstep in Central America between right-wing dictatorships and Marxist guerrillas in Nicaragua, El Salvador, Honduras and Guatemala; and was faced, in November 1979, with the ignominy of 52 of its countrymen being held hostage by Islamic students in Teheran who demanded the return of the hospitalised Shah.

During this troubled period, the Carter administration still earnestly sought to improve its relations with the Soviet Union and effect a new arms limitation agreement. However, its constant criticism of Soviet civil rights abuses repelled and embarrassed an increasingly anti-American Moscow. A limited and modest arms control treaty, SALT-2, was eventually signed by the two superpowers in Vienna in June 1979, but its prospects of ratification by the Senate appeared slim as Republicans and 'Defense Democrats' united in opposition. They vanished completely when, on Boxing Day of 1979, Soviet troops suddenly invaded Afghanistan, deposed and executed its troubled ruler Hafizullah Amin and placed in power a puppet administration run by Babrak Karmal.

This action, coming hard on the heels of Teheran, completely changed President Carter's perception of Soviet intentions, and led to a radical U-turn in America's foreign policy. The President felt betrayed by Leonid Brezhnev and was determined to exact a penalty for Soviet transgressions. He thus introduced a range of economic and diplomatic sanctions against the Soviet Union, which included a grain embargo, a suspension of high-technology sales and the boycott of the forthcoming Moscow Olympics. Second, he launched a major new arms modernisation drive with the aim of establishing a new Rapid Deployment Force (RDF) for the Gulf and West Asian region; of deploying medium-range Cruise and Pershing-2 nuclear missiles in Western Europe; and of boosting military expenditure by 4.5% per annum in real terms between 1981 and 1985.

The Carter administration's foreign policy had thus gone full circle by 1980 and relations with the Soviet Union had deteriorated to a level not seen since the Cuban missile crisis of 1962. Public opinion in the United States similarly shifted away from mid 1970s isolationism, being further influenced by the Soviet-backed repression of the Solidarity free trade union movement in Poland in 1980. However, President Carter, though moving with this changing popular mood, failed to benefit in the election of November 1980. The events of November 1979–January 1981 were seen instead as an indictment of the weak and vacillating policy pursued during the preceding three years and as a vindication of its conservative critics. These critics, headed by the Republican candidate, Ronald Reagan, promised rapidly to redress the imbalance in power and to restore American paramountcy. The incumbent administration remained by contrast impotent. It failed to gain the release of the Teheran hostages or to persuade the Soviet Union to withdraw from Afghanistan, and its one attempt at a military solution – the April 1980 Teheran rescue mission – ended in bungling failure in the sands of Iran and led to the resignation of the disapproving State Department Secretary Vance and his replacement by Edmund Muskie.

The Carter administration's 'new foreign policy' was launched in 1977 with the best of intentions, but four years later the balance sheet was one of overriding failure. Ill fortune played a part in this failure – most evidently in the hazardous Teheran rescue mission, which, if successful, may well have saved the Carter presidency[1] – but the policies themselves and their poor execution were also to blame, contributing to destabilisation in many regions. As was the case with domestic policy during the Carter presidency, a sense of priorities, consistency and coherence was lacking in the conduct of foreign affairs.

The New Cold War – Foreign Policy under President Reagan

Ronald Reagan had earned a reputation as a fervent anti-communist during his years of stump oratory at Republican fund-raising functions. He promised during the election campaign of 1980 to restore America's military strength and dominance over world affairs. Thus the onset of the Reagan presidency in January

1981 promised to inaugurate a new 'cold war' era in American-Soviet relations and herald a period of rearmament and Third World interventionism.

The new President, like his predecessor, was unusually inexperienced in international affairs, and thus, while holding strong views and a broad vision of his own, relied heavily for tactical advice on his administration team. The most powerful member of this team was the new Secretary of State, General Alexander Haig, an ambitious, industrious and imposing figure who had served as President Nixon's Chief-of-Staff (1973–4) and as NATO's Supreme Allied Commander (1974–9). Haig shared the President's concern to restore America's military strength – having been instrumental in persuading NATO ministers to accept a strategy to increase military spending by 3% per annum in real terms after 1977 – and its ability to defend the crucial Middle Eastern oil region. He was also, however, willing to show flexibility if the Soviet Union reciprocated American advances. He was thus in the mould of Henry Kissinger and was distrusted by Reaganite hardliners. In his conduct of affairs, Haig sought to re-concentrate power in the hands of the State Department and downgrade the role of the National Security Adviser which had recently been inflated by Kissinger and Brzezinski. Staff numbers at the NSC were reduced and the State Department given more White House committee chairmanships, but the shift in power was only partial. William Clark, a former Chief-of-Staff and Supreme Court judge in California who was a close personal friend of President Reagan, was placed at the side of Alexander Haig as a conservative counterweight.

There were four other checks and counterweights in the new administration: the powerful new Defense Secretary, Caspar Weinberger – another former Californian colleague of the President and a man who had earned a reputation as a budget-cutting Scrooge ('Cap the Knife') when director of President Nixon's OMB – who was given the brief of building up the nation's military arsenal in a cost-effective and efficient manner; the new CIA Director, William Casey (a member of the Office of Strategic Services during the Second World War and veteran of the Nixon and Reagan's Californian administrations); and two 'neo-conservative' Democrat academics, National Security Adviser Richard Allen (Georgetown/Hoover Inst) and UN Representative Jeane Kirkpatrick (Georgetown/AEI).[2] Allen and Kirkpatrick injected a new southern and west coast perspective into the conduct of America's foreign policy, being interested in extending

US influence in the expanding Pacific basin and Latin American region and becoming impatient with the perceived timidity of America's European allies. They favoured the nation's adoption of a more 'unilateralist', America-first, approach to foreign affairs. Reagan, Clark, Weinberger and Meese were attracted by this new outlook, while the State Department and Vice-President Bush fought for a more cautious and traditional Atlanticist policy. This created a perpetual tension in the new administration, with the State Department usually, but not always, emerging the victor.

Under the Reagan administration, America's approach to international relations radically altered. Emphasis shifted away from North-South and human rights issues towards the East-West balance. Soviet expansionism was to be contained through the strengthening of America's strategic allies and military and intelligence capabilities, with the eventual aim of being able to bargain from a position of strength. The first element in this policy involved major drives to supply sophisticated arms to allies in key strategic regions. In the Gulf and West Asia, US bases were established in Oman, Kenya and Somalia, and Saudi Arabia, Turkey and Pakistan were targeted for support. In Africa, relations with mineral-rich South Africa were improved; in Western Europe, added impetus was given to NATO's arms modernisation drive; in Central America, arms sales to the brutal El Salvador regime were resumed; and, at home, a major defence programme was launched, with prominence being given to the new MX ICBM missile and with the mothballs being dusted off the defunct neutron bomb and B-1 bomber projects.[3] Increased resources were also now pumped into the CIA and a freer rein was given to its covert activities as attempts were made to topple the new communist regimes in Afghanistan and Nicaragua. A number of these initiatives were first set in train by the Carter administration during its final year in office, making December 1979 rather than November 1980 the true turning point for US foreign policy. However, the Reagan administration was far more committed to this 'cold war' approach than the reluctant Carter team ever were or seemed likely to be.

There were, however, limitations upon the extent to which the Reagan administration could turn the clock back towards the national dominance of 1950–63. These were imposed by political and military realities and by the views of America's European allies and domestic public opinion.

During the Polish crisis of 1981, which ended in the imposition of martial law by General Jaruzelski in December 1981, the United States was as powerless to affect the outcome as in Hungary in 1956, in Czechoslovakia in 1968 or in Afghanistan in 1979–80. The military option was unacceptable and inconceivable, while the economic sanctions which were imposed on the Soviet Union in 1981 and 1982 had little impact and fell apart as a result of the lack of Western unity. This demonstrated that America could only hope to check and contain Soviet expansionism in areas outside the latter's sphere of direct influence and that, even when acting in a limited containment role, the Reagan administration had to work with often fickle public opinion and with its allies. At home, the experience of Vietnam had not been fully exorcised. The public still refused to countenance prolonged direct American military involvement in Central America or the Middle East, and they remained concerned with the threat of nuclear war. This became particularly evident during 1982 and 1983 with the sudden growth of the 'freeze movement' and the reaction to the rising death toll among American troops sent out to police the troubled city of Beirut. It was reflected in Congress by its temporary refusal to grant funds for the MX programme in December 1982 and by the House vote in favour of a nuclear freeze in May 1983. These concerns were even more strongly held in Western Europe, the home of a burgeoning peace movement, and impelled the American government to attempt to maintain a dialogue with the Soviet Union.

Arms control talks thus recommenced in Geneva (medium-range) in November 1981, when President Reagan put forward his 'zero option'.[4] They were subsequently, however, stalled by the imposition of martial law in Poland and by the resignation of the disenchanted Alexander Haig in June 1982. This resignation allowed the hawks within the Reagan administration to gain a temporary ascendancy, before George Shultz, the new Secretary of State, was able to establish his authority.[5] One indication of this was the increased influence of the National Security Adviser, William Clark,[6] who insisted on the right to report directly to the President, rather than via Special Counselor Meese, as had been the case with his predecessor.

The low point of deteriorating American-Soviet relations was reached in September 1983 when a South Korean commercial airliner, KAL 007, which had strayed into Soviet airspace, was shot down with the loss of 269 lives, including that of a US

Congressman, Lawrence McDonald. The Soviet Union claimed meekly that the plane had been deliberately sent on a spy mission at the time of an important missile test near its Sakhalin Island military base. This, however, failed to convince American opinion, which became more sympathetic to the President's hardline anti-Soviet policy. Support inside Congress for the MX missile and B-1 bomber projects suddenly increased and the popular mood changed sufficiently to enable the Reagan administration to launch the symbolic anti-Marxist invasion of the tiny island of Grenada on 25 October 1983.

By 1984 the strong-minded policy of the Reagan administration had achieved a number of successes and had gained the overwhelming backing of the American public. The President could claim that, following the four years of substantial growth in the military budget, the country's military dominance had been restored and Soviet expansionism halted.

In Western Europe, NATO's strength had been significantly increased, though at the cost of a temporary straining in individual countries' relations with the United States, following the stationing of Cruise and Pershing-2 missiles and a sustained period of real growth in each member country's defence budget. This had been achieved at a time of economic recession and had been made possible by the willingness of the key conservative governments in West Germany and the United Kingdom to follow the American lead. It was aided by disarray in Moscow, which was racked by debilitating succession struggles following the death of two leaders in as many years, and by mounting economic problems. In the Gulf region, the military capabilities of the United States and its allies had been strengthened with the establishment of the 222000-man RDF and a 25% increase in the strength of the US navy. During this same period the hostile powers of Iran and Iraq had become ensnared in a war of attrition and the Soviet Union remained bogged down by mujaheddin rebels in Afghanistan. In Central America, the spread of the Sandinista revolution had been checked and, though civil war still ravaged the whole region, the balance had been tilted towards the incumbent pro-American regimes in El Salvador, Honduras and Guatemala, while indications of growing support for moderation were to be found in the elections of this period. In South-east Asia, relations with China continued to improve, although Taiwan still remained a stumbling block. Attempts were also made to strengthen links with the repressive regimes of South Korea and the Philippines and to persuade Japan to take a greater share of the burden for the defence of the Pacific zone. In Africa, these years were ones of unusual stability, with a Libyan-backed rebellion in Chad being checked by French and American technology. Only in the Middle East had the situation deteriorated since 1980, following Israel's invasion of Lebanon (June 1982), its annexation of the Golan Heights and its determination to continue to settle on the West Bank and Gaza Strip.

The Reagan administration's handling of foreign affairs between 1981 and 1984 caused periods of acute anxiety for American liberals and for her overseas allies. Superpower relations deteriorated dangerously – the Soviet Union walked out of the Geneva START (Strategic Arms Reduction Talks) in December 1983 following the deployment of Cruise missiles in Europe and snubbed the July 1984 Los Angeles Olympics – and the prospect of the irruption of a new Vietnam in El Salvador or Nicaragua appeared always imminent. However, the State Department – supported from September 1983 by the National Security Adviser Robert McFarlane[7] – in combination with public opinion and Congress, managed to keep the belligerent Defense Department of Caspar Weinberger and his hardline assistant Richard Perle in check. The Reagan administration wisely chose only limited targets for direct US military intervention and aggression – Libyan fighter planes in 1981, Grenada in 1983, and the *Achille Lauro* in October 1985. These symbolic gestures maintained a fear and credibility in the use of America's new military muscle in what became a close-chested poker game between East and West. Elsewhere, in Central America, Africa and West Asia, the Reagan administration acted indirectly or covertly, and when it found itself bogged down in Beirut, with casualties mounting, a pragmatic withdrawal was accepted in February 1984.[8]

Thus, with its military strength and credibility restored, the Reagan administration was by 1985 in a position to undertake a 'constructive dialogue' with the Soviet Union from a position of strength, in which, with the new 'Star Wars' Strategic Defense Initiative, it would be holding the trump cards. These serious discussions commenced in September 1984 with the meeting between President Reagan and the Soviet foreign minister Andrei Gromyko in Washington. With the coming to power in March 1985 of the young new Soviet leader Mikhail Gorbachev, the frequency of top-level diplomatic contacts increased significantly

and meaningful arms control talks recommenced. Both sides ban-
died about contradictory arms reduction offers and fought to win
over world opinion. However, the amicable Reagan-Gorbachev
summit in Geneva in November 1985 raised hopes that a new
longer-term accommodation between the superpowers might be
at hand, based around a revised and harder-nosed version of
detente. During 1986, the Reagan administration's refusal to join
the Soviet Union in a nuclear testing moratorium or to agree to
bargain on its Strategic Defense Initiative (SDI), the replacement
of the pragmatic McFarlane by Vice-Admiral John Poindexter as
NSA,[9] and America's air strikes on Libya during March and April,
resulted in a sharp deterioration in US-Soviet relations. However,
flexibility on the side of the Soviet Union paved the way for a
second Reagan-Gorbachev mini-summit at Reykjavik in Iceland
in October 1986. Dramatic progress in talks concerning sweeping
cutbacks in long- and medium-range nuclear weapon forces was
achieved, but negotiations broke down once more on the SDI
issue.

However, the damage inflicted to the prestige of the Reagan
administration by the 'Irangate' affair of November 1986–March
1987, which served to bring to the fore a moderate core of
pragmatists centred around the figures of State Department
secretary George Shultz, Chief-of-Staff Howard Baker, National
Security Adviser Frank Carlucci[10] and CIA director William Webster, coupled with the continued flexibility exhibited by the Soviet
Union, vaulted arms reduction very much to the head of the
administration's agenda during its final 18 months in power. The
negotiation of an arms-cutting treaty became viewed as a means
of 'rescuing' the presidency and rehabilitating, for posterity,
Reagan's personal reputation as an able statesman. Work thus
began in earnest in Geneva during the spring and summer of
1987 to put together the outlines of two potential treaties: one
concerned with the elimination of all superpower Intermediate-
Range Nuclear Forces (INF) and some shorter-range weapons in
Europe – an updated version of the 'zero option' – and the other
with securing substantial reductions, of between 35–50%, in each
side's long-range strategic nuclear arsenal. Hardliners within the
Defense Department objected to these initiatives and in March
and November 1987 respectively Perle and Weinberger resigned.
The latter was replaced by Carlucci, a low-profile Atlanticist,
with his deputy and protégé at the NSC, Lt General Colin
Powell (50), a highly decorated former NATO commander and

black Vietnam veteran, taking over as NSA. This completed the transformation of the Reagan foreign policy team from one of confrontation to one of consensual accommodation and in December 1987, at the Soviet-American Washington summit, an historic treaty providing for the elimination of superpower INF in Europe was signed by Reagan and Gorbachev. This agreement, which was duly ratified by the Senate and Supreme Soviet (USSR parliament) in March and May 1988 respectively, provided for the Soviet Union's destruction, within three years, of 1752 missiles to the United States' 867.

The Soviet Union had hoped that this INF pact would soon be followed at the succeeding summit, the fourth of the Reagan presidency that had been arranged for May–June 1988 in Moscow, by agreement upon an even more ambitious START treaty. Such an accord was, in the light of the mounting US budget deficit and the fast deteriorating condition of the Soviet economy, widely perceived as being in the material interests of both superpowers. However, President Reagan's stubbornness on the SDI issue, coupled with Pentagon discord over what mix of missile types (land, air and sea-borne) it should seek to maintain and unease about the effectiveness of verification, scuppered these hopes. Instead, at the Moscow summit both national leaders had to be content with limiting their work to the formal public signing of the 1987–8 INF Treaty and a collection of more minor 'confidence-strengthening' notification and verification agreements. This outcome disappointed both pragmatists within the Reagan administration and liberal Democrats outside. However, at Moscow the draft outlines of a possible future START treaty were agreed upon in principle, thus preparing the ground for more detailed negotiations by the succeeding American administration.

While the 'Irangate' affair had significant repercussions upon the Reagan administration's conduct of East-West relations and, in particular, its approach to the issue of arms control, it also had a profound impact upon foreign policy organisation. Under the respected new broom of Frank Carlucci the NSC was restaffed and radically restructured, being forced, during 1987–9, to restrict itself to the purely advisory and policy co-ordinating role that had initially been envisaged by the President in 1981. Additionally, the 'Irangate' affair effectively brought to an end what had become termed the 'Reagan doctrine' – America's direct and covert support for 'freedom fighters' in Afghanistan, Angola, Namibia and

Nicaragua with the aim of 'rolling back' communist revolutions. Faced with a hostile Democrat-controlled Congress, the President, during his closing two years in power, was to find it impossible to repeat his pre-1985 and his 1986 successes in securing military aid for counter-revolutionaries in Central America and West Asia – only small amounts of 'non lethal' humanitarian aid being voted – and had to endure tighter restrictions being imposed upon CIA covert activities. This persuaded the administration, under the lead of State Department Secretary Shultz and with the support of the Soviet Union, to back UN-sponsored solutions to a range of regional conflicts during 1988, including those of Afghanistan, Angola, Cambodia and Namibia. In these regards, 'Irangate' appeared to mark a decisive turning point, comparable to November 1979, for American foreign policy, heralding an era of renewed detente and reassessment of America's place in the world.

Beyond the Cold War – Foreign Policy in the Bush Era

Unlike his three immediate predecessors, the new occupant of the Oval Office from January 1989, George Bush, was a politician brimming with specialist experience and knowledge of international affairs, more so even than had been the case with Richard Nixon in 1969. During the early and mid 1970s, he had spent more than six years as, successively, US ambassador to the UN, Special Envoy to China and Director of the CIA. Thereafter, since 1981, as Vice-President, Bush had made frequent overseas tours, establishing in the process close relationships with ruling heads of government. With this background, the new President was determined, in contrast to his detached predecessor, to take an active personal interest in both the formulation and execution of foreign policy and, indeed, mindful of his intractable domestic budgetary difficulties, was anxious to give high priority to overseas initiatives.

To work alongside him, Bush recruited a diplomatic team of State and Defense Department Secretaries and under-secretaries and White House advisers that was arguably the most high-powered since the Nixon and Ford detente eras.

At the head of this team, occupying the position of State Department Secretary, was Bush's close friend and former

Reagan administration colleague, James Baker. Although a relative novice to the international scene, Baker, during the course of the Reagan presidency, had built up a formidable reputation for political shrewdness, intelligence and tactical savvy. Known as the 'Velvet Hammer', he was unrivalled in his ability to 'sell' policies both to his executive colleagues and to Congress and the media and was renowned for his pragmatic realism. Diplomatically, his record as Treasury Secretary showed him to be a committed internationalist, sharing a world view broadly similar to that of his respected predecessor, George Shultz. To work alongside Baker, as Deputy Secretary for State, President Bush appointed Lawrence Eagleburger, a highly experienced former US Ambassador to Yugoslavia and longtime Kissinger aide. Baker also inducted into the State Department, to the chagrin of its permanent officials, a team of trusted personal counsellors and advisers, headed by Robert Zoellick and Margaret Tutwiler, who had previously worked closely with him at the White House and the Treasury.

To fill the post of NSA,[11] President Bush turned to Lt General Brent Scowcroft, another Nixon-Ford 'old hand' and Kissinger protégé, who had previously occupied the same position, and with distinction, more than a decade earlier in 1975–6, at the time when Bush had charge of the CIA.[12] Scowcroft was thus personally close to the President and, being drawn from the same generation, also shared a similar world view. To work alongside Scowcroft, as Deputy NSA, Robert Gates, a much more hawkish conservative, was transferred from his duties as Deputy Director of the CIA. In addition, Scowcroft personally recruited an impressive coterie of foreign policy experts to take charge of sub-sections of the NSC. They included: Robert Blackwill, European and Soviet affairs; Richard Haas, Middle East; and Karl Jackson, Asia and the Pacific Rim.

Completing the top echelon of the new foreign policy team, Dick Cheney, an experienced conservative Republican Congressman, was appointed, following the failure of the Tower nomination (see page 163), Defense Secretary. Here he was given the brief of restoring order and efficiency to the Pentagon's procurement process after it had fallen into disrepute as a result of the uncovering of a series of corruption and overcharging scandals during the Weinberger ('Cap the Shovel') era of rapid budgetary expansion. Cheney, a longstanding fishing companion of the President's and a Ford administration colleague of both Baker and Scowcroft, was also assigned the task of overseeing a far-reaching defence spending review, with the aim of establishing where economies could best be secured and of deciding which new weapon programmes should be continued and which abandoned. The final two members of the new foreign affairs team were William Webster, who was retained as Director of the CIA, and Thomas Pickering, a career diplomat, who replaced General Vernon Walters (now reassigned as US ambassador to Bonn) as America's UN Representative. Departing from previous administration practice, neither of these two appointees was granted cabinet-level status.

In its broad complexion, the Bush foreign policy team contrasted sharply with that recruited by Ronald Reagan in 1981, being staffed at its uppermost levels predominantly by pragmatic, internationalist 'Rockefeller Republicans' and, in particular, by men closely linked to Henry Kissinger, a figure who, as the architect of detente, was loathed by the Republican far-right. In addition, although two of its key figures, Bush and Baker, were drawn from Texas and, as a consequence, had a keen interest in adjacent Central American affairs, the Bush foreign policy team adhered fundamentally to a traditional Atlanticist world view. In this regard, their outlook appeared to be in line with that of the Shultz-Carlucci-Powell 'establishment troika' that had dominated US foreign policy-making during the closing 14 months of the Reagan presidency.

However, despite such experience and apparent concordance of policy vision, the opening months of the new Bush presidency were to be marked, in the diplomatic sphere, by a surprising directionless uncertainty. This rudderlessness was particularly apparent in the sphere of East-West relations where, notwithstanding immediate post-election urgings by the Soviet side that a new heads-of-government summit meeting should swiftly be convened so as to give impetus to the START process, the American side elected for a period of 'cooling' and stock-taking.

One of the factors that explained this initial diplomatic hiatus was a desire on the part of the administration to 'put some distance' between itself and its immediate predecessor so as to make clear to the outside world that the Bush presidency did not mark a simple continuation of the Reagan era, but, instead, was ready to think anew and would offer its own distinctive style and approach to foreign policy issues. A second factor was that much of administration's time during its early months was simply occupied with recruiting and overseeing the confirmation of new staff, a process which, as a result of the 'Tower affair', was to be surprisingly protracted during 1989. A third, partly linked, factor was that both NSA Scowcroft and State Department Secretary Baker chose to accord initial priority to reorganising their respective departments and to liaising with both potential Congressional and external allies, so as to get a 'feel' for the outside mood.

The most fundamental restructuring occurred at the NSC. Here Scowcroft, somewhat departing from his own Tower Commission recommendations, moved swiftly to increase his institution's authority, at least in the policy formulation and recommendation spheres. He secured for himself the seat of chairman of the co-ordinating 'principals' committee, the key committee on which all cabinet members with an involvement in foreign policy sit: previously the State Department Secretary had headed this committee. He also sponsored the creation of a new 'deputies committee', chaired by his assistant Gates, which, including amongst its members the Deputy Director of the CIA and the vice-chairmen of the Joint Chiefs of Staff, brought together, for the first time, sub-cabinet level members of government agencies which had an interest in foreign affairs. Both of these moves were designed to promote closer government foreign policy consensus, in the hope of ensuring that the semi-public NSC, State and Defense Department wranglings that had blighted the Reagan presidency would be averted. They also served, however, to establish Scowcroft as the administration's dominant backroom policy co-ordinator and detailed strategist. This left State Department Secretary Baker to concentrate on liaison and the public execution of policy, concentrating, in particular, upon the five key 'glamour' areas of East-West relations, the Middle East, Latin America, Western Europe and Japan.

It was, however, the momentous changes that were occurring in the world outside that were the most important factor behind the new administration's uncertainty in the foreign policy sphere during the spring of 1989. The postwar global order was apparently being torn asunder as one of its key elements, the Soviet empire, began to disintegrate. This called into question the relevance of existing American strategic thinking, setting off a wide-ranging debate both within and outside government circles.

The Soviet imperial collapse commenced at the periphery during 1988–9 as the USSR's reformist leader, Mikhail Gorbachev, switching priority from guns to domestic butter, began to retrench overseas, deciding to cease bankrolling unpopular puppet regimes and guerrilla movements in Africa and Asia and, instead, to seek negotiated settlements to regional disputes. As a consequence, Soviet troops were withdrawn from Afghanistan during 1988–9, as, under Soviet prompting, were those of Vietnam from Cambodia and, more gradually, those of Cuba from Angola. Closer to home, Gorbachev also made a critical decision during 1988–9 to renounce the post-1968 'Brezhnev Doctrine' of Soviet intervention to ensure the maintenance of 'correct socialism' within its sphere of influence and, instead, now made clear his willingness to allow the Soviet satellite regimes of Eastern Europe the freedom to determine their own futures, whether as socialist republics or as pluralist democracies. As a consequence, the existing neo-Stalinist regimes of the region were to be rapidly overthrown during 1988–9 variously as a result of internal reformist coups, as was the case in Hungary (October 1989) and Bulgaria (November 1989); of the electoral process, as in Poland (September 1989); of peaceful 'people's power' demonstrations, as in East Germany (October–November 1989) and Czechoslovakia in (November 1989–January 1990); or of violent civil strife, as in Romania (December 1989 – January 1990). This drive towards autonomy and pluralism also rippled over the Soviet borders during 1989–90, the 'year of revolution', igniting the Baltic and Trans-Caucasus Republics to such an extent that the very unity of the Soviet federation became imperilled.

Beyond the 'Soviet sphere', significant changes also took place in the key region of the Middle East during 1988–9. Here the PLO's renunciation of the use of terrorist violence and their recognition of Israel's right to exist promised to ease a diplomatic logjam and render the search for a negotiated settlement to the West Bank-Gaza Strip issue potentially feasible. Further to the northeast, the ending, during 1988, of the long-running Iran-Iraq war and the death, in June 1989, of Iran's fundamentalist leader Ayatollah Khomeini also seemed to provide a 'window of opportunity' for America in the region.

However, perhaps most fundamentally, as the Reagan presidency closed and the Bush era opened, there began to develop a sense, in academic, diplomatic and political circles, that the postwar bipolar superpower cold war age was at last drawing to a close and that a new post-superpower global order was in the making. This post cold war epoch seemed likely, as result of

Europe's moves towards closer unity – with a 'Greater Germany' situated at its core – and Japan's continuing economic advance, to be dominated by four power blocks: Europe, the US, Japan and the Pacific Rim and, economically weakest of all, the Soviet Union. In this new quadripolar world, such cold war structures as NATO and the Warsaw Pact would require remodelling and, within the 'Western community', military 'burden sharing' reviewed.

In the light of these far-reaching developments, the new Bush administration chose wisely, at its outset, to institute a 'grand review' of US foreign policy in all of its areas, though with special focus being accorded to the key topic of East-West relations in the era of glasnost (openness), perestroika (economic restructuring) and Soviet decolonisation. For several months, between January and March 1989, a battle raged within the administration between conservatives, headed by Deputy NSA Gates, Defense Secretary Cheney, and Vice-President Quayle, and moderates, led by State Department Secretary Baker, over whether the comprehensive reforms instituted by Gorbachev were, first, genuine and, second, likely to succeed. Conservative strategists doubted both and argued that Gorbachev's reforms were doomed to fail and that a belligerent hardliner would replace him at the Soviet helm. The more moderate Baker was similarly by no means certain as to Gorbachev's ability to survive. However, whilst the Soviet reform process was underway, he believed it prudent to grasp the 'historic opportunity' then available for the negotiation of a series of sensible arms reduction deals (chemical, conventional and strategic). Baker also believed that the West should work to try and improve the odds on the success of the perestroika and glasnost reforms and to encourage moves towards even greater pluralism by granting to the Eastern bloc economic carrots in the forms both of financial aid and the easing of restrictions on technology transfers. Initially, President Bush and NSA Scowcroft adopted a non-committal, intermediate position in this 'hawks' versus 'doves' debate, both voicing grave reservations as to the viability of the Gorbachev reform programme. Eventually, however, when the foreign policy review was formally completed in April 1989, they chose to side with the Baker camp. This gave the green light to a rapid thawing of Soviet-American relations.

The earliest indication that the battle had been won by the proponents of a new 'constructive detente' was the announcement, on 25 April 1989, by Defense Secretary Cheney that a five-year rolling programme of what he described as 'very, very painful' economies (amounting to $64 billion) in the defence budget had been agreed upon by the administration. These included a reduction in military personnel of 17200 and a supra-20% cutback in funding for the SDI programme. This was then followed, in May 1989, by President Bush's unveiling, in a speech at the NATO summit in Brussels, of a plan to reduce, by 1993, US conventional forces in Europe (CFE) by 20% to a ceiling of 275000 on the understanding that the Soviet Union would asymmetrically cut its Atlantic-to-Urals troop levels by more than 50% to the same figure. Two months later, during visits to Poland and Hungary, the President made clear his willingness to increase significantly the level of American financial aid to these reforming countries so as to help underpin their reform movements. In Geneva, meanwhile, considerable progress began to be made during the summer of 1989 towards the agreement of a potential draft US-Soviet treaty for the banning of chemical weapons and towards removing the obstacles that lay in the path of a START accord. These advances were furthered during informal talks held by State Department Secretary Baker and the Soviet Foreign Minister, Eduard Shevardnadze, at Jackson Hole, Wyoming on 22–23 September 1989 and during a brief 'floating summit' which was held between Bush and Gorbachev on their respective naval vessels moored off Malta harbour on 2–3 December 1989.

Although no substantive treaties were signed by the two nations during 1989, the warming in relations that was apparent from April seemed set to bear fruit in potential subsequent agreements on chemical weapons, CFE reduction – to a projected figure of below 195000, following a further Bush initiative in February 1990 – within a Helsinki-2 framework and, helped by Soviet movement on the SDI issue, START between 1990–2. After a cautious beginning, the Bush administration thus appeared, following the victory of Baker and the State Department 'doves' in the spring policy review, to have, by the close of 1989, begun to build imaginatively upon the initiatives taken by the Shultz-Carlucci-Powell troika during 1987–8 and to have embraced with enthusiasm an enlightened new policy of 'constructive detente'. This policy marked, as the President outlined in a major speech on East-West issues delivered in Texas on 12 May 1989, a significant advance 'beyond [the doctine of] containment' towards the ambitious goal of both securing the freeing of Eastern Europe from authoritarianism, and its uniting with Western Europe, and the 'integration of the Soviet Union into the community of nations'.

In other strategic areas, changes in emphasis from the policies pursued by the Reagan administration also became evident as the Bush presidency progressed. In the case of Europe, the close 'special relationship' that had existed between the US and the United Kingdom during the Reagan years began to be weakened as new emphasis was placed upon both targeting West Germany as the key player in the European field and upon supporting a quickening of the process of European Community integration. In the case of South Africa, contacts with black organisations and institutions were broadened. In the Middle East, an effort began to be made to revivify the peace process in Israel-Palestine. Finally, in Central America, a gradual retreat began to be made from the Reagan policy of staunch backing of the Contras towards a more constructive encouragement of democratisation by persuasion rather than force. This was evidenced by the administration's entering into an agreement with Congress that, for 1989–90, it would merely seek humanitarian (food and housing assistance), and not military, aid for the Contras, pending the holding of free elections promised by the Sandinista regime during 1990. In all of these areas, the Bush administration, under the lead of State Department Secretary Baker, had made substantive moves towards more centrist positions. In the process, it hoped to re-establish a bipartisan, administration-Congress, consensus over foreign policy issues that had been noticeably absent during the Reagan and even the Carter presidencies.

The Bush administration's cautious, low-key start in the diplomatic sphere during the spring of 1989 led, domestically, to charges of weak, vacillating, 'wimpish' presidential leadership, and, to confusion among both America's allies and the Soviet side. However, many of these criticisms were assuaged by the launching of the President's well-received detente initiative during his early summer tours of Western and Eastern Europe. In the light of this 'peace initiative', the President's public approval ratings rose sharply. They briefly dipped during October 1989, following renewed charges of indecision over the President's unwillingness to commit US military forces in the support of an attempted coup that had been made on 3 October 1989 against Panama's corrupt strongman, General Manuel Noriega, a man whose extradition to America was sought on drugs-running charges. However, in December 1989, Bush finally laid to rest all charges of timidity by two decisive actions. First, on the opening day of the month, the President sanctioned the requested deployment of US F-4 Phantom jets to control the skies above Manila so as to ensure the survival of the Philippines leader, Corazon Aquino, whose democratically elected government was faced by overthrow by renegade forces. Then, on the eve of Christmas, Bush oversaw the launching of an assault by 24 000 American troops, half of whom were drawn from the US's adjacent Canal Zone bases, on the army barracks of Panama city which succeeded, at the loss of 23 GI lives, in toppling the Noriega regime and, eventually on 3 January 1990, securing the capture and safe transfer to American soil of the reviled dictator. The latter invasion, which involved the largest use of US military power since Vietnam, was viewed by American eyes, despite the high toll of life on the Panamanian side (314 troops and at least 220 'unarmed civilians') as a striking military success. It constituted for Bush his 'Grenada'. In its wake, his public approval ratings soared into the high seventies – polls showing that 80% of Americans approved of the invasion, including 74% of Democrat voters – as a new reputation for toughness and decision had been established.

The US forces' successful action in Panama brought to a close a year in which America's foreign policy had been subtly remoulded. In some respects the Panama action, in which, as also in the October 1989 failed coup attempt, CIA operatives had been intimately involved, represented a reversion to the gung-ho 'America first' policy in the Central American sphere that had characterised the Reagan years. However, this appeared to be an exception. As the Bush presidency developed, the more general trend in foreign policy appeared to be a softening of both rhetoric and actions in traditionally polarising areas and a move towards positions of greater consensus. In particular, a new more constructive relationship with the East was apparent, from which a useful 'peace dividend', in the form of defence economies, showed signs of accruing. This promised to be of value in helping the administration to deal with its pressing domestic budgetary difficulties. Much, however, in the international sphere remained uncertain, being dependent to a substantial extent upon the outcome of the reform process in the Soviet Union.

APPENDIX A

THE STATES, CITIES AND OVERSEAS TERRITORIES OF AMERICA

TABLE A1   THE SIZE AND POPULATION OF AMERICA'S 50 STATES*

	Area (sq km)	Est 1987 Population (000)	Date of Joining the Union	State Capital
Alabama	133,665	4,083	1819	Montgomery
Alaska	1,518,539	525	1959	Juneau
Arizona	295,023	3,386	1912	Phoenix
Arkansas	137,533	2,388	1836	Little Rock
California	411,013	27,633	1850	Sacramento
Colorado	270,240	3,296	1876	Denver
Connecticut†	12,973	3,211	1788	Hartford
Delaware†	5,328	644	1787	Dover
Florida	151,700	12,023	1845	Tallahassee
Georgia†	152,500	6,222	1788	Atlanta
Hawaii	16,705	1,083	1959	Honolulu
Idaho	216,412	998	1890	Boise
Illinois	146,075	11,582	1818	Springfield
Indiana	93,994	5,531	1816	Indianapolis
Iowa	145,790	2,834	1846	Des Moines
Kansas	213,063	2,476	1861	Topeka
Kentucky	104,623	3,727	1792	Frankfurt
Louisiana	125,675	4,461	1812	Baton Rouge
Maine	86,027	1,187	1820	Augusta
Maryland†	27,394	4,535	1788	Annapolis
Massachusetts†	21,385	5,855	1788	Boston
Michigan	150,777	9,200	1837	Lansing
Minnesota	217,735	4,246	1858	St Paul
Mississippi	123,584	2,625	1817	Jackson
Missouri	180,455	5,103	1821	Jefferson City
Montana	381,085	809	1889	Helena
Nebraska	200,036	1,594	1867	Lincoln
Nevada	286,300	1,007	1864	Carson City
New Hampshire†	24,100	1,057	1788	Concord
New Jersey†	20,295	7,672	1787	Trenton

233

Table A1   The Size and Population of America's 50 States (cont)

	Area (sq km)	Est 1987 Population (000)	Date of Joining the Union	State Capital
New Mexico	315,133	1,500	1912	Santa Fe
New York[†]	128,400	17,825	1788	Albany
North Carolina[†]	136,523	6,413	1789	Raleigh
North Dakota	183,020	672	1889	Bismarck
Ohio	106,714	10,784	1803	Columbus
Oklahoma	181,088	3,272	1907	Oklahoma City
Oregon	251,180	2,724	1859	Salem
Pennsylvania[†]	117,412	11,936	1787	Harrisburg
Rhode Island[†]	3,144	986	1790	Providence
South Carolina[†]	80,432	3,425	1788	Columbia
South Dakota	199,550	709	1889	Pierre
Tennessee	109,412	4,855	1796	Nashville
Texas	692,407	16,789	1845	Austin
Utah	219,931	1,680	1896	Salt Lake City
Vermont	24,887	548	1791	Montpelier
Virginia[†]	105,711	5,904	1788	Richmond
Washington	176,615	4,538	1889	Olympia
West Virginia	62,629	1,897	1863	Charleston
Wisconsin	145,438	4,807	1848	Madison
Wyoming	253,595	490	1890	Cheyenne
District of Columbia	179	622		
All America	9,363,404	243,400		Washington DC

[*] Below the State level there are 3100 counties, over 18 000 municipalities and almost 17 000 townships.

[†] The 13 original States which joined the Union and ratified the US constitution between 1787 and 1790.

TABLE A2   THE CONTEMPORARY POLITICAL PROFILE OF
THE UNITED STATES

	Presidential Electoral College Votes	1989–90 H of R Seats		1989–90 Senate Seats		Total* Seats in Statehouses		Jan 1990†
		D	R	D	R	Upper	Lower	Governor
Alabama‡	9	5	2	2	0	35	105	Guy Hunt (R)
Alaska	3	0	1	0	2	20	40	Steve Cowper (D)
Arizona‡	7	1	4	1	1	30	60	Rose Mofford (D)
Arkansas‡	6	3	1	2	0	35	100	Bill Clinton (D)
California‡	47	27	18	1	1	40	80	George Deukmejian (R)
Colorado‡	8	3	3	1	1	35	65	Roy Romer (D)
Connecticut‡	8	3	3	2	0	36	151	William O'Neill (D)
Delaware‡	3	1	0	1	1	21	41	Michael Castle (R)
Florida‡	21	10	9	1	1	40	120	Bob Martinez (R)
Georgia‡	12	9	1	2	0	56	180	Joe Harris (D)
Hawaii	4‡	1	1	2	0	25	51	John Waihee (D)
Idaho‡	4	1	1	0	2	42	84	Cecil Andrus (D)
Illinois‡	24	14	8	2	0	59	118	James Thompson (R)
Indiana‡	12	6	4	0	2	50	100	Evan Bayh (D)
Iowa	8	2	4	1	1	50	100	Terry Branstad (R)
Kansas	7	2	3	0	2	40	125	Mike Hayden (R)
Kentucky‡	9	4	3	1	1	38	100	Wallace Wilkinson (D)
Louisiana‡	10	4	4	2	0	39	105	Buddy Roemer (D)
Maine	4	1	1	1	1	33	151	John McKernan (R)
Maryland‡	10	6	2	2	0	47	141	William Schaefer (D)
Massachusetts	13	10	1	2	0	40	160	Michael Dukakis (D)
Michigan	20	11	7	2	0	38	110	James Blanchard (D)
Minnesota	10	5	3	0	2	67	134	Rudy Perpich (DFL)
Mississippi‡	7	4	1	0	2	52	122	Ray Mabus (D)
Missouri‡	11	5	4	0	2	34	163	John Ashcroft (R)
Montana‡	4	1	1	1	1	50	100	Stan Stephens (R)
Nebraska‡	5	1	2	2	0	49	—	Kay Orr (R)
Nevada‡	4	1	1	2	0	21	42	Bob Miller (D)
New Hampshire‡	4	0	2	0	2	24	400	Judd Gregg (R)
New Jersey‡	16	8	6	2	0	40	80	Jim Florio (D)
New Mexico‡	5	1	2	1	1	42	70	Garrey Carruthers (R)
New York	36	21	13	1	1	61	150	Mario Cuomo (D)
North Carolina‡	13	8	3	1	1	50	120	James Martin (R)
North Dakota	3	1	0	2	0	53	106	George Sinner (D)
Ohio‡	23	11	10	2	0	33	99	Richard Celeste (D)
Oklahoma‡	8	4	2	1	1	48	101	Henry Bellmon (R)

Table A2   The Contemporary Political Profile of the United States (contd)

	Presidential Electoral College Votes	1989–90 H of R Seats D	1989–90 H of R Seats R	1989–90 Senate Seats D	1989–90 Senate Seats R	Total* Seats in Statehouses Upper	Total* Seats in Statehouses Lower	Jan 1990[†] Governor
Oregon[‡]	7	3	2	0	2	30	60	Neil Goldschmidt (D)
Pennsylvania[‡]	25	12	11	0	2	50	203	Bob Casey (D)
Rhode Island	4	0	2	1	1	50	100	Edward DiPrete (R)
South Carolina[‡]	8	4	2	1	1	46	124	Carroll Campbell (R)
South Dakota[‡]	3	1	0	1	1	35	70	George Mickelson (R)
Tennessee[‡]	11	6	3	2	0	33	99	Ned McWherter (D)
Texas[‡]	29	19	8	1	1	31	150	Bill Clements (R)
Utah[‡]	5	1	2	0	2	29	75	Norman Bangerter (R)
Vermont[‡]	3	0	1	1	1	30	150	Madeleine Kunin (D)
Virginia[‡]	12	5	5	1	1	40	100	Douglas Wilder (D)
Washington[‡]	10	5	3	1	1	49	98	Booth Gardner (D)
West Virginia	6	4	0	2	0	34	100	Gaston Caperton (D)
Wisconsin	11	5	4	1	1	33	99	Tommy Thompson (R)
Wyoming[‡]	3	0	1	0	2	30	62	Mike Sullivan (D)
District of Columbia[§]	3	1**	0	0	0	10[††]	—	Marion Barry (D) Mayor
All America	538	260	175	55	45	2003	5464	

* The legislative arrangements for each State vary substantially in terms of the size of local Statehouses (see Table above), the frequency of elections and the length of sittings. All States, with the exception of unicameral Nebraska (whose members are, in addition, elected without party designation), possess two-chamber legislatures. In most States, members of the upper house are elected for four-year terms; the exceptions are Connecticut, Georgia, Idaho, Maine, New Hampshire, New York, North Carolina, Rhode Island, South Dakota and Vermont, where terms last for only two years. All lower houses, with the exception of Alabama, Louisiana, Maryland and Mississippi (which each have four-year terms), are elected at two-yearly intervals. Legislatures in most of the larger States meet on an annual basis for sessions of considerable length. By contrast, a number of, primarily, smaller State legislatures meet only once every two years in either odd (Arkansas, Montana, Nevada, North Carolina, North Dakota, Oregon, Texas and Vermont) or even years (Kentucky). In Minnesota, New Mexico, Rhode Island, South Dakota and Utah the State legislatures sit for sessions of less than 60 days per annum.

[†] Most State Governors serve terms of four years. New Hampshire, Rhode Island and Vermont are the exceptions, enjoying terms of only two years. In 31 States there are no restrictions on the numbers of terms a Governor can

serve. However, in Kentucky, Mississippi, New Mexico, South Carolina and Virginia, Governors are debarred from serving consecutive terms in office; in Alabama, Florida, Indiana, Maryland, Missouri, Nebraska, New Jersey, Oregon, Pennsylvania, South Dakota and West Virginia the limit is two consecutive terms; while in Delaware, Georgia and North Carolina the limitation is a maximum of two terms consecutive or otherwise. In Vermont there are special regulations for the election of Governors, successful candidates needing to gain a clear majority, not just a plurality, in gubernatorial contests, with the State legislature having the final say over selection in the January following the November election if no clear majority has been gained.

‡   States in which capital punishment is in force.

§   The District of Columbia, being the site of the Federal legislature and executive, was administered directly by three commissioners appointed by the President until 1967 and its citizens were unable to vote in presidential elections until the passage of the 23rd Constitutional Amendment in 1961. Between 1967-74 the local governance of the District of Columbia was entrusted to a mayor-commissioner and a nine-member City Council, all of whom were appointed by the President subject to the approval of the Senate. In May 1974, however, a Home Rule Charter was approved by the local citizens under which the mayor and, now 13-member, City Council became subject to popular election and the District gained the right to levy its own taxes, subject to continuing Congressional veto rights. The District has also enjoyed representation in Congress since 1971 in the form of one delegate to the House of Representatives who can vote in committees but not in floor debates. A Constitutional Amendment designed to give the District of Columbia full, State-level, voting representation in Congress was passed by the House of Representatives and Senate in 1978 but failed to gain ratification by the necessary 38 State legislatures within the stipulated seven-year term.

**   Non-voting member on House floor.

††   City Council.

Politics in the USA

TABLE A3   STATE SOCIO-ECONOMIC DATA BY REGIONS IN 1986

Region & State	Pop Change 1980–6 (%)	% of Population Black	% of Population Hispanic	Per Capita Income ($)	Rate of Unemployment (%)
CENTRAL	+ 7.8	3.7	7.3	13,301	7.1
Colorado	+13.1	3.5	11.8	15,113	7.4
Kansas	+ 4.1	5.3	2.7	14,379	5.4
Montana	+ 4.1	0.2	1.3	11,904	8.1
Nebraska	+ 1.8	3.1	1.8	13,777	5.0
New Mexico	+13.5	1.8	36.6	11,037	9.2
North Dakota	+ 4.1	0.4	0.6	12,284	6.3
Oklahoma	+ 9.2	6.8	1.9	12,368	8.2
South Dakota	+ 2.5	0.3	0.6	11,850	4.7
Wyoming	+ 8.0	0.7	5.2	13,230	9.0
NORTH-CENTRAL	+ 0.6	9.5	2.1	13,929	7.6
Illinois	+ 1.1	14.7	5.6	15,420	8.1
Indiana	+ 0.2	7.6	1.6	12,944	6.7
Iowa	− 2.2	1.4	0.9	13,222	7.0
Kentucky	+ 1.9	7.1	0.7	11,129	9.3
Michigan	− 1.3	12.9	1.7	14,064	8.8
Minnesota	+ 3.4	1.3	0.8	14,737	5.3
Missouri	+ 3.0	10.5	1.0	13,657	6.1
Ohio	− 0.4	10.0	1.1	13,743	8.1
Wisconsin	+ 1.7	3.9	1.3	13,796	7.0
NORTH-EAST	+ 2.0	11.3	4.8	16,288	5.7
Connecticut	+ 2.6	7.0	4.0	19,208	3.8
Delaware	+ 6.5	16.1	1.6	15,010	4.3
District of Columbia	− 1.9	70.4	2.8	N/A	N/A
Maine	+ 4.3	0.3	0.4	12,709	5.3
Maryland	+ 5.8	22.7	1.5	16,588	4.5
Massachusetts	+ 1.7	3.9	2.5	17,516	3.8
New Hampshire	+11.5	0.4	0.6	15,922	2.8
New Jersey	+ 3.5	12.6	6.7	18,284	5.0
New York	+ 1.2	13.7	9.4	17,118	6.3
Pennsylvania	+ 0.2	8.8	1.3	13,944	6.8
Rhode Island	+ 2.9	2.9	2.1	14,670	4.0
Vermont	+ 5.8	0.2	0.6	12,845	4.7
West Virginia	− 1.6	3.3	0.7	10,530	11.8

State Socio-Economic Data by Regions in 1986 (contd)

Region & State	Pop Change 1980–6 (%)	% of Population Black	% of Population Hispanic	Per Capita Income ($)	Rate of Unemployment (%)
SOUTH	+11.3	19.6	7.0	12,882	7.7
Alabama	+ 4.1	25.6	0.9	11,115	9.8
Arkansas	+ 3.8	16.4	0.8	10,773	8.7
Florida	+19.8	13.8	8.8	14,281	5.7
Georgia	+11.7	26.8	1.1	13,224	5.9
Louisiana	+ 7.0	29.4	2.4	11,227	13.1
Mississippi	+ 4.1	35.2	1.0	9,522	11.7
North Carolina	+ 7.7	22.4	1.0	12,245	5.3
South Carolina	+ 8.2	30.4	1.1	11,096	6.2
Tennessee	+ 4.6	15.8	0.7	11,831	8.0
Texas	+17.3	12.0	21.0	13,523	8.9
Virginia	+ 8.2	18.9	1.5	15,374	5.0
WEST	+13.2	5.6	14.3	15,599	7.0
Alaska	+32.8	3.4	2.4	17,744	10.8
Arizona	+22.1	2.8	16.2	13,220	6.9
California	+14.0	7.7	19.2	16,778	6.7
Hawaii	+10.1	1.8	7.4	14,691	4.8
Idaho	+ 6.2	0.3	3.9	11,432	8.7
Nevada	+20.3	6.4	6.6	15,074	6.0
Oregon	+ 2.5	1.4	2.5	13,217	8.5
Utah	+14.0	0.6	4.1	10,743	6.0
Washington	+ 8.0	2.6	2.9	14,498	8.2
USA TOTAL	+ 6.4	11.7	6.5	14,450	7.0

TABLE A4 THE UNITED STATES' TWENTY-FIVE LARGEST CITIES IN JANUARY 1990

Ranking Number		State	Population	Mayor
1	New York	NY	7,262,700	David Dinkins (D)
2	Los Angeles	Calif	3,259,340	Tom Bradley (D)
3	Chicago	Ill	3,009,530	Richard Daley (D)
4	Houston	Texas	1,728,910	Kathryn J Whitmire (D)
5	Philadelphia	Pa	1,642,900	Wilson Goode (D)
6	Detroit	Mich	1,086,220	Coleman Young (D)
7	San Diego*	Calif	1,015,190	Maureen O'Connor (D)
8	Dallas*	Texas	1,003,520	Annette Strauss (D)
9	San Antonio*	Texas	914,350	Lila Cockrell (D)
10	Phoenix	Ariz	894,070	Tery Goddard (N-P)
11	Baltimore	Md	752,800	Kurt Schmoke (D)
12	San Francisco	Calif	749,000	Art Agnos (D)
13	Indianapolis	Ind	719,820	William Hudnut III (R)
14	San Jose*	Calif	712,080	Thomas McEnery (N-P)
15	Memphis	Tenn	652,640	Richard Hackett (N-P)
16	Washington	DC	626,000	Marion Barry Jr (D)
17	Jacksonville	Fla	609,860	Tommy Hazouri (D)
18	Milwaukee	Wis	605,090	John Norquist (D)
19	Boston	Mass	573,600	Raymond Flynn (D)
20	Columbus	Ohio	566,030	Dana Rinehart (R)
21	New Orleans	La	554,500	Sydney Barthelemy (D)
22	Cleveland	Ohio	535,830	Michael White (D)
23	Denver	Colo	505,000	Federico Pena (D)
24	El Paso	Texas	491,800	Johnathan Rogers (N-P)
25	Seattle	Wash	486,200	Norman Rice (D)

* Also governed by a professional 'City Manager'.
(N-P) = Non-partisan

TABLE A5   AMERICA'S OVERSEAS DEPENDENCIES*

	Area (sq km)	1986 Population (000)	Congressional Representation	Local Legislature U	Local Legislature L	Governor (In May 1989)
EXTERNAL TERRITORIES						
American Samoa	199	35	1	18	20	Peter Tali Coleman
Guam	541	125	1	21	–	Joseph Ada
Commonwealth of Puerto Rico	8,959	3,274	1	27	53	Rafael Hernandez-Colon
US Virgin Islands	343	111	1	15	–	Alexander Farrelly
FORMER UN PACIFIC TRUST TERRITORIES						
Republic of the Marshall Isles	180	35	0	33	–	(President) Amata Kabua
Federated States of Micronesia	691	85	0	79†	–	Yapese John Hagelgam
Commonwealth of the Northern Marianas Isles	471	20	0	9	15	Pedro Tenorio
Republic of Palau	367	14	0	–‡	–‡	Ngiratkel Etpison

U = Upper   L = Lower

* These overseas territories vary in their degree of dependency on the United States. The Pacific Trust Territories were administered by the United States on behalf of the United Nations (UN) during 1947–79 in preparation for full independence. Such independence was granted during the later years of the Carter administration when, under the designation 'Compacts of Free Association', new constitutions, involving the principles of self-government, were adopted by all the islands, with the sole

exception (before 1990) of Palau (Belau), and were ratified by the UN Trusteeship Council. The United States still guarantees, however, the defence and security of the Micronesia region and provides substantial economic aid. The United States retains closer links with the self-governing 'External Territories'. Each sends a delegate to the US House of Representatives, who can vote in committees but not on the floor of the House, and is subject to many federal laws and a number of federal taxes, for example, social security. Moreover, citizens of these territories enjoy special rights within the United States. Politically, these include that of participation in the primary process employed by the two principal 'mainland' parties in selecting a candidate to contest the US presidential election: for example, in 1988, 68 of the Democratic Party's National Convention delegates were chosen by Puerto Rico (56), American Samoa (4), Guam (4) and the US Virgin Islands (4) and a further 9, by mail ballot, by the 'Democrats Abroad' constituency. However, citizens of these 'External Territories do not have the right to vote in the actual November US presidential election. In recent years, the US overseas territories have grown in autonomy, with their executive Governors now being elected locally by universal adult suffrage rather than being appointed by the US government, as had occurred in Puerto Rico until 1977. However, in Puerto Rico, there is currently a movement afoot to secure full statehood for the Caribbean 'colony', with a plebiscite likely to be held on this subject in 1991. The opposition, Republican-leaning, New Progressive Party (PNP), along with almost half the population, favour statehood, but the concept is opposed by the ruling Popular Democratic Party (PDP) led by Rafael Hernandez-Colon. Instead, the PDP seeks enhancement of the territory's current semi-autonomous 'commonwealth' status. The more radical, socialist Independence Party (PIP) favours full autonomy and enjoys 10% public support. If Puerto Rico did become the 51st State in the Union, a possible development which President Bush has warmly welcomed, it would rank 27th in demographic terms and be entitled to two Senators and six or seven Representatives. With a per capita income barely two-thirds that of the current bottom ranking State of Mississippi and an unemployment level in excess of 15%, it would be the poorest State in the Union. It would also be the only fully Spanish-speaking State.

† Comprising four locally elected district, or State, legislatures of between 10 and 28 members apiece, with 79 legislators in all.
‡ Two-chamber legislature, membership numbers uncertain pending adoption of a new constitution.

Further information on the political structures, histories and party systems of these dependencies is provided in JD and ID Derbyshire, *Political Systems of the World*, Edinburgh, W & R Chambers, 1989, pp 842–54.

APPENDIX B

SUPPLEMENTARY TABLES ON POSTWAR PRESIDENTIAL, CONGRESSIONAL, JUDICIAL AND PARTY AFFAIRS

TABLE B1   POSTWAR PRESIDENTIAL ELECTION RESULTS

	Democrat	Popular Vote (m)	Electoral College Vote	Republican	Popular Vote (m)	Electoral College Vote	Voter Turnout* (%)
1948	HS Truman	24.18	303	TE Dewey	21.99	189	51.1
1952	AE Stevenson	27.31	89	DD Eisenhower	33.94	442	61.6
1956	AE Stevenson	26.02	73	DD Eisenhower	35.59	457	59.3
1960	JF Kennedy	34.23	303	RM Nixon	34.11	219	62.8
1964	LB Johnson	43.13	486	BM Goldwater	27.18	52	61.9
1968	HH Humphrey	31.28	191	RM Nixon	31.78	301	60.9
1972	G McGovern	29.17	17	RM Nixon	47.17	520	55.2
1976	JE Carter	40.83	297	GR Ford	39.15	240	54.4
1980	JE Carter	35.48	49	RW Reagan	43.90	489	52.6
1984	WF Mondale	37.57	13	RW Reagan	54.45	525	53.3
1988	MS Dukakis	41.81	111	GHW Bush	48.88	426	50.1

* The % of the voting-age population who cast a ballot.

243

TABLE B2 THIRD-PARTY CANDIDATES IN POSTWAR ELECTIONS

	Candidate	Party	Popular Vote (m)	Electoral College Vote
1948	J Strom Thurmond	States' Rights Dem	1.18	39
	Henry A Wallace	Progressive	1.16	0
	Norman Thomas	Socialist	0.14	0
1968	George C Wallace	American Ind	9.91	46
1972	John G Schmitz	American	1.10	0
1976	Eugene J McCarthy	Independent	0.76	0
1980	John B Anderson	Independent	5.72	0
1980	Ed Clark	Libertarian	0.92	0
1984	David Bergland	Libertarian	0.23	0
1988	Ron Paul	Libertarian	0.43	0

TABLE B3 PARTY SHARES IN CONGRESS AND GOVERNORSHIPS SINCE 1973*

	Number of Congress	House of Representatives	Senate	Governorships
1973–4	93rd	D–242 R–192	D–56 R–42	D–32 R–18
1975–6	94th	D–291 R–144	D–61 R–37	D–36 R–13
1977–8	95th	D–292 R–143	D–61 R–38	D–37 R–12
1979–80	96th	D–276 R–159	D–58 R–41	D–31 R–19
1981–2	97th	D–243 R–192	D–46 R–53	D–27 R–23
1983–4	98th	D–269 R–166	D–46 R–54	D–34 R–16
1985–6	99th	D–255 R–180	D–47 R–53	D–34 R–16
1987–8	100th	D–258 R–177	D–55 R–45	D–26 R–24
1989–90	101st	D–260 R–175	D–55 R–45	D–28 R–22

* Seats not listed in these totals were filled by independents or were vacant.

TABLE B4   POSTWAR CONGRESSIONAL AND SUPREME COURT LEADERS

Term	Senate Floor Leaders Majority	Party	Term	Minority	Party
1947–48	Wallace White (Me)	R	1947–48	Alben Barkley (Ky)	D
1949–50	Scott Lucas (Ill)	D	1949–50	Kenneth Wherry (Neb)	R
1951–52	Ernest McFarland (Ariz)	D	1951–52	Styles Bridges (NH)	R
1953–53	Robert Taft (Ohio)	R	1953–54	Lyndon Johnson (Tex)	D
1953–54	William Knowland (Calif)	R	1955–58	William Knowland (Calif)	R
1955–60	Lyndon Johnson (Tex)	D	1959–68	Everett Dirksen (Ill)	R
1961–76	Mike Mansfield (Mont)	D	1969–76	Hugh Scott (Pa)	R
1977–80	Robert Byrd (W Va)	D	1977–80	Howard Baker (Tenn)	R
1981–84	Howard Baker (Tenn)	R	1981–86	Robert Byrd (W Va)	D
1985–86	Robert Dole (Kan)	R	1987–	Robert Dole (Kan)	R
1987–88	Robert Byrd (W Va)	D			
1989–	George Mitchell (Me)	D			

Table B4 Postwar Congressional and Supreme Court Leaders (contd)

Term	Speakers of The House of Representatives	Party	Term	Chief Justices of the Supreme Court*
1947–48	Joseph Martin (Mass)	R	1946–53	Frederick Vinson (Ky)
1949–52	Sam Rayburn (Tex)	D	1953–69	Earl Warren (Calif)
1953–54	Joseph Martin (Mass)	R	1969–86	Warren Burger (Va)
1955–61	Sam Rayburn (Tex)	D	1986–	William Rehnquist (Ariz)
1962–70	John McCormack (Mass)	D		
1971–76	Carl Albert (Okla)	D		
1977–86	Thomas O'Neill (Mass)	D		
1987–89	Jim Wright (Tex)	D		
1989–	Thomas Foley (Wash)	D		

* State in brackets behind the Chief Justices name refers to the State in which he had last served before being appointed to the Supreme Court.

TABLE B5   SUPREME COURT JUDGES APPOINTED UNDER EACH PRESIDENCY SINCE 1933

President	Term of Office	S/C Judges Appointed	Number Still Serving	Justice	
Franklin D Roosevelt	1933–45	9	0		
Harry S Truman	1945–52	2	0		
Dwight D Eisenhower	1953–60	4	1	William J Brennan (NJ)	1956–
John F Kennedy	1961–63	2	1	Byron R White (Col)	1962–
Lyndon B Johnson	1963–68	2	1	Thurgood Marshall (NY)	1967–
Richard M Nixon	1969–74	3	2	Harry A Blackmun (Minn)	1970–
				William H Rehnquist (Ariz)	1972–
Gerald R Ford	1974–76	1	1	John Paul Stevens (Ill)	1975–
James E Carter	1977–80	0	0		
Ronald W Reagan	1981–88	3	3	Sandra Day O'Connor (Ariz)	1981–
				Antonin Scalia (DC)	1986–
				Anthony Kennedy (Calif)	1988–
George HW Bush	1989–	0	0		

TABLE B6   REPUBLICAN AND DEMOCRAT NATIONAL COMMITTEE CHAIRMEN SINCE 1970

Republican Party National Committee Chairmen since 1971		Democratic Party National Committee Chairmen since 1970	
Robert Dole (Kan)	1971–73	Lawrence O'Brien (Mass)	1970–72
George Bush (Tex)	1973–74	Jean Westwood (Utah)	1972–72
Mary Louise Smith (Iowa)	1974–77	Robert Strauss (Tex)	1972–77
William Brock (Tenn)	1977–81	Kenneth Curtis (Me)	1977–77
Richard Richards (Utah)	1981–83	John White (Tex)	1977–81
Frank Fahrenkopf Jr (Nev)	1983–88	Charles Manatt (Calif)	1981–85
Lee Atwater (SC)	1988–	Paul Kirk (Mass)	1985–89
		Ronald Brown (DC)	1989–

TABLE B7 'CONGRESSIONAL SUCCESS RATES'* (%) OF AMERICAN PRESIDENTS, 1953–89

Dwight D Eisenhower (R)		Gerald R Ford (R)	
1953	89.0	1974	58.2
1954	82.8	1975	61.0
1955	75.0	1976	53.8
1956	70.0	1974–76 Av	57.7
1957	68.0		
1958	76.0	James E Carter (D)	
1959	52.0	1977	75.4
1960	65.0	1978	78.3
1953–60 Av	72.2	1979	76.8
		1980	75.1
John F Kennedy (D)		1977–1980 Av	76.4
1961	81.0		
1962	85.4	Ronald W Reagan (R)	
1963	87.1	1981	82.4
1961–63 Av	84.5	1982	72.4
		1983	67.1
Lyndon B Johnson (D)		1984	65.8
1964	88.0	1985	59.9
1965	93.0	1986	56.5
1966	79.0	1987	43.5
1967	79.0	1988	47.4
1968	75.0	1981–88 Av	61.9
1964–68 Av	82.8		
		George H W Bush (R)	
Richard M Nixon (R)		1989	62.6
1969	74.0		
1970	77.0		
1971	75.0		
1972	66.0		
1973	50.6		
1974	59.6		
1969–74 Av	67.0		

* The 'Congressional Success Rate' is a record of the proportion of Presidential victories on roll-call votes on which he had taken a clear-cut position. This usually comprised between a fifth and a quarter of the total roll-call votes in Congress.

TABLE B8 PRESIDENTIAL VETOES OF CONGRESSIONAL PUBLIC BILLS, 1945–89*

President	Period Covered	Total of Public Bills Vetoed	Regular Vetoes	'Pocket Vetoes'	Number Overridden by Congress	% of Regular Vetoes Overridden
Truman	1945–52	83	54	29	11	20.4
Eisenhower	1953–60	81	36	45	2	5.5
Kennedy	1961–63	9	4	5	0	0
Johnson	1963–68	13	6	7	0	0
Nixon	1969–74	40	24	16	5	20.8
Ford	1974–76	46	35	11	8	22.8
Carter	1977–80	29	13	16	2	15.4
Reagan	1981–88	78	39	39	9	23.7
Bush	1989	10	9	1	0	0

* In addition, Truman vetoed 167 private bills; Eisenhower, 100; Kennedy, 12; Nixon, 3; Ford, 3; and Carter, 2.

TABLE B9   FRESHMEN/WOMEN ELECTED TO CONGRESS AND INCUMBENTS RE-ELECTED, 1974–88*

November	Freshmen/Women Elected		% of Incumbents Re-Elected	
	House of Representatives	Senate	House of Representatives	Senate
1974	92	11	87.7	85.2
1976	67	17	95.8	64.0
1978	77	20	93.7	60.0
1980	74	18	90.7	55.2
1982	81	5	90.6	93.3
1984	43	7	95.1	89.7
1986	50	13	98.0	75.0
1988	33	11	98.5	85.2

* These figures include those returning to Congress following a break in service. Between one to six Representatives and Senators fell into this category at each of the elections exhibited above.

TABLE B10 PARTY CONTROL OF STATE LEGISLATURES, 1979–89*

January	States with Both Chambers Controlled by One Party		States with Split Legislature Control
	D	R	
1979	31	12	7
1981	28	14	8
1983	34	12	4
1985	29	11	10
1987	29	8	12
1989	28	8	13

* Excludes Nebraska which has a unicameral assembly.

TABLE B11   THE 'CONSERVATIVE COALITION' IN CONGRESS – APPEARANCES AND VICTORIES, 1970–88*

Session	'Conservative Coalition' Appearances as a % of Total Recorded Congressional Votes	% Success Rate of 'Conservative Coalition' During its Appearances
1970	22	66
1971	30	83
1972	27	69
1973	23	61
1974	24	59
1975	28	50
1976	24	58
1977	26	68
1978	21	52
1979	20	70
1980	18	72
1981	21	92
1982	18	85
1983	15	77
1984	16	83
1985	14	89
1986	16	87
1987	8	93
1988	9	89
1989	11	87

*   The 'Conservative Coalition' is an informal voting alliance between Republicans and conservative southern Democrats against liberal northern Democrats in Congress. It is said to 'appear' whenever a majority of southern Democrats vote with a majority of Republicans against a majority of other Democrats and this table exhibits (in column 2) such 'appearances' as a proportion of total recorded votes for both chambers of Congress and shows (in column 3) the proportion of voting victories secured by the coalition whenever it has appeared.

APPENDIX C

THE WORKINGS OF CONGRESS AND THE CONGRESSIONAL COMMITTEE SYSTEM

Congress was established to perform three principal functions: to frame new legislation, to monitor the operations of the executive branch of government and to act as a forum for the debate of topical national issues. It exercises these functions in a decentralised manner through a network of powerful, specialist and largely autonomous standing and select committees. These committees are the hub around which the legislative process revolves, acting as 'little legislatures', framing new bills and amendments. For members of Congress they are the key institution to which they are assigned and in which they will spend their subsequent careers, slowly rising up the committee ladder to positions of increasing influence in a gerontocratic fashion.

The Legislative Process

New bills proposed by Senators and Representatives are, following a brief first reading during which they are sent to the clerk of the chamber for numbering and titling, sent to a relevant committee which is given the task of deciding whether to proceed with or abandon ('table') the measure. If adopted, the committee holds hearings in which the views of experts and interested parties are called and the committee's members debate and bargain over the bill clause by clause. The bill in its finally amended version is then voted on by the committee. If accepted, it is sent to the floor of the chamber for debate and further amendments during its second reading. Debate during this stage is, however, brief, particularly in the House of Representatives where strict closure ('cloture') rules apply, and members invariably back decisions made by the specialist committee which has had time to investigate the measure in greater detail. The bill is then given a third reading, in title only, after which a voice or electronic roll-call vote is effected. The legislation is then passed on to the other chamber of Congress where it may be defeated or passed, with or without amendments. If a substantially amended bill is approved, a joint Congressional Committee composed of senior members from both houses is appointed to iron out differences and agree on a compromise measure. This 'report' is then presented for ratification by each chamber.

Table C1 below sets out the legislative workload of Congress during recent years. These figures attest to the huge workload borne by the Congressional Committees, but highlight the small proportion of bills introduced which finally reach the statute book. In addition, these returns draw attention to the significant differences in legislative performances that exist between election (even – 1986 and 1988) and non-election (odd – 1985 and 1987) years.

TABLE C1   The Congressional Legislative Workload, 1985–8*

	1985	1986	1987	1988
(A) Bills and Resolutions Introduced	7777	3825	7532	3740
(B) Bills Signed into Public Law by the President	240	424	242	471
(C) As % of (A)	3.1	11.1	3.2	12.6
(D) Recorded Votes Taken	H–439	H–451	H–488	H–465
	S –381	S –354	S –420	S –379
(E) Number of Days Congress Met	H–152	H–129	H–170	H–137
	S –170	S –143	S –169	S –129

*   H = House   S = Senate.

Congressional Committees: Assignments, Sizes and Ranking

For the freshman Congressman one of the most crucial decisions that will influence his subsequent career is the choice of committee to which he is assigned. In the House of Representatives in 1989 there were 22 standing committees and five select committees with a combined membership of 991 and an average of 37 members. In such circumstances, Representatives can expect to serve on between two to three committees each, as well as a number of sub-committees. In the Senate in 1989 there were 16 standing committees and four select committees with a combined membership of 344 and average size of 17 members. (See Tables D5 and D6.) Senators thus find themselves serving on between three to four committees, as well as on a similar number of sub-committees.[1]

These committees, however, vary considerably in influence and importance. The four most influential 'blue-ribbon' committees are: Rules, which schedules and sets the parameters of debate for all major bills sent to the floor of each chamber; Appropriations, which authorises expenditure for bills; Ways and Means (and its counterpart in the Senate, Finance), which approves the raising of revenue and taxation to fund new measures; and Budget, which has grown increasingly important since the adoption of new budget regulations in 1974. These general authorisation and spending committees exert considerable influence over the remaining specialist committees within Congress, thus enabling their members to extract a wide range of reciprocal 'log-rolling' favours. Individual Congressmen also, however, seek to gain entry to committees which deal with subjects in which they have a particular personal interest and expertise or which deal with subjects of high media profile, for example foreign affairs. Above all, however, freshmen Congressmen, anxious to secure re-election in two to six years' time, seek out seats on committees which will provide the opportunity for furthering the interests of their local constituents. Thus, for example, Congressmen from the corn-belt Midwest States seek seats on the Agriculture Standing Committee, members from the oil- and gas-producing States of the South-west on the Energy and Natural Resources Standing Committee, while liberal freshmen from the industrial North-east battle for representation on the Labor, Public Works and Urban Affairs spending committees.

The assignment of freshmen to committees used to be entrusted in the case of House Democrats to the Ways and Means Committee, giving this body tremendous patronage power. Since 1975, however, appointments have been made by the Democratic Steering and Policy Committee, a body composed of the Speaker of the House, the Democratic Majority Leader, the chairman of the Democratic Conference and a cross-section of party House members. This new system of assignment is somewhat more just and democratic, but still allows for favouritism and the resort to 'trade-off' bargains in the allocation of plum committee seats. Democrat committee assignments in the Senate are similarly entrusted to the Steering Committee, a body which, until 1989, was chaired by the party's floor leader. The Republicans have adopted similar assignment systems for both chambers of Congress.

Once allocated to a committee, a Congressman used to rise slowly up the committee ladder following the precepts of the 'seniority system'. Under this system, the most important committee positions, including that of the committee chairman, who controls the agenda and scheduling of meetings and has charge of the spending of funds, had been filled by members from the majority party who could boast the longest record of service on the particular committee regardless of merit or ideological predilection. The 'seniority system' has been substantially undermined, however, as a consequence of the democratisation reforms introduced into Congress during the early and mid 1970s. These reforms have made committee chairs, and party leadership positions, subject to election in cases where strong objections emerge to particular individuals. In reality, more than three-quarters of committee chairs are still filled in accordance with seniority ranking, usually in an uncontested fashion. However, the existence of the threat of electoral challenge has served to change significantly the outlook of chairmen, forcing them to be less autocratic in their dealings with fellow committee members and to move towards more centrist and consensual party majority positions on controversial issues.

The authority of committee chairmen has, in addition, been weakened by the growing influence and independence of the more than two hundred sub-committees which function in both chambers of Congress and make many of the crucial substantive decisions on amendments to bills.

Such changes, coupled with the introduction of new Democrat House rules in 1971 which limited Representatives to the holding of one sub-committee chairmanship, have resulted in recent years in a dispersal of power within Congress and an upgrading of the authority and influence of individual Congressmen.[2] Served by a personal team of, usually, 18 'staffers' in the House and 36 in the Senate,[3] sitting on a variety of committees and frequently chairing a sub-committee, each Congressman now acts as his own individual legislator, engaging in numerous 'log-rolling' deals with party and opposition leaders over clauses and amendments to bills and establishing *ad hoc* coalitions both in support of and in opposition to measures of particular personal or constituency interest. These developments have made Congress a more atomised, volatile and unpredictable body than the chairman-dominated 'closed Congress' of the 1950s, as well as increasingly prey to the activities of high-profile single-issue activist groups.

APPENDIX D

THE 101ST (1989–90) CONGRESS

TABLE D1 SEATS AND LEADERSHIP POSTS IN THE SENATE AND HOUSE (NOVEMBER 1989)

Senate

Seats: Democrats 55   Republicans 45

Position	Party	Age	Year of Entry into Senate	Party Seniority Ranking
Majority Floor Leader*	D	56	1980	30
Majority Whip	D	75	1969	7
President Pro Tempore†	D	72	1959	1
Secretary of Democratic Conference (Caucus)	D	55	1979	24
Chairman of Democratic Steering Committee	D	65	1963	5
Chairman of Democratic Senatorial Campaign Committee‡	D	45	1987	41
Co-chairman of Democratic Policy Committee	D	41	1987	46
Chief Deputy Whip	D	62	1981	32
Minority Floor Leader	R	66	1969	4
Assistant Minority Leader (Whip)	R	58	1979	21
Chairman of Republican Conference (Caucus)	R	67	1976	12
Secretary of Republican Conference (Caucus)	R	51	1978	19

The names that appear in the table (by row):
- George Mitchell (Me)
- Alan Cranston (Calif)
- Robert Byrd (W Va)
- David Pryor (Ark)
- Daniel Inouye (Hawaii)
- John Breaux (La)
- Thomas Daschle (SD)
- Alan Dixon (Ill)
- Robert Dole (Kan)
- Alan Simpson (Wy)
- John Chafee (RI)
- Thad Cochran (Miss)

Table D1 Seats and Leadership Posts in the Senate and House (November 1989) (contd)

Senate

Position		Party	Age	Year of Entry into Senate	Party Seniority Ranking
Chairman of Republican Policy Committee	William Armstrong (Cl)	R	52	1979	23
Chairman of Republican Committee on Committees	Larry Presler (SD)	R	47	1979	25
Chairman of the National Republican Senatorial Committee‡	Don Nickles (Okla)	R	40	1981	31

* The Democrat Senate floor leader is also chairman of the party's Senate Conference (caucus) and Policy Committee.
† A post which is assigned to the most senior member of the majority party.
‡ Party campaign fund-raising post.

House of Representatives
Seats: Democrats 258   Republicans 177

Position		Party	Age	Year of Entry into House	Party Seniority Ranking
Speaker of House*	Thomas Foley (Wash)	D	60	1965	20
Majority Floor Leader	Richard Gephardt (Mo)	D	48	1977	79
Majority Whip	William Gray (Pa)	D	48	1979	103
Chairman of Democratic Conference (Caucus)	Steny Hoyer (Md)	D	50	1981	144
Vice-Chairman of Democratic Conference (Caucus)	Vic Fazio (Calif)	D	48	1979	103
Chief Deputy Whip	David Bonior (Mich)	D	44	1977	79
Chairman of Democratic Personnel Committee	Jack Brooks (Tex)	D	66	1953	3

Table D1   Seats and Leadership Posts in the Senate and House (November 1989) (contd)

Position	House of Representatives	Party	Age	Year of Entry into House	Party Seniority Ranking
Chairman of Democratic Congressional Campaign Committee (DCCC)†	Beryl Anthony Jr (Ark)	D	51	1979	103
Minority Floor Leader	Robert Michel (Ill)	R	66	1957	1
Minority Whip	Newt Gingrich (Ga)	R	46	1979	45
Chairman of Republican Conference (Caucus)	Jerry Lewis (Calif)	R	55	1979	45
Vice-Chairman of Republican Caucus	Bill McCollum (Fla)	R	45	1981	67
Secretary of Republican Conference (Caucus)	Vin Weber (Minn)	R	37	1981	67
Chief Deputy Whips	Steve Gunderson (Wis)	R	38	1981	67
	Robert Walker (Pa)	R	46	1977	35
	Mickey Edwards (Okla)	R	52	1977	35
Chairman of Republican Policy Committee	Duncan Hunter (Calif)	R	41	1981	67
Chairman of Republican Research Committee					
Chairman of National Republican Congressional Committee†	Guy Vander Jagt (Mich)	R	58	1966	8

*   Also chairman of the Democrats' Steering and Policy Committees.
†   Party campaign fund-raising post.

261

TABLE D2 SEAT DISTRIBUTION BY REGION IN 1989–90 (101st) CONGRESS

	House of Representatives		Senate		Both Chambers	
	Democrats	Republicans	Democrats	Republicans	D	R
Central*	14	14	9	9	23	23
North-Central†	63	47	9	9	72	56
North-East‡	66	42	15	9	81	51
South§	77	39	15	7	92	46
West**	40	33	7	11	47	44
All America	260	175	55	45	315	220

* Central = Colorado, Kansas, Montana, Nebraska, New Mexico, North Dakota, Oklahoma, South Dakota and Wyoming. Nine States with a combined population of 14.82 million in 1987.

† North-Central = Illinois, Indiana, Iowa, Kentucky, Michigan, Minnesota, Missouri, Ohio and Wisconsin. Nine States with a combined population of 57.81 million in 1987.

‡ North-East = Connecticut, Delaware, Maine, Maryland, Massachusetts, New Hampshire, New Jersey, New York, Pennsylvania, Rhode Island, Vermont and West Virginia. Twelve States with a combined population of 57.35 million in 1987.

§ South = Alabama, Arkansas, Florida, Georgia, Louisiana, Mississippi, North Carolina, South Carolina, Tennessee, Texas and Virginia. Eleven States with a combined population of 70.2 million in 1987.

** West = Alaska, Arizona, California, Hawaii, Idaho, Nevada, Oregon, Utah and Washington. Nine States with a combined population of 43.57 million in 1987.

TABLE D3   LENGTH OF SERVICE OF THE MEMBERS OF
THE 101ST CONGRESS*

Date of Entering Chamber	Senate†			House‡			Both Chambers		
	D	R	Total	D	R	Total	D	R	Total
1941–50	0	0	0	2	0	2	2	0	2
1951–60	2	1	3	8	3	11	10	4	14
1961–70	5	4	9	26	12	38	31	16	47
1971–75	8	5	13	40	18	58	48	23	71
1976–80	15	17	32	50	32	82	65	49	114
1981–85	9	10	19	85	70	155	94	80	174
1986–87	11	2	13	28	22	50	39	24	63
1988–89	5	6	11	20	17	37	25	23	48
Total	55	45	100	259	174	433	314	219	533

* As of January 1989.
† Thirty of these Senators (15 D : 15 R) had been former Representatives before being elected to the Senate; 8 had formerly been State Governors (7 D : 1 R); while one Senator elected in November 1988 had already previously served in the Senate between 1981 and 1987.
‡ Two seats were vacant in the House at this date.

TABLE D4   BACKGROUND OF MEMBERS IN THE 101st (1989–90) CONGRESS*

	House			Senate			Both Chambers Total
	D	R	Total	D	R	Total	
Male	246	164	410	54	44	98	508
Female	14	11	25	1	1	2	27
Black	24[†]	0	24	0	0	0	24
Hispanic	11[†]	0	12[‡]	0	0	0	12
Asians & Pacific Islanders	3	2[†]	5	2	0	2	7
RELIGION							
Roman Catholic	81	39	120	12	7	19	139
Methodist	38	25	63	9	4	13	76
Episcopalian	22	21	43	7	13	20	63
Baptist	33	10	43	4	8	12	55
Presbyterian	16	26	42	7	2	9	51
Jewish	26	5	31	5	3	8	39
Lutheran	10	10	20	3	1	4	24
United Church of Christ[§]	4	3	7	4	1	5	12
Mormon	3	5	8	1	2	3	11
Unitarian	5	2	7	1	2	3	10
Greek Orthodox	4	4	8	1	0	1	9
Other & Unspecified	18	25	43	1	2	3	46
OCCUPATIONS*							
Law	122	62	184	36	27	63	247
Business and Banking	66	72	138	13	15	28	166
Public Service/Politics	58	36	94	14	6	20	114
Education	25	17	42	6	5	11	53
Journalism	9	8	17	5	3	8	25
Agriculture	8	11	19	1	3	4	23
Law Enforcement	6	2	8	0	0	0	8
Professional Sports	3	1	4	1	0	1	5
Aeronautics	0	3	3	1	1	2	5
Engineering	2	2	4	0	0	0	4
Medicine	2	2	4	0	0	0	4
Clergy	2	0	2	0	1	1	3
Labor Officials	2	0	2	0	0	0	2
Actor/Entertainer	1	1	2	0	0	0	2
Average Age (Years)	52.3	51.8	52.1	55.9	55.3	55.6	52.8

*   The 'apparent winners', as of November 1988.

†   Includes one non-voting delegate from the District of Columbia or an American overseas possession.

‡   Also included is a non-voting delegate from Puerto Rico representing the Popular Democratic Party (PDP).

§   Congregationalist.

**   Some members gave more than one occupation. Hence the totals, when summed, exceed the membership of Congress.

TABLE D5 SENATE COMMITTEE CHAIRS AND PARTY STRENGTHS IN OCTOBER 1989

Standing Committees	Chairman (D)	Seniority Within Party*	Party Strength on the Committee		Sub-committees attached
			D	R	
Agriculture, Nutrition & Forestry	Patrick Leahy (Vt)	15	10	9	7
Appropriations	Robert Byrd (W Va)	1	16	13	13
Armed Services	Sam Nunn (Ga)	9	11	9	6
Banking, Housing & Urban Affairs	Donald Riegle (Mich)	17	12	9	4
Budget	Jim Sasser (Tenn)	20	13	10	0
Commerce, Science & Transportation	Ernest Hollings (SC)	6	11	9	8
Energy & Natural Resources	J Bennett Johnston (La)	10	10	9	5
Environment & Public Works	Quentin Burdick (ND)	2	9	7	5
Finance	Lloyd Bentsen (Tex)	8	11	9	8
Foreign Relations	Claiborne Pell (RI)	3	10	9	7
Governmental Affairs	John Glenn (Ohio)	12	8	6	5
Judiciary	Joseph Biden (Del)	11	8	6	6
Labor & Human Resources	Edward Kennedy (Mass)	4	9	7	6
Rules & Administration	Wendell Ford (Ky)	13	9	7	0
Small Business	Dale Bumpers (Ark)	14	10	9	6
Veterans' Affairs	Alan Cranston (Calif)	7	6	5	0

Table D5   Senate Committee Chairs and Party Strengths in October 1989 (contd)

Standing Committees	Chairman (D)	Seniority Within Party*	Party Strength on the Committee		Sub-committees attached
			D	R	
Aging	David Pryor (Ark)	24	10	9	0
Select Ethics	Howell Heflin (Ala)	27	3	3	0
Select Indian Affairs	Daniel Inouye (Hawaii)	5	5	3	1
Select Intelligence	David Boren (Okla)	25	8	7	0
Total			189	155	87

[1] Ranking in terms of length of service within the Senate.

TABLE D6   HOUSE COMMITTEE CHAIRS AND PARTY STRENGTH IN OCTOBER 1989

Standing Committees	Chairman (D)	Seniority Within Party*	Party Strength on the Committee D	R	Sub-committees attached
Agriculture	'Kika' de la Garza (Tex)	20	27	18	8
Appropriations	Jamie Whitten (Miss)	1	35	22	13
Armed Services	Les Aspin (Wis)	37	31	21	7
Banking, Finance & Urban Affairs	Henry Gonzales (Tex)	12	31	20	8
Budget	Leon Panetta (Calif)	79	21	14	6
District of Columbia	Ronald Dellums (Calif)	37	7	4	3
Education & Labor	Augustus Hawkins (Calif)	13	21	13	8
Energy & Commerce	John Dingell (Mich)	7	26	17	6
Foreign Affairs	Dante Fascell (Fla)	5	26	17	8
Government Operations	John Conyers (Mich)	20	24	15	7
House Administration	Frank Annunzio (Ill)	20	13	8	6
Interior & Insular Affairs	Morris Udall (Ariz)	11	23	14	6
Judiciary	Jack Brooks (Tex)	3	21	14	7
Merchant Marine & Fisheries	Walter Jones (NC)	26	26	17	6
Post Office & Civil Service	William Ford (Mich)	20	14	9	7
Public Works & Transportation	Glenn Anderson (Calif)	30	30	20	6
Rules	Joe Moakley (Mass)	42	9	4	2
Science & Technology	Robert Roe (NJ)	36	30	19	7
Small Business	John LaFalce (NY)	55	27	17	6
Standards of Official Conduct	Julian Dixon (Calif)	103	6	6	0
Veterans' Affairs	'Sonny' Montgomery (Miss)	27	21	13	5
Ways & Means	Dan Rostenkowski (Ill)	8	23	13	6

Table D6   House Committee Chairs and Party Strength in October 1989 (contd)

Standing Committees	Chairman (D)	Seniority Within Party*	Party Strength on the Committee D	R	Sub-committees attached
Aging	Edward Roybal (Calif)	13	39	26	4
Children, Youth & Families	George Miller (Calif)	55	18	12	3†
Hunger	Tony Hall (Ohio)	103	18	12	2†
Intelligence	Anthony Beilenson (Calif)	79	12	7	3
Narcotics Abuse & Control	Charles Rangel (NY)	37	18	12	0
Total			597	394	150

Joint Committees of Congress	Chairman & Vice Chairman	Seniority Within Party*	Party Strength on the Committee D	R	Sub-committees attached
Joint Economic	Chmn Rep Lee Hamilton (Ind)	20	H 6	4	8
	V-C Sen Paul Sarbanes (Md)	19	S 6	4	
Joint Library	Chmn Rep Frank Annunzio (Ill)	20	H 3	2	0
	V-C Sen Claibourne Pell (Ala)	3	S 3	2	
Joint Printing	Chmn Sen Wendell Ford (Ky)	13	S 3	2	0
	V-C Rep Frank Annunzio (Ill)	20	H 3	2	
Joint Tax	Chmn Rep Dan Rostenkowski (Ill)	8	H 3	2	
	V-C Sen Lloyd Bentsen (Tex)	8	S 3	2	
Total		H&S	30	20	8

* Ranking in terms of length of service within the Senate.
† Task-forces.   V-C = Vice-Chairman.

APPENDIX E

FEDERAL EXECUTIVE DEPARTMENTS AND AGENCIES IN 1990

Attached to Executive Office of the President	Date Established
Central Intelligence Agency (CIA)	1947
Council of Economic Advisers (CEA) (3)*	1946
Council on Environmental Quality (3)*	1969
National Security Council (NSC)	1947
Office of Administration	1977
Office of Management and Budget (OMB)	1970
Office of Science and Technology Policy	1976
Office of the US Trade Representative	1963
Office of Policy Development	1981
Office of National Drug Control Policy	1989
Office of Federal Procurement Policy	1989

EXECUTIVE DEPARTMENTS

Department of State	1789†
Department of Treasury	1789
Department of Defense	1947
Department of Justice	1789
Department of the Interior	1849
Department of Agriculture	1862
Department of Commerce	1903‡
Department of Labor	1884
Department of Health and Human Services	1953§
Department of Housing and Urban Development	1947**
Department of Transportation	1966
Department of Energy	1977
Department of Education	1979
Department of Veteran Affairs	1989††

---

* Number of members.
† Prior to 1789, known as Department of Foreign Affairs.
‡ Known as Department of Commerce and Labor during 1903–13.
§ During 1939–53 the Federal Security Agency functioned in its stead.
** During 1947–65 it functioned as the Department of Housing and Home Finance.
†† Previously, since 1930, the Veterans Administration.

MAJOR INDEPENDENT AGENCIES – 33

These include: the Environmental Protection Agency (EPA – established in 1970); Equal Employment Opportunity Commission (EEOC – 1965); Farm Credit Administration (FCA – 1916); Federal Communications Commission (FCC – 1934); Federal Election Commission (FEC – 1974); Federal Reserve Bank Board of Governors (1913); Federal Trade Commission (FTC – 1914); Interstate Commerce Commission (ICC – 1887); National Aeronautics and Space Administration (NASA – 1958); National Labor Relations Board (NLRB – 1935); National Science Foundation (NSF – 1950); Nuclear Regulatory Commission (NRC – 1975); Securities and Exchange Commission (SEC – 1934); Tennessee Valley Authority (TVA –1933); US Arms Control and Disarmament Agency (1961); US Commission on Civil Rights (1957); US International Trade Commission (1916); and the US Postal Service (1789).

MINOR INDEPENDENT AGENCIES – 23

These include: the Appalachian Regional Commission (1965); Federal Labor Relations Authority (1978); Panama Canal Commission (1979); and the Peace Corps (1961).

LEGISLATIVE DEPARTMENTS – 6

These include: the General Accounting Office (GAO) and the Library of Congress.

APPENDIX F

AMENDMENTS TO THE US CONSTITUTION

Amendment Number	Date Passed	Principal Provisions of the Amendment
1–10	1791	The 'Bill of Rights', granting:
1	1791	Freedom of worship, speech, assembly, the press and to petition the government.
2	1791	The right to keep and bear arms.
3	1791	Protection against the quartering of soldiers in private houses during peacetime and in times of war in the absence of special legal permission.
4	1791	Rights to ensure protection against unreasonable search and the seizure of property.
5	1791	The right not to be 'deprived of life, liberty or property without due process of law' or be compelled in a criminal case to be a witness against oneself (i.e. the right to remain silent).
6	1791	The right to speedy and public trial by an impartial jury and to call witnesses and be served by a defence counsel.
7	1791	The right to trial by jury.
8	1791	Protection against the imposition of excessive bail, fines or 'cruel and unusual punishments' upon those accused or found guilty. (An Amendment often quoted by opponents of capital punishment.)
9–10	1791	The restriction of the powers of the central (Federal) government to those specifically delegated to it by the constitution. The States and the people are reserved powers in residual areas. (This Amendment is frequently referred to by supporters of States' rights).
11	1798	Established the limits of US judicial power to within the nation's borders.
12	1804	Established the rules for electing the President and Vice-President by popular vote.
13–15	1865–70	These Amendments, often referred to as the 'Reconstruction Amendments', ended slavery, enfranchised blacks and guaranteed all citizens, regardless of race or colour, equal protection under the law.

13	1865	Prohibited slavery and 'involuntary servitude'.
14	1868	Granted citizenship to all persons born or naturalised in the United States and guaranteed citizens legal rights within the States. For States who practised discriminatory franchise laws, the number of Congressional Representatives was to be reduced according to the number of voters disenfranchised.
15	1870	Forbade the withholding of the right to vote in Federal or State elections on the grounds of race, colour or 'previous conditions of service'.
16	1913	Established a Federal income tax.
17	1913	Changed the system of electing Senators from one based on indirect election by State legislatures to one of direct popular election by citizens of the State.
18	1919	Prohibited the manufacture, sale or transportation of 'intoxicating liquor'.
19	1920	Enfranchised women.
20	1933	Established the date for the commencement of Congressional sessions as 3 January, thus ending the previous December–March 'lame duck' session when Congressmen defeated in November had been allowed to continue to influence legislation. This Amendment also established the date for the handover of Presidential power on 20 January.
21	1933	Repealed Amendment 18, thus ending 'prohibition'.
22	1951	Restricted Presidents to a maximum of two terms in office.
23	1961	Gave residents of Washington DC the right to vote in presidential elections, assigning the city the same number of 'electoral college' votes as that enjoyed by the least populous State in the Union.
24	1964	Prohibited the imposition of a poll tax as a prerequisite for voting in Federal elections. (This Amendment was designed to enfranchise southern blacks who had previously been debarred from voting by such regulations.)
25	1967	Established specific rules for the selection of a new Vice-President when the office becomes vacant. (i.e. the President was now to nominate a new deputy who required approval from both chambers of Congress). This Amendment also established new rules for the temporary assumption of power by a Vice-President when the President became incapacitated.
26	1971	Lowered the voting age from twenty-one to eighteen years.

NOTES

Part One

CHAPTER 1

[1]   Contemporary, and thus far unsuccessful, examples of attempts at amending the US constitution have been the Equal Rights Amendment and the campaigns to give the District of Columbia full Congressional representation and for a balanced budget amendment, which was first proposed by State legislatures.

[2]   American 'liberalism' differs from traditional European liberalism which, with its roots in the nineteenth century, stresses individualism and liberty. US liberalism is concerned with social justice and minority rights and advocates government intervention to alleviate social ills.

[3]   The number of Democrat primaries increased from 17 in 1968 to 23 in 1972, 29 in 1976 and 35 in 1980 before falling to 26 in 1984, with an increased proportion also becoming binding. The Republicans followed suit in this democratisation process, the number of Republican presidential primaries rising from 16 in 1976 to 34 in 1980, before falling back to 25 in 1984. In 1988, the Democrats held presidential primaries in 34 States and the Republicans in 36.

[4]   In addition, there has been a trend toward a greater national orientation on the part of the press: the *New York Times* having introduced a national edition in 1980 and Gannet Co Inc having successfully launched *USA Today* as the country's first national general interest paper in 1982. Much of the remainder of the press remains, however, strongly localised and parochial.

[5]   PACs account for 41% of funds spent in House elections and 25% in Senate contests and provide 38% of Democrat candidates' funds compared with 29% of Republican.

Part Two

CHAPTER 2

[1]   President Johnson issued 7 'pocket' and 6 regular vetoes (none being overridden), President Nixon 16 'pocket' and 24 regular vetoes (5 being overridden). (See Appendix Table B8.)

[2]   By 1976 success in primaries was now essential to win the nomination, with 73% of Democrat National Convention delegates being chosen this way (compared to 41% in 1968) and 68% of Republican delegates.

³   Carter drew together a blackneck-redneck coalition in the South, capturing almost all the black vote and half the white vote.

CHAPTER 3

¹   In 1977 southern Democrats held only 22% of the standing committee chairmanships in the House and 40% in the Senate and in 1979 23% and 27%, with the northern liberals Edward Kennedy and Frank Church now controlling the Senate Judiciary and Foreign Relations committees.

²   In Georgia, Carter, while continuing to increase the provision of welfare services, abolished 278 of the 300 executive agencies attached to the State government and introduced a novel system of 'zero-based budgeting' which forced administrative departments annually to justify and 'prioritize' their budget requests for funds.

³   The new members of the cabinet were W Miller (former head of the Federal Reserve Bank) – Treasury; Mrs P Harris – HEW; CW Duncan (former president of Coca-Cola) – Energy; M Landrieu (former New Orleans Mayor) – HUD; B Civiletti (the then Deputy Attorney-General) – Attorney-General; and N Goldschmidt (Mayor of Portland) – Transportation. The UN Ambassador, A Young, resigned soon afterwards following an unofficial meeting with the PLO and was replaced by his black deputy, D McHenry. A final reshuffle in November and December 1979 brought in Shirley Hufstedler at the head of new Department of Education and Philip Klutznick as Secretary of Commerce.

⁴   Edward Kennedy's third and eldest brother, Joseph Patrick Jr, had died in an air crash in 1944.

⁵   Brown withdrew from the contest in April 1980, having been unable to garner more than 10% of the party vote.

⁶   President Carter won a total of 23 primaries contested, more than 50% of the party vote and 60% of the Democrat delegates.

⁷   The 'balanced budget movement', which was spearheaded by the National Taxpayers' Union, sought to gain the support of two-thirds (34) of the State legislatures to force the establishment of a special Constitutional Convention with the intention of introducing a new 27th Amendment which would compel the mandatory balancing of Federal budgets.

⁸   The forceful Texan conservative, John Connally, and the 53-year-old moderate Minority Leader, Senator Howard Baker of Tennessee, were expected to put in a serious challenge, but they withdrew from the contest in March 1980 after making little impact.

⁹   The 'platform' (manifesto) adopted by the Democrats at their 11-14 August National Convention included, in addition, a massive $12 billion anti-recession jobs, railroad renewal and housing programme, inserted by the Kennedy wing of the party. President Carter was, however, a less enthusiastic supporter of this more traditionalist 'make work' approach and made equivocal his intentions concerning its implementation if re-elected.

[10] The scandal concerned the involvement of President Carter's controversial younger brother Billy (1937-88) as a lobbyist for the Libyan government and his receipt of a 'loan' of $220,000 from Tripoli.

[11] The recent deaths of Mayor Daley of Chicago in December 1976 and Hubert Humphrey (the Minnesotan DFI, leader) in January 1978 and the retirement of many Southern Democrat bosses marked the end of an era in a number of traditional Democrat States.

[12] Jews were dissatisfied with a number of the apparently pro-Arab policies pursued by the Carter administration; blue-collar workers were attracted by Ronald Reagan's macho 'Main Street' image and promise of an economic turnaround.

[13] At the State level, the Republicans gained 200 legislature seats in November 1980. This followed a gain of 300 seats in 1978.

[14] These measures included bills designed to restrict development on Federal land in areas of outstanding beauty, including oil-rich Alaska, and imposing tighter regulations on industrial safety; the extension, in 1978, of the deadline for ratification of the Equal Rights Amendment by three years; and the inclusion of an unprecedented number of women (40), blacks (38) and Hispanics (16) among the President's 262 new appointments to the US Court of Appeals and US District Courts.

[15] The Carter administration also succeeded in commencing a process of deregulation which was to be continued under the Reagan presidency: piloting through legislation aimed at reducing restrictions and injecting greater competition into the air, rail and trucking industries.

Part Three

CHAPTER 4

[1] In 1932 President Herbert Hoover (R) was also briefly faced with a 'split Congress' when Republican deaths deprived his party of a majority in the House.

[2] This measure, the Economic Recovery Tax Act, involved a three-year phasing of tax reductions, with the highest Federal income tax rate falling from 70% to 50%. Business tax rates were also reduced, with new depreciation rules being set.

[3] The 'freeze movement' began among middle-class radicals in New England and attracted strong support in California and New York (800,000 gathering in Central Park in June 1982). It reached its peak during the November 1982 elections when there was a 2:1 vote in favour of a 'freeze' in referendums covering 30% of the total US electorate.

[4] In North Carolina and West Virginia, for example, 'New Right' candidates were heavily defeated, while elsewhere liberal Democrat Senators targeted by NCPAC survived.

[5] Produced by the refusal of, on the one side, the President to sanction tax increases and of, on the other hand, Congress to acquiesce in further major spending cuts.

[6] Overall, the number of Federal-State grant programmes was reduced from 361 to 259 between 1981 and 1984.

[7] During the Carter presidency, 12% of the Federal administration's posts went to blacks, 12.1% to women and 4.1% to Hispanics. During the succeeding Reagan presidency, blacks were to hold only a 4.1% share of the top-level posts, women 8% and Hispanics 3.8%. Twenty-eight of the Reagan administration's top 100 posts went, indeed, to millionaires.

[8] This decision had made possible the execution, in 1977, of the convicted murderer Gary Gilmore in what had been the first exercise of capital punishment anywhere in the United States since 1967. By the early 1980s, the numbers being annually executed had climbed to double figures.

[9] The 'legislative veto', which was first introduced in 1933, was a convenient device by which Congress reserved the power to review and, if necessary, later overturn the decisions of Federal Regulatory Commissions and executive agencies of which it disapproved. This veto had been built into 196 statutes and covered matters such as immigration (the Chadha case), trade and energy regulations, and even foreign policy (the War Powers Resolution). Its proscribing promised, in the short term, to extend greater power to executive agencies and, in the longer term, to force Congress to be more precise and detailed in its framing of statutes.

[10] Of the nine members of the Supreme Court in 1984, Justices William Brennan (78, an Eisenhower appointee), and Thurgood Marshall (76, a black Johnson appointee), aging survivors of the 'Warren court', and Justice Harry Blackmun (75, a Nixon appointee) occupied the liberal wing; Justice John Paul Stevens (64, a Ford appointee), Lewis Powell (76, a Nixon appointee) and Byron White (67, a Kennedy appointee) the centre; and Justices William Rehnquist (60), Warren Burger (77) (both Nixon appointees) and Sandra Day O'Connor (54) the conservative wing.

[11] Membership of the National Organization for Women (NOW), the National Association for the Advancement of Colored People (NAACP) and the Environmental Action liberal pressure groups all increased significantly between 1980 and 1984.

CHAPTER 5

[1] In March 1982 44% of people polled identified themselves as Democrats, 24% as Republicans and 30% as independents; a position almost identical to that of the early 1970s. In the same year, the Democrats held 64% of the elected seats in the State legislatures.

[2] Examples of recent liberal PACs aiming to target prominent 'New Right' Republicans for defeat have been Morris Udall's Independent Action, Averell Harriman's Democrats for the '80s, and George McGovern's Civil Liberties Association.

[3] These reforms, which were based upon the recommendations of a party commission established in July 1981 under the chairmanship of James Hunt (Governor of North Carolina), meant that almost half the Democrats' national Convention delegates would be selected in the five weeks between the opening of the Iowa caucuses of 27 February and 31 March 1984 and that barely 53% would be chosen by the primary system, compared with 75% in 1980.

[4] As Vice-President, Mondale had acted as a peripatetic diplomat, flying out on special missions to China, Africa, Europe, the Middle East and South-east Asia, and serving as a crucial bridge with Congress, dutifully exerting pressure on liberal Democrat colleagues to accept unpalatable cuts in spending programmes, often against his personal wishes.

[5] The other candidates comprised two elderly radicals, Senator Alan Cranston (69, California) and the former Senator and presidential nominee George McGovern (61, South Dakota); two southern conservatives, Senator Ernest Hollings (62, South Carolina) and former Governor Reubin Askew (55, Florida); and one moderate centrist, Senator John Glenn (63, Ohio), the former astronaut and first American to orbit the earth, who was initially viewed as a strong contender in 1984 but proved to be an ineffective campaigner and rapidly faded, despite accruing campaign debts in excess of $3 million.

[6] During the 1960s Hart worked as an attorney at the US Department of Justice (1964-67), before moving to Colorado where he established a private law practice in 1967.

[7] Attention was focused, in particular, upon two curious actions by Hart: the shortening of his name at birth, Hartpence, to the more electorally appealing Hart, and the shaving off of a year from his true age in the information given in his promotional material.

[8] The other candidates considered for this post – Hart having ruled himself out – were Tom Bradley and Wilson Goode (both black Mayors); Martha Layne Collins (Governor of Kentucky); Dianne Feinstein (San Francisco Mayor); Henry Cisneros (the Hispanic Mayor of San Antonio); and Michael Dukakis (the Greek-American Governor of Massachusetts). However, Ferraro was not the first-ever female vice-presidential nominee. Minor party presidential candidates had selected female running-partners before: for example the Comanche Indian woman La Donna Harris had been on the Citizens Party ticket in 1980, while as early as 1872 the suffragette Victoria Claffin Woodhull had stood for the presidency at the head of the National Radical Reformers Party ticket. Two female minor party candidates appeared on the ballot paper of several States in November 1984, Sonia Johnson and Gavrielle Jones (see Table 13).

[9] Ferraro graduated from the New York Law School and established a successful law practice during 1961-74. In 1974 she became assistant district attorney for the Queens District of New York and went on to work at the Supreme Court in 1978-80, before being elected to Congress in November 1980.

[10] By the end of the nomination campaign Mondale had won 39% of the Democrat votes, 12 primaries and 13 caucuses and boasted the backing of 55% of the Convention delegates (one-third of these were union-linked). His expenditure in the campaign had totalled $18 million. Hart had captured 36% of the votes and

delegates and had prevailed in 12 primaries and 13 caucuses. He had spent $11 million and was left with debts of $4.7 million. Jackson had gained 18% of the votes (made up of younger and churchgoing blacks and progressive whites, but few Hispanics) and had recorded victories in two primaries (Louisiana and the District of Columbia) and three caucuses (Mississippi, South Carolina and Virginia), but had captured only 9% of the National Convention delegates. He had spent a mere $3 million in what was a shoestring campaign, leaving him with debts of only $0.06 million. Jackson's performance exceeded that of the previous black candidate, Shirley Chisholm in 1972, who had captured only 3% of the delegate vote.

[11]   Anderson, who had recently established a new National Unity Party (NUP), failed to collect sufficient signatures to appear on all State ballots in 1984 and thus decided not to contest the election. He gave strong endorsement to the Mondale-Ferraro ticket during the campaign of September–November 1984.

[12]   Two such localised contests were the Senate races in North Carolina, where the 'New Right' fundamentalist Republican, Jesse Helms, narrowly held off (by 52:48%) a challenge from the Democrat ex-Governor James Hunt, in a race that, involving outlays of more than $23 million, broke new spending records, and in Illinois, where the moderate Republican, Charles Percy, was ousted following targeting by NCPAC and Zionist groups who were opposed to his allegedly pro-Arab policies as head of the Senate Foreign Relations Committee (FRC). The somewhat more conservative Richard Lugar (Indiana) replaced Percy as chairman of the FRC in January 1985.

[13]   In the House races, the Republicans captured 48% of the popular vote, but gained only 41% of its seats as a result of gerrymandering during recent redistricting by Democrat-controlled State legislatures. They did capture, however, 17 (63%) of the 27 'open seats' (those not being contested by incumbents) in the House.

[14]   The number of southern Democrat 'Boll Weevils' totalled between 30 and 35, with barely 20 being certain to vote regularly with the Republicans on conservative 'roll-call' votes.

Part Four

CHAPTER 6

[1]   Baker (b. April 1930) came from a wealthy patrician Texas family which controlled Houston's most influential law firm as well as a major bank. Following brief service in the US Marines and education at Princeton, he became a successful corporate lawyer in a rival law firm to scotch allegations of nepotism. Initially a Democrat, after striking up a close friendship with George Bush, Baker later switched to the Republicans and served as Under-Secretary in the Commerce Department in the Ford administration, before going on to manage the 1976 and 1980 Ford and Bush presidential campaigns.

2 Regan (b. December 1918 in Cambridge, Mass), whose father had been a railway security guard, enjoyed the distinction of having been the youngest US Marine major on active service during the Second World War. He had earlier attended Harvard as a part-time classmate of John F Kennedy, studying English and economics. After the war he joined the Merrill Lynch brokerage firm as a salesman in 1946, rising to become its president in 1968.

3 Stockman left his $75,000 per annum government post for a $1 million per annum position at the Saloman Bros investment bank and proceeded to write, in return for a $2.4 million advance, a major critique, *The Triumph of Politics*, of the 'Reagan experiment' which covered his years at the OMB. This work in particular drew attention to the Reagan team's only partial understanding of the supply-side philosophy and its unwillingness to accept either swinging across-the-board departmental budget cuts or emergency tax increases in order to bring the Federal Budget closer to balance. Deaver, Reagan's renowned 'imagemaker', left to set up a multi-million-dollar Washington lobbying company, utilising his White House connections. This proved to be most controversial and led to Congressional inquiries into possible breaches of 'ethics in government' rules. Later, in December 1987, Deaver was convicted of perjury and in September 1988 was fined $100,000 and given a three-year suspended prison sentence for lying about his lobbying activities.

4 President Reagan, who gained the reputation of being the 'Great Communicator', paid unusual attention to the way his views and image were projected. In contrast to his 'open house' predecessors, Carter and Ford, who had each held an average of 15 press conferences a year, Reagan carefully rationed these adversarial meetings, holding an average of only six press conferences per annum. Only the reclusive Richard Nixon (7) among recent Presidents, came close to matching this low figure. In addition, President Reagan's appearances were skilfully stage-managed, in terms of backdrop and location, to evoke strong images of symbols which would remain in the minds of the public.

5 The rate of US economic growth fell to 2% between July 1984 and August 1985 and the visible trade deficit climbed to $145 billion (a rate double that registered in 1983).

6 According to Stockman's memoirs, the idea of a 'flat-tax' originated with George Shultz, who converted President Reagan to the concept during a golf round in 1982.

7 The House plan allowed pensions to rise with inflation but froze defence spending; the Senate plan froze pensions but allowed defence spending to rise by 3% in real terms.

8 Key elements of GRH were subsequently, however, declared unconstitutional in July 1986 by the Supreme Court, which ruled that the law violated the separation of powers by granting the Comptroller-General (an official who, as head of the General Accounting Office, was ultimately responsible to and removable by Congress) authority to make automatic cuts in an executive manner. Congress would thus need either to vote again on cuts made, removing the 'automatic trigger', or change the status of the Comptroller-General, turning him into a fully independent figure.

9   The trade deficit exceeded$160 billion in August 1986 despite the innovative action of Treasury Secretary Baker, who had overseen an internationally co-ordinated devaluation of the dollar by 40% vis-à-vis the Yen and Deutschmark since February 1985, and the adoption of a firmer stance in trade negotiations by Commerce Secretary Baldrige and Trade Representative Clayton Yeutter.

10   The final joint budget resolution passed in October 1986 entailed the lowest increase in government outlays for 20 years. It involved a defence spending figure $30 billion lower than the Defense Department had requested (including a 33% reduction in the President's request for his SDI programme), cuts in health outlays for the poor and a number of related domestic programmes, the decision to privatise Conrail (the nationalised rail network) in 1987 and a holding of all other programmes to a rate of spending increase in line with inflation. By such means, and aided by a projected $11 billion adjustment windfall that would accrue as a result of the implementation of the new tax reform programme, the Federal budget deficit was expected to be reduced from its 1986 level of $221 billion to a figure of $170–180 billion in 1987.

11   The final act was a compromise between the Reagan administration's initial proposals, the House's more liberal measure and the Senate's radical bill which had bravely defied the pleadings of special interest lobbies. It involved the creation of two broad new tax bands at 15% and 28%, with, in addition, a third special 'phantom tax bracket' at 33% for exceptionally high income earners. Second, it reduced the top rate of corporation tax on businesses from a level of 40% to one of 34%, but ended tax credits for investment and introduced harsher terms for depreciation. Overall, the act reduced Federal income taxes by 6% on average, but, unlike the 1981 Reagan reforms, benefited the poor as well as the rich and exempted 6.5 million low-income taxpayers from payment altogether.

12   During President Reagan's first five years in office his 'Congressional success rate' by chamber had been: in 1981 Senate (S) – 88%, House (H) – 72%; in 1982 S – 82%, H – 56; in 1983 S – 86%, H – 48%; in 1984 S – 86%, H – 52%; and in 1985 S – 72%, H – 45%.

13   These items included the President's recurrent call for Congress to pass a balanced-budget amendment to the constitution and to grant him new 'line-veto' powers which would enable him to take personal responsibility for budget-cutting operations.

14   In 1986, however, there was evidence that this foreign policy consensus was beginning to crumble, as pressure mounted for the President to adopt a more conciliatory line in arms negotiations with the Soviet Union, the House voting in August 1986 to halt further US nuclear tests if the USSR maintained its test-ban moratorium and refusing to finance spending on strategic arms which breached the SALT-2 limits.

15   Indeed, overall during the Reagan presidency the number of Federal regulations was cut by more than a fifth, from 10 343 to 8004.

16   Rehnquist was duly confirmed as Chief Justice by the Senate on 17 September 1986 by the margin of 65 voters in favour to 33 against, receiving more negative votes than any Justice or Chief Justice previously confirmed by the Senate. Judge Scalia, the Court's first Associate-Justice of Italian-American descent, was confirmed by 98 votes to nil.

17   The new Rehnquist Supreme Court still, initially, retained a majority in favour of upholding the 1973 *Roe v Wade* abortion ruling and supportive of race employment quotas.

18   Only 30 (8.1%) of the 370 Federal Appeals and District Court judges appointed by President Reagan between 1981 and 1988 were female, only seven (1.9%) were blacks and only 14 (3.8%) were Hispanics; 21%, in contrast, were millionaires.

19   In the State legislature contests the Democrats gained more than 150 seats and control of four more State legislatures. (See Appendix Table B10.)

20   In the House of Representatives, however, incumbents enjoyed, once more, an unusually high 'return rate' of 98.5%.

21   In these leadership and committee chairmen 'elections' the custom of seniority was largely adhered to, with Wright, for example, stepping up from the number two position of Majority Floor Leader in the House and the former Majority Whip, Thomas Foley (Washington), being promoted to floor leadership. Only the vacant Majority Whip's post, filled by Tony Coelho (44 – California), the former chairman of the fund-raising Democratic Congressional Campaign Committee, was vigorously contested.

22   Later, in January 1989, at the very close of the Reagan administration, two Libyan MIG-23 fighter aircraft were shot down by US F-14 jets over the Mediterranean amidst American accusations that Libya was preparing to commence production of chemical weapons at a factory near Tripoli.

23   Ayatollah Ruholla Khomeini (1902–89), Iran's spiritual leader, eventually died in June 1989.

24   The CIA were, however, later to learn in September 1985 that Buckley had been secretly murdered by his captors in the spring of 1985, forcing the US to accept the release of the Rev Benjamin Weir as compensation.

25   Special Prosecutors (also known as Independent Counsels) are appointed by and report to a special three-judge court. They operate in strict secrecy, collecting evidence for subsequent prosecutions, until their investigations are completed.

26   Casey, who emerged from later testimonies as the key Svengali figure in the affair, subsequently died in hospital in May 1987.

27   These charges were vehemently refuted by Regan in his subsequent memoirs, *For the Record*. In addition, in this work Regan drew damaging ridicule upon the Reagan presidency by revealing that the President's calendar was determined by a Californian astrologer, Joan Quigley, who sent, to Nancy Reagan, advance notice of forthcoming 'good' and 'bad' dates for official appearances.

28   Howard Baker had not been the first choice for this post. The President had first approached former Transport Secretary Drew Lewis and then ex-Senator Paul Laxalt, but both had refused the offer.

29   In this report, the office of President was accused of deceiving Congress, acting unlawfully and abusing its powers. Furthermore, the Joint Committee, while accepting that no evidence was available that President Reagan actually knew of

the Contra diversion, asserted that he bore 'ultimate responsibility' in that he had allowed a 'cabal of the zealots' to take control of policy. The Committee's majority report recommended improved procedures of Congressional notification of covert operations and of administrative oversight at the White House.

30   Robert McFarlane was fined $20,000 in March 1989 and placed on probation for two years for unlawfully withholding information from Congress concerning the administration's clandestine funding of the Contras. Lt-Col North was convicted in May 1989 by a Federal court in Washington of three charges of obstructing Congress, of unlawfully destroying government documents and of accepting an illegal gratuity. He was fined $150,000, given a three-year suspended prison sentence and automatically disqualified for life from holding Federal office. In April 1990 Vice-Admiral Poindexter was convicted of conspiring to obstruct Congressional inquiries into 'Irangate' and making false statements.

31   Both David Stockman and Donald Regan in their memoirs draw critical attention to this detached leadership style, nothing that, on and after their appointments, they were never given specific job guidelines or goals, but were just asked to 'get on with the job' in conformity with the President's perceived 'wishes'. As Regan commented: 'The President never told me what he wanted to accomplish in the field of economics . I had to figure these things out like any other American, by studying his speeches, and reading the newspapers.'

32   Webster's appointment marked the end of attempts instituted by Donald Regan controversially to nominate Robert Gates, the former Deputy Director of the CIA during the 'Iran-Contragate' period, as the new director. Webster had headed the FBI since 1978.

33   The US trade deficit had increased by 10% over the preceding year to $170 billion in 1987, while the Federal budget deficit, benefiting from the phasing of tax reform, had fallen by 32% to $150 billion (3.5% of GNP), but showed signs of resuming an upward course.

34   These 'overrides' were on the Clean Water Act (February 1987), the Highway Reauthorisation Bill (April 1987) and the Civil Rights Restoration Act (March 1988).

35   In October 1987 William Verity (70), the former chairman of the US Chamber of Commerce, replaced Commerce Secretary Baldrige, who died in a rodeo accident, and James Burnley (39) took over as Transportation Secretary; in November 1987 Frank Carlucci (57) became Defense Secretary and Lt General Colin Powell (50) the country's first black NSA; in December 1987 Anne McLaughlin (46), a former Treasury official, took over as Labor Secretary; in June 1988, Chief-of-Staff Howard Baker retired as a result of his wife's illness and was replaced by his deputy Kenneth Duberstein (44); in July 1988, following investigations into his financial affairs by an Independent Counsel, Attorney-General Meese resigned and was subsequently replaced by Richard Thornburgh (56); in August 1988 Nicholas Brady (58) took over as Treasury Secretary; and in September 1988 Lauro Cavazos (61) became Education Secretary and the country's first ever Mexican-American cabinet member.

36   Between 1981 and 1983, despite cutbacks in grants to State and local governments and cutbacks in non-mandatory and non-entitlement domestic programmes

(particularly 'discretionary' programmes such as housing and low-income energy assistance), Federal government outlays rose from 22.7% of GNP to 24.3%. Only thereafter, largely as a result of the effects of buoyant general GNP growth, did it decline to 22.8% in 1987.

CHAPTER 7

[1]   Indeed, between 1980 and 1984 the Republicans' share of Statehouse seats fell from 40% to 36%, only returning to the 40% mark after the elections of 1986.

[2]   By December 1985, the Republicans had attracted 50,000 of the 100,000 defections anticipated from this campaign. These defectors included six prominent Georgia State officials and five senior political opponents who were to become gubernatorial candidates in November 1986. The campaign was particularly widespread in Florida, Louisiana, Pennsylvania and Texas.

[3]   The DLC included the figures of Missouri Representative Richard Gephardt, Georgia Senator Sam Nunn, ex-Virginia Governor Charles Robb, Florida Governor Robert Graham and Arizona Governor (to 1987) Bruce Babbitt, who represented a new, younger breed of Democrats used to governing in the harsh conditions of the late 1970s and early 1980s when difficult social choices had to be made in balancing State and Federal budgets. They had sought, but failed, to secure the election of Terry Sanford (the former Governor of North Carolina) to the party chairmanship and were the driving force behind the idea of a Southern 'Super Primary' on 8 March 1988 in an effort to improve the chance of a moderate Democrat capturing the party's presidential nomination.

[4]   The Young Democrat organisation (headed by William Belk) was revamped and made more active at the campus level, while an Ethnic Council was founded by Arizona Senator Dennis De Concini in an effort to retain the support of German, Italian and Polish Americans who had recently begun to defect to the Republican camp.

[5]   The Democrat majority in the Senate had already been reduced to 54:46 by the death in March 1987 of Edward Zorinsky (Nebraska) and his replacement for the final two years of his term by the Republican David Karnes at the discretion of Governor Kay Orr (R).

[6]   Overall, Dukakis, after spending the maximum permitted nomination contest sum of $27.6 million, had finished first in 21 State primaries and nine caucuses; Jackson, excluding DC, in five and four respectively: Gore in five and two; Gephardt in two and one; and Simon in one primary. Of the 22.7 million people who voted in the Democrats' primaries, 43% supported Dukakis and 29% Jackson, a considerable advance on his 1984 candidacy. Of the Democrat blacks participating in the primaries, 92% voted for Jackson, as well as 30% of the Hispanics and 12% of whites.

[7]   Bentsen, the son of a self-made millionaire landowner-entrepreneur, held a DFC for his wartime military service and, after making his own fortune in life insurance in Houston, was elected to the US Senate in 1970, after defeating George Bush. Chairman of the Senate Finance Committee since 1986, Bentsen was a renowned expert on financial affairs.

[8] By February 1988, the Robertson campaign had raised $28 million and spent $22 million, This compared with Bush's $27 million raised ($15 million spent); Dole's $21 million ($16 million); and Kemp's $16 million ($15 million).

[9] The Democrats' Atlanta platform (manifesto) had been a deliberately vague document which had emphasised party themes and goals rather than specific policy commitments. In the economic sphere, it called for the creation of 'good jobs at good wages', the fostering of closer public-private partnership in the development of new technologies and of increased emphasis upon the revival of depressed regions. The Republicans' adopted platform , a 30,000-word document, included the commitment to reduce the current rate of capital gains tax and 'to oppose any attempts to increase taxes', as well as the call for a 'flexible freeze' on current government spending. The chief party differences in the economic sphere centred around the Democrats' pledge to introduce an indexed minimum wage – which the Republicans castigated as 'inflationary and job destroying' – and the Republicans' call for a balanced budget amendment to the constitution and for a presidential line-item veto. In the social sphere, both parties agreed upon the need for increased child-care facilities, educational investment and for the appointment of a special Drug Czar, but while the Democrats called for a reassertion of 'progressive values', the Republicans' platform made plain its opposition to abortion and support for 'voluntary prayers at school'. Differences were also notable in the diplomatic sphere, the Democrats advocating the imposition of comprehensive sanctions against the 'terrorist state' of South Africa - something the Republicans opposed – as a well as the 'halt[ing] of all nuclear weapons testing', whilst the Republicans championed continuance, of the SDI programme and support for the Nicaraguan Contras.

[10] In reality, Dukakis though, like Carter, difficult to categorise accurately, was broadly a fiscal conservative but social and defence liberal. He opposed capital punishment, restrictions on busing, the B1 bomber and MX missile programmes and aid to the Contras; supported gun control, the Federal funding of abortions and the establishment of a comprehensive, employer-financed, health-care plan; and was equivocal on SDI funding.

[11] Born, February 1947, into a wealthy Indianapolis newspaper/publishing family, Quayle was the heir to a fortune of more than $500 million. He had degrees in political science (DePauw University) and law (Indiana Law School) and, after being admitted to the bar in 1974, initially worked in the family's business before being elected to the House of Representatives in 1976 and the Senate in 1980, where he had specialised in defence and labour issues.

[12] The spending limit set by the Federal Election Commission for each candidate had been $46 million in public funds. In actuality, however, a further $69 million of 'soft money' – including $29 million by State party organisations and $27 million in the form of private and corporate donations of $100,000 apiece – had been raised by the Republicans and spent indirectly in support of the Bush-Quayle ticket and $59 million similarly by the Democrats. More than two-thirds of the overall campaign spending went on television advertising.

[13] Turnout was highest in the Midwest and New England, reaching 66% in Minnesota, where election day registration is permitted. It was lowest in the South, South-west and industrial North-east, attaining only 39% in Georgia. Traditionally, low turnouts have usually been viewed as favourable to the Republicans. In

1988, however, this did not appear to be the case, with opinion poll surveys of non-voters – 42% of whom were under the age of 30 – revealing Bush to have been preferred by a wider margin (50:34 percent) than had been the case among actual voters.

[14]   These are the States of Alaska, Arizona (which has consistently voted Republican in presidential contests since 1948), California, Colorado, Idaho, Illinois, Indiana, Kansas, Montana, Nebraska, Nevada, New Hampshire, New Jersey, New Mexico, North Dakota, Oklahoma, South Dakota, Utah, Vermont, Virginia and Wyoming.

[15]   In November 1988, the electorate was also presented with the opportunity in 41 States, of voting on a variety of referendum questions or proposals. In all, 238 proposals were placed on State ballot-papers, including 29 in California, where voters approved a Ralph Nader-sponsored proposal to enforce supra-20% reductions in the level of car insurance premiums and for the imposition of a 'health sales tax' on cigarettes. In Arkansas, Colorado and Michigan bans on the State funding of abortions were approved.

CHAPTER 8

[1]   Mitchell, indeed, was the co-author, with Senator William Cohen (Me), of an insider account of the Iran-Contra hearings, *Men of Zeal*, which had concluded, contrary to the 'Tower Report', that George Bush had been a full player in the conspiracy to sell arms to Iran.

[2]   The previous three, Henry Clay in 1814, Andrew Stevenson in 1834 and Schuylet Colfax in 1869, had left to take up posts, respectively, as a member of the US Peace Commission, as Ambassador to the UK, and as Vice-President.

[3]   If, however, there is an economic 'hard landing' between 1990 and 1992 culminating in a recession – defined as real GNP growth of below 1% during two successive quarters or a forecast of zero real growth – then there is provision, under the terms of GRH, for its annual deficit targets to be disregarded temporarily.

[4]   The party's 'neo-liberal' torchbearer of 1988, Michael Dukakis is unlikely to be a candidate for the party's nomination in 1992, to the relief of its leadership. A series of family tragedies – his wife, Kitty, checked into a Rhode Island alcoholism treatment centre for a month in February 1989 and was hospitalised in November 1989 after suffering a 'severe reaction' from drinking rubbing alcohol – and budget crises in Massachusetts, whose economy was hit by defence cutbacks, have led to a plummeting in his popularity rating in the State to a figure of barely 19% by August 1989, severely denting his credibility as a potential presidential candidate.

[5]   At the Congressional and State levels, the Democratic Party remains in a much healthier position. Despite the threat of reapportionment, it appears likely that, as occurred in 1982, the party, with its dominance at the Statehouse and gubernatorial levels, will be able to control the process of redistricting – electoral boundary redrawing – in such a manner that the actual loss of House seats will be limited

to single figures. The party, moreover, has high hopes of making crucial gains in the Congressional and Statehouse elections of November 1990, the last that will take place before reapportionment, since, during the postwar era, the party of the incumbent President has endured net losses at the House level, of an average of 26 seats, at the midterm stage. In the case of the Senate, the Republicans will, in 1990, be defending 18 of the 34 seats to be contested and, as a result of retirements creating 'open contests' and of the Democrats fielding unusually popular candidates, appear to face strong challenges in up to seven of these. If the party was to achieve a net gain of five seats or more it would have sufficient voting power in the Senate to invoke the cloture rule to shut off debate. However, any gains secured in 1990 are likely to be reversed in 1992, in which year, following the party's strong performance in 1986, the Democrats will be defending at least 20 of the 34 Senate seats at stake.

Part Five

CHAPTER 9

[1]   Arizona, California, Colorado, Florida, Georgia and Texas accounted for 57% of US population growth during 1970-87. Alaska's population grew by 74%.

[2]   The new 'high-tech' sector employs now more than 3.3 million people (3.2% of the total workforce), half a million of whom are to be found in California.

[3]   Gains were made by Florida (4 seats), Texas (3), California (2), Tennessee, New Mexico, Arizona, Colorado, Utah, Nevada, Oregon and Washington (1 each). Losses were suffered by New York (5), Pennsylvania, Ohio, Illinois (2 each), Missouri, South Dakota, New Jersey, Massachusetts, Michigan and Indiana (1 each).

[4]   The recent 1985 takeover of the influential 15-million-member Southern Baptist Convention by conservative Christian groups is likely to give additional impetus to Republican gains among southern whites, 39% of whom described themselves as Republicans in 1988 compared with a mere 14% three decades earlier. In contrast, more than 90% of black voters in the South view themselves as Democrats.

[5]   The number of foreign-born persons in the United States increased between the 1970 and 1980 censuses from 9.6 million (4.7% of the total population) to 14 million (6.2% of the total), reversing a 30-year downward trend in net immigration.

[6]   During the decade and a half since 1975 the number of Hispanic elected officials has doubled to more than 3200, nearly half of whom are to found in the State of Texas. A key factor behind this growing local success has been the registration drives launched by the late Willie Velasquez's San Antonio-based 'South-West Voter Registration Education Project'. Still, however, in national presidential elections, Hispanic voter turnout reaches barely 30%, compared with figures of 50-55% for blacks and 60% for whites.

7   Since Reconstruction, there has been only one black Senator, E Brooke (R, Mass 1967–78), and one black Governor, D Wilder (D, Virginia 1990–).

8   In 1989 only four of the full-voting black Representatives came from the States of the South: one each from Georgia, Mississippi, Tennessee and Texas. Four came from urban portions of California, four from New York and 11 from the northern industrialised States of Illinois (3), Maryland (1), Michigan (2), Missouri (2), New Jersey (1), Ohio (1) and Pennsylvania (1). Of these 23 Representatives, only two, Ronald Dellums (Berkeley and Oakland, Calif) and Alan Wheat (Kansas City, Mo), represented districts in which the black population did not enjoy a voting plurality. At the same time, moreover, there was only one further House district available, the New Orleans-based Louisiana 2nd, in which black voters were in the majority but the sitting representative, in this case the veteran liberal Democrat Lindy Boggs, was white. This suggested that the 'easy' period of expansion in black Congressional numbers was over.

9   Bradley (1917–), a sharecropper's son and former police lieutenant who has continuously been Mayor of Los Angeles since 1973, had already fought for the California governorship as the Democrat nominee in 1982.

10   In 1987 31% of black families were below the official US poverty line of $9069, compared with 27% of Hispanic families and 11% of white; in 1983-4, the average family income for blacks was $15 432 compared with $27 686 for whites; average unemployment 18% (compared with 9% for whites), with that for black teenagers exceeding 40%; and only 45% owned their own homes compared with 65% of whites. The position of Hispanics was intermediate, with Hispanic teenage unemployment, for example, standing at 21%.

11   The ERA sailed through Congress in 1971–2 and was approved by 22 States in its first year and by 35 States by 1977 (three short of the necessary target), but then ran into mounting opposition from anti-abortion and New Right fundamentalist groups, particularly Phyllis Schafly's 'Eagle Forum', and deliberate stalling in the southern States. Despite an extension of the time limit for State ratification in 1978, it eventually died in 1982, becoming only the sixth constitutional amendment (and the second this century) to fail to secure State ratification after passage through Congress.

12   Seven other women unsuccessfully contested for governorships in Alaska, Arizona, Connecticut, Maine, Nebraska, Nevada and Oregon in November 1986 and one, in Missouri, in November 1988, while Madeleine Kunin was re-elected for further terms on both occasions.

13   Union membership did increase by 35% in the burgeoning service sector between 1973 and 1983, but its overall unionisation rate remains low at only 11% (compared with a rate of 24% for the industrial sector). The fastest growing service unions are the 0.85-million-member Service Employees International Union (SEIU), the 1.3-million-member United Food and Commercial Workers International Union and the 1-million-member American Federation of State, County and Municipal Employees (AFSCME).

14   Kirkland succeeded George Meany, a vehemently anti-communist conservative, who had headed the AFL-CIO from 1955 to 1979. Meany's departure led to the reaffiliation of the liberal UAW in 1981, which had left on personal

and ideological grounds in 1966. Another important union, the Teamsters, a body which represented truck drivers and related trades and which, with 1.7 million members, was the country's largest single labour union, was also later, in November 1987, readmitted to the AFL-CIO after a 30-year ban. This was a controversial move since traditionally the Teamsters, who had been expelled from the AFL-CIO in 1957 for refusing to abide by its ethics code, has close links with organised crime. It was also notoriously pro-Republican in its political stance, having endorsed Ronald Reagan for the presidency in both 1980 and 1984.

[15] Under the terms of the National Labour Relations Act (1935), American labour unions are accorded the right to bargain collectively (representing all workers) in a workplace if they are able to secure a majority of votes in an election approved by the NLRB. Each year thousands of elections are held to decide whether such bargaining rights should be extended to a new workplace. Since 1974 unions have never won more than half of such contests. Additionally, a smaller, but since 1974, increasing number of 'decertification elections' are held to determine whether or not a union should be expelled from a particular workplace.

Part Six

CHAPTER 10

[1] It has since been asserted in a number of works that renegade ultra-conservative elements within the CIA who were opposed to the re-election of Carter may have actively sabotaged this rescue mission and have worked deliberately to postpone the release of the American hostages held in Teheran until after the presidential election. Such assertions remain, however, unproven.

[2] Allen had been Richard Nixons's foreign policy adviser during the 1968 presidential campaign and had expected to become NSA in 1969, but was pipped by the Harvard academic and Rockefeller Republican, Henry Kissinger.

[3] Defence spending increased in real terms by 5.9% in fiscal 1981, by 9.7% in 1982, 7.5% in 1983, 4% in 1984 and by 7.5% in fiscal 1985.

[4] This proposed America's cancellation of the deployment of Cruise and Pershing-2 land missiles in Western Europe in return for Russia's dismantling of its SS-20 missiles. Requiring, as it did, asymmetrical Soviet concessions, it was viewed as an unrealistic, propagandistic proposal. However, subsequently, in 1987, it was to be accepted by the Soviet side.

[5] Shultz had served as Labor Secretary, OMB director and as Treasury Secretary in the Nixon administration, before becoming vice-chairman of the Bechtel construction corporation. He was an experienced economist – serving as Reagan's chief economic adviser between 1980 and 1982 – and was a pragmatic Atlanticist in foreign affairs in the vein of Haig and Kissinger, but quieter and less assertive and more a loyal team player.

6   Clark became NSA in January 1982 following Richard Allen's resignation over allegations (unproved) that he had accepted $1000 from a Japanese magazine for arranging an exclusive interview with Nancy Reagan.

7   McFarlane, a former Marine, Kissinger aide and deputy NSA, took over when William Clark moved to the Interior Department. He was a pragmatic conservative, who sought to restore the lost authority of the NSC. This he succeeded in doing during 1984, but he later found his authority checked by Donald Regan.

8   During February 1986 the Reagan administration displayed similar pragmatism when it exerted late pressure to help oust the unpopular but pro-American 'Baby Doc' and Marcos dictatorships in Haiti and the Philippines.

9   Admiral John Poindexter, a nuclear physicist and former US Navy rear-admiral who had been hand-picked by Chief-of-Staff Donald Regan, took over as NSA following Robert McFarlane's resignation in December 1985.

10   Carlucci (b. 1930 in Scranton, Pa), educated at Princeton and Harvard Business School, enjoyed a lengthy career in government and diplomatic service. He had been a diplomat in Africa during the 1950s and 1960s; had worked in the Office of Economic Opportunity, OMB and Department of Health during the Nixon administration; and had served as US Ambassador to Portugal between 1974 and 1976, as Deputy Director of the CIA in 1977–80 and as Deputy Secretary of Defense, under Weinberger, between 1981 and 1982.

11   Lt General Powell, the previous NSA, resumed his military career, being subsequently promoted in September 1989, by which time he was a Major-General, to the armed forces' senior most position, that of chairman of the Joint Chiefs-of-Staff.

12   Born in Utah in March 1927, Scowcroft was a graduate of the US Military Academy West Point (1947) and had secured a PhD in International Relations from Columbia University in 1967. Having previously been in the US Airforce, he had served as military assistant to President Nixon from 1972.

Appendix C

1   There are 150 sub-committees functioning in the House of Representatives and 87 in the Senate.

2   Today more than 50% of Senators and 40% of Representatives are committee/sub-committee chairmen.

3   By 1989, Congressional staff numbers exceeded 19 300, a figure 15% up on the 1980 level, and the overall annual cost of running Congress was more than $1 billion.

ABBREVIATIONS AND GLOSSARY OF POLITICAL TERMS

ABM Treaty (1972) Soviet-American anti-ballistic missile treaty.

Achille Lauro The name of an Italian cruise ship which, while in the Mediterranean off Egypt and with 400 persons aboard, was hijacked on 7 October 1985 by Palestinian terrorists. The hijackers, who unsuccessfully demanded the release of 50 Palestinians held by Israel and who murdered one American passenger, were, on 10 October, turned over to the Italian authorities when US Navy F-14 fighter jets forced down the Egyptian plane on which they had taken flight.

ACLU American Civil Liberties Union. Liberal/libertarian pressure group founded in 1920 to protect the constitutional rights of the individual. Membership 250 000.

ACU American Conservative Union. A conservative pressure group formed in 1964. Since 1971, the ACU has annually published ratings of the ideological stance of individual Congressmen based on an analysis of their voting record with respect to contentious bills.

ADA Americans for Democratic Action. Liberal pressure group founded in 1947. Membership 75 000. Since its inception, it has annually published ratings of the 'liberalism' of individual Congressmen based on an analysis of their voting records.

AEI American Enterprise Institute. Washington DC-based conservative academic think tank.

AFDC Aid for Families with Dependent Children. A State-administered, means-tested, cash assistance programme funded jointly by the Federal and State governments for families with dependent children and a parent who is absent, incapacitated and (in some States) unemployed.

Affirmative Action Term for 'positive discrimination' in terms of job quotas etc in favour of ethnic minorities.

AFL-CIO American Federation of Labor-Congress of Labor. Umbrella organisation for 93 affiliated labour unions. Membership 14 million.

AIP American Independent Party. Conservative breakaway party from Democrats founded by George Wallace of Alabama in 1968.

Appropriations Bill A bill sanctioning the grant of money to fund programmes 'authorised' in separate measures by Congress.

Bakke Case 1978 Supreme Court case concerning the 'affirmative action' ethnic selection quotas employed by the University of California Medical School. The Court ruled that in this specific case the quotas violated white applicants' rights under the 14th Amendment, but continued to give general support to the idea of 'affirmative action'.

Balanced Budget Amendment Movement State-level movement spearheaded by the National Taxpayers' Union and National Tax Limitations Committee during the late 1970s and early 1980s to force the passage of a Federal balanced budget amendment to the constitution. By 1983 32

States had passed resolutions in favour of such an amendment. Thereafter, however, the momentum behind the movement faded.

B-1 Bomber New generation US bomber aircraft designed to replace the B-52 and penetrate Soviet air defences.

Bill of Rights Term given to Amendments 1–10 of the constitution which guarantee specific civil rights against the actions of the government.

Black Muslims Religious grouping founded in 1931 by Elijah Muhammad (1897–1975) after a vision of Allah. It developed into a black separatist movement from the 1950s under the leadership, initially, of Malcolm X (1925–65) and, more recently, of Louis Farrakhan.

Block Grant Funds granted to State and local governments by the Federal government for specified broad purposes, but for whose spending in detail considerable discretion is allowed to the former bodies: much greater than in the case of grants-in-aid. There has been a progressive switch away from the traditional categorical grant-in-aid systems towards block grants since the Nixon presidency.

Boland Amendment Legislation promoted by the Massachusetts Representative, Edward Boland (D), and passed by Congress in October 1984 (Boland II) which specifically prohibited any 'agency or entity of the United States involved in intelligence activities' from spending any money on direct or indirect support of military operations in Nicaragua during fiscal 1985. The amendment was breached in the 1985–6 'Irangate' affair.

'Boll Weevil' Nickname, derived from the name of a famous cotton pest, given to conservative southern Democrats who frequently align in Congress with Republicans on roll-call votes.

Budget and Impoundment Control Act (1974) This Act gave Congress a central role in the budget-making process, forcing it to consider the budget as a whole according to a strict timetable. It led to the establishment of the CBO and to the creation of new Budget Committees in the House and Senate. It also prohibited the President's impoundment of funds unless both chambers approved within 45 days.

Capitol Hill Site of US Congress.

Caucus A closed meeting of party members used to select candidates for election and delegates to National Conventions. The term also applies to party members within each house of Congress, when they meet together at the start of each legislative session to elect their House and Senate leaders.

CBO Congressional Budget Office. Independent Congressional agency of professional budget analysts.

CDF Conservative Democratic Forum. Grouping of conservative southern Democrat Congressmen.

CEA Council of Economic Advisers. Established in 1946, the CEA, which is composed of three academic economists, advises the President on economic affairs, providing an alternative source of advice to the Treasury Department.

Chadha Case June 1983 Supreme Court judgment on a case concerning Jagdish Chadha (a British subject and native of Kenya) who had entered the United States on a student visa in 1966 and was ordered for deportation in 1972 when, after his visa had expired, Congress overturned the Immigration and Naturalization Service's decision to allow him to remain as a resident alien. The Supreme Court ruled that the Legislative Veto used by Congress in this case violated Article 1 of the constitution.

Chief-of-Staff The head of the White House Office whose task it is to co-ordinate the presidential cabinet and act as the chief aide to the President.

CIA Central Intelligence Agency. Federal bureau created in 1947 to co-ordinate and carry out espionage and intelligence activities. It is based in Langley, Virginia.

Citizens Party Minor party founded by Barry Commoner in 1980 which comprises former liberal Democrats and environmentalists.

Civil Rights Commission Independent Agency civil rights watchdog established in 1957. Half of its eight members are appointed by the President and half by Congress.

Cloture The process by which a filibuster can be brought to an end. In the Senate, a cloture motion requires the signature of 16 Senators to be introduced. It is then voted on by the full chamber two days later, requiring the support of at least 60% of the entire Senate membership to be successful. Between 1917 (when the 'cloture rule' was introduced) and 1988 of the 273 cloture votes taken 92 (34%) were successful.

'Common Cause' A public-interest pressure group which was formed in 1970 by John Gardner, formerly HEW Secretary in the Johnson administration. Anxious to bring an end to America's involvement in the Vietnam War, it campaigned originally, and successfully, for an ending to the seniority system in selecting Congressional committee chairmen as a means of securing the removal of conservatives who had repeatedly blocked votes on war policy. Also during the 1970s, it lobbied for reform of the election campaign finance laws and for the passage of the 1978 Ethics in Government Act and during the 1980s it opposed funding of the Reagan administration's MX missile and SDI programmes. The pressure group, with Fred Wertheimer as president, boasts a membership of 275000 and an annual budget of $11 million.

Congress House of Representatives and Senate. Both chambers meet continuously for eight months between January–August, before recessing during the summer.

Congressman Member of House of Representatives or Senate. The term is also sometimes used more specifically to refer to a House member.

Conservative Caucus Grassroots 'new conservative' organisation formed in 1974 by Howard Phillips.

'**Conservative Coalition**' Term given to the informal voting coalition of 'boll weevil' southern Democrats and the majority of Congressional Republicans for votes on conservative issues. First formed in 1937, in opposition to Roosevelt's 'New Deal' programme, it dominated the House of Representatives during the 1950s and early 1960s, and was re-activated in 1981.

Constitutional Amendment Under Article 5 of the constitution, to become law constitutional amendments require the initial approval of a two-thirds majority from both houses of Congress and subsequent ratification by three-quarters (38) of the United States' fifty State legislatures within a seven-year timespan. Constitutional amendments can, alternatively, be initiated by two-thirds of State legislatures calling for the establishment of a special National Constitutional Convention. Measures adopted at this Convention then require subsequent approval by Constitutional Conventions in 38 States to become law.

COPE Committee on Political Education. Political wing of the AFL-CIO.

Confederate States Term given to the 11 southern agrarian States (S Carolina, Mississippi, Florida, Alabama, Georgia, Louisiana, Texas, Virginia, Arkansas, N Carolina and Tennessee) which seceded from the Union during 1860–1 and fought the northern industrial States in the American Civil War of 1861–5.

Contras Anti-communist forces in Central America opposed to the Nicaraguan Sandinista government.

Cruise Missiles Medium-range American nuclear missiles stationed in Western Europe from 1983.

D Democrat

DFL Democratic Farmer-Labor Party. Democratic Party organisation in Minnesota built up by Eugene McCarthy and Hubert Humphrey.

DNC Democratic National Committee.

DSG Democratic Study Group. Research and co-ordinating body formed in 1959 by House Democrats of a liberal hue in an effort to counteract the, then dominant, 'Conservative Coalition'. It supported the 'New Frontier' and 'Great Society' legislation of the 1961–8 Kennedy and Johnson administrations. The DSG provides its Congressional members with weekly reports and fact sheets on bills about to come to the House floor, as well as vote summaries and campaign 'ammunition' to use against Republican opponents.

Electoral College Name given to college used to elect the President. Each State is granted the same number of electors as the sum of its Senators and Congressional Representatives and each State party nominates slates of would-be electors committed to their presidential candidates. Voters cast their ballots for presidential candidates in early November, but, in fact, elect the slates of aligned electors, whose task it is later formally to vote *en bloc* in their State capitals in mid December for the presidential nominee to whom they are pledged.

ERA Equal Rights Amendment.

Ethics in Government Act (1978) Law which bars senior officials from lobbying their former agencies for a year after leaving office, with a lifetime ban on lobbying being imposed upon matters with which they were 'personally and substantially' involved.

FBI Federal Bureau of Investigation. The agency of the Justice Department charged with investigating violations of Federal laws and responsible for internal security.

Federal Election Campaign Act (1974) Introduced strict limits on party-political and business contributions to the primary and final campaign spending of Federal election candidates and provided for the State funding of presidential contests.

Federal Reserve Board Seven-member board of governors in charge of the Federal Reserve Bank, setting the level of bank interest rates and controlling monetary policy. Members are appointed by the President (subject to Senate confirmation) and serve 14-year terms. The chairman (since 1987 Alan Greenspan) and vice-chairman are appointed from among the board's members by the President and serve renewable four-year terms.

Filibuster Term given to the deliberate prolongation of debate in order to prevent voting on, and hence the passage of, legislation. In the House of Representatives strict cloture rules restricting the time for debate prevent filibusters. In the Senate, however, filibusters can only be defeated if a special 'cloture motion' is supported by a 60% majority.

Food Stamps A federally financed and State-administered aid system, through the grant of food coupons, for needy groups.

FRC Foreign Relations Committee (Senate).

GAO General Accounting Office. Specialist body created by Congress in 1921 to oversee and review government programmes.

GE General Electric company.

Gerrymandering Term given to deliberate manipulation in the drawing of constituency boundaries to favour the party in power.

GNP Gross National Product.

GOP 'Grand Old Party'. Traditional nickname of the Republican Party.

Gramm-Rudman-Hollings (GRH) Balanced Budget Act The 'Balanced Budget and Emergency Deficit Control Act', proposed by Senators Phil Gramm (R – Texas) , Warren Rudman (R – New Hampshire) and Ernest Hollings (D – S Carolina) and signed into law in December 1985, which provided for the graduated and statutory reduction in the size of the Federal budget deficit, ending in its elimination by 1991. Key elements of this Act were subsequently ruled unconstitutional by the Supreme Court in July 1986. Thus, in 1987, the Act was amended to make the OMB's budget deficit forecast, rather than the GAO's, the decisive one for determining whether statutory cuts in the defence and 'non exempt' domestic programmes were necessary. In addition, 1993 was now made the target year for a balanced budget.

Grant-in-Aid Payment by the Federal government to State and local governments in support of specified programmes.

'Great Society' Term given to the 1960s social and welfare reforms introduced by President Johnson during 1963–8 following his call for 'an all-out-war' on poverty.

Gubernatorial State governorship.

'Gypsy Moths' Nickname given to liberal northern Republicans who sometimes align themselves with northern Democrats in Congress on roll-call votes.

Heritage Foundation Conservative think tank formed in 1973 by Paul Weyrich and Edwin Feulner.

HEW Department of Health, Education and Welfare (1953–77).

Hispanics Term given to ethnic groups of Spanish and Central and Latin American descent.

Hiss Hearings 1948 investigations by the House of Representatives' Un-American Activities Committee into allegations that the former State Department official Alger Hiss (1904–) had committed perjury in 1938 when, before a Federal Grand Jury, he had denied charges of having passed secret administration papers to Whittaker Chambers (editor of *Time* and a self-confessed communist). Richard M Nixon played a leading role on the committee pressing charges against Hiss and gained a national reputation for his work. Hiss was subsequently convicted of perjury in 1950, but was released from prison in 1954 and continued to protest his innocence.

House of Representatives 435-member lower house of Congress elected at regular two-year intervals every even year in November. All spending bills must, according to Section 7 of Article 1 of the constitution, originate in the House, thus rendering its financial committees particularly influential bodies. The House also has sole powers of instigating impeachment proceedings.

HUD Department of Housing and Urban Development (1965–).

ICBM Intercontinental ballistic missile.

Impeachment A proceeding brought against a Federal government official for an offence committed in office. A bill of impeachment must first be voted by a simple majority in the House of Representatives. The Senate then hears the case as a jury, with a two-thirds vote of its members being required for conviction and the removal of the offender (President, judge etc.) from office.

Impoundment The refusal by the executive to spend money appropriated by Congress. The President's ability to impound funds has been severely restricted by the 1974 Budget and Impoundment Control Act.

IRS Inland Revenue Service.

Legislative Re-Organization Act (1970) The first in a series of acts which radically reformed and democratised the operations of Congress. This act introduced a number of important procedural innovations, the two most important being the switch from teller to 'roll-call' votes within committees, with the results being made public, and the grant of the right of minorities on committees to file minority reports, hire staff and call witnesses to the committee's hearings. It also required Congress to issue oversight reports every two years.

Legislative Veto Term given to the proviso built into much legislation between 1932 and 1983 whereby Congress delegated considerable rule-making authority to government agencies but retained the authority to annul any new rule of which it disapproved by a simple majority vote. This was ruled unconstitutional by the Supreme Court in the Chadha case, since it was seen as violating Article 1 of the constitution under which all new laws needed to be approved by both chambers of Congress as well as being signed by the President.

Libertarian Party Far-right/anarchic minority party founded in 1971 which opposes all forms of government (regulation and taxation) interference in life, supports free trade and a return to the gold standard, and favours an isolationist foreign policy. The party is strongest in Alaska (where it has boasted local State legislators) and the States of the West.

'Log-rolling' Term given to bargaining process in Congress by which Congressmen make private agreements to support amendments on bills in return for similar reciprocal favours on other measures.

'Main Street' Term given to conservative, rural, small-town wing of the Republican Party.

Majority Leader In the Senate, the head of the majority party in the Chamber who is elected by his party colleagues and serves as its chief spokesman and strategist. Along with the Minority Leader (the floor leader of the minority, or opposition, party) he directs the Senate's legislative schedule. In the House, the Majority Leader ranks second to the Speaker.

McCarthyism Term given to the practice of making unsupported allegations of communist leanings derived from the 1950–5 Senate investigations instigated by the Republican Senator Joseph McCarthy (1908–57).

MDD McDonnell Douglas Corporation. Aerospace grouping.

Medicaid Health care service for the poor administered by the States and jointly funded by the State and Federal governments.

Medicare Federally administered and financed health care insurance service for people over the age of 65 introduced in 1965.

MX Missile New generation of land-based, rail-mobile, multi-warhead, American ICBMs to be sited in Wyoming and replace the Minuteman missile force.

NAACP National Association for the Advancement of Colored People. Moderate black rights pressure group founded in 1909. Membership 450000.

Nader, Ralph (1934–) Public interest/consumer activist. Nader rose to prominence in 1966 when his recommendations to a Congressional committee investigating car safety were incorporated in the national Traffic and Motor Vehicle Safety Act. Thereafter, he encouraged the formation of 'civic interest lobbies' to pressurise Congress, State legislatures, regulatory commissions and company boards to improve their standards of consumer and environmental protection. In 1980, he became head of the Public Citizen Foundation.

National Convention The national meeting of delegates selected by the State organisations of each party which is held in the summer of a presidential election year to elect the party's presidential and vice-presidential candidates and adopt an election 'platform' (manifesto). The number of delegates apportioned to each State is based on the party's performance in the State during the preceding Congressional, gubernatorial and presidential elections (i.e. the number of Democrat or Republican Representatives, Senators and Governors it can boast) and delegates are selected within the States by either primaries, caucuses or committee meetings. A few votes-at-large are also assigned to US overseas territories. In 1988 4162 accredited delegates attended the Democratic Party National Convention and 2277 the Republicans'.

NATO North Atlantic Treaty Organisation.

NEA National Education Association. 1.7-million-member teaching union.

'New Deal' Term given to the interventionist economic policies of F D Roosevelt's 1933–40 administrations designed at guaranteeing, through the agency of the Federal government, the minimum conditions of life and which sought to overcome the curse of unemployment.

New England Designation given to the six States of the far North-east – Connecticut, Maine, Massachusetts, New Hampshire, Rhode Island and Vermont.

'New Frontier' Term given to the social and civil rights reforms of the early 1960s mapped out by John F Kennedy in his January 1961 inaugural address.

NIC Newly Industrialising Country.

NCPAC National Conservative Political Action Committee.

NOW National Organization for Women. Organisation formed in 1966 to campaign for equal rights for women.

NSA National Security Adviser. The director of the NSC and personal adviser to the President on security matters.

NSC National Security Council. Council established in 1947 to provide alternative foreign policy advice to the President and co-ordinate strategic actions.

OECD Organisation for Economic Co-operation and Development.

OMB Office of Management and Budget. Body of presidential advisers who prepare the administration's budget and legislative proposals to be presented to Congress.

OPEC Organisation of Petroleum Exporting Companies.

'Open Contest' An election not contested by an incumbent.

PAC Political Action Committee. A lobbying organisation which collects and channels funds to politicians who support its policy stance and which engages in general media campaigns.

PERSHING-2 Medium-range, high-velocity American nuclear weapons stationed in West Germany since the autumn of 1983.

PLO Palestine Liberation Organisation.

Pocket Veto Term given to the defeat of legislation at the end of Congressional sessions by the President's deliberate refusal to sign a bill in the knowledge that Congress will adjourn before the ten-day limit elapses, thus killing the measure.

Populist Term given to quasi-socialist midwestern radicals (q.v. Progressive) who follow the tradition of the 1892–1908 People's (Populist) Party, an agrarian reform movement. The New Populist Forum, led by Senator Tom Harkin (D – Iowa), is the contemporary heir to this tradition.

'Pork-Barrel' Legislation' Term given to the addition of numerous minor amendments and clauses to bills which result in the grant of constituency favours to individual Congressmen in return for their agreement to support the broader bill.

President Head of the Federal executive government. Candidates must be at least 35 years of age and be natural-born citizens of the US with at least 14 years of residence. Under the 22nd Amendment, Presidents are restricted to a maximum of two four-year terms in office.

President pro Tempore A position filled by the most senior-ranking figure from the majority party within the Senate. The officeholder presides over the Senate whenever the Vice-President is absent.

Primary Intra-party election used to select candidates who will subsequently stand for elective office under the party banner or to select delegates to attend the National Convention. In an 'open' primary, any voter may participate, regardless of party affiliation. In a 'closed' primary, only registered party supporters may vote. In Democratic Party presidential primaries, delegates are usually apportioned between candidates on a proportionate basis, with a 15% of the vote cut-off limit applying. In Republican Party primaries, a mix of proportionality and winner-takes-all is the norm. In 1988, 35 million people voted in the presidential primaries held by the two parties: 22.7 million in the Democrats', and 12.3 million in the Republicans'.

Progressive Term given to farmbelt, quasi-socialist radicals, seeking to represent the small farmer against big business interests, following the brief rise of 'Fighting Bob' La Follette's Progressive Party during the early 1920s and its successor, led by Henry Wallace, during the later 1940s. The heirs to this tradition are the Midwestern-based Citizen Action grouping and, more controversially, Lyndon LaRouche's National Democrats.

Proposition An electoral device employed at State level by which citizens can, by gathering a stipulated number of signatures for an initiative, have propositions included on the ballot paper in State elections which, if supported by a majority of voters, become binding on the government.

Public Bill A legislative proposal which deals with general questions and becomes a 'public law' if ratified by Congress and the President. It is distinct from a private bill which deals with such individual matters as personal claims against the government in immigration and land title and which, if approved, becomes a 'private law'. A substantial number of private bills used to be passed by Congress during the nineteenth and early twentieth centuries. Today, however, while several hundred are introduced each annual session, barely a dozen are ratified.

PUSH People United to Serve Humanity. Organisation directed at black economic advancement established by the Rev Jesse Jackson.

R Republican.

RDF Rapid Deployment Force. US military force established to police the Gulf region during the early 1980s.

Reaganomics Nickname given to the tax-cutting, de-regulationary, 'supply-side' economic programme propounded during the Reagan administration.

Reconstruction 1865–77 post Civil War period when the South was reorganised and reintegrated into the Union.

Reconstruction Finance Corporation Government-run industrial bank which functioned between 1932–53, providing capital to industry, banks, farmers and railways to prevent bankruptcies.

Redistricting System of re-apportioning House of Representatives seats between States according to population sizes following each decennial census. The associated re-drawing of constituency boundaries is controlled by State legislatures and Governors, subject to judicial approval on the grounds of 'fairness'.

Regulatory Commissions Agencies established by the Federal executive to regulate economic and social activities and protect the general public interest. Their executive boards, which contain nearly equal numbers of Democrats, and Republicans, enjoy considerable autonomy.

Representative Member of the House of Representatives. Candidates for election must be at least 25 years of age and a US citizen of seven years' standing and must reside in the State in which they are standing. They are elected in constituencies which comprise populations of between 400–650000, serve two-year terms and are debarred from concurrently holding a government or an executive administration post.

Resolution A Congressional motion, usually to do with procedural rules, which does not require passage by the other chamber or the President's approval. Resolutions are also passed to express Congress's views on foreign policy actions by the executive or to express condolences. They differ from 'Joint Resolutions', which after approval by both chambers and signature by the President, can become laws. 'Joint Resolutions' are thus similar to bills, but deal with more limited matters, such as a single appropriation.

RNC Republican National Committee.

Roe v Wade 1973 landmark Supreme Court case in which the Court prohibited States from banning abortion during the first three months of pregnancy, permitted abortion on medical grounds during the second trimester (months 4–6), but outlawed it after six months of pregnancy. The Court's 1989 decision in the *Webster v. Reproductive Health Services* case, which allowed individual States to exercise greater control over the availability of abortion has, however, seriously undermined the *Roe v. Wade* ruling.

'Roll-Call' Vote A vote in Congress in which the stand of each member is recorded. In the Senate, this is effected by asking each Senator to answer 'yeah', 'nay', or, if he wishes to abstain, 'present'. In the House, an electronic voting system has been used since January 1973.

SALT Strategic Arms Limitation Treaty. The SALT-1 accord was signed by President Nixon and Leonid Brezhnev in 1972 and was subsequently ratified by the US Senate. SALT-2 was signed by Presidents Carter and Brezhnev in June 1979, but failed to gain formal ratification by the US Senate.

SDI Strategic Defense Initiative. Programme unveiled by President Reagan in March 1983 which seeks to create a satellite-based defence system against strategic nuclear weapons. The USSR opposes SDI as a potentially destabilising innovation.

Select or Special Committee A committee in the House of Representatives or Senate which is established for a special purpose and, usually, for a limited period. Most such special committees are investigative and lack legislative authority.

Senate 100-member upper chamber of Congress whose members are elected for staggered six-year terms at regular biennial intervals. Consent from the Senate is required for the appointment of Federal administrators, members of the presidential cabinet and top-level judicial officers, while a two-thirds Senate vote is necessary for the ratification of treaties with foreign powers. In addition, it is the Senate which hears cases of impeachment brought against Federal officials.

Senator Member of the Senate. Candidates for election must be at least 30 years of age and a US citizen of nine years' standing and must be resident in the State in which they are standing. They are elected in a State-wide contest for six-year terms and are debarred from concurrently holding a government or an executive administration post.

Seniority System Traditional system of assigning committee chairs and party leadership positions to majority members with the longest record of service on the relevant bodies. The system has been undermined by 'democratisation reforms' within Congress since the early 1970s, but is still adhered to in large measure.

Social Security Federal welfare insurance programme introduced in 1935 which protects workers and their families against income loss resulting from retirement, disability and the death of a breadwinner. Retirement pensions constitute the principal item in the social security budget.

Speaker Leader of the majority party in the House of Representatives.

The Speaker presides over floor debates and enjoys considerable patronage powers, controlling appointments to the House's influential Rules Committee. He is second in line of succession to the President after the Vice-President.

Standing Committee A committee in the House of Representatives or Senate to which legislation is referred and which subsequently reports bills and resolutions to its respective chamber. Unlike standing committees in the British parliament, which are temporarily established to consider specific legislative measures and which have only limited amending authority, US Congressional standing committees are powerful permanent bodies which effectively 'make' legislation. Each specialises in a specified range of activities and, invariably, boasts under its aegis several, more specialist, sub-committees. Standing and sub-committees are well staffed and hold open hearings at which interested parties and members of the executive branch give evidence in support of, or in opposition to, proposed bills. Currently there are 22 standing committees in the House and 16 in the Senate to which 138 and 86 sub-committees are respectively attached.

START Strategic Arms Reduction Talks. Soviet-US arms negotiations which began in Geneva in July 1982.

'Supply-side' economics An economic theory which emphasises the need to maximise efficiency in the supply end of the economy through removing regulations and reducing taxes, and opposes government manipulation of demand in a Keynesian fashion.

Supreme Court Constitutional watchdog body comprising nine judges nominated by the President and approved by the Senate who are removable only by impeachment.

'Tabling Motion' A Congressional motion to end debate and effectively 'kill' a bill.

Ticket Term given to list of party names for elective offices presented in each State on polling day.

U-2 Incident Incident in May 1960 when an American U-2 reconnaissance aircraft was shot down while on a spy mission over the central Soviet Union and its pilot, Gary Powers, taken prisoner.

UAW United Auto Workers Union. 1.2-million-member labour organisation covering workers in the car, aerospace and agricultural implements industries.

UMWA United Mine Workers of America. Labour union with 0.07 million members. It is not affiliated to the AFL-CIO.

UN United Nations.

USSR Union of Soviet Socialist Republics (Soviet Union).

USWA United Steel Workers of America. Labour union with 0.8 million members.

Veto The rejection of a bill passed by Congress by the President and its return to the chamber of origin with a message clarifying his objections. Such vetoes must be imposed by the President within 10 days of the receipt of the bill, otherwise it automatically becomes law without his signature. They can, moreover, be overridden by a two-thirds majority in each chamber.

Vice-President Elected to serve as deputy to the President, the Vice-President serves in an *ad hoc* role in the President's cabinet and also functions as the formal President of the Senate, being granted a casting vote if the Senate evenly divides on a measure.

Voting Rights Act (1965) A product of the 1960s civil rights movement, the law provides for Federal intervention to help enroll voters in districts where in excess of 50% of those old enough to vote remain unregistered. Aimed principally to raise black registration in the southern States, it was extended to the States of the South-west, where large unregistered Hispanic minorities exist, in 1975.

'Wall Street' Term given to urban, north-eastern liberal wing of the Republican Party.

War Powers Resolution (1973) Act passed by Congress which requires Presidents to inform the legislature of any hostile use of American troops overseas within 48 hours. Congressional approval (which is not subject to Presidential veto) is required after 60 days if the action is to be continued.

Weber v USWA 1979 Supreme Court case concerning voluntary 'affirmative action' quotas, which were ruled to be permissible.

BIBLIOGRAPHY

GENERAL US POLITICS

JE Chubb & PE Peterson (eds) *The New Direction in American Politics* (Washington DC: Brookings Institution, 1985)

Congressional Quarterly Almanacs, 1976–88 (Annual)

PJ Davies & FA Waldstein (eds) *Political Issues in America Today* (Manchester: Manchester University Press, 1987)

D McKay *Politics and Power in the USA* (Harmondsworth: Penguin, 1987)

RA Maidment & AG McGrew *The American Political Process* (New York: Sage, 1986)

RA Maidment & M Tappin *American Politics Today* (Manchester: Manchester University Press, 3rd edn, 1989)

M Malbin (ed) *Money and Politics in the US* (Washington DC: American Enterprise Institute, 1984)

H Smith *The Power Game: How Washington Works* (Glasgow: Fontana/Collins, 1988)

The Parties

FW Austin *Political Facts of the United States since 1789* (New York: Columbia University Press, 1986)

L Epstein *Political Parties in the American Mold* (Wisconsin: University of Wisconsin Press, 1986)

SM Gillon *Politics and Vision: The ADA and American Liberalism* (Oxford: Oxford University Press, 1987)

A L Hamby *Liberalism and its Challenges: FDR to Reagan* (Oxford: Oxford University Press, 1985)

X Kayden & E Mahe *The Party Goes On* (New York: Basic Books, 1986)

G Peele *Revival and Reaction: The Contemporary American Right* (Oxford: Oxford University Press, 1984)

N Polsby *Consequences of Party Reform* (New York: Oxford University Press, 1983)

NC Rae *The Decline and Fall of the Liberal Republicans: From 1952 to the Present* (Oxford: Oxford University Press, 1986)

A Ware *The Breakdown of Democratic Party Organization, 1940–1980* (Oxford: Oxford University Press, 1985)

MP Wattenberg *The Decline of American Political Parties 1952–1980* (Cambridge, Mass: Harvard University Press, 1984)

Congress

CJ Bailey *The US Congress* (Oxford: Blackwell, 1989)

MD McCubbins & T Sullivan (eds) *Congress: Structure and Policy* (Cambridge: Cambridge University Press, 1987)

T O'Neill & W Kovak *Man of the House* (London: Bodley Head, 1988)
JL Sundquist *The Decline and Resurgence of Congress* (Washington DC: Brookings Institution, 1981)

The Presidency

N Bowles *The White House and Capitol Hill: The Politics of Presidential Persuasion* (Oxford: Oxford University Press, 1987)
G Hodgson *All Things to All Men* (Harmondsworth: Penguin, 1984)
B Kellerman *The Political Presidency: Practice of Leadership from Kennedy through Reagan* (Oxford: Oxford University Press, 1984)
A King (ed) *Both Ends of the Avenue: The Presidency, the Executive Branch and Congress in the 1980s* (Washington DC: American Enterprise Institute, 1983)
TJ Lowi *The Personal President: Power Invested Promise Unfulfilled* (Ithaca, NY: Cornell University Press, 1985)
M Shaw (ed) *Roosevelt to Reagan: The Development of the Modern Presidency* (New York: C Hurst, 1987)

Supreme Court

V Blasi *The Burger Court: The Counter Revolution That Wasn't* (New Haven, Conn: Yale University Press, 1983)
RH Williams *The Politics of the US Supreme Court* (London: Allen & Unwin, 1980)

States and Federal System

R Bahl *Financing State and Local Government in the 1980s* (New York: Oxford University Press, 1984)
TL Beyle (ed) *State Government: CQ's Guide to Current Issues and Activities, 1985–86* (Washington DC: Congressional Quarterly Press, 1985)
RL Kemp *Coping with Proposition 13* (Lexington, Mass: Lexington Books, 1980)

ELECTIONS AND ELECTION CAMPAIGNS 1976–84

HE Alexander *Financing the 1976 Election* (Washington DC: Congressional Quarterly Publications, 1979)
HE Alexander *Financing the 1980 Election* (Lexington, Mass: DC Heath & Co, 1983)

M Bosnow *Diary of a Dark Horse: The 1980 Anderson Presidential Campaign* (Carbondale: Southern Illinois University Press, 1983)

E Drew *Portrait of an Election: The 1980 Presidential Campaign* (London: Routledge & Kegan Paul, 1981)

T Ferguson & J Rogers (eds) *The Hidden Election: Politics and Economics in the 1980 Presidential Campaign* (New York: Pantheon Books, 1981)

P Goldman, T Fuller et al *The Quest for the Presidency: 1984* (New York: Bantam Books, 1985)

TE Mann & NJ Ornstein *The American Elections of 1982* (Washington DC: American Enterprise Institute, 1983)

M Nelson (ed) *The Elections of 1984* (Washington DC: Congressional Quarterly Press, 1985)

G Pomper (ed) *The Election of 1984: Reports and Interpretations* (Chatham, NJ: Chatham House, 1985)

A Ranney (ed) *The American Elections of 1980* (Washington DC: American Enterprise Institute, 1981)

A Ranney (ed) *The American Elections of 1984* (Duke University Press, 1985)

KL Schlozman (ed) *Elections in America* (Winchester, Mass: Allen & Unwin, Inc, 1987)

F Smallwood *The Other Candidates: Third Parties in Presidential Elections* (Dartmouth College: University of New England, 1983)

THE 1988 PRESIDENTIAL ELECTION

J Germond & J Whitcover *Whose Broad Stripes and Bright Stars? The Trivial Pursuit of the Presidency 1988* (New York: Warner, 1989)

C Kenney & RL Turner *Dukakis: An American Odyssey* (Boston, Mass: Houghton Mifflin Company, 1988)

GM Pomper et al *The Election of 1988: Reports and Interpretation* (Chatham, NJ, Chatham House, 1989)

P Simon *Winner and Losers* (New York: Continuum, 1989)

AMERICAN POLITICS 1974–90

The Ford Administration: 1974–6

JJ Casserly *The Ford White House: The Diary of a Speechwriter* (Boulder, Col: Associated University Press, 1977)

GR Ford *A Time to Heal: The Autobiography of Gerald R Ford* (London: WH Allen, 1979)

H Kissinger *The White House Years* (London: Weidenfeld & Nicolson, 1979)

AJ Rechley *Conservatism in an Age of Change: The Nixon and Ford Administrations* (Washington DC: Brookings Institution, 1981)

R Reeves *A Ford, Not a Lincoln: The Decline of American Political Leadership* (London: Hutchinson, 1976)

The Carter Administration 1977–80

G Abernathy, DM Hill & P Williams *The Carter Years: The President and Policy Making* (London: Frances Pinter, 1984)

B Adams & K Kavanagh-Baran *Promise and Performance: Carter Builds a New Administration* (Lexington, Mass: Heath, 1979)

J Carter *Keeping Faith; The Memoirs of a President* (London: Collins, 1982)

W Christopher et al *American Hostages in Iran: The Conduct of a Crisis* (New Haven, Conn: Yale University Press, 1985)

TR Dye *Who's Running America? The Carter Years* (London: Prentice & Hall, 1979)

GM Fink *Prelude to the Presidency: The Political Character and Legislative Leadership Style of Governor Jimmy Carter* (Westport, Conn: Greenwood Press, 1980)

H Jordan *Crisis: The Last Year of the Carter Presidency* (London: Michael Joseph, 1982)

B Mazlish & E Diamond *Jimmy Carter: A Character Portrait* (New York, Times Books, 1978)

LH Shoup *The Carter Presidency and Beyond: Power and Politics in the 1980s* (Palo Alto, Calif: Ramparts Press, 1980)

M Thompson *President Carter: 1980* (Washington DC: Congressional Quarterly Publications, 1981)

C Vance *Hard Choices: Critical Years in American Foreign Policy* (New York: Simon and Schuster, 1983)

J Wooton *Dasher: The Roots and Rising of Jimmy Carter* (London: Weidenfeld & Nicolson, 1978)

The Reagan Administration: 1981–8

M Anderson *Revolution* (New York: Harcourt Brace Jovanovich, 1988)

S Blumenthal & T Edsall (eds) *The Reagan Legacy* (New York: Pantheon, 1988)

M Boskin *Reagan and the Economy* (New York: ICS Press, 1988)

R Brownstein & N Easton *Reagan's Ruling Class: Portraits of the President's Top One Hundred Officials* (New York: Pantheon Books, 1983)

R Dallek *Ronald Reagan: The Politics of Symbolism* (Cambridge, Mass: Harvard University Press, 1984)

M Deaver & M Herskowitz *Behind the Scenes* (New York: William Morrow, 1988)

R Dugger *Reagan: The Man and the Presidency* (New York: McGraw-Hill, 1984)

PD Erickson *Reagan Speaks: The Making of an American Myth* (New York: New York University Press, 1985)

DM Hill et al *The Reagan Presidency* (London: Macmillan, 1988)

CO Jones (ed) *The Reagan Legacy: Promise and Performance* (Chatham, NJ,: Chatham Press, 1988)

JD Lees & M Turner *Reagan's First Four Years: A New Beginning?* (Manchester: Manchester University Press, 1988)

J Mayer & D McManus *Landslide: The Unmaking of the President, 1984–1988* (New York: Houghton Mifflin, 1988)

Modern Studies Association *The Reagan Years* (Glasgow: MSA, 1987)

NJ Ornstein *President and Congress: Assessing Reagan's First Year* (Washington DC: American Enterprise Institute, 1982)

JL Palmer & IV Sawhill (eds) *The Reagan Record: An Assessment of America's Changing Domestic Priorities* (Washington DC: Urban Institute, 1984)

R Reagan & RG Hubler *Where's the Rest of Me? My Early Life* (London: Sidgwick & Jackson, 1981)

DT Regan *For The Record: From Wall Street to Washington* (London: Century Hutchinson, 1988)

PC Roberts *The Supply-Side Revolution: An Insider's Account of Policy Making in Washington* (Cambridge, Mass: Harvard University Press, 1984)

LM Salmon & MS Lund (eds) *The Reagan Presidency and the Governing of America* (Washington DC: Urban Institute, 1985)

DA Stockman *The Triumph of Politics: Why the Reagan Revolution Failed?* (London: Bodley Head, 1986)

G Wills *Reagan's America: Innocents at Home* (London: Heinemann, 1988)

The Intra-Contra Affair

B Bradlee, Jr *Guts and Glory: The Rise and Fall of Oliver North* (London: Grafton Books, 1988)

W Cohen & G Mitcheel *Men of Zeal* (New York: Viking, 1988)

D Martin & J Walcott *Best Laid Plans* (New York: Harper & Row, 1988)

Economic and Social Change

MF Berry *Why ERA Failed: Politics, Women's Rights and the Amending Process of the Constitution* (Bloomington, Ind: Indiana UP, 1986)

M Bradshaw *Regions and Regionalism in the United States* (London: Macmillan, 1988)

W Greider *Secrets of the Temple: How the Federal Reserve Runs the Country* (New York: Simon & Schuster, 1988)

J Hagstrom *Beyond Reagan: The New Landscape of American Politics* (New York: Norton, 1987)

W Issel *Social Change in the United States, 1945–1983* (London: Macmillan, 1985)

IC Magaziner & RB Reich *Minding America's Business: The Decline and Rise of the American Economy* (New York: Harcourt Brace Jovanovich, 1982)

M Manning *Black American Politics* (London: Verso Press, 1985)

RM Miller & GE Pozzetta (eds) *Shades of the Sunbelt: Essays on Ethnicity, Race and the Urban South* (Westport, Conn: Greenwood Press, 1988)

AL Reed *The Jesse Jackson Phenomenon: The Crisis of Purpose in Afro-American Politics* (New Haven, Conn: Yale University Press, 1986)

GK Wilson *Interest Groups in the United States* (Oxford: Oxford University Press, 1981)

Foreign Policy

JE Dougherty & RL Pfaltzgraff *American Foreign Policy: FDR to Reagan* (New York: Harper & Row, 1986)

MH Hunt *Ideology and American Foreign Policy* (New Haven, Conn: Yale University Press, 1987)

E Tivnan *The Lobby: Jewish Political Power and American Foreign Policy* (New York: Simon & Schuster, 1987)

E Van Den Haag & TJ Farer *US Ends and Means in Central America* (New York: Plenum, 1988)

B Woodward *Veil: The Secret Wars of the CIA 1981–1987* (New York: Simon & Schuster, 1987)

CHRONOLOGY OF RECENT EVENTS: 1977–90

1977 Jan, Carter (after winning Nov 1976 presidential election against Ford) takes office. Sept, Lance resigns from OMB.

1978 June, Proposition 13 approved in California. Sept, Camp David Middle East accord. Oct, energy bill passed. Nov, Republican midterm election gains. Dec, relations with China normalised.

1979 Jan, Shah flees Iran. March, Egypt-Israel peace treaty. June, SALT-2 signed in Vienna. July, Camp David reappraisal and cabinet shake-up. 4 Nov, Iranian students take over US embassy in Teheran. 26 Dec, Soviet Union invades Afghanistan.

1980 Jan, sanctions against Soviet Union. April, failed Teheran rescue mission – Vance resigns. Nov, Reagan defeats Carter in presidential election – Republicans capture Senate.

1981 Jan, Reagan takes office; Teheran hostages released. March, Reagan shot in Washington. July, tax-cut bill passed. Sept, O'Connor appointed to Supreme Court; march on Washington. Nov, Reagan announces 'zero option'. 13 Dec, martial law imposed in Poland; Reagan announces sanctions package against USSR.

1982 June, Haig resigns; New York peace rally; ERA defeated; Supreme Court rules against legislative veto. Nov, Brezhnev dies – Andropov new Soviet leader; Democrat midterm gains; unemployment reaches post-war peak of 10.8%; Siberian pipeline sanctions lifted.

1983 Sept, Soviet Union shoot down S Korean airliner; death of H Jackson. Oct, US marines invade Grenada. Nov, cruise missiles deployed in Europe – Soviet Union walks out of START talks.

1984 Feb, US marines withdraw from Beirut; Andropov dies – Chernenko new Soviet leader. June, unemployment falls to 7%. July, Ferraro (D) first female vice-presidential nominee. August, Los Angeles Olympics. Nov, Reagan defeats Mondale in presidential race; Republican gains in House.

1985 Jan, Reagan second term begins, DT Regan new Chief-of-Staff. March, Chernenko dies – Gorbachev new Soviet leader. June, Beirut hostage crisis. July, Reagan's colon operation; Stockman leaves OMB. Oct, *Achille Lauro* incident. Nov, Reagan-Gorbachev Geneva summit. Dec, GRH balanced budget act accepted.

1986 April, oil price halved; US raid on Libya. June, Congress approves $100 million Contra aid bill; Senate approve their own tax reform bill. July, Supreme Court rule against parts of GRH act. Sept, Senate confirmation of William Rehnquist as new Chief Justice of the Supreme Court. Oct, Reagan-Gorbachev Reykjavik 'mini-summit'; passage of tax reform act. Nov, Republicans lose Senate majority following Congressional elections; irruption of 'Irangate' scandal; forced resignation of NSA Poindexter and assistant North.

1987 Feb, report of Tower Commission on 'Irangate'; dismissal of Chief-of-Staff Regan to be replaced by Howard Baker. April, first arrests by Special Prosecutor in 'Irangate' affair. May, Senate and House joint Select Committee commences 'Irangate' public hearings; Hart withdraws from presidential race after 'Rice affair'. June, Volcker replaced by Greenspan as Federal Reserve Board chairman. July, Poindexter and North testify before Congressional 'Irangate Committee'. Oct, Wall Street 'Black Monday' crash; Senate reject Reagan's nomination of Judge Robert Bork to replace retiring Justice Powell on the Supreme Court. Nov, bipartisan two-year budget agreement accepted; publication of damning report on 'Irangate'. Dec, signing of INF treaty at US-Soviet Washington DC summit.

1988 Feb, Judge Anthony Kennedy approved as new Supreme Court Justice; Dole (R) and Gephardt (D) win Iowa caucuses, Bush (R) and Dukakis (D) the New Hampshire primary. March, Bush sweeps towards nomination contest victory on 'Super Tuesday', Democrat race remains divided. April, Dukakis triumphs in crucial New York primary. May–June, INF treaty formally ratified at Moscow summit. July, resignation of Attorney-General Meese. July–August, Dukakis-Bentsen and Bush-Quayle presidential tickets approved by Democrat and Republican National Conventions. August, ceasefire in Iran-Iraq war. Nov, Bush elected President, Democrats strengthen Congressional position. Dec, unemployment level falls to 5.3%, a post-1974 low.

1989 Jan, Bush is inaugurated as 41st President. Feb, Ron Brown (D) elected as first black major party chairman. March, Senate rejects Bush's nomination of Tower as Defense Secretary; USSR withdraws fully from Afghanistan. May, Speaker Wright forced to resign over ethics issue; North convicted by Federal Court on three felony charges. June, Chinese massacre of 'democracy movement' in Tiananmen Square; death of Ayatollah Khomeini. July, Supreme Court ruling tightens abortion law. August, Maj-Gen Powell becomes first black to head the US armed forces. Sept–Dec, collapse of communist regimes in eastern Europe. Nov, Wilder (D – Virginia) is elected first black State Governor and Dinkins (D) as New York's first black Mayor. Dec, Bush-Gorbachev 'floating summit' off Malta; US troops overthrow Panamanian dictatorship of General Noriega.

1990 Jan, Noriega captured and flown to Miami to face drug-trafficking charges; Bush rated the most popular Republican President since Theodore Roosevelt (1901–9). Feb, Washington's Mayor Barry indicted on cocaine possession charges; Sandinistas lose power after Nicaraguan election. April, ex-NSA Poindexter convicted of lying to Congress. May, START agreement outlined at US-Soviet Washington summit.

INDEX

INDEX

317

Kemp-Roth proposal, 61
Kennedy, Edward, 42–4, 71, 75, 96, 120, 121, 124, 129, 167, 185
Kennedy, John F, 9, 18, 43, 73, 93, 120, 127, 143, 173, 182
Kennedy, Judge Anthony, 114, 116
Kennedy, Robert, 73
Kerrey, Bob, 157
Keyes, Alan, 203
Khomeini, Ayatollah, 100, 228
King, Ed, 128
King, Rev Martin Luther, 72, 124, 127, 203
Kinnock, Neil, 122
Kirbo, Charles, 32
Kirkland, Lane, 71, 208
Kirkpatrick, Jeane, 132, 217
Kirk, Paul, 118, 119, 185
Kissinger, Henry, 20, 22, 23, 162, 212, 213, 217, 225, 226
Koch, Ed, 126, 130
Kopechne, Mary Jo, 44
Korean War, 127, 137
Kristol, Irving, 46
Kunin, Madeleine, 205

L
Labor unions' decline, 206–10
Laffer, Arthur, 45
Laird, Mel, 20, 22
Lance, Bert, 32, 33, 124
Landon, Alfred, 205
Lang, Russell, 37
La Rouche, Lyndon, 141
Laxalt, Paul, 59, 93, 105, 117, 120, 132
Leahy, Patrick, 168
Legislative Reorganization Act 1970, 23
Lewis, Jerry, 169
Libertarian Party, 51, 78, 146
Lieberman, Joseph, 157
Lott, Trent, 157, 168
Lucas, William, 203
Lujan, Manuel, 171

M
machine politics, 8, 16, 50, 72
Mack, Connie, 157
Mahon, George, 34
Mallick, George, 169
Manatt, Charles, 69, 75, 118
Mankiewicz, Frank, 127
Mansfield, Mike, 34, 168
Marshall, Justice Thurgood, 116, 203
Martin, Lynn, 169
Mathias, Charles, 93
McCarthy, Eugene, 27, 146

McClellan, John, 34
McCloskey, Peter, 137
McClure, Fred, 164
McDonald, Alonzo, 41
McFarlane, Robert, 84, 99, 102, 108, 221, 222
McGovern, George, 19, 25, 52, 73, 74, 139, 142
McIntyre, James, 33
Medicaid, 61, 87
Medicare, 18, 61, 87, 176, 177, 178, 179
Meecham, Evan, 206
Meese Commission, 91
Meese, Ed, 58, 82, 84, 90, 101, 102, 114, 132, 169, 180, 218, 219
Melcher, John 'Doc', 157
Michel, Robert, 80, 97, 168
Mikulski, Barbara, 205
Mills, Wilbur, 34
Mitchell, George, 167, 168, 178
Moakley, Joe, 169
Mofford, Rose, 206
Mondale, Walter, 27, 31, 33, 45, 71–2, 73, 74, 75, 77, 79, 120, 121, 122, 128, 129
monetarism, 12, 45
Moore, Arch, 158
Moore, Frank, 32, 33
'Moral Majority' movement, 46, 49
Moretti, Bob, 59
Mosbacher, Robert, 165, 166
Moynihan, Patrick, 9, 45
MX ICBM programme, 218, 219, 220

N
NAACP (National Association for the Advancement of Colored People), 73
National Conservative Political Action Committee (NCPAC), 46, 52, 77, 113
National Convention, 13, 24
National Endowment for the Preservation of Liberty, 106
National Labor Relations Board (NLRB), 209
NATO (North Atlantic Treaty Organisation), 103, 182, 217, 218, 220, 222, 229, 230
NEA (National Education Association), 72
'neo-liberal', 73, 118, 120, 121, 122, 184, 188, 201
'New Deal', 5, 8, 9, 18, 48, 52, 61, 62, 64, 73, 117, 197
'New Federalism', 63
'New Frontier', 18, 120, 133, 141, 165, 183
'New Realism', 54